for Stan
— with gratitude,
admiration, and affection —
Bob Kagan

Stan,
This is just one of
hundreds of books that
you and your work has inspired.
Thank you —
affectionately,
Patty

To Stan —
This is one small token —
of my gratitude —
There are few in our
field who have had, + ever
a positive + lasting
impact on so many —
thanks for everything.
Austin

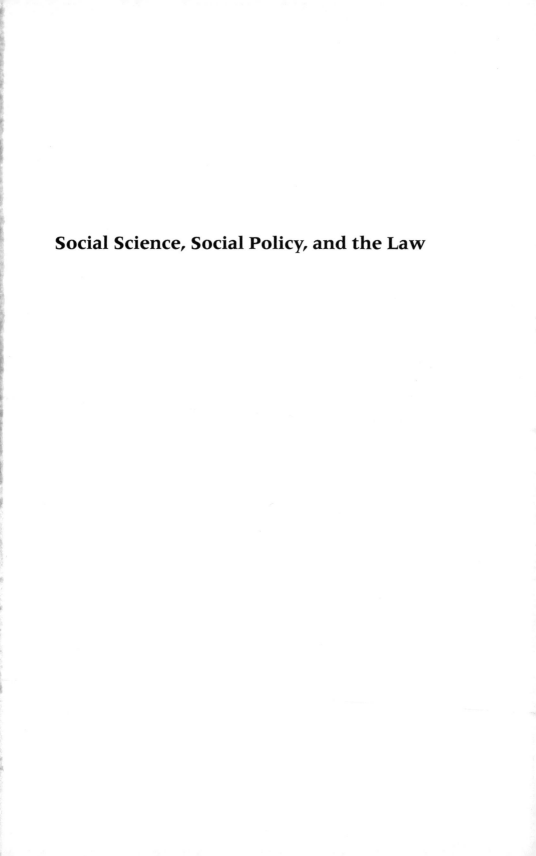

Social Science, Social Policy, and the Law

Social Science, Social Policy, and the Law

Patricia Ewick

Robert A. Kagan

Austin Sarat

EDITORS

Russell Sage Foundation
New York

The Russell Sage Foundation

The Russell Sage Foundation, one of the oldest of America's general purpose foundations, was established in 1907 by Mrs. Margaret Olivia Sage for "the improvement of social and living conditions in the United States." The Foundation seeks to fulfill this mandate by fostering the development and dissemination of knowledge about the country's political, social, and economic problems. While the Foundation endeavors to assure the accuracy and objectivity of each book it publishes, the conclusions and interpretations in Russell Sage Foundation publications are those of the authors and not of the Foundation, its Trustees, or its staff. Publication by Russell Sage, therefore, does not imply Foundation endorsement.

Library of Congress Cataloging-in-Publication Data

Social science, social policy, and the law / edited by Patricia Ewick,
    Robert Kagan, Austin Sarat.
        p.   cm.
    Includes bibliographical references and index.
    ISBN 0-87154-426-1
    1. Sociological jurisprudence—Congresses.   2. Social policy
—Congresses.   3. Law—Social aspects—United States—Congresses.
I. Ewick, Patricia.   II. Kagan, Robert A.   III. Sarat, Austin.
K367.S585   1999
340'.115—dc21   98-52431
                                                                       CIP

RUSSELL SAGE FOUNDATION
112 East 64th Street, New York, New York 10021
10 9 8 7 6 5 4 3 2 1

Dedication

To Stanton Wheeler, teacher, scholar, friend, in honor of his re-
markable contribution to the field of law and social science.

Contents

Contributors   ix

Acknowledgments   xi

Introduction   Legacies of Legal Realism: Social Science,   1
               Social Policy, and the Law
               Patricia Ewick, Robert A. Kagan, and Austin Sarat

PART I   HISTORICAL AND STRUCTURAL ANALYSES   39
               OF LAW

Chapter 1   Privatization and Punishment: Lessons   41
               from History
               Malcolm M. Feeley

Chapter 2   On Stage: Some Historical Notes   68
               About Criminal Justice
               Lawrence M. Friedman

Chapter 3   Beyond the Law of Evidence: Facts and   101
               Inequality in Criminal Defense
               Kenneth Mann

PART II   BARRIERS TO INFLUENCE   137

Chapter 4   A Bad Press on Bad Lawyers: The Media Sees   139
               Research, Research Sees the Media
               Deborah L. Rhode

Chapter 5   Maps, Gaps, Sociolegal Scholarship, and   170
               the Tort Reform Debate
               Neil Vidmar

Chapter 6   Hunting for Bias: Notes on the Evolution of   210
             Strategies for Documenting Invidious
             Discrimination
             Jack Katz

Chapter 7   Good for What Purpose? Social Science,   258
             Race, and Proportionality Review in New Jersey
             David Weisburd

PART III   LAW AND THE REORDERING OF   289
             SOCIAL RELATIONS

Chapter 8   Boundary Work: Levels of Analysis, the   291
             Macro-Micro Link, and the Social Control
             of Organizations
             Diane Vaughan

Chapter 9   When You Can't Just Say "No": Controlling   322
             Lawyers' Conflicts of Interest
             Susan P. Shapiro

Index   377

Contributors

PATRICIA EWICK is associate professor of sociology and associate dean at Clark University.

ROBERT A. KAGAN is professor of political science and director of the Center for Law and Society at the University of California at Berkeley.

AUSTIN SARAT is William Nelson Cromwell Professor of Jurisprudence and Political Science at Amherst College and president of the Law and Society Association.

MALCOLM M. FEELEY is Claire Sanders Clements Professor of Law at the University of California at Berkeley.

LAWRENCE M. FRIEDMAN is Marion Rice Kirkwood Professor of Law at Stanford University.

JACK KATZ is professor of sociology at the University of California at Los Angeles.

KENNETH MANN is associate professor of law at Tel-Aviv University and chief public defender for the State of Israel.

DEBORAH L. RHODE is Ernest W. McFarland Professor of Law at Stanford University.

SUSAN P. SHAPIRO is senior research fellow at the American Bar Foundation.

DIANE VAUGHAN is professor of sociology at Boston College.

NEIL VIDMAR is Russell M. Robinson II Professor of Law and professor of psychology at Duke University.

DAVID WEISBURD is director of the Institute of Criminology at Hebrew University Law School and senior research scientist at the Police Foundation.

Acknowledgments

We are grateful for financial support from the Russell Sage Foundation and Yale Law School as well as for administrative support provided by Amherst College's Department of Law, Jurisprudence, and Social Thought. We also want to thank the friends, colleagues, former students, and admirers of Stan Wheeler who have contributed to this volume and to the many people who enthusiastically participated in the symposium at which these essays were first presented. This book is but one small tribute to Stan's extraordinary career and to the virtues of generosity and excellence, which have been combined so powerfully in Stan Wheeler the person. We seek to recognize his deep and selfless investment in a generation of scholars who he did so much to nurture and his superb example of what it means to be a scholar. We are all deeply in his debt.

Legacies of Legal Realism: Social Science, Social Policy, and the Law

Patricia Ewick, Robert A. Kagan, and Austin Sarat

What can social science contribute to the study of law? Can the use of social science methods enrich our understanding of law? Can and should it help us to formulate more reasoned and effective legal policy? These questions provided the basis for a symposium of leading sociolegal scholars who were brought together in April 1997 to consider the relationships among social science, social policy, and law. The purpose of this symposium was to take stock of what social science has contributed, what it might contribute, and what barriers stand in the way of using social science more effectively to make and implement social policy.

The symposium was also an opportunity to honor Stanton Wheeler, professor of law and of sociology at Yale Law School, for his long-standing leadership in sociolegal studies.[1] At the heart of Professor Wheeler's vision of law and social science is a conviction that, as law becomes more deeply implicated in societies everywhere, empirically grounded studies of law in action become more important and more consequential for generating basic knowledge of society and for informing policymakers. Social science applied to the understanding of law would be a form of enlightened critique, but also an aid to social and legal reform.

The dream of enlisting social science in efforts to understand law and inform legal policy is not new. In this century it traces its lineage at least to the work of the legal realists.[2] As is by now well known, realism emerged as part of a progressive response to the collapse of the nineteenth-century laissez-faire political economy. By the beginning of the twentieth century, state involvement in a variety of arenas was substantial, and "wise and far-thinking advocates of the 'status quo'" such as Theodore Roosevelt and Woodrow Wilson urged policies to accommodate the pressures of urbanization, big labor, and concentrated wealth. Careful and caring policies, they believed, would both socialize violent individualism and preserve the main features of the existing social order (Hofstadter 1955). Realists picked up these political themes and espoused "policy-oriented intervention by the state. . . . The espousal by the Realists of a favorable response to socioeconomic legislation . . . was in essence a plea for a readjustment of the legal order to social developments" (Hunt 1978, 39).

By attacking the classical conception of law with its assumptions about the independent and objective movement from preexisting rights to decisions in specific cases (Cohen 1935; Llewellyn 1931b), realists opened the way for a vision of law as policy, a vision in which law could and should be guided by pragmatic and utilitarian considerations (Llewellyn 1940).[3] By exposing the difference between law on the books and law in action, realists established the need to approach lawmaking and adjudication strategically with an eye toward difficulties in implementation. By exploring the ways in which law in action—for example the law found in lower criminal courts—was often caught up in politics, realists provided the energy and urgency for reform designed to rescue the legal process and restore its integrity.[4] Realism attacked "all dogmas and devices that cannot be translated into terms of actual experience" (Cohen 1935, 822); it criticized conceptualism and the attempt by traditional legal scholars to reduce law to a set of rules and principles that they insisted both guided and constrained judges in their decisions. The boldness of that assertion prompted Holmes (1881) to write that tools other than logic were needed to understand the law. Law was a matter of history and culture and could not be treated deductively.

Nonetheless, no realist believed that legal rules and concepts were entirely irrelevant. They sought, instead, to move the focus from the words of law to legal action and the consequences of legal behaviors. Legal rules are one of the many constraints that shape legal behavior, but other factors are also important. It was here, in the realm of behavior and action, that the empirical claims of realism became prominent. Realists saw the start of the twentieth century as a period of the explosion and transformation of knowledge (Reisman 1941). Some saw in both the natural and emerging social sciences the triumph of rationality over tradition, inquiry over faith, and the human mind over its environment (McDougal 1941). They took as one of their many projects the task of opening law to this explosion and transformation. They argued that the law's rationality and efficacy ultimately depended on an alliance with positivist science (see Schlegel 1980). By using the questions and methods of science to assess the consequences of legal decisions, realists claimed that understanding what law *could* do would help in establishing what law *should* do (Llewellyn 1931a and 1931b). As Yntema (1934, 209) put it,

> Ultimately, the object of the more recent movements in legal science . . . is to direct the constant efforts which are made to reform the legal system by objective analysis of its operation. Whether such analysis be in terms of a calculus of pleasures and pains, of the evaluation of interests, of pragmatic means and ends, of human behavior, is not so significant as that law is regarded in all these and like analyses as an instrumental procedure to achieve purposes beyond itself, defined by the conditions to which it is directed. This is the Copernican discovery of recent legal science.

Realism initiated a dialogue between law and social science by staking a claim for the relevance of phenomena beyond legal categories (Cardozo 1921; Pound 1923; Llewellyn 1925, 1940).[5] Many realists saw in social science methodology the potential to make explicit, and thus purge, moral values in science and knowledge. Ironically, the pursuit of legal values would be better realized, they believed, through the accumulation of value-free facts. Although Dewey had rejected the idea of complete objectivity, he nonetheless insisted on the need for a scientific study of social problems and "the supremacy of method" (Dewey 1960). Others sought truly value-neutral inquiry, and they believed that what social science could make available to legal decisionmakers was an accurate and relatively undistorted portrait of social relations and processes. Social science dealt "with things, with people, with tangibles, with definite tangibles, and observable relations between definite tangibles, and

not with words alone." Science would help get at the positive, determinative realities, "the tangibles which can be got at beneath the
words . . . [and would] . . . check ideas, and rules and formulas by
facts, to keep them close to facts" (Llewellyn 1931b, 1223). For law
to be effective and legitimate, it had to confront such definite, tangible, and observable facts; to ignore the facts of social life was folly.
Social science could aid decisionmaking by identifying the factors
that limited the choices available to officials and, more important, by
identifying the determinants of responses to those decisions. Aware of
those determining conditions, the informed decisionmaker could and
should adopt decisions to take account of what was or was not possible in a given situation.

   The intellectual and institutional success of realism was enormous
(Schlegel 1979). After World War II, the behaviorist and functionalist orientations that had been urged by the scientific realists became
conventional in mainstream social science and in mainstream legal
analyses and teaching. For social science, the unmasking of legal formalism and the opening of legal institutions to empirical inquiry offered, at one and the same time, fertile ground for research and the
opportunity to be part of a fundamental remaking of legal thought.
The possibility of influencing legal decisions and policies further allied social science and law (see Whyte 1986). Rather than challenge
basic norms or attempt to revise the legal structure, realism ultimately worked to increase confidence in the law (Brigham and
Harrington 1989) and to foster the belief that legal thinking informed
by social knowledge could be enlisted to aid the pressing project of
state intervention. Realism thus invited law and social science inquiry to speak to social policy, an invitation that many, although by
no means all, of its practitioners have taken up.

From Legal Realism to Law and Society

The legacy of realism has been realized in the past three decades by
the modern law and society movement. Indeed, the beginnings of
the modern period of sociolegal research might be set with the formation of the Law and Society Association in 1965. Although there
is, and was, more to sociolegal research than can be encapsulated by
the formation of that association, its creation marked an important
step forward for empirical studies of law. The Law and Society

Association self-consciously articulated the value of empirical research for informing policy (see Schwartz 1965).

The emergence of the modern law and society movement coincided with one of those episodes in American legal history in which law is regarded as a beneficial tool for social improvement, in which social problems appear susceptible to legal solutions, and in which there is, or appears to be, a rather unproblematic relationship between legal justice and social justice (Trubek and Galanter 1974). Moreover, the rule of law served to distinguish the West from its adversaries in the communist world, and hence the full and equal implementation of legal ideals was, to many reformers, essential. By the mid-1960s, liberal reformers seemed once again to be winning the battle to rebuild a troubled democracy; the political forces working, albeit modestly, to expand rights and redistribute wealth and power were in ascendancy. The national government was devoting itself to using state power and legal reform for the purpose of building a Great Society. The courts, especially the Supreme Court, were out front in expanding the definition and reach of legal rights. Because law was seen as an important vehicle for social change, those legal scholars who were critical of existing social practices believed they had an ally in the legal order. Pragmatic social change was an explicit agenda of the state and an equally explicit part of the agenda of law and society research. Legality seemed a cure rather than a disease (Scheingold 1974); the aspirations and purposes of law seemed unquestionably correct. Thus, the modern law and society movement, like the realist movement before it, grew up in, and allied itself with, a period of optimism about law. The period was one in which

> liberal legal scholars and their social science allies could identify with national administrations which seemed to be carrying out progressive welfare regulatory programs, expanding protection for basic constitutional rights, and employing law for a wide range of goals that were widely shared in the liberal community and could even be read as inscribed in the legal tradition itself. [Trubek and Esser 1987, 23]

This period was, of course, also a period of extraordinary optimism in the social sciences, a period of triumph for the behavioral revolution, a period of growing sophistication in the application of quantitative methods in social inquiry (see Eulau 1963).

The awareness of the utility of social science for policy can be seen clearly in the standard form of many law and society presentations, which begin with a policy problem, locate it in a general theoretical context, present an empirical study to speak to that problem, and sometimes, though not always, conclude with recommendations, suggestions, or cautions. (For a discussion of this approach, see Abel 1973; Nelken 1981; Sarat 1985.) It appears with striking clarity in some of the most widely respected, widely cited work in the field, although often social science serves legal policy by clarifying background conditions and making latent consequences manifest with little or no effort to recommend new or changed policies.

Take, for example, Abraham Blumberg's "The Practice of Law as a Confidence Game" (1967), which described the ways in which the organization of criminal courts worked to support the interests of court officials and defense attorneys to the detriment of the due process claims and rights of criminal defendants. The importance of Blumberg's work is its insistence on the reasonableness of the actors and the absence of malfeasance, malevolence, or incompetence. Read alongside a number of equally detailed studies, for example Skolnick's *Justice without Trial* (1966), Blumberg's work produced a compelling indictment of structural inequities in the criminal justice system. If Skolnick revealed the contradictions in police work born of the demand for law enforcement and peacekeeping—what he called the law and order dilemma—Blumberg demonstrated the contradictions between social organization and due process rights. The reasonable behavior of well-meaning people earning a living by working in the criminal justice system would nonetheless subvert the best intentions of the law. Moreover, it appeared that the unequal distribution of resources that seemed consistently to threaten liberal ideals not only was a product of class and status distinctions but also was created through the ordinary patterns of interaction that characterized membership and exclusion.

Blumberg begins his analysis paradoxically by identifying himself with the policy project of progressive legal reform. Early in his article, Blumberg (1967, 16) argues that

Very little sociological effort is expended to ascertain the validity and viability of important court decisions which may rest wholly on erroneous assumptions about the contextual realities of social structure. A particular decision may rest upon a legally impeccable rationale; at the same time it may be rendered nugatory or self-defeating by contingencies imposed by aspects of social reality of which lawmakers are themselves unaware.

He takes as his point of departure "important court decisions" whose logic or content he does not wish to question or interrogate. In this way, he both affiliates with and distinguishes himself from traditional doctrinal analysis; his is after all a "sociological" effort. Blumberg's work begins with the same legal act that doctrinal scholarship begins with—"important court decisions"—but Blumberg's project is quite different from doctrinal analysis. Although he wants to "ascertain the validity and viability" of court decisions, for Blumberg validity is an extension of viability; viability is understood in terms of effectiveness, that is, whether court decisions are consistent with social facts and thus have the capacity for realizing their goals.

From his sociological perspective, Blumberg worries that "important court decisions" may rest on "wholly erroneous assumptions about the contextual realities of the social structure." Sociology provides access to the reality of the determining social conditions that will influence whether "impeccable" legal reasoning is viable and therefore valid. The sociologist may be able to save the lawmaker or judge from error, to help prevent decisions that are "rendered nugatory" or that defeat themselves. Thus the sociological project involves the education of lawmakers, whose good works fail because of the contingencies imposed by "aspects of social reality" of which they are "themselves unaware." Blumberg's article (1967, 31) relies heavily on metaphors of concealment or invisibility (such as "the lack of visible end product"; "the lawyer-client confidence game . . . seems to conceal this fact"). These metaphors portray his research as a project of revelation, of bringing the unseen to light; while others are deceived by, or are unaware of, the true nature of the process, the sociologist can get at that which is concealed or that which is not readily visible. He worries that unless those things are taken into account, presumably by those who are responsible for making decisions, "recent Supreme Court decisions may have a long-range effect which is radically different from that intended or anticipated" (Blumberg 1967, 39). Here again, we see one of the legacies of legal realism's effort to unmask the hidden structures of law.

The use of social science to inform social policy and law is by no means limited to studies of the administration of criminal justice. It is found in research on the impact of legislation, the practices of lawyers in civil matters, and the operations of the administrative process (see Macaulay 1979; Weitzman 1985). Moreover, an interest in using social science in the service of better policy is not only embedded in many important empirical studies. It also is clearly present in commentaries on the tradition and direction of sociological research. Thus one does not have to read very closely, or very far, to find exhortative statements urging sociologists of law to heed policy. Victor Rosenblum, in his president's message to the Law and Society Association delivered in August 1970, quotes approvingly the words of one of his students (Rosenblum 1970, 3–4):

> In today's world the relationship between law and social change seems to me to be the overriding problem facing any person or group concerned with the relationship between law and society. . . . The social-scientific investigation of the variables which produce [varying degrees of legal effectiveness] carried on with the aim of formulating a general theory of the limits of effective legal action seems to be essential to the understanding of the relationship between law and social change. Such a theory should be useful to lawmakers as a guide in using law as an instrument of social policy. Another service the social scientist can and should provide the lawmaker is the pragmatic evaluation of the social consequences of specific rules of law to determine how well they achieve their ends and how they might be modified to better achieve those ends.

What was, for some, a hope in 1970—a hope of influencing legal decisionmakers—has, in the view of two more recent past presidents of the Law and Society Association, become a reality. Thus Herb Jacob (1983, 420) praises the contribution of law and society scholarship to the study of trial courts and argues that, "We can begin to inform policymakers about some of the probable nonanticipated consequences of their actions even if we cannot state with certainty the outcome of reforms." Marc Galanter is even more confident in his assertion that law and society scholarship can and should speak to policy, arguing that the policy debate about the litigation explosion has "both utilized and promoted law and social science research" (Galanter 1985, 541). Concerning proposed reforms designed to alleviate the alleged litigation crisis, Galanter suggests that, "It is the work of the law and society community that supplies much of the conceptual basis, methodology, and data for public debate on these proposals." He continues,

> Debate about legal policy remains a game of persuasion in which the canons of evidence are breathtakingly permissive, reflecting the tendency of mainstream legal learning to rely on causal surmise about patterns of practice and systematic effects. The presence of law and society scholarship, with its accumulation of empirical data and critical apparatus, exerts pressure towards institutionalizing norms of intellectual accountability in the discourse. [Galanter 1985, 541]

This description of the elevating effects of law and society scholarship, although much less direct than Rosenblum's suggested role for sociolegal research in the policy process, is, nevertheless, an indication that the interest in the relationship among social science, social policy, and law did not die with the last gasp of Great Society liberalism, with the resulting change in the political direction of policy elites, with the accumulated evidence of repeated policy failure, or with the coming of age of a new generation of more skeptical law and society scholars. Interest in using social science in the service of social policy is as great today as ever. Everywhere people are striving to realize the rule of law and are demanding equal treatment, rational regulation, and a framework of rules within which to pursue economic liberalization.[6] Interest in policy continues to be seen with striking regularity in the pages of the major journals of the field as scholars grapple with the long-standing questions raised by legal realism: In what ways is law a product of society, and how can knowing the answers to this question aid in the formulation of effective law and the attainment of a just society?[7]

Revisiting and Revising Existing Paradigms

Yet in the past few decades the social scientific study of law has complicated these questions. Although it is true that much law and society research is still oriented toward an effort to explain why the law is the way it is and to understand the conditions under which legal rules have an impact, or make a difference in society (Kagan 1995b), many scholars have radically reformulated the conceptual categories and the empirical focus animating their inquiries. As originally posed by the first few generations of legal realists and sociologists of law, questions concerning the relationship between law and society left unexamined the clarity and coherence of those terms. The phrase "law and society" unproblematically assigns to law a distinctive and recognizable form, independent from something called society. Similarly, the conjunction "and" assumes a more or less clear boundary demarcating the two spheres of social life. Finally, the surface question regarding the relationship between law and society instructed scholars to focus on the events and interactions that occur across or at that boundary. More recently, each of these assumptions has been challenged (see, for example, Hunt 1980; Brigham 1996; Sarat et al. 1998a). With these challenges, the original legal realist project has not been abandoned as much as it has been expanded in ways that have opened up new lines of inquiry.

In many ways this expansion was a direct outgrowth of the legal realist project. Earlier empirical studies of law clearly demonstrated that the law lacks the uniformity, coherence, and autonomy that are often assumed. Instead, the law refers to assorted social acts, organizations, and persons, including lay as well as professional actors, and encompasses a broad range of values and objectives (Brigham 1996). Recognition of this complexity led scholars to expand the sorts of material and social practices that constitute the law. It inspired them to study not only how, why, and by whom the law is used, but also when and by whom it is not used and, for that matter, to reassess what using the law might mean (Ewick and Silbey 1998). One of the most obvious consequences of reconceptualizing the law in this way is that it renders the old law and society question incomplete. It is incomplete because it presupposes the very thing that is now understood to be problematic: how is it that law emerges out of, or is constituted within, local, concrete, and historically specific situations? If the law is now understood to be an internal feature of social situations, rather than an autonomous force acting on them, it is necessary to identify the ways in which these situations are constructed by law (Sarat and Kearns 1993).

Following from this transformation, a good deal of research has shifted away from simply tracking the causal and instrumental relationship between law and society toward tracing the presence of law in society (see Sarat et al. 1998b). Thus, law is now understood to constitute partially the very activities and persons that, previously, it was thought merely to be acting on (Garth and Sarat 1998). This insight has critical implications for understanding the relationships among social science, law, and social policy. Law is no longer seen as merely an instrument of social change or regulation. It is now conceptualized as being of a piece with larger historical and structural conditions and thus implicated in that which it would change or regulate. For instance, as a number of essays in this volume discuss, law is sometimes used by actors as a resource to accomplish ends that are extra-legal or only minimally related to the legal system. Trials are theater and narrative played to diverse audiences (Friedman, chapter 2; Mann, chapter 3); a regime of criminal punishments are entrepreneurial opportunities (Feeley, chapter 1). The law is more than a means to achieving various ends; it becomes an object of direct social action. As persons and groups invoke, evade, brandish, or celebrate the law, they enact legality. Whereas legal realism tended to see law as operating to shape social action, here it is understood to be a form of social action. Moreover, as it is enacted, the character of the law changes as it is deployed in new situations for unanticipated purposes and with novel consequences (Ewick and Silbey 1998).

The web of relationships that are now recognized as existing between and among society and law humble efforts to effect social change through social policy in any straightforward way. Policies are transformed as advocacy organizations and lawyers use the complex, slow, and costly procedures of the law strategically to increase their bargaining power (McCann 1994; Kagan 1995a, 1996). Within organizations and communities, local cultural and structural factors (such as professional cultures, organizational size, and wealth) mediate, compete with, and sometimes amplify legal norms. Research has suggested, for instance, that in some cases law is rendered irrelevant by local norms of informality (Ellickson 1991). In other contexts, professionals within organizations interpret the significance of law in such a way as to shape the day-to-day operation of the organization. These interpretations may overstate the relevance (or threat) of law or, alternatively, downplay its role, depending on organizational priorities and professional interests and perspectives (Weick 1979; Edelman, Erlanger, and Lande 1993; Heimer 1993; Vaughan, chapter 8; Shapiro, chapter 9). Of course, how social actors interpret and comprehend law in various social situations, ranging from formal organizations to families and neighborhoods, exerts a profound influence on how law might effect behavior within those settings. Moreover, to the extent that these interpretations determine levels of compliance with legal rules or shape decisions to invoke legal mechanisms, they should be understood to be shaping the character and reach of the law.

Finally, social scientists have not left unexamined or untheorized the overlap between their own activities and law and policy. Even as they deny law the autonomy it often claims for itself, recent sociolegal studies have begun to focus on the ways in which their own research is received, interpreted, and redeployed in the making of law and policy (Sarat and Silbey 1988). Knowledge is reconceived as emergent, incomplete, and contextual and, like law itself, as a resource subject to a variety of uses and interpretations.[8] A number of essays in this volume squarely address this aspect of the social science, law, and social policy nexus (Rhode, chapter 4; Vidmar, chapter 5; Katz, chapter 6; Weisburd, chapter 7).

In light of these developments, the time seemed right to convene a symposium to speak to the growing pervasiveness of law, the controversies that surround it, and the status of social science as a tool for knowing law and for assessing its contribution to social life. The time seemed right to take up specific lines of inquiry that were fostered by Stanton Wheeler and to ask about the role of social science in examining, assessing, and aiding social policy.

The essays in this book were first presented at that symposium. They take up the role of social science in guiding and responding to social policy in two different ways. Some do so by conducting a social scientific study of a particular policy problem; others do so by writing about what it means for social science to inform social policy or about the barriers that stand in the way of a more effective partnership of social science, social policy, and law.

Essays in the first part (chapters 1 through 3) examine the role of history and larger cultural forces in shaping a particular area of legal policy and institutional development, namely the adjudication of crime and punishment. In the United States and Europe, there have been important recent changes in law's response to crime, and the essays in this part seek to explain and assess those changes. In this context, we ask whether the inequalities that are inevitably a part of social life are also inevitably a part of legal life.

The second part of the book (chapters 4 through 7) examines the success and failure of social scientists and social science in influencing legal policy. Specifically, it discusses the mechanisms through which social science is translated for public consumption and the extent to which our research shapes public debate. Particular attention is paid to the role of the news media in this process of translation. Although history and culture know their own laws, the question that animates the essays in this part is whether social science can contribute to more rational social policy.

The third, and final, part (chapters 8 and 9) takes up what we call the problem of law's ability to penetrate and reorder social relations. Social scientists have traditionally drawn attention to the gap between law on the books and law in action. More recently, research has tried to move beyond the mere documentation of the gap to ask under what conditions does or can law have a role in controlling or reordering social practices and to what effect.

Historical and Structural Analyses of Law

The first three essays in this book—the chapters by Malcolm Feeley, Lawrence Friedman, and Kenneth Mann—take up the relationships among social science, social policy, and law by examining the relationship between law and social structure. They use social science to illustrate the pushes and pulls of society on law and seek to make manifest the latent social forces that operate in the domain of legal policy. The vision that their respective studies afford us belies the promise of legal realism or the optimism of the early law and society movement. This view suggests that law is embedded in, and therefore subject to, structures that are more diverse, wide-ranging, and intractable than imagined. The "lessons" that their analyses provide include a sobering one regarding the difficulty of attempting to alter social relations and social practices through law, precisely because of the embeddedness of law in social life. Also, by revealing the broad cultural, economic, and political factors that give shape and content to law, these authors make an implicit claim regarding the crucial role of social science in any such attempt at purposive social change. To proceed without the theoretical or historical view afforded by social scientific analyses is almost certainly to fail.

Chapter 1 describes the emergence of transportation to the colonies as a criminal sanction adopted by European states beginning in the seventeenth century. Feeley rejects the characterization of transportation as having been adopted as an alternative to the ghastly executions that were the principal sanction of the premodern period. According to him, such a narrative of progressive social change is refuted by the simple fact that the number of executions declined precipitously well before the widespread or routine use of transportation. Thus, rather than displacing execution in the state's arsenal of criminal sanctions, transportation represented an independent innovation in social control, one introduced and practiced by private entrepreneurs who not only received a subsidy from the state for transporting criminals, but then sold exiled convicts' labor in the colonies.

Although the practice of transportation might well have been more humane than execution, it was also more efficient, effective, and profitable. As a result, transportation could be used more routinely, more frequently, and more widely. It thus extended the reach of social control to persons and behaviors that were otherwise likely to escape any sanction at all.

Feeley uses this historical examination of an innovation in punishment policy as a lens through which to examine a contemporary innovation, namely the trend toward the privatization of criminal justice in the United States. Recently privatization has included entrepreneurial involvement in the management of prisons, the provision of low-security custodial programs for juveniles and shallow-end offenders, and the development and implementation of new technologies of surveillance and control. As was true of transportation, Feeley claims that the efficiency and effectiveness of these contemporary practices have expanded the reach of the state's control over citizens.

In tracing the implicit collaboration between free market activities and criminal justice, Feeley rejects the picture of the venality or power of private economic interests capturing the state. The conclusion he draws is that legal institutions and practices are shaped not merely by legal ideas (such as notions of proper punishment) but also by organizational and political imperatives playing out a certain logic. Thus governments have political incentives to control crime, maintain order, and appear to punish wrongdoing and rebellion, while doing all of this in the most economical way possible. In fact, Feeley shows that the adoption of any policy—such as the implementation of a new type of punishment—implicates many actors with varying motives. In the case of transportation, the profit motive of entrepreneurs converged with the interests of the state in finding an effective and fiscally plausible way of handling a mounting crisis of law and order. Even the families of convicted offenders collaborated in the development of transportation, because they willingly arranged for the removal of loved ones in order to avoid harsher penalties. This picture presents an additional lesson for understanding the limits of law to effect social life: the difficulty of addressing the complex web of interests, motives, practices, and relationships that produce and sustain social arrangements, including law. In short, law and structures of legality operate in different spheres and for different purposes, and they represent different things to different groups. As such, they defy both easy explanation and easy alteration.

In chapter 2, Lawrence Friedman addresses the public meanings of the criminal trial from a historical perspective. Likening the trial to theater—full of human drama, suspense, roles, scripts, and staging—he attributes to the trial profound didactic functions. The plot and its resolution, as enacted in the trial, announce before a rapt audience social values and norms (at least in the sensational trials that dominate the media). In this way, the records of criminal trials stand as informative archives of social and cultural history.

In his analysis, Friedman acknowledges however, as do Feeley and Mann, the complex and subtle ways in which law and other social arrangements are related. Law, in the form of criminal trials, does not simply broadcast lessons regarding moral boundaries to a waiting public. Extra-legal values and norms insinuate themselves into the law, informing and changing it, even as law informs and changes the social world.

This situation of mutual effect is possible because the trial is not just theater; it is interactive theater played to more than one audience. In particular, the jury is distinguished from the public by virtue of the fact that it is empowered not only to watch the developing drama but also to write the ending and thus determine what the exact "moral of the story" will be. Moreover, because jury deliberations are secret and not subject to review or held to standards of rationality, they become the channel through which extra-legal considerations, conflicting values, or irrelevant considerations are incorporated into law and through which they can subvert the explicit goals of legal rules and policy.

Friedman points out that, when considered against the trial as spectacle, this discretionary power of the jury is ironic.

> The great trials are as public a display, as theatrical a social event, as is possible in this society. Yet the power of the trials to *change* norms and rules is vested in a secret body: the jury. And the actual work of modifying law, of chipping away at doctrine, of subtly altering patterns, takes place in an arena that, up to now, the media cannot penetrate at all.

The implications of this insight for understanding the possibilities and limitations of policy interventions through law are clear. Whenever purposive legal change is sought through criminal prosecution (or civil law suits), this effort can never circumvent or eliminate the power of the public, in general, or the jury, in particular, to reject, alter, ignore, or interpret, and thus change, the law. In this regard, Friedman notes that

> One thing is clear: the rules are not made only in the usual way: by fiat or enactment. Some of them are developed in the course of dramas of high visibility; others by underground evolutions, changes in direction . . . ; they grow and develop beneath the surface, so to speak, until they burst out during such high, hot episodes as criminal trials.

In chapter 3, Kenneth Mann focuses not on the high drama of notorious trials, but on the day-to-day workings of criminal law. His essay provides a sophisticated inquiry into the extra-legal causes of legal inequality that, he suggests, permeate the everyday world of law. Despite the best efforts to design fair processes and eliminate the bias of decisionmakers, legal institutions inevitably reflect and incorporate wider social inequality.

By presenting a witness-by-witness, blow-by-blow account of a particular criminal adjudication in Israel, Mann demonstrates how the efforts of competing lawyers to bring out seemingly small factual details can change the perception of what occurred between the alleged victim and the alleged perpetrator and, hence, about where responsibility should be placed. Second, Mann shows just how difficult and costly the lawyers' job of "constructing the facts" actually is:

"Proving factual reality is, relative to other goods and services in society, a high-cost endeavor." And that costliness, Mann reminds us, is a constant threat to legal equality.

In his analysis, Mann suggests that one source of inequality derives from the fact that "most trials are conducted with resources insufficient for exploiting fact-finding procedures." Within those constraints, defendants' lawyers, who bear the burden of constructing "an exculpatory image," as Mann puts it, will vary in their energy, commitment, ability, and available time and resources. Richer defendants, who can afford better lawyers and more of their time, are likely to do better in this regard than those who depend on government-funded legal services. Ironically, defendants entitled to government-funded legal services may be less disadvantaged than slightly better-off defendants who must rely on the low end of the private market for attorneys.

By demonstrating how material resources affect the possibilities of justice, Mann poses one of the most crucial questions for sociolegal studies: How do different institutional arrangements and procedures magnify (or reduce) the almost inevitable disparities in parties' ability to influence the construction of legal facts and the realization of justice? In posing this question, moreover, Mann addresses the larger issue raised by both Feeley and Friedman: In what ways are law and the operation of the legal system captives of larger structural conditions?

Barriers to Influence

In the chapters by Feeley, Friedman, and Mann, social science remains outside the frame of analysis. It is what they practice, as they collect, examine, and interpret historical data, but social science, as a social and cultural enterprise in its own right, is not part of their object of study. The four chapters in the next part of this volume, in contrast, focus their analytic gaze squarely on the role of social science as they seek to understand the relationship between law and social policy.

These chapters remind us that in the past thirty years, social science has indeed become deeply embedded in the processes of legal policymaking, particularly in the United States.[9] Comparing the American legal system with that of England, Atiyah and Summers

(1987, 404) write that, "The dominant general theory of law in America" can now be characterized by the term "instrumentalism," which "conceives of law essentially as a pragmatic instrument of social improvement" rather than as a received set of authoritative legal rules and principles. An instrumentalist view of law leads policy-makers to be concerned about the actual empirical consequences of current or proposed rules and institutions. Accordingly, legislatures, courts, and administrative agencies have become increasingly open, or eager to appear to be open, to considering sociolegal research and to building requirements for empirical assessment into the policy-making and policy-evaluation process.

Yet most academic sociolegal scholars do not conduct research that is quite so applied. Their relationship to the legal policy process typically is more indirect; they seek, through their research, to illuminate the dynamics of legal processes, to discern general tendencies, and to illuminate unexamined assumptions and biases underlying legal rules and processes.[10] Sometimes these studies are read by legislative staff members, administrators, and lawyers on the lookout for new insights. Often they are not. It probably can be said, however, that academic sociolegal studies have played a significant role in legitimating the use of theory and empirical evidence in debates concerning legal policy and institutional reform and, indeed, in enabling well-founded research findings sometimes to prevail, if properly mobilized, over untested assertions.

Chapters 4 through 7 reflect the assumption that social scientific evidence not only should but, based on our recent history, plausibly might be expected to influence legal policymaking. Based on that set of assumptions, they explore, in different ways, factors that limit sociolegal scholars' influence on the law.

Deborah Rhode, in chapter 4, acknowledges the formative role of the news media in shaping public and elite images regarding law, in this case tort litigation, often in ways that neglect and upstage the more systematic research conducted by sociolegal scholars. Journalists, Rhode claims, frame their coverage of legal cases in accordance with the constraints of their market and craft. Reported events must be newsworthy (meaning interesting or extreme). Stories must be generated under tight deadlines and with limited resources. As a consequence, the picture of the legal system that is generated as a result of this process tends to be biased, incomplete, and typically sensational.

Most important, this picture, Rhode asserts, no matter how extreme and empirically indefensible, cannot be simply dismissed as biased or distorted. The media do not just reflect some underlying reality, but, in their depictions, they may actually reshape the legal world they claim to be merely representing. By drawing on the sensational, the media generate public sentiments and produce preferences, intentions, and motives that, in turn, can influence legal behaviors and decisions.

In her critique of the media's role in representing the legal system, Rhode traces the complicity of legal academics and sociolegal scholars who, all too frequently, defer to (or remain oblivious to) the media's depictions and their cultural and political implications. Constraints of the academic craft mean that most scholars have neither the time, incentive, nor ability to present accurate and intelligible accounts of the legal system to the general public. Nonetheless, by not actively participating in the responsible dissemination of knowledge about the legal world, academics conspire in producing the misapprehensions and distrust of the public in relation to the law that are generated by the media's fixation on atrocity stories and extreme examples of abuse of the legal process. Rhode suggests, as a possible corrective to this situation, a dual strategy whereby the press become a more sophisticated consumer of information and research about the legal system and the law. Similarly, she argues, legal academics must become more sophisticated participants in public discussions.

Neil Vidmar, in chapter 5, also examines depictions of the law and the significance of these depictions in public discourse and policy efforts. Turning to the debates over the litigation crisis and tort reform, Vidmar analyzes the ways in which depictions of the system by interest groups and politicians all too often displace the careful mapping by sociolegal scholars in the policy debate. He illustrates this displacement using the growing body of research concerning medical malpractice litigation to puncture the politically generated stereotypes concerning the existence of a litigation crisis, an explosion of frivolous lawsuits, and an irresponsible jury system.

Vidmar begins his analysis by considering the so-called "gap" between the aspirations of law and its enactment (Sarat 1985). The particular gap that is perceived to exist in the case of medical malpractice, he argues, is in part manufactured by the various interest groups involved directly or indirectly in litigation and in legislative debates.

Law is known and enacted in a highly politicized arena, where formidable economic and professional interests can manufacture a "crisis" and generate legal changes. Once again, as in Feeley's research, we see that a multiplicity of actors—both legal and nonlegal—shape legal policy.

Vidmar jumps into this political arena armed with an array of relevant studies. In so doing he takes up the challenge that Rhode defines for social scientists. Vidmar examines a number of the most frequently heard and damning criticisms of medical malpractice, offering us, not a picture of a gap, but what he calls a "map" of the legal terrain or an accurate reckoning of how legal decisions are made and legal processes enacted. By examining the role of the jury and the character of settlements, Vidmar dispels, or corrects, many of the most widely held misapprehensions regarding medical malpractice. Reviewing social science data regarding issues such as the magnitude of compensatory awards, pain and suffering awards, and punitive awards, Vidmar concludes that juries, on balance, are neither irresponsible nor inclined to hand out excessive awards. Similarly, in regard to the settlement process, he concludes that the tort system is relatively effective in winnowing out cases without merit. Indeed, the most recurrent finding by sociolegal scholars, Vidmar notes, is that the American tort system systematically undercompensates seriously injured persons.

Vidmar concludes his assessment of the tort system by considering, as did Rhode, the role of sociolegal scholarship. He notes that although empirical sociolegal research cannot resolve the disputes over value that revolve around controversial legal policies—such as whether the tort system should emphasize prompt, economical, and widespread compensation, or punishment and deterrence of negligent behavior—sociolegal research, by accurately and dispassionately mapping the performance of legal institutions "can set terms around which the dialogue must center and focus policymakers on the real issues." Despite some failures in this regard, he notes some successes, and he urges the production of the kind of "maps" that have been produced in other areas of the law. He cautions scholars not to be discouraged by "spectacular failures, like the rejection or evasion of social science findings about the death penalty." He holds out hope that although the influence of social science may not be complete, immediate, or easily detected, it can and should shape the policy debate.

If social science is to influence policy and to overcome barriers to that influence, social scientists must be able to communicate clearly and be clear about the meaning of the core concepts of their research. Unfortunately, such clarity is rarely achieved. Jack Katz, in chapter 6, examines the efforts of sociolegal scholars to address issues of inequality in the legal system.[11] He provides an insightful history and analysis of social scientists' engagement with the problem of inequality—or "bias" as it is often termed—in the operation of legal institutions. Katz notes that researchers have asked whether legal processes are biased against a widening array of social groups—the poor, racial and ethnic minorities, women, gays and lesbians, immigrants—and in a widening array of institutional settings, from police cars and lower courts to the location of hazardous waste storage sites and the offices of institutions governed by antidiscrimination law, from schools and bank lending departments to apartment complexes and car dealers. Moreover, Katz observes, the focus of studies of bias has expanded conceptually. Beginning with a definition of bias as the expression of (1) individual psychological prejudice on the part of police or judges or employers, researchers have also conceptualized bias as (2) unequal organizational or institutional outcomes (such as higher imprisonment rates for African American defendants), regardless of whether there is or is not evidence of prejudice on the part of decisionmakers in the relevant institutions, and as (3) unequal patterns of pressures on decisionmakers, as when victims of securities fraud by upper-class businessmen ask enforcement officials not to prosecute (which would inhibit the victim's hopes of getting restitution), while victims of street crime demand prosecution of jobless assailants.

Katz goes on to analyze the different methodological and interpretive problems that have impeded efforts to document each kind of bias. For example, societal successes in banning discrimination and stigmatizing overt manifestations of bias have made public officials and employers much more circumspect about what they say, and hence it is much more difficult for researchers to document the incidence of personal prejudice in decisionmaking institutions. In research concerning unequal organizational outcomes, Katz observes, well-documented racially disparate capital punishment of black men in southern states helped to produce U.S. Supreme Court opinions that banned capital punishment for rape and that mandated closer statutory and judicial controls of prosecutorial and jury discretion in

murder cases. But it then became methodologically much more difficult to establish what role race played in capital cases—as David
Weisburd's chapter in this volume further demonstrates. Increasingly,
the search for bias has been pushed to earlier, less formal steps in the
legal process. Thus although research has indicated that white-collar
offenders are sentenced just as heavily as street criminals, that does not
settle the matter, Katz argues. The researcher must also study the pretrial screening of cases, which, it turns out, is biased toward middle-
and upper-class offenders, so that only a particularly egregious subset
of that group reaches the sentencing stage.

Partly because the intensity and incidence of conscious bias have
declined or been driven underground and partly because the analysis and moral interpretation of various kinds of inequalities have become more complicated, the social scientific search for bias, Katz concludes, has become "increasingly sophisticated" and "labyrinthine,"
while "its findings have become increasingly ambiguous in their policy implications." The simple demonology of earlier studies of bias is
no longer viable. Thus Katz concludes that researchers interested in
legal inequality must acknowledge "a more complex view of the distribution of morality in society" and must study legal and employment processes in all their social complexity and causal origins, if
they are to interpret adequately the incidence and etiology of
inequality.

David Weisburd, in chapter 7, nicely exemplifies the complexities
in proving bias that Katz mentions and the barriers to effective influence that social researchers face, even when their research is solicited by legal officials. Those complexities are greatest, this chapter
suggests, when social science analyses are invoked to help resolve
specific legal cases or policy issues. One of the most dramatic uses of
social science in court stemmed from research conducted by David
Baldus and his colleagues on homicide cases in Georgia in the 1970s.
Reviewing 2,000 Georgia murder cases, Baldus and his colleagues
found evidence that prosecutors were more likely to seek the death
penalty in cases in which black or white defendants had slain white
victims than in cases in which the homicide victim was black. The
disparities persisted when the researchers controlled for the number
of statutory "aggravating factors" (Baldus et al. 1983).[12] Nevertheless,
the U.S. Supreme Court ruled, in a five to four decision, that the statistical evidence fell short of proving that the state had acted with un-

constitutionally discriminatory purpose in the case at hand (*McCleskey v. Kemp*, 481 US 279 [1987]).

Weisburd's essay concerns yet another effort to use social scientific analysis to test the fairness of capital punishment, this time in the courts of New Jersey. The New Jersey legislature mandated appellate review of death sentences, instructing the state supreme court to determine whether the sentence imposed is "disproportionate to the penalty imposed in similar cases." The New Jersey supreme court then appointed Professor Baldus as special master to produce a database of relevant cases and a method for determining proportionality in particular cases. Weisburd carefully describes the methodological challenges faced by Baldus and his successors. The special master's analysis of prior cases indicated that blacks convicted of murder were slightly more likely than whites to have received a death sentence, as were defendants of either race who had killed white as opposed to black persons. Yet, as in *McCleskey*, the state's analysts criticized the results, arguing that the measures were inadequate and that the results were statistically unreliable. In a series of cases, the New Jersey supreme court grappled seriously with a progressively more sophisticated series of statistical debates, carefully described by Weisburd. But in each case, the court declined to find the proportionality analysis submitted by the special master to be sufficiently reliable to support a conclusion that the death sentence should be reversed on grounds of disproportionality or on grounds of "race-based disparities in sentencing."

The problem, Weisburd explains, was that the number of cases in the database was small (only thirty-nine death sentence cases) and hence the special master's statistical model for determining whether the offender in any particular case was equally culpable as others who had been sentenced to die generated results with wide "confidence intervals" or margins of error. Weisburd says that the special master used the best available social science methods to deal with the small-sample problem and the instability of the outcomes produced by the model. Yet what is good for social science may not be good enough for law. The statistical method still failed to meet the normative or policy standard that the court insisted on. Before the court would rule that police, prosecutors, and juries had acted unconstitutionally, the data would have to show that racial considerations had played a convincing or "relentless" role.

Weisburd's New Jersey story seems to reaffirm Katz's conclusion that the methodological and conceptual problems involved in the establishment of bias have become increasingly complex, so that research often yields ambiguous results. But Weisburd's analysis does not mean that social scientists have little to contribute to the search for equal justice. In the New Jersey capital punishment setting, social scientists were given an extraordinarily ambitious assignment: to build a predictive model, based on many variables and relatively few cases, that would determine the fairness of the sentence in a particular case. Moreover, the legal debate concerning capital punishment and race is politically explosive, bearing some resemblance in that respect to the highly politicized arena of tort reform discussed by Rhode and Vidmar. In those realms, empirical research is perhaps least likely to influence legal policy, as contending interest groups draw conflicting normative conclusions from the same empirical findings or invoke distorted accounts of social science studies.

More often, social scientific studies are intended not to determine case decisions or policy changes, but rather to provide political or legal policymakers with data or analyses that can inform their normative debates and choices. In many areas of legal policy, moreover, decisionmakers are eager for useful information or are eager to appear eager. In a complex society, findings of inequality, although surely important, often are not in themselves policy-determinative but rather are weighed against other values. In addition, as Katz's analysis reminds us, Weisburd's New Jersey story occurred after years of close legal and journalistic oversight that sharply diminished the most extreme manifestations of racial bias, thus making the proof of bias much more difficult to obtain. In other institutional spheres, systematic research into the often subtle ways in which social and economic inequalities affect legal processes is likely to remain both meaningful from a policy standpoint and central to the agenda of sociolegal studies.

Law and the Reordering of Social Relations

A recurrent set of questions in sociolegal studies revolve around the capacity of law to penetrate, influence, and change established social patterns and practices. Those questions have become increasingly salient as governments have become more ambitious, promulgating sweeping constitutional rights and regulatory programs that prohibit or demand sharp reductions in pollution, racial and gender discrimination, product-related risks, police brutality, securities fraud, and so on. When and why, sociolegal scholars have asked, do such ambitious laws and regulatory programs induce the desired behavioral changes? When and why do they instead lead only to symbolic responses or, at the other extreme, have large effects that are unanticipated and undesirable? How do interactions between regulatory officials and regulated entities, or between complainants and regulated entities, transform the meaning, the application, and the legitimacy of regulatory rules? How do changes in the political or economic context affect the implementation of regulations and the vindication of legal rights? Answering these questions may, in some instances, inform policymakers in ways that allow them to devise strategies to close the gap between law on the books and law in action.

Addressing such questions, many sociolegal scholars have turned to field research, conducting detailed case studies of regulatory enforcement in fields ranging from consumer fraud (Silbey 1984) and securities law (Shapiro 1984) to workplace safety (Kelman 1981), industrial pollution (Hawkins 1984; Shover et al. 1984), and quality of care in nursing homes (Braithwaite 1993). Other scholars have examined the dynamics of compliance, evasion, and adaptation to legal obligations in governmental agencies such as police departments (Skolnick 1966), welfare administrations (Mashaw 1971), and school districts (Kirp 1982). The chapters in this volume by Diane Vaughan and Susan Shapiro represent and extend this research tradition. Both employ the difficult, but rewarding, research strategy of probing deeply into the culture and practices of regulated organizations to determine the import and limits of external legal influences.

In chapter 8, Diane Vaughan emphasizes that if it is to be effective, regulation often must go beyond a legalistic "command and control" approach, backed by the threat of penalties. Regulated organizations, she notes, are not unified, profit-maximizing monoliths, responsive only to the threat of immediate sanctions imposed by law or the market. She tells us that deviant behavior in complex organizations arises from the interaction of such external legal pressures with the motives and perceptions of individuals within the organization and the interorganizational culture and structures that affect those motives and perceptions. Consequently, legal interventions must be attentive to the context-specific structural and cultural dynamics of organizational life, and sociological scholars, to aid that process, must do the "boundary work" of examining both the macro- and micro-level dynamics of organizational behavior.

Vaughan illustrates her point by discussing the tragic 1986 decision by the National Aeronautics and Space Administration (NASA) to launch the ill-fated space shuttle *Challenger*. The dominant explanation has been that NASA's managers, desperate to maximize the agency's political and budgetary position by maintaining a frequent launch schedule, overrode objections by engineers in the contracting aerospace company concerning the hazards of launching in unprecedentedly cold weather. But Vaughan's examination of archival records suggests that the launch decision violated no safety-oriented regulations and that the dominant opinion of the engineers, after completing the prescribed safety checks and discussions, was that it was safe to fly. The fatal decision, Vaughan tells us, was made because of an institutionalized practice, built up over a sequence of successful flights, of accepting incrementally larger risks as "normal."

The *Challenger* explosion, Vaughan points out, occurred even though NASA had established a regulatory system and decision structure that called for repeated analyses and critiques by knowledgeable engineers at each step of the prelaunch process. Moreover, this professionalized internal attention to safety was reinforced by the external political and legal environment, which presumably would impose huge costs on both NASA and the contractors in the event of a disaster. So why were the fatal flaws not detected or sufficiently emphasized? Vaughan's analysis points, among other factors, to (1) the false assurance that NASA engineers and managers drew from their faithful adherence to the safety procedures called for by the regulations and (2) their own working culture, which emphasized the inevitability of a certain degree of "satisficing" in adapting engineering theory to real-world conditions and the need for definitive scientific evidence (rather than mere engineering intuition) as a basis for changing existing procedures. One important lesson, Vaughan observes, "is that the potential deterrent impact of sanctions" can easily be nullified when "behavior that is considered objectively deviant to outsiders is considered normal and legitimate within an organization."

In one sense, the *Challenger* story conveys a discouraging message about law's capacity to prevent organizational error and misbehavior. But NASA's regulatory task, we ought to remember, is extraordinarily demanding: to produce absolute perfection in a complex process that extends the boundaries of engineering and organizational coordination and in which even small deviations can lead to disaster. In other, more mundane settings, where the operative goal is gradual progress in reducing the incidence of harmful acts, sociolegal scholars have shown that law often has been reasonably effective. By modifying organizational incentives and norms, regulation—to mention just a few examples—has reduced emissions of most major air and water pollutants, cut the mortality rate in coal mines (Lewis-Beck and Alford 1980), and curtailed smoking in transportation, restaurants, and offices (Kagan and Skolnick 1993). Using the tools of litigation, lawyers have stimulated significant improvements in southern prison conditions (Feeley 1996) and effective efforts in many police departments to curtail dangerous, brutal, and intrusive police practices (Orfield 1987; Skolnick and Fyfe 1993; Walker 1993). That is not to say that law always, or perhaps even usually, succeeds in such ambitious efforts; much depends, as Vaughan reminds us, on a variety of legal and contextual factors (Kagan 1994). Studies both of law's successes and of law's failures, however, converge in supporting Vaughan's central conclusion: law most efficiently and reliably affects complex organizations when it creates mechanisms that directly affect intraorganizational cultures and priorities.[13]

If Vaughan's chapter nicely represents the sociolegal literature that investigates the obstacles that law faces in building safeguards against organizational failure or misconduct, Susan Shapiro's chapter represents the tradition that explores the consequences of regulatory law when regulated entities (as they usually do) vary widely in size, risk of legal surveillance, and resources for compliance. The legal rules whose impact is traced in her study of 128 Illinois law firms are aimed at lawyers as service providers. Just as explicit governmental regulations governing used car dealers, banks, and corporate pension funds codify norms designed to protect consumers, the American Bar Association Code of Professional Responsibility seeks to protect lawyers' customers (and the integrity of legal processes) by ensuring that a lawyer will not take cases from clients whose interests conflict with the interests of other clients represented by the same lawyer or by others in the firm.

At first blush, one might ask whether hard-driving, profit-seeking law firms take these ethical rules seriously. As firms get larger, Shapiro's research shows, the number of potential conflicts among clients grows exponentially and the more burdensome it is to detect them. At the same time, like many other rules of the modern regulatory state, the rules extend far beyond precluding harmful acts; they are prophylactic and extraordinarily cautious, seeking to prevent conflicts that might result in harm to a client's interests under circumstances in which the client's attorney also violates other, more immediate duties of loyalty. Moreover, as in the case of many other regulatory regimes, violations of the rules often are difficult to detect. Yet apart from a handful of small Illinois firms (whom Shapiro classifies as "ostriches," since they simply hope the problem will go away), Shapiro finds that law firms do take these regulations seriously. Some smaller firms whom she labels "elephants" rely only on the memory of senior partners to detect conflicts. But most invest an extraordinary amount of time and money in creating archival and (as they grow larger) computerized databases and review systems.

The bar's ethical injunctions have teeth, Shapiro shows, partly because a law firm's adversaries can petition courts to disqualify a law firm on grounds of a conflict of interest and because lawyers can be sued for malpractice if they fail to detect and disclose conflicts. Fighting disqualification motions and malpractice suits is very costly and may hurt the firm's reputation. In addition, Shapiro finds that legal malpractice insurance companies, especially a mutual company created by large law firms themselves, pressure firms to adopt ever more elaborate "conflict-detecting" systems. This comports with sociolegal studies of other regulatory regimes, which suggest that law gains its greatest potency in shaping business behavior when it stimulates the creation of intraorganizational "shadow-regulators" who are charged with buffering the organization from "trouble" with regulatory agencies or the courts (Bardach and Kagan 1982).

Indeed, one of the most interesting aspects of Shapiro's study is how passively the lawyers seem to accept the regulatory regime. In large firms whose conflict-detecting systems are so advanced that Shapiro labels them "cybersurveillance" or "technoblitz," certain senior partners spend more time watching out for potential conflicts of interest than they do on "client work," and "on a complex case with many coparties, it may cost more to do a conflicts search than the client will be billed in fees." This, together with parallel findings in some other studies, suggests that even beyond the economic risks that motivate enterprises to comply with the law, legal compliance systems in organizations often take on a life of their own, institutionalizing new values in the entity's day-to-day operations (Edelman, Abraham, and Erlanger 1992). At least in countries with a strong cultural commitment to the rule of law, Shapiro's chapter implies, law usually can affect organizational norms and behavior, although those effects typically are more elusive with respect to small, less "visible," and less well-endowed entities (see also Kagan and Axelrad 1997).

Conclusions

The relationship among social science, social policy, and the law is nothing if it is not complex, contingent, and variable. As a result, the lessons that can be drawn from this collection of essays are, of course, multiple. Sometimes our work identifies where policy fails and helps us to understand why; sometimes it shows what works and points the way for a greater investment in those things. Yet always what social science offers to law is a broadening of perspective and a deepened awareness of the latent forces that constrain legal policy and the latent consequences that accompany any legal decision. This broadening of perspective comes at a cost to both law and social science. Law has to act in the world and act with whatever information it has, however, partial, incomplete, or biased. The cost to social science is that its power as critique may be diminished as it seeks influence and that it may lend an appearance of rationality and legitimacy to a process that is itself deeply political. And, as the essays suggest, social science information competes with anecdote, horror story, and myth for the attention of policymakers. What we offer is complexity and often increased uncertainty. This is hardly the stuff to win friends when decisions have to be made and sides have to be taken.

The essays collected in this volume remind us that, as Susan Silbey (1997, 233) points out, we must pursue social science knowledge of law "because without that theoretically informed analysis of the social organization of power and law . . . critical questions of justice cannot be answered."

Notes

1. Stanton Wheeler is Ford Foundation Professor of Law and the Social Sciences at Yale Law School and Master of Morse College of Yale University. He was educated at Pomona College and the University of Washington and is the author or editor of ten books including *Controlling Delinquents, Crimes of the Middle Class, Social History and Social Policy,* and *Sitting in Judgment: The Sentencing of White Collar Criminals.* He is widely recognized as the "father" of an entire generation of law and society scholars, several of whose work is represented in this volume.

2. Much of the following analysis is taken from Sarat and Silbey (1988).

3. Legal realism was by no means, however, a unified or singular intellectual movement. At one and the same time, the label legal realist has been applied to people like Felix Cohen (1935), who took what Gary Peller (1985) later categorized as a deconstructive approach—a radical skepticism that challenged the claims of logical coherence and necessity in legal reasoning—and to others like Karl Llewellyn (1930) who embraced and believed in science and technique. Moreover, realism embodied three distinct political perspectives. It included a critical oppositional strand that sought to undermine the law's ability to provide legitimacy for political and economic elites by exposing the contradictions of classical legal formalism and the hypocrisy of legal authority. Realism also included a strand of scientific naturalism whose proponents attempted to advance a more enlightened, rational, and efficient social order by using the methods and insights of the empirical sciences to understand a wide range of human, political, and social phenomena. Among these scientific realists, there were divisions between the pragmatic followers of Dewey and James and those realists who pursued a more positivistic version of empirical science. Finally, legal realism was a practical political effort that did more than merely support or legitimate political elites; some of its members were themselves the officials designing, making, and enforcing reform policies.

4. Not all strands of realist inquiry were, however, equally confident that law could, or should, be rescued or that its integrity could, or should, be restored. The deconstructivist strand, which came to be viewed by mainstream legal scholars as dangerously relativistic and nihilistic, tried to reorient legal thought by emphasizing its indeterminacy, contingency, and contradiction. According to Peller, "This deconstructive, debunking strand of realism seemed inconsistent with any liberal notion of a rule of law distinct from politics, or indeed any mode of rational thought distinct from ideology . . . This approach emphasized contingency and open-ended possibilities as it exposed the exercises of social power behind what appeared to be the neutral work of reason" (Peller 1985, 1223).

5. By pointing to the scientific impulse in realism, however, we do not want to suggest that only one model of empirical social science was available for adoption by those who pursued a more "constructivist" approach. Institutionalists of such varied stripes as Walton Hamilton, William Douglas, Rexford Tugwell, John Commons, and A. A. Berle attacked the metaphysics and psychological abstractions of classical economics and organization theory, producing detailed descriptive histories and analyses of organizational behavior and legal doctrine (Hamilton and Wright 1926; Commons 1924). Making space for this style of realism, only a small number of scholars went so far as to embrace a full-fledged operationalism, that is, defining concepts in terms of a set of physical operations, observable actions external to and removed from the human mind, and "probably half of the active social scientists of the period accepted the outlines of [a] broader [less stringent] quantitative behaviorism" (Purcell 1973, 39). The work of the largest majority of social scientists was even more generally particularist and functional without sharing the tenet of the most extreme objectivism of some. Particularism meant specificity and attention to detail; it eschewed generalization and categorization. If a concept was to be valid and meaningful, it had to refer directly to an individual concrete thing. Functionalism meant that those details—specific facts, cases, and things—were to be understood in terms of their social and economic consequences; it denied the possibility of a further standard for determining the worth of anything (Purcell 1973, 42). Many of the social scientists who shared a generally functionalist approach, and who participated in the spread of scientific naturalism in the 1920s and 1930s, nonetheless criticized what they considered to be its excesses: too extreme a "concern with measurement and an abuse of statistical techniques" (Purcell 1973, 39; see also Hamilton 1931; Ogburn 1934). There was a strong pragmatic impulse; fact finding was to be related to practical problem solving, according to Merriam and Berle (Karl 1969). Dewey "argued that the quantitative behaviorists distorted the scientific method in their desire to reduce social science to purely 'factual' data" (Purcell 1973, 40; see also Dewey 1931).

6. Yet at the same time, law has come to seem more vexed and vexing. As the O. J. Simpson trial showed, the more we see of law, the less we like it. Legal legitimacy is more strained, the closer we come to the triumph of liberal legality.

7. To the extent some sociologists of law continue to orient themselves to social policy, they are likely to be led, like the realists, to try to establish credibility with that audience by claiming that they offer a posture of "deliberate detachment" (Friedman 1986, 780). This is not to say that interest in policy is the only force encouraging sociologists of law to adhere to, or to adopt, the posture and canons of normal science; there are

certainly others. Nonetheless, it is worthwhile noting the powerful effect of that interest in encouraging sociologists of law to characterize their empirical work in the language of science (see Dror 1975). It encourages sociologists of law to operate as if social behavior could be understood in terms of a tangible and determinate world of facts (see Rein and White 1977; Rich 1977), to treat data as if they were an undistorted window on the social world, to treat the ambiguity of what we observe in an unambiguous way. Sociologists of law are invited to act as if there were a clear congruence between our representations of things and the things themselves and to accept the model of value-free, detached, objective inquiry in which empirical research seeks generally valid propositional knowledge about "reality." This is one of the results of attempting to speak convincingly to the powerful (see Trubek 1984; Black 1976).

8. At the same time as we refine our theories and develop more sophisticated methods of social investigation, the status of value-neutral inquiry in the academy is viewed with greater skepticism and is under greater scrutiny than ever before (see, for example, Sarat 1994).

9. In the 1960s, social scientists conducted studies of police practices, criminal courts, and race relations for the Kerner Commission and the National Commission on Violence appointed by President Lyndon Johnson. Since then, policy-oriented sociolegal research has been systematically supported by the National Institute of Justice, the National Sentencing Commission, the National Research Council, the American Bar Foundation, and the Rand Corporation Institute for Civil Justice. Congress and several presidents have instructed regulatory agencies to conduct cost-benefit analysis of proposed regulations. The Justice Department schedules recurrent crime "victimization" studies, based on surveys of household experience. Court administrators, drawing on social science methodologies, study the determinants of delay in court and the effects of experimental changes in pretrial policies. Law review articles arguing legal policy issues routinely cite sociolegal research. Psychologists advise lawyers on jury selection. The New Jersey Supreme Court, David Weisburd's chapter in this volume tells us, appointed a sociolegal scholar as a special master to construct a database and statistical model to help guide the court's decisionmaking in capital punishment cases.

10. Chapters 1, 2, and 3 in this volume are good examples of this tendency.

11. The normatively freighted relationship between law and inequality has long been an important, perhaps a paramount, focus of sociolegal research. (This emphasis may be partially responsible for the development of a lively scholarly counterstream, the law and economics movement, in which the relationship between law and economic efficiency has been the primary focus.) But in the pages of the *Law & Society Review*

and in the conference rooms of the Law and Society Association, sociolegal scholars have presented studies examining whether police officers treat white and minority complainants and suspects differently (Reiss 1971), whether African Americans convicted of crime receive heavier sentences than whites with comparable offenses and prior records (Spohn et al. 1981–82), whether white-collar defendants get lighter sentences than lower-class offenders (Weisburd et al. 1991), whether "the haves come out ahead" in lower courts (Galanter 1974) and state supreme courts (Wheeler et al. 1987), and the consequences of police officers' tendency to forgo arrest more often in spousal abuse cases than in other kinds of assaults (Sherman 1992).

12. To use Katz's terminology, lawyers for Warren McCleskey, a black man sentenced to die for killing a white police officer in an Atlanta suburb, argued before the U.S. Supreme Court that these racially disparate outcomes provided evidence of psychological prejudice, perhaps unconscious, in the charging process, thereby showing that the death penalty was arbitrarily and hence unconstitutionally applied. By a five to four majority, the court rejected McCleskey's argument, reasoning that the statistical evidence fell short of proving that "the decisionmakers in McCleskey's case acted with discriminatory purpose" (*McCleskey v. Kemp*, 481 U.S. 279 [1987]).

13. Today, the most interesting regulatory policymaking and enforcement programs in the United States and abroad build on this insight, providing incentives for intra-agency, intracorporation, or industry-wide self-regulation, auditing, and disclosure (Gunningham and Rees 1997).

References

Abel, Richard. 1973. "Law Books and Books about Law." *Stanford Law Review* 26: 175.

Atiyah, P. S., and Robert Summers. 1987. Form and Substance in Anglo-American Law: A Comparative Study of Legal Reasoning, Legal Theory, and Legal Institutions. Oxford: Clarenden Press.

Baldus, David, Charles Pulaski, and George Woodworth. 1983. "A Comparative Review of Death Sentences." *Journal of Criminal Law and Criminology* 74: 661.

Bardach, Eugene, and Robert A. Kagan. 1982. *Going by the Book: The Problem of Regulatory Unreasonableness*. Philadelphia: Temple University Press.

Black, Donald. 1976. *The Behavior of Law*. New York: Academic Press.

Blumberg, Abraham. 1967. "The Practice of Law as a Confidence Game." *Law & Society Review* 1: 15.

Braithwaite, John. 1993. "The Nursing Home Industry." In *Beyond the Law: Crime in Complex Organizations,* vol. 18: *Crime and Justice,* edited by Michael Tonry and Albert J. Reiss, Jr.. Chicago: University of Chicago Press.

Brigham, John. 1996. *The Constitution of Interests: Beyond the Politics of Rights.* New York: New York University Press.

Brigham, John, and Christine Harrington. 1989. "Realism and Its Consequences." *International Journal of the Sociology of Law* 17: 41.

Cardozo, Benjamin. 1921. *The Nature of the Judicial Process.* New Haven: Yale University Press.

Cohen, Felix. 1935. "Transcendental Nonsense and the Functional Approach." *Columbia Law Review* 34: 809.

Commons, John R. 1924. *The Legal Foundations of Capitalism.* New York: Macmillan.

Dewey, J. 1931. "Social Science and Social Control." *New Republic* 67: 276.

———. 1960. *The Quest for Certainty.* New York: Minton, Balch.

Dror, Yehezkel. 1975. "Applied Social Science and Systems Analysis." In *The Use and Abuse of Social Science.* 2d ed., edited by I. L. Horowitz. New Brunswick, N.J.: Transaction Books.

Edelman, Lauren, Steven Abraham, and Howard Erlanger. 1992. "Professional Construction of Law: The Inflated Threat of Wrongful Discharge." *Law & Society Review* 26: 47.

Edelman, Lauren, Howard Erlanger, and John Lande. 1993. "Employers' Handling of Discrimination Complaints: The Transformation of Rights in the Workplace." *Law & Society Review* 27: 497.

Ellickson, Robert. 1991. *Order without Law: How Neighbors Settle Disputes.* Cambridge, Mass.: Harvard University Press.

Eulau, Heinz 1963. *The Behavioral Persuasion in Politics.* New York: Random House.

Ewick, Patricia, and Susan Silbey. 1998. *The Common Place of Law: Stories from Everyday Life.* Chicago: University of Chicago Press.

Feeley, Malcolm. 1996. "Federal Courts in the Political Process: Assessing the Consequences of Prison Conditions Litigation." In *Courts and the Political Process,* edited by Austin Ranney. Berkeley, Calif.: Institute of Governmental Studies Press.

Friedman, Lawrence. 1986. "The Law and Society Movement." *Stanford Law Review* 38: 763.

Galanter, Marc. 1974. "Why the 'Haves' Come out Ahead: Speculations on the Limits of Legal Change." *Law & Society Review* 9: 95.

———. 1985. "The Legal Malaise; Or, Justice Observed." *Law & Society Review* 19: 537.

Garth, Bryant, and Austin Sarat. 1998. "Justice and Power in Law and Society Work: On the Contested Careers of Core Concepts." In *Justice and Power in Sociolegal Studies,* edited by Bryant Garth and Austin Sarat. Evanston, Ill.: Northwestern University Press.

Gunningham, Neil, and John Rees. 1997. "Industry Self-Regulation: An Institutional Perspective." *Law and Policy* 19: 363–414.

Hamilton, Walton. 1931. "Methods in Social Science: Three Reviews of the Rice Book." *Journal of Political Economy* 39: 633.

Hamilton, Walton, and Helen R. Wright. 1926. *The Case of Bituminous Coal.* New York: Macmillan.

Hawkins, Keith. 1984. *Environment and Enforcement: Regulation and the Social Definition of Deviance.* Oxford: Oxford University Press.

Heimer, Carol. 1993. "Competing Institutions: Law, Medicine, and Family in Neonatal Intensive Care." American Bar Foundation Working Paper 9308. American Bar Foundation.

Hofstadter, Richard. 1955. *The Age of Reform.* New York: Vintage Books.

Holmes, O. W. 1881. *The Common Law.* Boston: Little, Brown & Co.

Hunt, Alan. 1978. *The Sociological Movement in Law.* Philadelphia: Temple University Press.

———. 1980. "The Radical Critique of Law." *International Journal of the Sociology of Law* 8: 33.

Jacob, Herbert. 1983. "Trial Courts in the United States." *Law & Society Review* 17: 407.

Kagan, Robert A. 1994. "Regulatory Enforcement." In *Handbook of Administrative Law and Regulation,* edited by David Rosenbloom and Richard D. Schwartz, pp. 383–422. New York: Marcel Dekker Inc.

———. 1995a. "Adversarial Legalism and American Government." In *The New Politics of Public Policy,* edited by Mark Landy and Martin Levin. Baltimore, Md.: Johns Hopkins University Press.

———. 1995b. "What Socio-Legal Scholars Should Do When There Is Too Much Law to Study." *Journal of Law and Society* 22: 140.

———. 1996. "American Lawyers, Legal Culture, and Adversarial Legalism." In *Legal Culture and the Legal Profession,* edited by Lawrence Friedman and Harry Scheiber. Boulder, Colo.: Westwood Press.

Kagan, Robert A., and Lee Axelrad. 1997. "Adversarial Legalism: An International Perspective." In *Comparative Disadvantages? Social Regulations and the Global Economy,* edited by Pietro Nivola. Washington, D.C.: Brookings Institution.

Kagan, Robert A., and Jerome Skolnick. 1993. "Banning Smoking: Compliance without Coercion." In *Smoking Policy: Law, Policy, and Politics,* edited by Robert Rabin and Stephen Sugarman. New York: Oxford University Press.

Karl, Benjamin D. 1969. "Presidential Planning and Social Science Research: Mr. Hoover's Experts." In *Perspectives in American History,* edited by Bernard Bailyn and Donald Fleming. Cambridge, Mass.: Harvard University Press.

Kelman, Steven. 1981. *Regulating America, Regulating Sweden: A Comparative Study of Occupational Safety and Health Policy.* Cambridge, Mass.: MIT Press.

Kirp, David. 1982. *Just Schools: The Idea of Racial Equality in American Education.* Berkeley: University of California Press.

Llewellyn, Karl. 1925. "The Effects of Legal Institutions upon Economics." *American Economic Review* 15: 665.

———. 1930. "A Realistic Jurisprudence: The Next Step." *Columbia Law Review* 30: 431.

———. 1931a. *The Bramble Bush.* Dobbs Ferry, N.Y.: Oceana Press.

———. 1931b. "Some Realism about Realism." *Harvard Law Review* 44: 1222.

———. 1940. "On Reading and Using the Newer Jurisprudence." *Columbia Law Review* 40: 581.

Lewis-Beck, Michael, and James Alford. 1980. "Can Government Regulate Safety? The Coal Mine Example." *American Political Science Review* 74: 745.

Macaulay, Stewart. 1979. "Lawyers and Consumer Protection Laws." *Law & Society Review* 14: 115.

Mashaw, Jerry. 1971. "Welfare Reform and Local Administration of AFDC in Virginia." *Virginia Law Review* 57: 818.

McCann, Michael. 1994. *Rights at Work: Law and the Politics of Pay Equity.* Chicago: University of Chicago Press.

McDougal, Myres. 1941. "Fuller v. the American Legal Realists." *Yale Law Journal* 50: 827.

Nelken, David 1981. "The 'Gap Problem' in the Sociology of Law." *Windsor Access to Justice Yearbook* 1: 35.

Ogburn, W. F. 1934. "The Limitation of Statistics." *American Journal of Sociology* 40: 12.

Orfield, Myron. 1987. "The Exclusionary Rule and Deterrence: An Empirical Study of Chicago Narcotics Officers." *University of Chicago Law Review* 54: 1016.

Peller, Gary. 1985. "The Metaphysics of American Law." *California Law Review* 73: 1152.

Pound, Roscoe. 1923. "The Theory of Judicial Decision." *Harvard Law Review* 36: 641.

———. 1931. "The Call for a Realist Jurisprudence." *Harvard Law Review* 44: 697.

Purcell, Edward. 1973. *The Crisis of Democratic Theory.* Lexington: University of Kentucky Press.

Rein, Martin, and Sheldon White. 1977. "Can Research Help Policy?" *The Public Interest,* 49: 119.

Reisman, David. 1941. "Law and Social Science." *Yale Law Journal* 50: 636.

Reiss, Albert J., Jr. 1971. *The Police and the Public.* New Haven, Conn.: Yale University Press.

Rich, Robert. 1977. "Uses of Social Science Information by Federal Bureaucrats." In *Using Social Research in Policy Making,* edited by Charles Weiss. Lexington: D. C. Heath.

Rosenblum, Victor. 1970. "Presidential Message." *Law & Society Review* 5: 3.

Sarat, Austin. 1985. "Legal Effectiveness and Social Studies of Law: On the Unfortunate Persistence of a Research Tradition." *Legal Studies Forum* 9: 23.

———. 1994. "Leading Law into the Abyss: What (If Anything) Has Sociology Done to Law?" *Law and Social Inquiry* 19: 609.

Sarat, Austin, and Thomas Kearns. 1993. "Beyond the Great Divide." In *Law in Everyday Life,* edited by Austin Sarat and Thomas Kearns. Ann Arbor: University of Michigan Press.

Sarat, Austin, and Susan Silbey. 1988. "The Pull of the Policy Audience." *Law and Policy* 10: 97.

Sarat, Austin, Marianne Constable, David Engel, Valerie Hans, and Susan Lawrence. 1998a. "The Concept of Boundaries in the Practices and Products of Sociolegal Scholarship: An Introduction." In *Crossing Boundaries: Traditions and Transformations in Law and Society Research,* edited by Austin Sarat, Marianne Constable, David Engel, Valerie Hans, and Susan Lawrence. Evanston, Ill.: Northwestern University Press.

———. 1998b. "Ideas of the 'Everyday' and the 'Trouble' Case in Law and Society Research." In *Everyday Practices and Trouble Cases,* edited by Austin Sarat, Marianne Constable, David Engel, Valerie Hans, and Susan Lawrence. Evanston, Ill.: Northwestern University Press.

Scheingold, Stuart. 1974. *The Politics of Rights.* New Haven: Yale University Press.

Schlegel, John. 1979. "American Legal Realism and Empirical Social Science. I." *Buffalo Law Review* 28: 459.

———. 1980. "American Legal Realism and Empirical Social Science. II." *Buffalo Law Review* 29: 195.

Schwartz, Richard. 1965. "Introduction." *Law and Society: Supplement to Social Problems* 4: 1.

Shapiro, Susan. 1984. *Wayward Capitalists: Target of the Securities and Exchange Commission.* New Haven, Conn.: Yale University Press.

Sherman, Lawrence. 1992. "The Influence of Criminology on Criminal Law: Evaluating Arrests for Misdemeanor Domestic Violence." *Journal of Criminal Law and Criminology* 83: 1.

Shover, Neil, et al. 1984. "Regional Variation in Regulatory Law Enforcement: The Surface Mining Control and Reclamation Act." In *Enforcing Regulation,* edited by Keith Hawkins and John Thomas. Boston: Kluwer-Nijhoff.

Silbey, Susan. 1984. "The Consequences of Responsive Regulation." In *Enforcing Regulation,* edited by Keith Hawkins and John Thomas. Boston: Kluwer-Nijhoff.

———. 1997. " 'Let Them Eat Cake': Globalization, Postmodern Colonialism, and the Possibilities of Justice." *Law & Society Review* 31: 207.

Skolnick, Jerome. 1966. *Justice Without Trial.* New York: John Wiley.

Skolnick, Jerome, and James Fyfe. 1993. *Above the Law: Police and the Excessive Use of Force.* New York: The Free Press.

Spohn, Cassia, John Gruhl, and Susan Welch. 1981–82. "The Effect of Race on Sentencing: A Re-Examination of an Unsettled Question." *Law & Society Review* 16: 71.

Trubek, David 1984. "Where the Action Is." *Stanford Law Review* 36: 575.

Trubek, David, and John Esser. 1987. "Critical Empiricism." In "American Legal Studies Paradox Program,or Pandora's Box." *Law and Social Inquiry* 14:3.

Trubek, D., and Marc Galanter. 1974. "Scholars in Self-Estrangement." *1934 Wisconsin Law Review* 1062.

Walker, Samuel. 1993. *Taming the System: The Control of Discretion in Criminal Justice, 1950–1990.* New York: Oxford University Press.

Weick, Kenneth. 1979. *The Social Psychology of Organizing.* Reading, Mass.: Addison Wesley.

Weisburd, David, Stanley Wheeler, Elin Waring, and Nancy Bode. 1991. *Crimes of the Middle Classes: White-Collar Offenders in the Federal Courts.* New Haven, Conn.: Yale University Press.

Weitzman, Lenore. 1985. *The Divorce Revolution.* New York: Free Press.

Wheeler, Stanton, Bliss, Cartwright, Robert A. Kagan, and Lawrence Friedman. 1987. "Do the 'Haves' Come out Ahead? Winning and Losing in State Supreme Courts, 1970–1970." *Law & Society Review* 21: 403.

Whyte, William F. 1986. "On the Uses of Social Science Research." *American Sociological Review* 51: 555.

Yntema, Hessel E. 1934. "Legal Science and Reform." *Yale Law Journal* 37: 468.

Part I

Historical and Structural Analyses of Law

Chapter 1

Privatization and Punishment: Lessons from History

Malcolm M. Feeley

In this essay, I examine two seemingly unrelated episodes in the history of penal sanctioning: transportation of felons from England to North America in the seventeenth and eighteenth centuries and the movement for the privatization of corrections in contemporary America. I link these two seemingly disparate policies separated by centuries and continents by focusing on features they share in common. I want to show that the same dynamics and consequences that are readily observable in the past policy of transportation (owing perhaps to historical distance and perspective) also occur in contemporary policies on correctional privatization. This effort will reveal what I think is the most dramatic feature of the privatization of corrections: the capacity of entrepreneurs to innovate and expand the nature and forms of criminal sanctions.

My argument, however, depends on a somewhat distinctive interpretation of the effects of transportation. Contrary to standard historical interpretation, which characterizes transportation as an "alternative" or "substitute" or "replacement" for capital punishment, I argue that this new form of punishment was an innovation of gigantic proportions, one that multiplied many times over the state's capacity to punish. To characterize it as an alternative or substitute for executions is to fail to comprehend that it was an innovation that profoundly expanded the state's capacity to punish and thus radically transformed the criminal justice system of the time.

I connect this earlier experience to the contemporary movement for privatization in corrections, because like transportation the contemporary effort is an innovation of gigantic proportions that has expanded the state's capacity to punish. And like transportation, its significance has also been obscured by a tendency to characterize it as an "alternative" or "substitute" for public prisons and by a preoccupation with the alleged efficiencies of private contractors in contrast to public agencies. I have two purposes in comparing these two quite diverse efforts: (1) to underscore the ease with which dramatic differences can be seen as functional equivalents and, more important, (2) to underscore the most distinctive feature of correctional privatization—not its alleged efficiencies, but rather the capacity of entrepreneurs to sense and meet or create the demand for an expanded repertoire of punishments. This lesson is most clearly revealed in the historical examination of transportation. But it is a lesson that applies to the contemporary movement for privatization of corrections as well.

In drawing parallels between two widely divergent episodes in penal history separated by time and form, I have accepted Stan Wheeler's invitation to social scientists to explore policy history not so much to trace the distant origins of a current policy, but to identify underlying patterns and recurring dynamics, in other words to see if in at least certain policy arenas, the past sheds light on the present (Rothman and Wheeler 1981). I hope to show that just as the early experiment in privatization of transportation led to a dramatic expansion of the state's capacity to punish, so too is the current privatization movement contributing to an expansion of punishment, and for essentially the same reasons. The lesson suggested by the history explored here is that, with respect to penal policy, private entrepreneurs are influential innovators who sense new demands, exploit new technologies, and develop new forms of social control.

Transportation to the Colonies

Shortly after arriving in Virginia in 1607, the first colonists were followed by a handful of convicted felons, transported there as a condition of pardon to be sold into a type of slavery or indentured servitude for periods of seven or fourteen years. This set into motion a new penal system that operated successfully for nearly 250 years. For the second half of this period, transportation constituted England's dominant mode of punishment for more serious property offenders. Emerging as a response to what was widely perceived as an ineffectual criminal justice system, transportation to the New World was a marriage of efficiency and effectiveness. It was efficient in that its costs were borne by profit-seeking merchants selling their human cargo and by planters purchasing it. It was effective in that it sanctioned thousands of offenders who otherwise would have gone unpunished.

One estimate is that fully half of the immigrants to the Americas during the eighteenth century were transported convicts or indentured servants (Smith 1965). During the long North American phase of transportation, from the early 1600s to 1776, some 50,000 convicts were shipped across the Atlantic to Virginia, the Carolinas, and Maryland where they were sold as agricultural laborers (Smith 1965; Ekrich 1987). Following the War of Independence the policy of transportation was modified and redirected to Australia. Between the time the first convict ship sailed into Botany Bay in 1789 and the time transportation ended in 1868, more than 100,000 convicts were put to task in Australia as agricultural workers, sheepherders, and manual laborers. However, this essay focuses only on North American transportation, a system—in contrast to Australia's—that was almost wholly administered by private entrepreneurs (Oldham 1933).

Why one form of punishment loses favor and another is instituted may not be readily answerable. At any given period, a number of alternatives may be employed simultaneously, and one may predominate. Banishment and forced labor, for instance, have been used as forms of punishment in diverse societies throughout history. The precise reasons for the rise of the transportation system in seventeenth-century England may not be fully understandable, but the policy cannot be divorced from the failure of the experiment with galleys, the development of mercantilism, and the colonial experience.[1] It began with the first settlement in North America and grew in rough proportion to the flow of English settlers to the Americas and the flow of cotton and tobacco from Virginia, Maryland, and the Carolinas to England.

Transportation began as an outgrowth of the trade in indentured servants; the same social and economic conditions that induced people to relocate to the New World also generated indentured servitude. And it was this same set of inducements that led to transportation. In his monumental book on the subject, *Colonists in Bondage*,

Abbot Emerson Smith pinpoints the primary economic impulse that gave rise to and sustained this process:

> From the complex pattern of forces producing emigration to the American colonies one stands out clearly as most powerful in causing the movement of servants. This was the pecuniary profit to be made by shipping them. Labor was one of the few European importations which even the earliest colonists would sacrifice much to procure, and the system of indentured servitude was the most convenient system next to slavery by which labor became a commodity to be bought and sold. [Smith 1965, 4–5]

These observations about the trade in indentured servants apply equally well to the trade in convicts. Smith (1965, 6) writes, "Even the convicts were handed over to private individuals. They shipped them to Maryland and Virginia and sold them at an excellent profit to the same planters who denounced the English government for allowing them to come at all." Indeed the two groups, indentured servants and convicts, were often indistinguishable in the public's mind, which was inclined to view both groups as scoundrels and ne'er-do-wells. Intellectuals and public officials, duty-bound to address concerns about potential mob unruliness among the "dangerous classes," lumped both groups together as a sort of surplus underclass for whom the colonies served as an overflow valve. Colonial landowners viewed both servants and convicts as sources of cheap labor. And merchants saw them as cargo to be commingled in the holds of their ships and sold to the highest bidders on the other side of the Atlantic.

In North America, transportation developed from a simple ad hoc arrangement to a sophisticated enterprise that enabled the state to sanction thousands of felons at little or no public cost and concomitantly provided handsome returns to private investors. At the outset, transportation was imposed as a condition of pardon by the crown after a court-issued sentence of death. Specific arrangements were left to the offender, his or her family, and some time later the county. If the family was unable to raise money for passage, convicts might languish in dockside jails for months or years. Some were able to negotiate free passage in exchange for allowing the captain to sell them into bondage. With growing experience and increasing profit in the indentured servants trade, shippers realized the economic potential of this new market for convicts and sought to rationalize it by securing government subsidies and exclusive transportation contracts. Once developed, their businesses generated a steady supply of convicts who were sent to North America in specially designed ships and auctioned off throughout the mid-Atlantic colonies. Without government contracts, shippers had previously profited only by transporting able-bodied males, but with subsidies they were able to take all sorts of offenders—women, children, elderly, and infirm—and still turn a profit.

This success is reflected in a series of commissions of the Privy Council through the eighteenth century that expanded authorization for transportation and granted exclusive charters for transportation to a select number of shippers (Ekrich 1987, 97–111). Indeed, in 1763 the demand for convicts in the Carolinas and Virginia was so intense that the crown was able to negotiate contracts that eliminated the subsidy of £5 per person. Shippers could make sufficient profits without it. This arrangement continued for another twelve years until the American Revolution put an abrupt halt to it (Oldham 1933).[2]

It is impossible to know who first seized on the idea of convict transportation. Was it entrepreneurs, experienced in the profitable trade in indentured servants and anxious to increase their westbound cargo? Or was it government officials desperate to find cheap ways to cope with a mounting crisis of law and order? Or was it the families of convicted offenders who sought to save the lives of loved ones by arranging for pardons and agreeing to remove them from English society?

Whatever its precise origins, transportation was ultimately deemed an overwhelming success. In an era when the idea of a central government, and particularly a strong centralized criminal justice system, was anathema to large segments of English society, the strategy of a decentralized, privately administered system of punishment was attractive. Transportation multiplied many times over the state's penal capacity and at no or low public expense. From the vantage point of those who established it and those who benefited from it, the marriage of efficiency and economy, of penal reform and mercantilism, of conscience and convenience was a welcome and progressive innovation.

The genius of this vast system of privately administered sanctions may more fully be appreciated when one realizes that it was put into place and functioning well more than one hundred years before parliament authorized the appointment of the first full-time, paid judge and nearly two hundred years before the first professional police force was established or the first prison was built in London. When they eventually came, all these developments were at first fiercely resisted by both the working class, which feared greater repressiveness from a stronger central government, and the aristocracy, which viewed a strong central government and a strong criminal justice system as encroachments on their traditional domains of privilege.

Misreading History

On the whole, English transportation to North America has been given short shrift by historians of the development of modern penalty.[3] But when it has been considered, it has often been characterized as a replacement for or alternative to capital punishment, a transitional punishment between the decline in the use of the death penalty and the rise of the prison. For instance in his monumental study of the history of the development of modern English penal policies, Sir Leon Radzinowicz (1948) characterizes transportation and, later, imprisonment as being "alternatives" that "superseded" capital punishment. Similarly in *Crime and the Police in England: 1700–1900*, J. J. Tobias portrays transportation as the culmination of a societal campaign against capital punishment that virtually eliminated the death sentence for offenses other than murder. He writes, "The alternatives to hanging were transportation, first to America and later to Australia" (Tobias 1979, 183). Even Philip Jenkins, who painstakingly reconstructed the number and rate of executions in sixteenth- and seventeenth-century England and established that the most dramatic decline occurred in the mid-sixteenth century, nevertheless views transportation as an all-encompassing "alternative" to the death penalty. He observes, "Every prisoner transported to America or the Caribbean would have stood an excellent chance of hanging if their crimes had occurred in Tudor times" (Jenkins 1990, 144). This may be true, but, as he points out elsewhere, the rate of executions had declined precipitously well before transportation was institutionalized. Certainly in numbers, transportation and then imprisonment did come to be relied on much more frequently than executions. But it is a mistake to treat them as alternatives that "superseded" or "replaced" executions. Indeed, I argue that transportation—and later the prison—is significant precisely because it did *not* simply replace other sanctions; it was an innovation that dramatically *expanded* the state's repertoire of punishments and its capacity to punish.

Transportation emerged as a practical and well-managed form of punishment in its own right and remained so for nearly 250 years; for the second half of this period, it constituted England's major form of punishment for serious offenses. It was an innovation whose impact was of gigantic proportions, one that radically transformed the administration of criminal justice. Long before England developed a complex administrative apparatus and long before it expanded state judicial and policing capacities, the otherwise weak and poorly developed central government managed to develop a massive capacity to punish.[4]

Although transportation was certainly a more merciful alternative for those who otherwise would have been hanged, its greatest applicability was to those who ran little risk of execution. Even after transportation was in full swing after the adoption of the Criminal Justice Act of 1718, those few who were guilty of the very worst offenses or were otherwise considered irredeemable were still likely to be hanged. Transportation had little or no impact on their cases. It was not until well into the nineteenth century, when legislation severely curtailed the scope and use of the death penalty, that these most serious offenders could expect to avoid the gallows. By this time, transportation to Australia had almost come to a halt, and long-term imprisonment had already become well-established in England.

Rather transportation was an "alternative" for those offenders who once could successfully have claimed benefit of clergy and escaped punishment altogether, those who otherwise might have been convicted of lesser offenses and received an unconditional pardon, and, after 1718, those who would have been convicted of petty larceny, a noncapital felony that until then had been punishable only by a whipping or a fine.[5] Moreover, the likelihood of transportation over execution meant that victims were more willing to prosecute, and juries to convict, and to convict without reducing the offense, because they now knew that offenders would not be subject to the death penalty if convicted.[6]

Comparisons of figures for executions and transportation in the seventeenth and eighteenth centuries do *not* reveal any marked decline in executions offset by a corresponding increase in transportation. Although from the sixteenth to the eighteenth century, there was a significant decline in executions—from a national high of as many as 560 executions per year in the early 1500s to around 65 in 1800—the greatest declines took place in the early seventeenth century,[7] long before transportation was widely used, and fully one hundred years before serious political opposition to the death penalty began to gain popular support (Radzinowicz 1948; Jenkins 1990).[8] There was a marked decrease in executions by 1630, but transportation was not widely used until much later in the century. This initial decline in executions appears to have little if anything to do with the new, but as yet little used, option of transportation and much more to do with increased political stability (Radzinowicz 1948; Jenkins 1990).[9] And when transportation finally became commonplace, its primary effect was not to displace executions (although it certainly had some moderating effect), but to enhance exponentially the capacity to punish those who would not have faced the gallows and who might have escaped serious punishment altogether. Figures are too sketchy to document the precise nature of this process, but the general pattern is clear.

To illustrate: between 1630 and 1660, the number of executions at Tyburn (for London and Middlesex) remained steady at about ninety per year (Radzinowicz 1948). One hundred years later (1750 to 1754), the number of executions had declined to an average of forty-eight per year and dropped still lower, to an average of twenty-two per year in the last decade of the century. Thus from the beginning to the end of this period, there was a decrease of about seventy executions per year. But during this same period, the number transported from London and Middlesex increased dramatically and far exceeded the reduction in the number of executions. Figures gathered by John Howard in the second part of the eighteenth century show that between 1749 and 1755, there were 306 executions, slightly less than forty-five per year; between 1756 and 1763, there were 139 executions or an average of slightly more than ten per year; between 1764 and 1771, there were 233 executions or an average of eighteen per year.[10] However, during this same period—between 1749 and 1771—5,600 offenders, on average 430 per year, were transported to North America (Howard 1929). Even taking into consideration increases in population and in the crime rate, it is clear that transportation did much more than displace the gallows. For the vast majority of those transported during this period—perhaps as many as 90 percent—transportation was an alternative not to the gallows but to an outright pardon, an exercise of benefit of clergy, a fine, a whipping, or a brief period in jail.

John Beattie's analysis of the impact of the Transportation Act of 1718 in Quarter Sessions Court in Surrey points to the same conclusions (Beattie 1986). He shows how for a large number of property offenses, the act effectively transferred sentencing discretion from the jury to the judge and, in so doing, dramatically increased the number of offenders transported. An important provision of the act blurred the distinctions between petty and grand larceny, which resulted in stiffer penalties for these offenses. Before the act, those convicted of petty larceny, a noncapital offense, would have been whipped or forced to pay a fine. After adoption, the act permitted them to be transported. And those who previously had been subject to a death sentence for the more serious forms of larceny could now be sentenced to transportation by the court.

To sum up, the provisions in the act had three radical consequences: (1) those who previously would have been convicted of petty larceny, and received a whipping or a fine, were now routinely transported; (2) those who previously would have been charged with grand larceny, but whose juries would have refused to convict in order to avoid the death penalty, could now be transported; and (3) those who once would have been convicted, and then received a pardon or benefit of clergy and escaped punishment altogether, could now be transported.[11] The act meant that for the first time a huge and heterogeneous group of criminal offenders was now directly punishable by transportation rather than by either lighter or heavier sanctions. Figures for Surrey reveal how immediate the act's impact was, especially for the lesser offenses (Beattie 1986).

Transportation revolutionized English penal policy. Its stunning cost-effectiveness fundamentally transformed the capacity of the state to punish long before there developed an administrative apparatus, the political will, and the material resources to support other components of a modern criminal justice system. By sheer confluence of circumstances, it was probably the first step toward development of the modern penal process. That is, it was the first successful effort to develop a significant punishment that could be applied to huge numbers of offenders in a standardized and routine manner.

And as we have seen, administrative and financial responsibility for transportation, at least until its Australian phase, was almost wholly in the hands of entrepreneurs who operated it as a highly profitable business. Indeed for a long period, the central government had little knowledge of and virtually no control over its administration. Pardons were sought and issued on an ad hoc basis, and shipment of offenders was arranged by poorly coordinated efforts of their families, the county sheriff, and the shippers themselves. Even after 1718, when transportation was institutionalized and expanded, its administration rested largely in the hands of local officials and shippers, although of course the central government paid subsidies to the latter. Indeed its genius lay in the fact that transportation was a new and more palatable form of sanctioning that overcame, on the one hand, the squeamishness that would have accompanied any impulse to escalate capital punishment and, on the other, the fierce opposition to the cost and propriety that would have accompanied any widespread use of domestic imprisonment or a system of forced labor. Finally it permitted a policy of massive sanctioning without having to develop a large state bureaucracy to administer it.

Historians of crime have tended to miss an important feature of North American transportation.[12] Focusing on the mechanics of the process at the judicial level and treating it as an alternative to capital punishment, they have ignored the revolutionary impact it had on expanding the state's capacity to punish. Typically transportation is portrayed as a brief transitional chapter, sandwiched between the era of capital and corporal punishment and the rise of the prison. But it was neither a "brief" era—it lasted roughly as long as the modern prison has existed—nor simply an "alternative" to capital punishment. Transportation radically augmented the state's authority to punish. It multiplied many times over—perhaps five or sixfold or more; it is difficult to tell—the number of people subject to severe criminal sanctions. Indeed it may have been the fulcrum used to catapult the English state toward its modern mass-scale punitive capability.

Parallels in Contemporary Penology

David Rothman (1971) has characterized the history of early American prison policy as an idealistic enterprise that went astray, as conscience was displaced by convenience. According to him, the penitentiary was conceived by high-minded reformers who hoped to redeem lost souls through a combination of "moral architecture" and a strict regimen of prison life. But their schema did not work and instead instituted a reign of numbing pain and terror. My reading of the history of the origins of the modern prison is not so sanguine.[13] It appears to me that many of the initial advocates for prisons were practical entrepreneurs who believed that these institutions could and should be run as profitable businesses (Bentham 1843; Livingston 1873; McKelvey 1977).[14] These early prophets of the prison understood the success of transportation and sought to emulate it, hoping to adapt a penal system designed for a plantation economy into a form suitable for a manufacturing economy. Prison factories were their solution (Feeley 1991). It was for this reason, and certainly not for the satisfaction of reformist consciences alone, that the idea of the prison finally took hold in England and the United States. Indeed, this innovation probably succeeded precisely because conscience and convenience coincided from the outset.

Contemporary entrepreneurs who promote "alternatives" to traditional custodial sentences, and other advocates of "privatization," represent a historically similar situation. They present their reforms as both cheaper and more effective. But these new methods of punishment, like their earlier counterpart, must be understood as augmentations to and not replacements for older or disfavored or more expensive forms of sanctioning (Shearing and Stenning 1983).

These new approaches to incarceration have taken several forms. Some of the most well-known are the new minimum- and medium-security facilities built and operated by Corrections Corporation of America, the Wackenhut Corporation, and other security companies. These private contractors claim that the discipline of the market allows them to own and operate prisons substantially more efficiently than can the state. By many reliable accounts, they do in fact operate these institutions somewhat more efficiently than do state agencies (Logan 1990). Perhaps they really are viable private "alternatives."

However, such efforts constitute only a small portion of contemporary privatized corrections. There are also a host of other, less visible, new forms that, when taken together, are much more significant than the handful of private contractors who have assumed management of traditional minimum- and medium-security prisons. These new correctional institutions are considered "softer" approaches to custody, control, and surveillance. Indeed, private programs today house more youngsters under the custody of juvenile courts than do state and county facilities. A feature common to many of these new private correctional arrangements is that they depend on new technologies and respond to a frustration with traditional arrangements, which are regarded as too rigid, too expensive, or inadequate to deal with a set of new problems. Thus private entrepreneurs both respond to and articulate new demands.

In this section I examine three new types of private correctional efforts that are often presented as "alternatives." But, as I show, each has expanded the net of social control: treatment programs, new types of custodial institutions, and new technologies that merge surveillance and custody. Just as transportation during its earliest years depended on discretion attendant to the pardon and benefit of clergy, so too these modern programs depend, for their activation, on the discretionary features of probation, parole, and prosecution (Blomberg 1991; Blomberg and Lucken 1994). And for the same reasons that it is a mistake to understand transportation as an *alternative* to capital punishment, so too these new forms of control should not be seen as "alternatives" or "substitutes" that replace other forms of incarceration in state-run prisons. Like transportation, the most distinctive features of these privately initiated and administered efforts is that they extend the reach of the state's capacity to punish.

Private Sector Treatment Programs

Supervised treatment programs, usually imposed as a condition of probation, include drug abuse, alcohol abuse, and job training programs. Virtually nonexistent forty years ago, they are now commonplace in the criminal justice system. Most are private, and many are run for profit (Ewick 1993); almost all derive their clients and most of their income from contracts with local governments. Some are designated as long-term, residential facilities, and others are designated as outpatient clinics. Program philosophies vary widely: some are organized with strict, military-like discipline; others are based on quasi-religious commitments; some are devoted to group therapy; other stress rugged individualism and self-reliance.

Some of these programs were started in the 1960s and early 1970s with support from the Law Enforcement Assistance Administration (LEAA; Feeley and Sarat 1982). Many were initially justified in terms of "community corrections," an idea that promised to keep less-serious offenders in more-effective alternatives "in the community" rather than in state prison and at lower cost. Although many were eliminated in federal cutbacks of the late 1970s and 1980s, these programs nevertheless established a private sector beachhead in corrections and have remained a part of it ever since. And growing concern with drugs in the 1990s has breathed new vigor into some of these programs, which typically obtain clients by means of a sentence that imposes "voluntary" participation as a condition of probation. However, some are pretrial diversion programs, and a few secure clients through an arrangement with private insurers. However structured, a common denominator is that they all obtain clients against the backdrop of the threat of criminal sanction.

Despite their growing numbers and significance, these private programs are largely ignored in discussions of correctional privatization. This may be because such programs are regarded as "services" rather than as integral components of the penal process or because they are small and less visible to public scrutiny. Still, voluntary participation is likely to be in name only—"clients" participate as a condition of probation or prosecutorial discretion. It would be wrong to characterize such programs as an incidental feature of the penal system. In the aggregate, they affect large numbers of criminal offenders. They have become an established component of a developed and expanding system of social control, and their operations depend wholly on the criminal process. In a review of recent developments in privatized corrections, Richard Ericson, Maeve McMahon, and Donald Evans make a similar point. Summarizing developments in both private corrections and private policing, they liken privatization to a form of franchising: "In correctional franchising," they observe, "the state functions as the franchisor and the various nonstate correctional agencies as the franchisees," which produces a "dispersal of social control involving a complex web of state and nonstate interests, organizations, and social forces" (Ericson, McMahon, and Evans 1987, 361). Such a process, they conclude, "allows for the apparent decentralization of control of offenders, community involvement, and distancing from the state. In effect, however, it secures 'publicization': centralized control of nonstate agencies through the conditions of contract and attendant monitoring and auditing functions" (Ericson, McMahon, and Evans 1987, 362). Evaluation research bears out this observation; private community corrections programs are typically "add-on" sanctions that widen and deepen the net of the state's capacity to punish (Blomberg 1991; Blomberg and Lucken 1994; Cohen 1985; Scull 1977).

Low-Security Custodial Programs

Although there is no comprehensive list, the growing number of low-security custodial facilities includes programs with names such as community work-release centers, work camps, prerelease centers, short-term detention facilities, restitution centers, return-to-custody facilities, residential treatment programs, and the like. Many of the newest and most innovative of these institutions have been designed and operated by private for-profit companies to serve both adults and juveniles. And some of these same contractors have helped to develop and operate new types of facilities to house persons detained by the Immigration and Naturalization Service. Indeed, division of labor may be emerging, with private contractors specializing in low-risk, low-security populations, and public corrections assuming responsibility for higher-risk offenders.

These new institutions are often presented under the banner of "community corrections," a term coined in the 1960s to describe a set of state-funded correctional programs that were to be administered by officials at the county level in an effort to keep state expenditures down. Community corrections continue to be promoted as a cheaper, local-based alternative to state prisons, but the term "community" is something of a misnomer because many of these alternatives confine offenders in custody rather than permit them to live at home. Furthermore, evaluations of community corrections consistently reveal that they rarely successfully target offenders who otherwise would have received state prison sentences (Blomberg 1991; Blomberg and Lucken 1994; Cohen 1985). Instead they are directed at offenders who otherwise would have received less-restrictive sentences of probation.

Connecticut law, for instance, provides for a network of public and private agencies to offer services, including custody at the local level, for offenders who otherwise would be imprisoned. Colorado has come to depend on an extensive network of private vendors to operate minimum-security facilities. Maryland provides state funding for local community correction centers, which, in some locations, are run by private contractors. Still other forms of privately administered sanctioning under the rubric of community corrections include pre-release centers for offenders about to complete prison terms, "restitution centers" that require community service or work release, and residential substance abuse programs.

Private sector involvement in community corrections is increasing, and there are indications that it will continue to grow especially as prison populations exceed capacity and pressures mount to develop less costly forms of custody. Although community corrections does not necessitate involvement by private contractors, it does generate pressures to find innovative and less expensive alternatives for some prisoners. This in turn leads to the search for more finely graded classifications and the desire for newer and cheaper alternatives for housing low-risk offenders. Private entrepreneurs have been especially quick to rationalize such classification systems and to develop new types of institutions for lower-risk populations.

Private entrepreneurs are also effective in devising and employing new technologies to identify the populations to be housed in these new types of custodial institutions. Only a few years ago, for instance, drug tests were a costly and time-consuming process only occasionally performed by a state crime laboratory. Now private drug-testing laboratories can provide fast, cheap, and reliable tests to detect a large variety of illegal substances, and as a consequence drug testing has become a staple of probation and parole. The expanded use of inexpensive and reliable tests has significantly increased the likelihood that drug use will be detected, and this has dramatically increased the number of known parole and probation violators. The growth of these violators, returned to custody to serve out the short balance of their terms, has generated demand for specialized short-term, low-security facilities more akin to jails than to full-service prisons. Here, too, entrepreneurs have been quick to respond. They have established a new niche by building and operating no-frills institutions that are more like jails than prisons in that they are designed for short- and not longer-term detainees. For instance, Texas, faced with an overcrowding crisis and a court order limiting the number of inmates in its prisons, turned to the Corrections Corporation of America and the Wackenhut Corporation to build and run new low-frills, low-cost "return-to-custody centers." Thus a new technology that permits easier detection of technical violations of probation and parole has created a demand for a new type of custodial institution. The private sector was able to respond quickly.

New Technologies for Surveillance and Control

A number of electronics companies and software service providers have developed and marketed devices to monitor the movement of individuals. Originally designed to provide monitoring for the elderly and the frail, these devices were quickly picked up by probation departments for remote surveillance of their clients. Electronic bracelets of various sorts provide continuous surveillance and make feasible confinement at home (or other specified and variable locations) without the need for custody or intensive personal supervision (Friel, Vaughn, and del Carman 1987). Still in its infancy, this new industry is growing by leaps and bounds. To date, probation departments have usually assumed responsibility for electronic monitoring. But this is not a traditional probation function, and probation departments—the weakest link in the criminal justice system—may not be up to the challenge of mastering and keeping abreast of this expanding new technology. If not, private entrepreneurs, who now only lease the hardware for monitoring or only supply software, may seek to administer directly the surveillance and control programs as well. Indeed there are ample signs that this is occurring. In California, Florida, and elsewhere, a number of private contractors are working directly with courts to provide both hardware and monitoring services for offenders whose noncustodial sentences include severely restricted movement (home, work, and the like) and the need to wear an electronic monitoring bracelet. In Nevada, a company that began by marketing a software system to keep track of restitution payments in bad-check cases for prosecutors' offices quickly expanded its business by contracting not only to supply the record keeping system but also to manage the entire restitution payment process. And once it assumed this function, it expanded again, developing and marketing its own special pretrial diversion program for chronic bad-check writers, which is financed by a surcharge on offenders' restitution payments.

Juvenile Institutions

One of the great successes in juvenile justice reform in the late 1960s and early 1970s was the movement to close state "training schools," large-scale custodial facilities for seriously delinquent juveniles.

Everywhere they were attacked as being dangerous, debilitating, and costly. Perhaps the best-known and most successful attack on these institutions took place in Massachusetts, where then-commissioner of youth corrections, Jerome Miller, literally overnight removed virtually all the young wards from these facilities and temporarily housed them in dormitories at the state university until he could locate community-based alternatives. The success of this removal has been recounted numerous times, as has its impact on the development of community-based juvenile "alternatives" elsewhere. However, what has not been explored so carefully is precisely how often these "alternatives" are now used or what the full implications of this shift have been.

The rapid and successful attack on large-scale state institutions was motivated not only by concern about their terrible conditions, but also by a distaste for such use of custodial sentences altogether. However, the architects of the attack had a clearer idea of what they disliked about the state training schools than they did about what would replace them. Some envisioned smaller, more caring facilities closer to home. But the impetus was not so much a vision for a new regime for treating troubled youths as it was a hatred of old-style state institutions. It was for this reason that many could unite behind the cause of "community corrections," although this was little more than a slogan meaning quite different things to different people.

The overnight victory against the training schools led to an intense demand for "alternatives" that could be set up and run almost immediately. The vacuum created by the abrupt change in policy was quickly filled by entrepreneurs who proffered a great variety of "community" alternatives. Among the most rapid to respond were locally based private organizations already in the helping business. They often had staff, a history of social service contracting, and experience with problematic clients. Consequently, such institutions came to replace large state-run programs.

Perhaps because there are so many of them and they are so small and scattered, there is little policy analysis of any sort about these institutions. Indeed, scholars and governmental agencies struggle to obtain an accurate count of how many there are and how many people they serve. Still, enough is known about enough of them to allow us to address some of the issues raised in this chapter. Nationwide more than half of all youths under the supervision of juvenile courts are now assigned to some type of private custodial facility (Flanagan and Jamieson 1988). They range from foster homes to franchised, theme-based wilderness camps, to "schools," to small, secure, prison-like institutions.

Privatized juvenile facilities are notable for their flexibility. Small, often locally administered, they can adapt to various local circumstances and conditions. But in the aggregate, they are enormous. California, Florida, Massachusetts, Michigan, Pennsylvania, Rhode Island, and Washington, among other states, rely extensively on private contractors to house their wards. In a number of states, placement in private out-of-home settings constitutes the primary component of juvenile corrections policy; in some, private placements outnumber placements in public facilities (Farbstein and Associates 1988; Armstrong 1994). In California, for instance, more than half of all juveniles in the custody of courts are housed in private, "community-based" facilities. This may be linked to that state's willingness to place juveniles in custody, because, next to Washington, D.C., California has the highest rate of juveniles in confinement in the nation. As of February 1985, California confined 430 per 100,000 juveniles in the population, up 10 percent from the year before and more than twice the nation's average of 185 per 100,000 (Flanagan and Jamieson 1988).

In Massachusetts, since the late 1960s when the state training schools were suddenly emptied, the state has come to rely heavily on private custodial placements for juveniles. Although its rate of custodial placements is not among the highest in the nation, the shift from state training schools to smaller, privately operated placements appears to have affected the way custody is regarded by many Massachusetts juvenile court judges. Under the earlier regime of custody in state institutions, judges were reluctant to commit juveniles to strictly run, but poorly managed and at times dangerous, state facilities. However, with the establishment of more benign "alternatives," judges became more willing to commit youths to custody, at least more willing to impose short-term custody as "shock therapy" to be used intermittently in conjunction with probation. Now, a higher proportion of Massachusetts youngsters under the custody of the court spend more time in community corrections facilities than they did in the older displaced state training institutions (Krisberg 1989).

Thus we cannot make the generalization that "community-based" and often private placements are smaller and more effective locally administered alternatives to state institutions. Often they are not alternatives to custody at all. Rather they extend the scope of juvenile custody (Blomberg 1991). Although they may serve as preferable alternatives for one set of youths, they also impose custodial sanctions on others who would not otherwise have received them. Here, too, entrepreneurs saw an opportunity to create a new set of institutions to meet a demand and in the process also expand that demand. And here, too, they established a niche in a new and expanding form of lower-cost social control.

Paul Lerman (1982, 1984) Barry Krisberg (1989), and others warn that private juvenile facilities have been used to create a two-tier system in juvenile corrections. Judges rely on private placements to deal with minor offenders and reserve public state facilities for more serious delinquents. Although a system of classification has considerable appeal, they warn that this system has produced two unwanted results: it has expanded the number of children who can be assigned to custody, and it has segregated these children by race, with the softer forms of control being used for white youths and the harsher forms for minorities. The image of benign professionalism and the great variety of special programs offered by the private sector, they warn, tend to obscure these two important features of these developments. This pattern appears to be growing. McDonald (1992) reports that in 1950 private placements for juveniles constituted about 20 percent of all placements, but in 1989, the figure was twice that.

Despite the dramatic expansion of custody that has accompanied the rise of private contracting in juvenile corrections, the topic has not been well researched and save for a handful of important exceptions (Lerman 1982, 1984; McDonald 1992; Armstrong 1994) has gone unnoticed by students of juvenile justice and even private corrections. Two related reasons account for this neglect. First, the "problem" for juvenile corrections beginning in the 1960s was the use of large state training institutions, which were widely regarded as counterproductive and failing, and so the emphasis and concern were on finding "alternatives" to them. What these alternatives were and the fact that they caught up a great many youths who otherwise would not have been placed in custody tended to be overlooked (Lerman 1982, 1984). Second, these "alternatives" were promoted not as "private facilities," but as "community corrections," a concept as benign in theory as it is misleading in practice. Promised that these new "community" programs would be more flexible and responsive to children's needs and be provided as well and at lower cost, they attracted widespread support of both liberals interested in instituting better policies and conservatives interested in reducing mushrooming costs. Such support rarely attaches to any new government initiative. Perhaps because of their initial image as benign alternatives to admittedly failing state training schools, no one at the time and few since have pointed out that these "alternatives" have facilitated the increase in the number of juveniles in custody and have rarely produced the cost savings that are claimed for them (Lerman 1982). And even in the current get-tough era, which has experienced a quantum jump in the number of juveniles tried as adults and is calling for harsher penalties for juvenile offenders, private "alternatives" for less-serious offenders have mushroomed as well.

This trend has been given a substantial boost by developments wholly unconcerned with the criminal process. The move to "reinvent" government and search for private alternatives for public agencies has not been motivated to any significant degree by a desire to "get tough" with criminals (Osborne and Gaebler 1992). Nevertheless it has contributed to the trend simply by virtue of promoting private alternatives over public agencies. The private alternatives—at least in the correctional arena—are not, as I have shown, merely cheaper, more efficient replacements, but in fact are often expanded functions of the state. Ironically (at least in this field) the movement to reinvent government—a movement designed to shrink both the functions and budget of the state—is doing neither. In the name of shrinking government, privatization in the correctional arena is expanding both the functions and the costs of government, but in such a way that both the functions are less accountable and the costs are less visible.

Conclusions

This chapter has offered a historical perspective on the contemporary policy of privatization of corrections. My purpose in doing this has not been to link punishment everywhere and always to some particular form of political economy. Rather, I have sought to show that new and expansive forms of punishment are easily obscured when they are developed by private contractors and presented as alternatives to existing forms of punishment. For this reason, I explored the English policy of transportation to North America, an experiment in privately provided punishments in the seventeenth and eighteenth century, which can be examined with the benefit of the hindsight of history. This examination yielded two important lessons. First, far from being what is viewed by some historians as a progressive "alternative" to capital punishment, transportation had at best only a marginal impact on executions. Its most dramatic effect was to apply a new form of punishment to other types of offenders who in its absence would have received lesser penalties. Net widening seems endemic to alternatives. Second, transportation suggests that one of the most distinctive feature of privatization is not that contractors can provide services more cheaply than government agencies, but that entrepreneurs have a capacity to respond quickly and successfully to demands for new forms of control.

Obviously there are a great many differences between transportation policy in the eighteenth century and the contemporary movement for privatization of corrections in the late twentieth century. The meaning and distinction between "public" and "private" has changed. The role and capacity of the state have grown enormously. The criminal process has been professionalized. The meaning and social significance of the criminal sanction have shifted. In short, the terms and concepts used in this essay have been reconstituted over the intervening 250 years. Still as Rothman and Wheeler (1981) have suggested, there is value in looking for enduring patterns over long periods of time, in this case the not-so-obvious consequences of entrepreneurs involved in providing penal sanctions.

I have not meant to suggest that the distinction between public and private has remained constant with respect to the criminal sanction or that nothing has changed. Rather, I have drawn certain parallels between the seventeenth- and eighteenth-century policy of transportation and modern correctional privatization in order to reveal the impact of entrepreneurs in both processes. Upon reflection, this should not be surprising. We are familiar with the claim that the private sector is more efficient and thus the belief that private alternatives may be cheaper. Indeed, this is how the debate and assessment of private contracting in corrections have been framed.

But another perhaps more important feature of the private sector is its entrepreneurial and innovative capacities. Sensing new needs and new demands or the desire for new products, entrepreneurs both respond to and help to generate new demands. Applying these lessons of history (or perhaps the market) to contemporary correctional privatization, this chapter has shown that new privately administered punishments that are commonly presented as alternatives to or substitutes for existing sanctions dramatically expand the reach of the criminal sanction. Like their counterparts who established transportation in the eighteenth century, contemporary entrepreneurs have been successful at tapping new technologies and identifying new forms of sanctions. If I am correct, much of the current debate about privatization, like the discussion of some historians about transportation, is off the mark. Whatever the initial motives, in both cases the consequences have been to expand dramatically the reach of the criminal sanction.

I wish to thank Nils Christie, Patricia Ewick, Kiara Jordan, Robert Kagan, Jack Katz, Shelly Messinger, John Langbein, Susan Silbey, Jerry Skolnick, and Stan Wheeler for comments on an earlier draft of this chapter.

Notes

1. Following the successes of France and Spain in putting a large number of criminals to work as oarsmen in large galleys, the English built some galleys in the late sixteenth century. However, galleys did not prove to be as workable on the rough North Sea as they were on the much calmer Mediterranean, and the experiment was abandoned almost immediately.

2. After prolonged consideration by the government, Australia was eventually selected as the site for a renewed policy of transportation. However, Australian policy was markedly different, especially at the outset. Convicts were the first colonists, and the government had to transport and maintain them in prison colonies rather than, as in North America, depend on private shippers and farmers in need of labor to handle the process. As a consequence, Australian transportation quickly became a costly and controversial public policy in ways that North American transportation never did.

3. For excellent accounts on transportation to North America, see Smith (1965) and Ekrich (1987). For an outstanding discussion of the impact of the 1718 transportation act on the courts, see Beattie (1986).

Although superlative studies, none of these books fully explores transportation in the context of the evolution of British penal practices.

4.   John Beattie (1986) provides a fine discussion of the rise of the use of transportation by the courts but does not couch this development in terms of the history of penal sanctions the way I do here. For a discussion of the rise of the modern administrative state in Great Britain, see G. R. Elton (1953), who argues that the Tudors developed a relatively sophisticated central administrative apparatus and that developments in the nineteenth century were only incremental extensions. In contrast, see Webb and Webb (1922).

5.   See John Beattie's (1986) discussion of the effects of the 1718 act, which allowed courts to sentence noncapital felons (those convicted of petty larceny) directly to transportation. This act had the effect of transferring sentencing discretion from the jury to the judge, in that juries had long downgraded grand larcenies to petty larcenies or acquitted the defendant altogether in order to avoid the death penalty and to avoid any serious punishments of any kind. After passage of the act, even if the jury did convict on the lesser offense, judges could impose transportation. But as Beattie (1986) and others have noted, the great jump in transported felons was the result of redirecting not gallows-bound offenders, but those who would have been pardoned or whipped.

6.   Eighteenth-century juries were loath to convict on capital offenses and would regularly acquit when evidence clearly pointed to guilt. And even when they did convict, they frequently convicted on lesser offenses, assessing downward the value of items stolen—even when they had objective valuations (such as money, silver, pewter)—below the 12p threshold that distinguished noncapital from capital theft.

7.   Philip Jenkins's estimates are much higher for some periods. For instance, extrapolating from detailed figures on executions in late sixteenth-century Essex, he estimates the annual average number of executions nationwide between 1597 and 1603 to be around 1300 and thus the decline by the mid-seventeenth century to be even more marked (Jenkins 1990). When these figures are expressed as rates per 100,000, or as a percentage of all those convicted of capital offenses, the declines are all the more dramatic. Still, my point is not that capital punishment did not decline, or that the decline was not influenced by the rise of transportation. Rather, I want to show that transportation did more, much more, than simply displace the gallows.

8.   See Philip Jenkins (1990). Jenkins is correct to argue that transportation has to be understood as a punishment in its own right, rather than as a transitional punishment that was used briefly between the regimes of capital punishment and imprisonment. Nevertheless, despite his own figures suggesting the contrary, he tends to regard transportation as a replace-

ment for execution rather than as an expansion of sanctioning power chiefly affecting those who would not have been executed. His discussion revealing that the greatest decline in executions preceded by nearly a century the widespread use of transportation, and Beattie's figures showing that transportation replaced the benefit of clergy and discharges, as well as whippings, does not support such a view.

9. Radzinowicz (1948) calculates based on Jeaffreson's figures for Middlesex that there were assumed yearly averages of executions at Tyburn of 140 and 560 (Henry VIII), 560 (Edward VI), 280 (Mary), 140 (Elizabeth), 140 (James I), 90 (Charles I), and 90 (Commonwealth).

10. Howard attributes the decline in capital punishment during this middle period to the war years, which redirected into naval service some offenders who otherwise might have been hanged.

11. I have presented a strong version of this argument. A weaker version is that although transportation may have displaced—and hence served as an "alternative" for—some executions, it did much more as well, by transporting vast numbers who stood little or no chance of being executed and otherwise would have received a whipping, a small fine, or an unconditional pardon. My point holds in either case, but my reading of the materials leads me to conclude that the decline in the use of the death penalty was almost entirely independent of transportation and that transportation appears to have displaced very few executions. I appreciate John Langbein pressing for clarification on this issue at the Wheeler symposium.

12. Perhaps because it was privately administered and privately financed, transportation to North America has received short shrift from historians of penal policy, even among those who have devoted great attention to transportation to Australia, which England established explicitly as a penal colony. See Hughes (1987).

13. I outline an entrepreneur-based history of the origins of the modern prison in Feeley (1991). See also Knepper (1991).

14. I do not, however, argue the thesis developed by Ruche and Kirchheimer (1939) that forms of punishment emerge to absorb surplus labor. My thesis is more modest (and more defensible): that at key junctures in the history of punishment, innovations have been developed by entrepreneurs in ways that simultaneously serve the interests of private and public convenience (and perhaps conscience).

References

Armstrong, Sarah. 1994. "Privatization of Juvenile Corrections." Jurisprudence and Social Policy Program, University of California at Berkeley. Unpublished paper.

Beattie, John M. 1986. *Crime and Courts in England: 1660–1800.* Princeton, N.J.: Princeton University Press.

Bentham, Jeremy. 1843. *Works,* edited by John Bowring. London: Russell and Russell.

Blomberg, Thomas. 1991. "Criminal Justice Reform and Social Control: Are We Becoming a Minimum Security Society?" In *Transcarceration: Essays in the Sociology of Social Control,* edited by John Lowman, Robert Menzies, and T. S. Palys. Aldershot, U.K.: Gower.

Blomberg, Thomas, and Karol Lucken. 1994. "Intermediate Punishment and Piling up of Sanctions." In *Criminal Justice: Law and Politics,* edited by George Cole. Belmont, Calif.: Wadsworth.

Cohen, Stanley. 1985. *Visions of Social Control: Crime, Punishment, and Classification.* Oxford: Polity Press.

Ekrich, A. Roger. 1987. *Bound for America: The Transportation of British Convicts to the Colonies, 1718–1775.* Oxford: Clarendon Press.

Elton, G. R. 1953. *The Tudor Revolution.* Cambridge, U.K.: Cambridge University Press.

Ericson, Richard V., Maeve W. McMahon, and Donald G. Evans. 1987. "Punishing for Profit: Reflections on the Revival of Privatization in Corrections." *Canadian Journal of Criminology* 29(4): 355–71.

Ewick, Patricia. 1993. "Corporate Cures: The Comodification of Social Control." *Studies in Law, Politics, and Society* 13: 137–59.

Farbstein, Jan, and Associates. 1988. *Statewide Needs Assessment of County Juvenile Facilities: Final Report.* Sacramento, Calif.: Department of Youth Authority.

Feeley, Malcolm. 1991. "The Privatization of Punishment in Historical Perspective." In *Privatization and Its Alternatives,* edited by William Gormley. Madison: University of Wisconsin Press.

Feeley, Malcolm M., and Austin Sarat. 1982. *The Policy Dilemma.* Minneapolis: University of Minnesota Press.

Flanagan, Timothy J., and Katherine M. Jamieson, eds. 1988. *Sourcebook of Criminal Justice Statistics—1987.* Washington, D.C.: U.S. Department of Justice.

Friel, Charles M., Joseph B. Vaughn, and Rolando del Carmen. 1987. *Electronic Monitoring and Correctional Policy: The Technology and Its Application.* Washington, D.C.: U.S. Department of Justice, National Institute of Justice.

Howard, John. 1929. *The State of Prisons.* 1792. Reprint, London: J. M. Dent.

Hughes, Robert. 1987. *The Fatal Shore: The Epic of Australia's Founding.* New York: Knopf.

Jenkins, Philip. 1990. "From Gallows to Prison? The Execution Rate in Early Modern England." In *Crime, Police, and the Courts in British History,* edited by Louis A. Knafla. Westport, Conn.: Meckler Corp.

Knepper, Paul. 1991. "Prison Historiography and the Modernity Question." Paper presented at the annual meeting of the American Society of Criminology. San Francisco, Calif. (November 20–24, 1991).

Krisberg, Barry. 1989. "Development in Juvenile Justice: Incarceration." Presentation given at the Center for the Study of Law and Society, University of California at Berkeley (April 17, 1989).

Lerman, Paul. 1982. *Deinstitutionalization and the Welfare State.* New Brunswick, N.J.: Rutgers University Press.

———. 1984. "Child Welfare, the Private Sector, and Community-based Corrections." *Crime and Delinquency* 30(1): 5–26.

Livingston, Edward. 1873. "A Code of Reform and Prison Discipline. Title 5." In *The Complete Works of Edward Livingston on Criminal Jurisprudence,* vol. 2, pp. 59–94. New York: National Prison Association.

Logan, Charles H. 1990. *Private Prisons: Cons and Pros.* New York: Oxford University Press.

McDonald, Douglas. 1992. "Private Penal Institutions." In *Crime and Justice: A Review of Research,* edited by Michael Tonry. Chicago: University of Chicago Press.

McKelvey, Blake. 1977. *American Prisons: A History of Good Intentions.* Montclair, N.J.: Patterson Smith.

Oldham, Wilfred. 1933. "The Administration of the System of Transportation of British Convicts, 1763–93." Ph.D. diss., University of London.

Osborne, David, and Ted Gaebler. 1992. *Reinventing Government: How the Entrepreneurial Spirit is Transforming the Public Sector.* Reading, Mass.: Addison-Wesley.

Radzinowicz, Sir Leon. 1948. *A History of the Criminal Law and Its Administration from 1750.* New York: Macmillan.

Rothman, David. 1971. *The Discovery of the Asylum: Social Order and Disorder in the New Republic.* Boston: Little, Brown & Co.

Rothman, David, and Stanton Wheeler, eds. 1981. "Introduction." In *Social History and Social Policy,* edited by David Rothman and Stanton Wheeler. New York: Academic Press.

Ruche, Georg, and Otto Kirchheimer. 1939. *Punishment and Social Structure.* New York: Columbia University Press.

Ryan, Mick, and T. L. Ward. 1989. *Privatization and the Penal System.* London: Open University Press.

Scull, Andrew. 1977. *Decarceration: Community Treatment and the Deviant, A Radical View.* 2d ed. London: Polity Press.

Shearing, C. D., and P. C. Stenning. 1983. *Private Security and Private Justice.* Montreal: Institute for Research on Public Policy.

Smith, Abbott Emerson. 1965. *Colonists in Bondage: White Servitude and Convict Labor in America, 1607–1776.* 1947. Reprint, Gloucester, Mass.: Peter Smith.

Tobias, J. J. 1979. *Crime and the Police in England: 1700–1900.* New York: St. Martin's Press.

Webb, Sidney, and Beatrice Webb. 1922. *English Poor Law History.* 2 parts. London: Longman's Green.

Chapter 2

On Stage: Some Historical Notes About Criminal Justice

Lawrence M. Friedman

Crime has been a major political issue in the United States for many years—certainly for most of the period since 1950. In recent years, according to television and the daily press, crime has become either the number one issue or something close to it; it has gained at the expense of health care, welfare reform, nuclear proliferation, the budget deficit, unemployment, toxic wastes, the high cost of living, the crisis in Yugoslavia, and whatever other rivals are out there.[1] Election campaigns are often heavily canted toward the issue of crime.

If crime is a major issue, then so is criminal justice: the network of roles, sites, and institutions (police, public defenders, courts, parole officers, judges, juries, jails, gas chambers) that are concerned with defining, catching, and punishing people who commit crimes. The public believes, rightly or wrongly, that the criminal justice system can control, through its policies, the amount and kind of crime committed in society.

This essay is about some aspects of the history of criminal justice; more specifically, it is about the *public* meanings of criminal justice, about links between that system and its audience. It is about the criminal justice system as a kind of social theater, as a web of communications, and as an aspect (or product) of popular culture, rather than as an engine of crime control.

People, in general, know or think they know far more about the basic contours of criminal justice than they do about other aspects of the legal system. People have all heard about "murder one," Miranda warnings, the gas chamber or the electric chair, and so on. Some of their information and misinformation comes, of course, from personal experience. Millions of people, after all, have direct contact with criminal justice. Some millions of men and women, over the course of their lifetime, will be arrested and even tried and imprisoned. Millions more have served on criminal juries. Throw in witnesses and other interested parties, and you have still more millions. Crime victims, too, have to deal with police and sometimes with trials and judges as well, and this too is a sizable category.

This still leaves us with many people, perhaps a majority, who, in their day-to-day existence, have little or nothing to do with the criminal justice system, except for a traffic incident now and then. And many of the others—witnesses, jurors, victims—have had only a partial or fleeting glimpse of the system at work. Most people get their "facts" about the criminal justice business from television, from the movies, from an occasional newspaper or magazine article, and from a few nuggets on the evening news. These sources project a few rather simple ideas about criminal justice, some of them extremely wrong-headed. (Moreover, impressions that flow directly from criminal trials are themselves often unreliable or misleading.)

From television, and from the political pulpit, come messages that somehow play into the public lust for more and tougher punishment. If we asked people what a criminal justice system is *for*, they would almost certainly tell us that the point of criminal justice is crime control. They might not use that phrase, but that would be the meaning. They would probably also say that the purpose is to punish criminals, almost as an end in itself.

These are, without doubt, two real-life functions of the criminal justice system. How well it does these jobs is another question. Another function is less obvious to the public. The criminal justice system is also a teacher and preacher. It announces, by word and deed, a code of behavior and marks the moral boundaries of society (Erikson 1966). Every state has a penal code—a *list* of behaviors to be outlawed, criminalized, and labeled as bad, blameworthy, or punishable. This catalog also contains relative weights and prices. The code tells us which crimes are worse than others and by how much. It does this by labeling some crimes as felonies and some as misdemeanors—that is, as major or minor offenses—and it adjusts the level of punishment accordingly. Reading the code would inform us, in case we did not know, that murder is a much worse crime than simple theft or tearing the label off a mattress.

These weights, measures, and prices are, of course, only on paper, and the general public does not make a habit of reading the penal code. But some of what the code contains is fairly common knowledge. Besides, the living, operating system also does its share of teaching and preaching. It provides moral lessons, in a vivid, expressive form. It dramatizes and makes concrete the norms of the community or at least the norms of some significant part of the community. It is, in short, didactic theater.

The system is theatrical too in a literal sense: it provides entertainment. Doubly so: in the first place, it is hard even to imagine popular culture (movies, radio, and television) without crime and punishment—without police, detectives, trials, juries, prisons, and executions. Literature (in the broad sense) would also be severely stunted. Only the criminal side of the legal system gets a fair shake in entertainment and the arts. Somebody wrote a great novel called *Crime and Punishment* and another one called *The Trial*. Nobody yet has written a masterpiece called *Antitrust Actions* or *A Tale of Two Bailments* or *Adventures in Chapter 11*.

Consider, too, how many people devour mystery and detective stories, "police procedurals," and the like. Bookstores have whole sections devoted to "true crime." The list of movies and plays containing courtroom scenes or trials would be very long.

The criminal trial is itself theatrical. People follow these trials as if they were actual dramas, which many of them are. What could have been more riveting than the Lizzie Borden trial over a century ago, or the Loeb-Leopold case, or the trial of Dr. Sam Sheppard, or, more recently, in the age of television, the trial of the Menéndez brothers or of O. J. Simpson, the most sensational trial of recent years. The trials and tribulations of this one defendant must have generated thousands of cubic feet of paper, and hundreds of millions of people all over the world watched it breathlessly, on the networks and on Cable News Network (CNN).

There are moral lessons, one supposes, in all of these affairs, a point we will come back to later in the chapter. But they also seem to be grand entertainment for vast numbers of people. Trials were vital entertainment, too, in the primitive days before movies and television, though in a much more localized way. "Court day" was an exciting time, in the dreary county seats of the middle west or south, in the nineteenth century, and in courts high and low, crowds turned out to hear silver-tongued lawyers do their thing.[2] Of course, the teaching and preaching function of criminal justice cannot be separated from its entertainment value. The "entertainment" value is often what gets the message across and makes it palatable.

The theatrical function of criminal justice is as old as the system itself in America. Justice in the colonial period, for example, was dramaturgical in an almost literal sense. The whole system was public, theatrical, and didactic from start to finish. To be sure, "trials" were not much like modern celebrity trials. They were, on the whole, quick and dirty affairs; in Massachusetts, say, in the seventeenth century, defendants were not represented by lawyers. They did not testify under oath. Perhaps the judge was not a lawyer either. The defendant was somebody who stole a pig, or played cards on Sunday, or was caught fornicating in the hay with a servant girl. One important object was to get the defendant, except when he could somehow explain his way out of the mess he was in, to confess his misdeeds (Langbein 1994; Moglen 1994). But in any event, all the proceedings were public. The trial was not a search for hidden truth or, for that matter, the kind of battle between lawyers that we expect in a modern celebrity trial. There was no Marcia Clark, no F. Lee Bailey, no Johnny Cochran. In an important sense, these cases were predecided. They were like modern summit meetings of politicians, where all that remains to be done is ritual and a final communiqué.

Not only was the trial public, but the punishment was public as well. It took place out of doors, for the most part, in the village square. If you were going to be whipped for your crimes, you were whipped in front of everybody. Under a Rhode Island statute of 1749, a person convicted of adultery was to be "set publickly on the Gallows in the Day-time, with a rope about his or her Neck, for the Space of one Hour," and then whipped.[3] Everyone has heard of the pillory and the stocks and of the scarlet letter. Adulterers, under a New Hampshire statute (1701) were to wear "for ever" a "Capitall Letter 'A' of two inches long and proportionable in Bignesse, cutt out in Cloath of a contrary Colour to their Cloathes," to be worn "in open View" (Laws N.H., Province Period, 1679–1702, 1, at 676, 1904). One Hannah Gray, in Massachusetts, in 1674, was ordered to "stand at the meeting house at Salem upon a lecture day, with a paper on her head on which was written in capital letters, I STAND HEERE FOR MY LACIVIOUS & WANTON CARIAGES"; this was her alternative to a public whipping (Records and Files of the Quarterly Courts of Essex County, Massachusetts, 5, at 291). For many crimes in New England, the punishment was branding—in 1674, two burglars in Massachusetts, after paying a fine, were ordered "Branded in their Forheades . . . with the letter B"; and in 1670, Nicolas Vauden, a servant and a persistent runaway, was sentenced to be "branded on the forehead with the letter R and to be severely whipped" (Smith 1961, 281; Records and Files of the Quarterly Courts of Essex County, Massachusetts, 4, at 234, entry for March 1670). For some crimes, the law decreed that the miscreant's ears were to be cut off. This was a lot more painful than a scarlet letter and more permanent, but with similar effect: the criminal was *publicly* marked for his crime.

The ultimate punishment, of course, was death by hanging, and this too was an outdoor activity. It was a show, an event, perhaps not quite an ˙entertainment, but definitely designed to provide moral lessons. A hanging was an especially good show, if the wretched criminal confessed and announced to the public how evil he had been and how deeply he repented. Best of all was when, standing in the very shadow of the gallows, people could see him and hear him as he begged his audience to learn from his miserable fate and adjured them to turn to lives of godliness and truth, while there yet was time (Williams 1986). James Morgan, executed in Boston in 1686 for "an horrible *Murder*," made a "last speech," which was then taken down "in Short-Hand." The speech began: "I Pray God that I may be a warning to you all . . . have a care of that Sin of Drunkenness, for that Sin leads to all manner of . . . Wickedness . . . O let all mind what I am a saying now . . . O take warning by me, and beg of God to keep you from this sin which has been my ruine" (Williams 1992, 71, 77–78). Esther Rodgers, executed in 1701 for infanticide, delivered a powerful speech at the gallows: "Young Ones, be not Disobedient, go not with bad Company, O my dear Friends—Take Warning by me"; she then prayed for "divine mercy" (Cohen 1993, 63).

The "show" did not necessarily end with execution. In 1710, in Virginia, after an Indian and a slave were hanged, the bodies were decapitated, then quartered, and the court ordered the heads and body parts to be displayed "in the most publick places" of Virginia, as an object lesson of the fate of those who committed treason (Rankin 1965, 119).

Well into the nineteenth century, all executions were exceedingly public. At one hanging, in Cooperstown, New York, in 1827, the crowd was so dense that a viewing stand gave way, killing two people. As late as 1880, in Tennessee, a landowner made more than $500 selling reserved seats and barbecue at a hanging. In the south, hangings were "powerful theater," and crowds, including school-children, were seized with "religious mania" as the "doomed man" was "launched into eternity" (Ayers 1984, 147–48).

All this seems barbaric to us today, but it was strong and salient education: a visible, horrifying show of the mighty hand of the law and the terrible fate of those who sinned. Criminal justice was both didactic and entertaining; the two aspects were interconnected. The excitement of a trial or a public hanging enhanced the power and the scope of the moral message. This was true in the colonial period, and it is no doubt true of trials today.[4]

In the nineteenth century, however, a long-term trend led away from these public dramas and toward privacy and concealment. Punishment ceased to be an affair of the open air. Major reforms of criminal justice resulted in a sharp reduction in the *public* aspects of punishment. To begin with, hangings retreated from the public square to the courtyard of the prison or jail. Pennsylvania began executing in private in 1834; New Jersey, New York, and Massachusetts followed with laws passed in 1835. Under an Illinois law passed in 1859, hangings were to take place "within the walls of the prison of the county" where the defendant was convicted "or within a yard or inclosure adjoining such prison." The invited guests were the judges, prosecuting attorney, and the clerks of court of the county, along with "two physicians and twelve reputable citizens" to be selected by the sheriff or deputy sheriff; the condemned man could name up to three "ministers of the gospel" and any "immediate relatives" he might want to attend. No one under twenty-one, except relatives of the condemned man—one wonders why they would want to watch—were allowed to witness the hanging.[5]

But even within these rather closed-off spaces, many people could still see the execution. When Lloyd Majors was executed in Oakland, California, in the jailyard, in 1894, crowds of people gathered in the streets, hoping for a glimpse of the show. Some people scrambled onto the roofs of houses, and "several boys . . . climbed into a tall poplar tree in front of the jail, in full view of the scaffold." This was already a shade anachronistic. A movement was under way to move executions deeper inside the bowels of the prison. The wonders of technology made this possible. In 1888, the legislature of New York passed an act providing that condemned men were to be "electrocuted" rather than hanged. This was the debut of the infamous "electric chair." An electric chair took up a lot less space than a gallows. Electrocuting somebody could take place in a small, intimate chamber of the prison, in front of a few carefully selected eyewitnesses and nobody else (Friedman 1993).[6] There would be no more boys climbing on trees.

Punishment in general had gone private; the public whipping post was also abandoned, and branding dropped out of the statute books after independence (in the northern states; it lingered longer in the south). Public hanging survived only in a few places: the last public hanging took place in Kentucky in 1936; 20,000 people attended, and there were "impromptu barbecues and . . . sporting activities" (Wright 1990, 257). But for most states, in the nineteenth century, the penitentiary became the normal mode of punishing those convicted of serious crimes. Convicts were locked up, out of sight, in grim fortresses. To be sure, Massachusetts, after it built its penitentiary, let visitors tour the prison, for a fee of $0.25. This practice was abolished by about the middle of the century (Hindus 1980).

The classic penitentiaries, built in the first half of the nineteenth century, or shortly afterwards, were massive, powerful buildings— austere, gloomy, and surrounded by high brick walls. They were visible expressions of an architecture of exclusion. The prisoners spent their long years inside solitary cells; they lived and worked in utter silence, and their lives were totally regimented. They ate only prison food, wore prison uniforms, and marched, if at all, in lockstep. Books were censored, mail was excluded or monitored, visitors were few and carefully screened. The outside world, in short, was rigorously shut off from their lives (Rothman 1971; Hirsch 1992).

What brought about this retreat from open, public punishment? Some scholars have pointed to structural and social changes in the social order. Colonial punishment focused on stigma and shame; it assumed a small, homogeneous audience. The milder punishments held deviants up to ridicule and public disgrace. More severe punishments, like hanging, were vivid, cathartic dramas, pointing to a stern moral lesson. These dramas were designed to be awesome and humbling. Nineteenth-century society was much more mobile—a society of big, anonymous cities or small communities full of strangers who came and went. Shame and humiliation lost some of their colonial bite (Hirsch 1992).

There was also a shift in elite attitudes toward public hangings. The appetite for such spectacles, among the leaders of society, particularly in the midwestern and northern states, began to cool off in the nineteenth century and by the middle of the century had become decidedly cold. In the nineteenth century, these outdoor events came to be denounced as "barbaric." Whipping was abolished in most states because it too was barbaric (Glenn 1984). But of course these were social judgments; what is barbaric is in the eye of the beholder, and definitions vary from place to place and from time to time. Future generations might find it barbaric to lock someone up for ten years in San Quentin.

Social judgments, of course, are not random; context determines them. Public hanging became "barbaric" because of a shift in legal culture. The ministers and leaders in old Massachusetts Bay thought of their people, by and large, as humble and deferential, eager to follow and obey—a respectful audience learning sound lessons or, at worst, child-like sinners to be educated in religion and morals. To nineteenth-century elites, the city crowd was different, looked different, and acted different. They were a mob, not a respectful audience. In fact, unruly crowds, riots, and urban disorders were all too common features of nineteenth-century city life (Feldberg 1980; Schneider 1980). Urban tumult was one of the reasons why city after city, toward the middle of the century, began to organize police forces (Miller 1977; Richardson 1974). To the respectable classes, an open display of cruelty and violence—a public hanging, for example—only pandered to the blood lust of the mob; such a spectacle was likely to bring out the beast inside the public breast.[7] The better sort of people began to avoid public hangings. These were not lessons in "civil and religious order" or "in morality and piety"; instead they evoked the "most debasing passions and appetites" (Masur 1989, 96–97).

Like the penitentiary, private hangings were a withdrawal from the community—a turning away from the idea that the *community* itself (the people) administered the punishment through shaming;

rather the people were feared and distrusted. The "community" was the *source* of criminality, not by any means the cure.

But although executions went private, the public continued to be present, if only vicariously. In a sense, the intention of the elites (if we have read this correctly) foundered on the rock of the mass media. The gentlemen and ladies of the press kept criminal justice in the public eye. The trial itself remained "public" in the limited, technical sense that the doors were open to anybody who wanted to attend and could find a seat. But more important, reporters were part of this audience; they came to the big, flashy trials and trumpeted the news to the world outside.

Executions were now completely closed to the public, but, like trials, they were favorite topics for newspapers and for rags like the *National Police Gazette*, the supermarket tabloid of its day. This was especially true in the late nineteenth century, the age of the so-called "yellow press." The press never showed its colors more shockingly than when it reported on crime, trials, and executions. The public, in general, loved to read the gory details; what the doomed man wore, how he acted, and what he ate. Thus, on December 22, 1924, the *Chicago Evening American* reported on Lester Kahl (the "Bride-Slayer") who, according to the paper, went to his death on an "icy gallows" with a "white carnation in the lapel of his coat and a gray cap at a jaunty angle." In Alameda County, California, the *Oakland Tribune* delighted in loathsome descriptions of executions, including a blow-by-blow description of how the rope nearly severed one man's head and how the blood spurted from his neck with a gurgling noise (Friedman and Percival 1981). Cameras, of course, were not allowed at executions; however, in 1928, a glorious day in the annals of capital punishment, a reporter for the *New York Daily News* smuggled a camera into the execution chamber, strapped to his ankle, and shot a picture of Ruth Snyder as she died in the electric chair (Friedman 1993).

The media also reported, minutely, the great trials, the headline trials, the packed courtroom trials. Some of these trials were media circuses: dozens of reporters crowded every available inch of space, while cameramen and artists worked feverishly to provide graphic detail. Thousands of words and pictures poured out, recounting every lurid aspect, every scandal, every twist and turn. Some newspapers were not above inventing juicy details on their own.[8] In any event, trials and punishments, and criminal justice in general, were for most people filtered, mediated, and even *experienced* by means of the daily press.

The sensationalism of the press did not, of course, go unnoticed. Lurid crime stories raised fears among some respectable elites, somewhat along the same lines as the fears evoked by public hangings. The media, in other words, were catering to the lusts and animal instincts of the rabble (Highfill 1926). Some states—Minnesota for example—took steps to make sure these lusts stayed hidden and suppressed. A Minnesota law of the late nineteenth century tried to make hangings as private as possible. The condemned convict was to be hung before sunrise "within the walls of the jail," and if the jail was not suitable, then "within an enclosure which shall be higher than the gallows, and shall exclude the view of persons outside." Moreover, no newspaper could lawfully publish any "account of the details of [any] . . . execution, beyond the statement of the fact that such convict was, on the day in question, duly executed according to law."[9]

Another related complaint was that the media swayed public opinion. The Cleveland survey of criminal justice, published in the 1920s, complained that newspapers overemphasized "human interest." Instead of "sober summary," their flashy style was "plainly intended either to condone or to condemn the accused" (Wisehart 1922, 515, 523).[10] In any event, the dramatic aspects of criminal justice survived in the form of trials and the media coverage of trials. There was, however, a change in the form and function of the trial, compared with colonial days. In the colonies, trials were more sermons than dramas—the results were, in the main, foreordained. The nineteenth-century trial was both a sermon *and* a drama: a drama, moreover, of suspense.

Whether distorted or not, full-scale criminal trials are fascinating. They are inherently theatrical. They are, to be sure, rather deviant forms of theater. Unlike a good stage play, a trial tends to be somewhat halting and incoherent. It is under much less control than the script of a play, and in major, contested trials there are two plots, not one, and they battle for primacy. There is also a definite tendency toward stereotyped plots and stock characters. A trial lawyer cannot afford to indulge in subtlety or ambivalence.

Indeed, trials are significant documents of social history precisely because they are so crude and so blatant. Each side tries to draw an idealized picture of its case and to demonize the other side. These conflicting images are important social indicators. The lawyers may play havoc with the truth, they may try to flummox the audience totally, but in spite of themselves they provide clear, precise evidence about the state of social norms and prejudices. They tell us what heroes and demons are *supposed* to look like, and act like, in the period in question.

Trial by Jury

At one time, the whole system of criminal justice was dramaturgic and intensely public. The situation changed in the nineteenth century. Punishment went private, and the public, dramatic, didactic side of criminal justice survived chiefly in the shape of the *trial,* at least the big show trials that were reported in the media.

The criminal trial is a sender of messages. That was true, of course, in the colonial period too. But the messages then were primarily top-down messages: lessons for the general public. The didactic role of the criminal trial in the nineteenth century was more complex. There were of course *official* lessons and messages, delivered mostly by the prosecution and by the judge in his instructions. Judge and prosecution powerfully shaped the thrust and point of the story, the drama that underlay the crime and the trial. But these messages were not sent solely to the public. They also went to the jury, and the jury was not a passive body. Through its work, it could send a countermessage; it could bend, reinforce, subvert, or redo the lessons and messages that came from judge and prosecution.

Of course, the jury also *is* the public, and it shares the views and attitudes of the public. In important trials, celebrity trials, trials that get into the newspapers—that tiny but crucial minority of trials—the unseen outside audience *may* have an impact on the trial itself—on its outcome and on its social meanings. The media, too, might have a direct effect. Jurors read newspapers, watch television, or talk about the case at home, even when a judge tells them not to. If the crime is sensational enough, *everybody* may have heard about the case. When a jury tries, say, Lizzie Borden or Dr. Sam Sheppard, it is too much to expect the members to be unaware of the basic facts of the crime.[11] How can one select a jury of twelve mental virgins, in a case where (as Mark Twain put it) the facts are known to "the very . . . stones in the streets" (Twain 1972, 308–9).[12] Commenting on the Loeb-Leopold case, a writer in the *New Republic* noted with alarm the enormous publicity, which would make "trial by jury a farce"; it was "scarcely probable that . . . there will be anyone of mediocre intelligence in this community who can go into the jury box with an open mind" (Lovett 1924, 121, 122).[13] In big trials, perhaps it would be too much to expect cool impartiality even from the judge.

Trials, then, are "public" also in an additional sense: twelve members of the public are drawn into the web of criminal justice and given full voice in the outcome. Our system, then, has this unique, *empowered* audience, twelve women and men who control the verdict, lay people who make the actual decision on innocence or guilt and, at times, even about life or death.

It is because of the jury that a trial, in our system, is particularly prone to the theatrical. The trial is not a dry search for evidence, a crabbed process of grubbing about for clues and indications. It is necessarily a drama—a story acted out as if onstage. The stories are primarily for the benefit of the jury, which, unlike the general audience, makes the actual decisions. The jury sits and listens. Normally, jurors do not even ask questions and are not allowed to. They seem totally passive throughout the trial. Nonetheless, trial by jury is not ordinary theater; it is interactive. The jury's contribution may be only a single word or two words, but they are incredibly powerful words. And they often carry a complex message in themselves.

This is because juries, in the aggregate, allow the legal system to exhibit a degree of normative complexity and subtlety that the official law does not permit and perhaps cannot permit, for whatever reason. The official rules of criminal law are relatively tight, clear, and brittle. They mince no words, and they draw bright, clear lines. There are official definitions of murder, manslaughter, and all the other crimes. But patterns of jury behavior give off more ambiguous and nuanced messages. In part, these messages tell us which norms are taken most seriously and which are not. The messages are not always easy to read. Jury decisions come with no overt explanation. They are hammered out in secret. They can be lithe and supple, cut to the individual case. Very little of the jury's subtlety is open and expressed.

The subtlety, in short, has to be inferred from what juries do. There is a great deal of research on jury deliberation, yet we rarely know exactly *what* a jury had in mind, in any particular case.[14]

Jurors deliberate in a locked room, and they issue a bald, naked verdict; unlike a judge, they never give reasons. Lately, in some hotly contested cases, jurors have granted interviews after the verdict or have even written books about their experiences. But this is exceptional. If we go back further in time, of course, jury behavior becomes even more obscure.

The ideology of the jury is (by now) fairly clear. The jury is supposed to find facts and to apply these facts to the law. At one time, it was usual to say that the jury was judge of law as well as fact (Nelson 1975, 165–71); that jurors could, in other words, ignore what the judge told them and craft their own legal rules. But that doctrine (or whatever it was) did not survive the nineteenth century in most jurisdictions. In two states, Maryland and Indiana, the power of the jury to decide law *and* fact survives as a constitutional principle, but even in these two states, judicial decisions have gutted the principle of any real meaning.[15] The jury is supposed to decide solely on the basis of the evidence presented. It would be wrong for a jury to toss a coin, and jurors are told to ignore sympathy, prejudice, and other raw emotions.

But the very structure of the system belies these platitudes. If the system really meant what it said, the jury would not be locked up in a room and told to deliberate in secret. The jury would not be allowed to pronounce its verdict like the Delphic oracle, as a bare fiat, without any explanation or supporting reasoning whatsoever. Perhaps a system that took seriously the idea of rational, legal decisionmaking would not use a jury at all or at least not a jury of twelve nobodies picked at random. Most legal systems in fact do not have juries; these systems put their faith in the power of professionals to come to just, careful conclusions. In other words, they put their faith in judges.[16]

In short, the jury's power to bend and sway, to chip away at the official rules, is built right into the system. Juries are not supposed to be "lawless," but the system is set up in such a way that lawlessness, of a sort, cannot be prevented or even detected. This can hardly be historical accident. So central a feature of an important legal institution might begin by chance but could not survive unless it met some deep-seated want or need. "Lawless" is merely a label for jury behavior that, in somebody's opinion, oversteps the invisible line between honest flexibility and wanton disregard for the rules.

In reality, there is evidence that most juries try hard to do their duty, as they see it and as they are told to do (Hans and Vidmar 1986, ch. 9). Moreover, there are very complicated rules of evidence, devised with the jury in mind. These rules help control the jury. Nobody presents raw, unadulterated "fact" to the jury. Rather "facts" are predigested, purified, and made into a kind of approved sauce before the jury is allowed to consume them. The jury only sees a corner of reality; Jurors are like somebody peeping into a keyhole, who cannot see the whole room.[17]

Still, within the limits imposed, the jury has awesome power. The jury, like the crowd in a Roman arena, turns thumbs up or thumbs down, and that decides the case. There is no appeal from the verdict of a jury. It has total finality when it acquits, and even a guilty verdict is untouchable on the facts. A lost defendant has to scrape around for "errors" of law to ground an appeal.

Trial by jury is a basic right, and Americans seem to value it, in part as a bulwark against the state. There is a downside of course. Juries do not always rise above the prejudices of their communities. Far from it. The way southern juries treated African American defendants before the civil rights revolution was a national scandal. Juries were all white, and they did not seem to think it was a real crime to kill a black man who violated rules of white supremacy. In theory, of course, juries are supposed to be panels of men and women who *deliberate*, who discuss, who "put aside narrow group allegiances" in search of consensus (Abramson 1994, 245). In today's world, some people think the jury has a somewhat different role. It has to exhibit "group representation" and reflect demographic diversity. This idea "fits the pluralist paradigm of democracy and interest group politics" (Abramson 1994, 245).[18]

In any event, jurors are and always have been human beings, lay people, people with hearts as well as heads. This is why, as everybody knows, lawyers work so hard to build up a sympathetic story; this is why they create stereotypes, why they try or defend the victim, why they whitewash the defendant or blacken his reputation. They want to convince the jury to see the facts of the case in the proper light. More especially, they want to advance *their* version of the plot, the drama, the script.

In short, the law permits and enhances, structurally, exactly those aspects of a jury trial that stress dramatic, nonlegal, nonlogical, emotional, didactic appeals. Lawyers are hamstrung as far as evidence is concerned, but it is not improper to make a jury laugh or cry—quite the contrary. In many ways, emotion and intuition are what jury trials are all about. For logic and legal reasoning, we have judges.[19]

Unwritten Laws

There are messages implicit in jury verdicts or, perhaps more accurately, in masses of jury verdicts. Because of the jury's freedom and power, jury verdicts in this country illustrate the strength of what are called "unwritten laws." That is, the verdicts illustrate or proclaim certain underground norms—social norms. The law ignores social norms on the official level, but they are nonetheless widely accepted. The practiced observer (or even the unpracticed one, from time to time) can detect these "unwritten laws" in patterns of jury behavior. Appeals to these norms are powerful tools in legal theater. There are no doubt many examples. One of the most famous, in the nineteenth century, was the "law" that a man was entitled to avenge the sexual dishonor of a wife, sister, daughter, or mother (Friedman 1993; Ireland 1992b; "Comment: Recognition of the Honor Defense under the Insanity Plea" 1934; Roberts 1922). This was in fact *the* "unwritten law," the one that gave the whole genre its name.

It is very likely that the history of jury behavior would turn up a number of "unwritten laws." Juries, of course, are not supposed to follow these norms; the norms are not given as part of the judge's instructions. Probably juries apply these "unwritten laws" most readily if they have some kind of fig leaf, some kind of legal excuse, however flimsy, to cover their nakedness. At least, this is a reasonable hypothesis. If so, then the history of jury behavior is also a history of these fig leaves, the legal hooks on which juries hang their verdicts.

One of these, which has figured in any number of sensational trials, is the doctrine of "temporary insanity." It is hard to know exactly when this magnificent concept got its start. "Temporary insanity" obviously takes off from the well-established notion that an insane person is not criminally responsible. Some insane people do have lucid intervals, and sane people might have episodes of insanity, too, presumably brought on by enormous passion or stress. Credit (if that is the word) for the first use of "temporary insanity" is often assigned to the trial of Congressman Dan Sickles, in Washington, D.C., in 1859

(Brandt 1991; Swanberg 1956; for an account of the trial, see Lawson 1919). That may not in fact be correct, but the Sickles trial certainly gave the concept a big push forward.[20] Sickles had a young wife, Teresa, and Teresa, alas, took herself a lover, Philip Barton Key, the son of Francis Scott Key. Sickles himself was no paragon of fidelity, but the double standard was in full flower in those days. An anonymous note tipped Sickles off; he confronted Teresa, who confessed her sins. The next day Sickles took his gun and shot Key dead on the streets of Washington, a few blocks from the White House.

The trial was a sensation in its day. Hundreds, including gentlemen of the press, lined up outside the courtroom, trying to get in. Sickles's lawyers made essentially two arguments: the first, hardly a legal argument at all, was that adulterers deserved to die. The bond of marriage was "sanctified by the law of God," they said, and the penalty for adultery "did not originate in human statutes; it was written in the heart of man in the Garden of Eden" (Lawson 1919, 708). In Biblical times, after all, adulterers were stoned to death.

This was, of course, an argument based on unwritten law. The rule may have been written in the heart of men, but it was conspicuously absent from the penal code. Hence the lawyers had to use some other bait for the jury. The concept of temporary insanity served this purpose. Adultery, so went the argument, could produce a towering rage in a man like Sickles, sending him into a "frenzy in which he is wholly irresponsible for what he may do" (Lawson 1919, 723). Popular opinion, as far as we can judge, was strongly on the side of the wronged husband. The jury, as it turns out, was also of this mind. Sickles was acquitted.

In the course of the nineteenth century and into the twentieth, there were many examples of the "unwritten law" in jury verdicts, and "temporary insanity" figured in any number of these trials.[21] In the 1870 trial of Daniel McFarland, who shot his ex-wife's lover to death, a Dr. Hammond testified to "cerebral congestion." The defendant's face and head were "abnormally hot" and, shown photographs of his wife, his pulse rose, and he started twitching. Tests on the "Dynamograph machine" proved that he "could not control his will." The good doctor swore that "the act itself was done during an attack of temporary insanity." The jury acquitted.[22] Paul Wright, in Glendale, California, shot his wife, Evelyn, and his best friend, John Kimmel, to death. Wright had been roused from sleep "by a single note, repeated over and over on the piano." He went down to the living room, where he found Evelyn and John sitting on the piano bench; John's fly was open. A "white flame exploded" in Paul Wright's brain, according to him. The jury acquitted here too (Wolf and Mader 1986, 143–47).[23]

Temporary insanity was also a defense in one of the most sensational trials in American history, the trial of Harry K. Thaw (1907). Thaw had killed Stanford White, the architect, in Madison Square Garden. The motive was sexual revenge—a variation on the theme of the unwritten law. White, according to Thaw, had defiled his wife, the beautiful Evelyn Nisbet Thaw, when she was young. Thaw's defense was temporary insanity, but the jury (at a second trial) found insanity of a more permanent type. Thaw was shipped off to the State Asylum for the Criminal Insane, in Matteawan, New York (O'Conner 1963, ch. 7 and 8; Friedman 1993).

Women who killed husbands and lovers were less successful than men in invoking the unwritten law (Ireland 1992a), but there are a fair number of examples. In 1894, Clara Fallmer went on trial for murder in Alameda County, California (Friedman and Percival 1981). Clara was fifteen or sixteen, and she had shot and killed her lover, Charlie La Due. Her story was an old, familiar one: she was seduced and abandoned. Like Dan Sickles, Clara shot her lover in broad daylight on the streets of Oakland, California. "I didn't do it" was therefore not a tenable defense. Once again, her lawyers trotted out the defense of temporary insanity: Clara shot Charlie during a "state of emotional insanity"; as she brooded over her fate, she became "unhinged." More significantly, the defense painted a picture of Clara as a tender young plant, innocent as fresh-fallen snow, and Charlie as a villain who deserved to die. Clara appeared every day in court, dressed in blue, with a veil covering her face, clutching a bouquet of violets. The prosecution sneered at this stage-managed image of Clara and tried to paint her as an abandoned young trollop.

To no avail. In the gender dramas of the 1890s, only two stock roles were available for Clara. She could be a flower or a whore; there was nothing in between. From our standpoint, Clara looks like just another sexually active teenager. But that was not a plausible story at the time. The two conflicting images, put forward by the opposing lawyers, tell us what was considered thinkable (or at least sayable) and what was not in the 1890s. The outcome was never in much doubt. Sympathy lay with the young defendant: weak, pale, distraught, and clutching violets. Moreover, the jury had their legal hook. Clara was quickly and easily acquitted.

These results seem obvious and predictable, and they raise a question: why are "unwritten rules" unwritten? Why are they not official, if they are genuinely popular? There are at least two answers. One is that law and practice reflect a kind of structural ambivalence. At one level, society disapproves of these underground norms; at another level, it likes them enormously.

But what does this mean? The "ambivalence," I suspect, is not a matter of psychology. It is an implicit theory of social control. Imagine a case in which an old man, weeping hysterically, gives a lethal dose of medicine to his beloved wife, terminally ill and suffering beyond human endurance. Technically, this might be murder. But many prosecutors would refuse to prosecute, and juries would almost certainly acquit. Yet the same prosecutors and jurors might well *oppose* making euthanasia legal. And why? Because then "everybody would do it," or the wrong people would do it. The present system—condemning euthanasia officially, but treating individual cases sympathetically—does a better job of keeping euthanasia within its proper limits, at optimal levels. At least one might think so.

The second answer is that some unwritten rules, though popular in certain quarters, may by no means command total consensus. Universal rules, consensus rules, rarely remain unwritten. They get absorbed into formal doctrine, in whole or in part. The ones that stay unwritten are often in some manner and form sharply contested. They thus lead to a kind of dual system, operating at two levels: an official level and a realm of behavior. The dual system acts as a kind of compromise or stalemate. Did most women, for example, really approve of the unwritten rule, in a case like that of Congressman Sickles? In any event, the historical study of patterns of jury decisions might reveal a whole new, unexplored country: a hidden realm of norms and patterns, many half-formed or inchoate, some exceedingly local, some widely diffused, some ephemeral, some longer-lasting.

Direct Action

In some of the cases of unwritten law just discussed, the defendant has executed an evil adulterer. These are cases of direct action—of a kind of vigilantism or, if you will, a kind of private or solitary act of lynch law.

"Direct action" is a euphemism for activities that violently circumvent ordinary legal process. Max Weber has a famous passage about the state as holding a monopoly of legitimate violence. Like many monopolies, this one is leaky about the edges.[24] Direct action includes mob violence, vigilante movements, urban riots and protests, and other ways of taking the law into one's own hands. Direct action by definition takes place outside the courtroom setting. Yet the show trial and direct action are not unrelated. Some forms of direct action are hidden and circumspect. But more often, direct action is open and notorious and is *intended* to be didactic theater. At times, it has even imitated ordinary legal process, including trial by jury. Often, it has been as public as possible and directed, like criminal trials, at a general audience.

Direct action comes in various shapes and sizes. Riots and mob action are perhaps at one end of the spectrum and have the least relationship to our general theme. Riots themselves are not all alike. Feldberg (1980), in his study of Jacksonian disorders, drew a distinction between various forms of riot—"preservatist riots" as against "expressive riots" and "recreational riots." "Preservatist riots," unlike the others, have a political aim: riots, for example, against blacks. These have historically served as a powerful weapon of racial suppression. Riots of protest and rebellion also fall into this category.

Vigilante movements, although they also take a bewildering multiplicity of forms, are also basically political acts. There have been dozens and dozens of these movements, in different times and places, from the colonial period on. But they are particularly associated with the American West and are concentrated in the last half of the nineteenth century.[25]

Nineteenth-century literature used to describe vigilantes as good, strong, macho men, fighting rustlers, no-goods, crooked sheriffs, and the like on behalf of law and order. Dimsdale's well-known book (1953) on the vigilantes of Montana positively swoons with admiration. But in fact many vigilante outbreaks—perhaps most of them—were not quite so benign; they represented some kind of culture clash or class conflict. Dimsdale described the frontier as lawless, yet there were courts and sheriffs and judges and juries and regular trials. His real complaint was that the juries refused to convict rough, violent men. Juries were very severe on cattle-rustlers, but they tended to acquit brawlers and gunfighters.

Dimsdale objected, in other words, to a *local* example of unwritten law. Local and, one might add, far from universal. The "code" of the jurors clashed with the code of the local elites, including Dimsdale. The vigilante outbreak in Montana was in good measure the result of this conflict. Vigilantes did, of course, have instrumental goals: getting rid of some particular bad hombre or a gang of such hombres, but they also sent a message and taught a lesson. This goal was in some ways the more important one. Direct action can, in other words, express its own unwritten rule, or it can act and teach in opposition to an unwritten rule that operates within the formal legal system.

Lynching rose to special prominence in the south in the late nineteenth and early twentieth centuries. At its dreadful climax, a hundred or so died each year at the hands of lynch mobs. A report of the National Association for the Advancement of Colored People (NAACP 1969) listed almost 3,000 southern victims (the northern toll was less than a tenth of that). Most victims had been accused of murder or rape; about four out of five were black.

Lynching, like most vigilante hangings, was quite *public*. It was mob action, and it often took place in front of crowds of people. In 1899, for example, in Newman, Georgia, a black man named Sam Holt was accused of murdering a white man and raping the man's wife. Holt was tortured, mutilated, and burned at the stake; a crowd of 2,000 people watched. Nobody in the crowd wore a mask or made any attempt to hide his identity (Ginzburg 1962). In some ways, this was a throwback to the bad old days of public hanging, although without even the slightest veneer of spirituality. Lynching was meant to teach a lesson in a blunt and brutal way. It was mainly a tool of white supremacy.[26] It enforced the southern white "code," and it was particularly virulent toward blacks who dared to transgress the sexual aspects of the code. In a federal system, the south did not totally control the formal law, which did not embody or enforce the "code" in its full rigor.

Direct action, in other words, has various roots. When a powerful local group feels that official justice is corrupt, or weak and inefficient, vigilante justice or some variant is a possible solution. More likely, some clash of norms or cultures lurks in the background. The

Ku Klux Klan arose during the reconstruction period because white supremacists felt that the formal law was in the hands of its enemies—blacks and carpetbaggers (see Randel 1965; for a contemporary account, see Tourgee 1880, pt. 2, "The Invisible Empire"). Lynch mobs felt that ordinary courts—even though these were, to our tastes, unbelievably severe to black defendants—were much too flabby and slow.

Today, almost every social movement has a radical fringe that is willing to take direct action: right-to-lifers who kill doctors, animal rights' extremists, and so on. A passionate belief, frustrated by normal processes, can sometimes curdle into violence. This violence is apt to be open violence—show violence—rather than terrorism, which tends to be clandestine. The public, quite naturally, despises fringe groups. Yet popular culture has a certain admiration for neo-vigilantes, if their goal is "law and order": Rambo or Dirty Harry or Bernhard Goetz, the real-life "subway vigilante." In part, this grudging admiration reflects public disgust with crime and impatience with laxity (as people see it) toward vicious thugs. A man (rarely a woman) who does quick, surgical justice appeals to something deep in the American soul. But the goal must be *justice;* vengeance is a more questionable aim. And justice often implies a kind of openness, even a theatrical quality, to the act. Americans have less tolerance for secret, dirty tricks or for death squads.

Like the celebrity trial, then, direct action tends to be on stage. It tends to be visible, to follow a flamboyant, violent script. The medium is supposed to convey the message. Sometimes the goal—also quite open—is to terrorize and paralyze the normal, official processes. Direct action, moreover, often concerns itself with unwritten laws. Nothing in southern penal codes made it a capital crime for a black man to raise a hand or open an impudent mouth to a white woman. No law in the west labeled certain bad *hombres* a community menace, to be disposed of by fair means or foul.[27]

Vigilante groups sometimes put on a semblance of a trial, before stringing up their victim.[28] They almost always claimed to act in the interests of a higher or better justice; they almost always claimed to represent the greater good. Almost always, too, they acted *in* public.

Because influential segments of the public approved of what they did, and protected them, vigilantes were almost never punished by the law. Leaders sometimes went on to high office and prestige.

Dr. John E. Osborne, of Wyoming, a vigilante, played a role in the killing of Big Nose George Parrott, an outlaw. Osborne skinned the corpse and openly exhibited objects made from the skin, including a pair of shoes. Was he arrested and prosecuted for any of this? Not at all. Later, in fact, he was elected governor of Wyoming (Brown 1975, 155).

Not all vigilante groups were concerned with thieves, rustlers, highwaymen, and urban corruption. Some were concerned with the moral code. It was standard practice in urban America in the nineteenth century for city officials and the police to wink at vice and sin and in fact to collect payoffs. Other segments of the public were less tolerant. Brothel riots, so-called, were common early in the century (Schneider 1980). In the late nineteenth century, there were the so-called "white caps," a vigilante group that enforced good old-fashioned morality. The white caps punished by whipping, and they singled out drunkards, wife beaters, immoral couples, and the like. There was at least one example of female white caps: twelve women of Nebraska who, in 1893, disguised with pillow cases on their heads, seized and flogged certain "immoral" young ladies. One of the floggers was the wife of a bank president (Friedman 1993, 187).

Direct action has never, of course, died out as a feature of American social life. Indeed, some sensational trials have concerned the intersection between direct action and criminal justice. The trial of Bernhard Goetz, the so-called subway vigilante, has already been mentioned.

Trial Drama Today

Today, in the age of television, movies, and public opinion polls, the great trials are more theatrical than ever, and theater (in the broad sense) is more than ever concerned with great trials. Millions devoured every last word of the Menéndez trials on Court TV. But the mother of all trials, in the era of television at any rate, was the O. J. Simpson trial. Tens of millions watched this case, like moths drawn to a naked bulb. This was the trial of trials: the defendant was a famous man, a sports hero, a movie star, in short, a *celebrity*, in an age fascinated by show business and by celebrities (Schickel 1985; Fowles 1992; Friedman 1990, ch. 7). Great trials can, of course, *create* celebrities. The defendant in a lurid or sensational case becomes an instant celebrity. The public is fascinated by celebrities, even (it seems) when they are murderers or criminals. Amy Fisher is a celebrity because she shot her lover's wife in the face. So are the Menéndez brothers, who killed their parents, and Lorena Bobbitt, who mutilated her husband. So too is John Gotti, a prominent mobster who was put on trial. Famous murderers on death row always get proposals of marriage. Hordes of fans gathered outside O. J. Simpson's house, after he was arrested, anxious to bathe in the mysterious aura of celebrity. T-shirts were huge sellers outside the L.A. courthouse during the trial. When Bruno Hauptmann was on trial for kidnapping and murdering the Lindbergh baby—perhaps the most sensational trial of this century—"certified locks of Baby Lindbergh's hair" (fake, of course) were sold on the streets of Flemington, New Jersey, where the trial took place, along with bookends in the shape of the courthouse, photographs of Lindbergh, and toy replicas of the ladder used by the kidnappers in snatching the baby from its home (Kennedy 1985, 259).

A celebrity society is under the spell of the media and especially of television, whose images dominate our daily lives. In the age of television, the dramatic aspects of trials become even more salient. But when the *entertainment* value of trials increases, what happens to the didactic aspects of public justice? What happens to the moral messages? Are they drowned out? Do they fade into the background? Are they replaced by the implicit messages of the modern mass media?

These are, of course, empirical questions, and I do not know the answers. Public justice always, perhaps, sent ambiguous messages. The messages, I suspect, are even more distorted today. The media mislead and misinform; some of the misinformation is deliberate, some merely market-driven. Consciously or unconsciously, the media present a false picture about criminal justice. John and Jane Public, as we know, get most of their information, such as it is, from television and newspapers, and much of this comes out of the world of the great show trials.

Some commentators think these trials are educational. People learn from what they see. The O. J. Simpson case taught the public lessons about criminal procedure and how it operates. But how valuable—or how accurate—is this "education"? Show trials give off two intense messages, which are in a way both wrong and contradictory. The first message is that the legal system is in deadly earnest about every aspect of due process. It takes days or weeks to pick a jury, the judge pays careful attention to procedure and evidence, the lawyers wrangle and argue and squabble over experts; "I object" is a constant refrain.

But all this posturing and maneuvering send another message. The trial is not about truth at all. It is exclusively theater, drama, and a lawyer's bag of tricks. Justice is a mountebank, a riverboat gambler, a con man, an impostor. Money and publicity bend justice. Enough of these two commodities, and the most ironclad case can turn to jello.

There is, of course, another system of criminal justice, the "real" system, the working system. This is a system of plea bargaining, copping pleas, and cutting deals; it is a world of slapdash, routine process. But this world is largely hidden from view. Hardly anybody seems to know much about it, except for the professionals and the scholars, and hardly anybody else seems to care.[29] In general, the public is wildly wrong about many facts about criminal justice. They imagine, for example, that the insanity defense is common; in fact, it is rare. People in one survey, in Wyoming, guessed that as many as a third of all felony defendants raised the insanity defense; in fact, the true figure was less than 0.5 percent (Maeder 1985).

People also believe that courts coddle criminals and that hardened criminals escape through chinks and cracks in the system. This is at least misleading, if not downright wrong. False information is one reason the public shows such bloodlust over crime and why politicians fall all over themselves competing to sound tougher and meaner than anybody else.

In a sense, too, all of public life has become theater—has become in some ways like the criminal trial writ large. A celebrity society is also a public opinion society. Political leaders, in such a society, are themselves celebrities, and they rise and fall like celebrities. Under these circumstances, the general public is both sovereign and manipulated. It has extraordinary power to influence policy through public opinion polls, focus groups, and the like. But at the same time, the government uses the tricks of the media trade to bend, mold, and distort public opinion. It shows only what it wants to show. It lies, it conceals, it stereotypes, it blusters. The public, then, is less in control than it thinks; someone else pulls invisible strings.

Of course, the government does not have everything its own way. There is, after all, an opposition, and it too tries to influence and persuade the public. It makes use of a bag of tricks, very much like the government's. This is why we can compare political life to the show trials of criminal justice. In politics, too, there are two opposing "sides" and two sets of arguments—defense and prosecution. The voting public has the role of the jury—powerful within its domain, but controlled by rules of evidence and shamelessly manipulated by lawyers. The public is, in short, systematically misled in much the same way that the jury is misled in a criminal trial. The information it gets is twisted and filtered. The two rival plots are distorted, rich in stock characterizations and empty rhetoric, and they pander to the most common social prejudices. The public tends to decide, not on the basis of "facts," but on the basis of personality, sincerity, and image. And all this is filtered through, and conducted by, the media.

A Concluding Word

This chapter has focused on expressive, didactic, dramaturgical functions of criminal justice and, in particular, the criminal trial. It looked at the nature of the jury and at the messages sent to the jury and to the wider world, it looked at the operation of unwritten laws, and it briefly discussed direct action and its relationship to the other themes of this chapter.

There is, of course, a lot we do not know about how criminal justice works, in any of its functions. The expressive and educational functions are perhaps least well understood or researched, despite a large "true crime" literature. The dry debates of law professors certainly do not capture the meaning and impact of criminal justice. And the speeches and rhetoric of politicians have to be taken with a whole mountain of salt.

Criminal justice has a deep and special meaning in a democratic society. Political theory talks about freedom of speech, voting, and other aspects of representative government, the constitution, the rule of law, and due process. But society is not governed only or even primarily by formal rules and constitutional structures. Due process is simply process. It is important in its sphere, but it does not get to the heart of justice. Justice is what people define as justice, and justice consists of outcomes as well as procedures. There is a formal system of justice, but there is also an informal, working system, and it is this system that actually runs the country, silently but powerfully. The *real* criminal justice system is based on social norms (of the public and of actors in the system—the police, for example) that are not necessarily part of the penal code. It includes unwritten rules, stereotypes, ideal pictures, images, and models of good and bad behavior.

These emerge most clearly in big, open trials. But stereotypes and unwritten rules pervade criminal justice, including the subterranean system—the routine parts of criminal justice. These unwritten rules are important rules of the game. They come out of society itself, not from the codes or from "model" laws. To be sure, judges and juries, prosecutors, and public defenders all have a role in defining or explicating norms.

The unwritten rules are not made by fiat or enactment. Some are developed in the course of dramas of high visibility; others are developed through underground evolutions, changes in direction, and processes of the kind described here. These grow beneath the surface, so to speak, until they burst out during the passions of criminal trials.

Here we confront a kind of paradox. The great trials are theatrical and public. Yet the power to *change* norms and rules is vested, at least in part, in the jury, which works in secret. Juries modify the law, they chip away at doctrine, and they subtly alter patterns of decisions, but in an arena that, up to now, the media cannot penetrate at all. This mixture of the visible and the invisible is not unusual in the legal system. The police, for example, are effective mainly because they are *visible*; they wear uniforms, they sound sirens, they patrol the streets openly, deterring by their very presence. But they are also secret, clandestine controllers, and they use methods at night or in the stationhouses that are (officially speaking) completely illegitimate, yet significant and real.

The great show trials shed light on the normative structure of society, openly and dramatically. But the law in action, in all its forms, also acts as a kind of X-ray, revealing bones and skeletons, the hidden, inner framework that plays an unacknowledged role in our society.

Notes

1. A poll conducted by the *New York Times* and CBS News on April 21–23, 1994, showed that "crime, violence, and guns" were the "most important problem facing" the country; the public ranked this cluster of difficulties ahead of economic issues and ahead of health care. This represented a dramatic shift since 1992. *New York Times*, May 10, 1994, national edition, A12.

2.   Sometimes the entertainment aspects of trial come out with unusual clarity. In *Roberts v. State*, 100 Neb. 199 (1916), the crime was murder, and it was the talk of the town in North Platte, Nebraska. So much so, and so desirable was a seat at the show, that the judge moved the trial from the courtroom to the Keith Theater, the local "opera house," because of the "insufficiency of the courtroom to seat and accommodate the people applying for admission." Judge, jury, and witnesses sat on the stage. At the end of one court day, the bailiff announced from the stage that the "regular show will be tomorrow; matinee in the afternoon and another performance at 8:30. Court is now adjourned." He may have been referring to the trial or, more likely, to an "exhibition" by a troop of actors, also scheduled for the theater; but in any event, the supreme court of Nebraska expressed shock and horror and sent the case back for a new and less overtly theatrical trial.

3.   Laws R.I. and Providence Plantation, 1749, at 53. John Godfrey, guilty of "wicked and most pernicious subborning of witnesses to the perverting of justice," was sentenced in Essex County, Massachusetts, to pay a fine and to "stand upon the pillory one hour, with this inscription written in capital letters upon a paper fastened upon him, 'JOHN GODFREY, FOR SUBBORNING WITTNESSES.' " Records and Files of the Quarterly Courts of Essex County, Massachusetts, 4, at 169 (April 1669).

4.   For this point, I am indebted to an anonymous reader of an earlier draft.

5.   Laws Ill., 1859, at 17. In addition, the sheriff could invite "such officers of the prison, deputies, and constables as shall by him be deemed expedient to have present." Only the categories mentioned were "permitted to be present" at the execution.

6.   The first person who had the honor to die in the electric chair was William Kemmler, in 1890. The U.S. Supreme Court held that electrocution was not cruel and unusual punishment, In re *Kemmler*, 137 US 436 (1890). The actual execution, though, did not go by as smoothly as the people who hustled this new method of killing claimed or hoped (see Denno 1994).

7.   This notion more or less survives today in the form of the argument that capital punishment is bad because it has a "brutalizing" effect. As one author put it, the "lesson" of executions is to "devalue life by the example of human sacrifice. Executions demonstrate that it is correct and appropriate to kill those who have gravely offended us" (Bowers, Pierce, and McDevitt 1984, 174).

8.   During the sensational trial of Chester Gillette for murdering his pregnant girlfriend, reporters for New York newspapers banged on the jail door and shouted "We want to lynch Gillette." This laid the basis for a story about a mob that surrounded the jail and tried to get in (Brandon 1986, 310).

9. Rev. Laws Minn. 1905, Sec 5422, at 1140; Laws Minn. 1889, Ch 20, at 66. This statute came before the U.S. Supreme Court in *Holden v. Minnesota*, 137 US 483 (1890). The question in the case was whether the statute was ex post facto as applied to a prisoner sentenced to death for a crime committed before the act was passed; the court upheld the statute.

   Another Minnesota law provided that no prisoner could be made to "labor, with ball and chain attached, upon the streets, parks, or other public works, nor, as a punishment for crime, be held, tied, or bound in public." Rev. Laws. Minn. 1905, Sec 5423, at 1140. This was in a way a total antithesis to the attitude of colonial jurisdictions toward the open, public nature of punishment.

10. For a more measured account than Fosdick's, see "Note: Crimes— Newspaper Publication—Contempt" (1912, 774). "It is easy, however, to exaggerate the pernicious influence of the . . . press . . . While the articles relating to a few sensational crimes may have this effect, it is to be remembered that the great majority of crimes receive but scant notice in the daily press."

11. Dr. Sheppard was accused of murdering his wife in 1954 in their home outside Cleveland. The trial was a sensation, and the local and national newspapers had a field day with it. They also dominated the courtroom scene. The jury was not sequestered during the trial. When the jury went out to look at the Sheppard home, where the murder took place, a pool reporter entered the house with them, while a helicopter circled overhead, taking pictures. This was only a sample of the goings-on at the trial. Sheppard was convicted, but his conviction was overturned, ten years later, by the U.S. Supreme Court in *Sheppard v. Maxwell*, 384 US 333 (1966). The opinion said, in essence, that the media madness had so poisoned the atmosphere at the trial that Sheppard had been denied his constitutional rights. He was acquitted on retrial. Sheppard's family insisted, all along, that he was innocent, and more recent literature makes a plausible case that Sheppard *was* innocent (Cooper and Sheppard 1995).

12. Twain was talking about Virginia City, Nevada. In small towns, it is probably true that prospective jurors would know about *every* felony trial, sensational or not.

13. In the event, Loeb and Leopold did not go to trial. They pleaded guilty, and the only issue, the sentence, was tried by a judge alone.

14. The research is, of course, extremely voluminous. Much of it is summed up in Hans and Vidmar (1986); see also the classic study by Kalven and Zeisel (1966).

15. Indiana Const, Art 1, Sec 19: "In all criminal cases whatever, the jury shall have the right to determine the law and the facts." Md. Const,

Declaration of Rights, Art 23: "In the trial of criminal cases, the Jury shall be Judges of Law, as well as of fact."

16. Or, in some cases, they throw the lay people onto a panel of professional judges, who tend to dominate the proceedings.

17. This was particularly true in the O. J. Simpson case. The vast television audience sometimes knew more about what was going on than the members of the jury, who were pushed out of the room whenever the lawyers wrangled over some point of law.

18. Abramson (1994) adds that this view is "openly skeptical about whether deliberation inside the jury room matters." It looks on juries, not as a body of rational discussants, but as a "microcosm of the biases and prejudices, the bartering and brokering among group interests." Jurors are seen as "voting their demographics."

19. Which (of course) is not to say that judges in fact *do* decide according to logic and legal reasoning.

20. Ireland (1993), reviewing Brandt (1991), asserts that the Sickles case was not, in fact, the first to "recognize the validity of the doctrines of temporary insanity." These had appeared at the trial of Thomas Washington Smith in 1858, according to Ireland. However, the Sickles trial did create the "ideological nucleus of the unwritten law which stated that a husband could justifiably assassinate his wife's paramour."

21. In a few states, parts of the unwritten law were embodied in the formal, written law. For example, in Texas, a man who killed his wife's lover, if he caught them in the act, was not guilty of murder, provided the killing took place "before the parties to the act of adultery have separated." Crim. Laws of Texas, 1881, Art 567, at 191.

22. Cooper (1994, 192–94). The courtroom was jam-packed for the final arguments. The defense spent most of its time arguing that "the compromise of a husband's honor" creates such strong feelings that "the Deity did not make man strong enough to stand a provocation like that." Cooper (1994, 216–17).

23. The defendant did not *always* win in cases that combined a kind of unwritten law with the defense of temporary insanity. In a Maryland case from 1888, the defendant, Spencer, shot Dawson to death. Dawson had assaulted Rachel, Spencer's wife, *before* the marriage. The assault (Rachel claimed) led to an illness, which eventually killed her. Spencer claimed he was obsessed with images of the "dead body of his wife," marked "with the scars inflicted by the deceased," and that his dreams were haunted by these images. The trial court excluded this evidence, and the jury convicted. Spencer lost on appeal. *Spencer v. State*, 69 Md 28, 13 Atl 809 (1888).

24. Of course, it is possible to *define* all nonstate violence as illegitimate, but that seems circular.

25. There is a large literature on vigilantes and vigilante movements. The most thorough and comprehensive is Richard Maxwell Brown (1975); see also Jordan (1970) and Friedman (1993, ch. 8). Senkewicz (1985) deals with the famous San Francisco vigilante movements.

26. The notorious lynching of Leo Frank, by a Georgia mob, in 1913, was a rare example of an antisemitic lynching (see MacLean 1991). In 1933, in San Jose, California, a mob stormed the jailhouse, overpowered the police, and lynched Jack Holmes and Harold Thurmond, who had kidnapped and killed Brooke Hart, a young man from a prominent local family. A large crowd of men, women, and children watched this gruesome event (Farrell 1993).

27. See the account of the death of Captain Slade, in Dimsdale (1953). Slade was executed, even though he had not been tried by a jury or convicted of any crime.

28. There were also "trials" of men accused of murder on the overland trail, far beyond the reach of ordinary processes of law, and these trials, with juries, were "often mirror images of American criminal justice." The travelers had a "felt need to think their trials were like those at home" (Reid 1997, 125).

29. There is a large literature on plea bargaining; see, for example, Heumann (1978). Plea bargaining accounts for vastly more convictions than juries do, but it is an obscure process, little known to the public. Plea bargaining shifts power from judge and jury to prosecutors and defense attorneys. For a recent view from the inside, see Lynch (1994).

References

Abramson, Jeffrey. 1994. *We, the Jury: The Jury System and the Ideal of Democracy.* New York: Basic Books.

Ayers, Edward L. 1984. *Vengeance and Justice: Crime and Punishment in the 19th Century American South.* New York: Oxford University Press.

Bowers, William J., Glenn L. Pierce, and John F. McDevitt. 1984. *Legal Homicide: Death as Punishment in America, 1864–1982.* Boston: Northeastern University Press.

Brandon, Craig. 1986. *Murder in the Adirondacks.* 2d ed. Utica, N.Y.: North Country Books.

Brandt, Nat. 1991. *The Congressman Who Got Away with Murder.* Syracuse, N.Y.: Syracuse University Press.

Brown, Richard Maxwell. 1975. *Strain of Violence: Historical Studies of American Violence and Vigilantism.* New York: Oxford University Press.

Cohen, Daniel A. 1993. *Pillars of Salt, Monuments of Grace*. New York: Oxford University Press.

"Comment: Recognition of the Honor Defense under the Insanity Plea." 1934. *Yale Law Journal* 43: 809.

Cooper, Cynthia L., and Sam Reese Sheppard. 1995. *Mockery of Justice: The True Story of the Sheppard Murder Case*. Boston: Northeastern University Press.

Cooper, George. 1994. *Lost Love: A True Story of Passion, Murder, and Justice in Old New York*. New York: Pantheon Books.

Denno, Deborah W. 1994. "Is Electrocution an Unconstitutional Method of Execution? The Engineering of Death over the Century." *William and Mary Law Review* 35: 554.

Dimsdale, Thomas. 1953. *Vigilantes of Montana*. 1866. Reprint, Norman: University of Oklahoma Press.

Erikson, Kai T. 1966. *Wayward Puritans: A Study in the Sociology of Deviance*. New York: John Wiley & Sons.

Farrell, Harry. 1993. *Swift Justice*. New York: St. Martin's Press.

Feldberg, Michael. 1980. *The Turbulent Era: Riot and Disorder in Jacksonian America*. New York: Oxford University Press.

Fowles, Jib. 1992. *Starstruck: Celebrity Performers and the American Public*. Washington, D.C.: Smithsonian Institution Press.

Friedman, Lawrence M. 1990. *The Republic of Choice: Law, Culture, and Authority*. Cambridge, Mass.: Harvard University Press.

———. 1993. *Crime and Punishment in American History*. New York: Basic Books.

Friedman, Lawrence M., and Robert V. Percival. 1981. *The Roots of Justice: Crime and Punishment in Alameda County, California, 1870–1910*. Chapel Hill: University of North Carolina Press.

Ginzburg, Ralph, ed. 1962. *One Hundred Years of Lynching*. New York: Lancer Books.

Glenn, Myra C. 1984. *Campaigns against Corporal Punishment: Prisoners, Sailors, Women, and Children in Antebellum America*. Albany: State University of New York Press.

Hans, Valerie, and Neil Vidmar. 1986. *Judging the Jury*. New York: Plenum Books.

Heumann, Milton. 1978. *Plea Bargaining: The Experiences of Prosecutors, Judges, and Defense Attorneys*. Chicago: University of Chicago Press.

Highfill, Robert D. 1926. "The Effects of News of Crime and Scandal upon Public Opinion." *Journal of American Institute of Criminal Law* 17: 40.

Hindus, Michael. 1980. *Prison and Plantation: Crime, Justice, and Authority in Massachusetts and South Carolina, 1767–1878*. Chapel Hill: University of North Carolina Press.

Hirsch, Adam J. 1992. *The Rise of the Penitentiary: Prisons and Punishment in Early America*. New Haven, Conn.: Yale University Press.

Ireland, Robert M. 1992a. "Frenzied and Fallen Females: Women and Sexual Dishonor in the Nineteenth-Century United States." *Journal of Women's History* 3: 95.

———. 1992b. "The Libertine Must Die: Sexual Dishonor and the Unwritten Law in the Nineteenth-Century United States." *Journal of Social History* 23: 27.

———. 1993. Review of Brandt, *The Congressman Who Got Away with Murder*. *Register of the Kentucky Historical Society* 91: 220.

Jordan, Philip D. 1970. *Frontier Law and Order: Ten Essays*. Lincoln: University of Nebraska Press.

Kalven, Harry, Jr., and Hans Zeisel. 1966. *The American Jury*. Boston: Little, Brown & Co.

Kennedy, Ludovic. 1985. *The Airman and the Carpenter*. New York: Viking.

Langbein, John H. 1994. "The Historical Origins of the Privilege against Self-Incrimination at Common Law." *Michigan Law Review* 92: 1047.

Lawson, John D., ed. 1919. *American State Trials*, vol. 12. St. Louis: Thomas Law Book Co.

Lovett, Robert Morse. 1924. "Crime and Publicity: Leopold, Loeb, and Chicago." *New Republic* 39 (June 25): 121.

Lynch, David. 1994. "The Impropriety of Plea Agreements: A Tale of Two Counties." *Law and Social Inquiry* 19: 115.

MacLean, Nancy. 1991. "The Leo Frank Case Reconsidered: Gender and Sexual Politics in the Making of Reactionary Populism." *Journal of American History* 78: 917.

Maeder, Thomas. 1985. *Crime and Madness: The Origins and Evolution of the Insanity Defense*. New York: Harper & Row.

Masur, Louis P. 1989. *Rites of Execution: Capital Punishment and the Transformation of American Culture, 1776–1865*. New York: Oxford University Press.

Miller, Wilbur R. 1977. *Cops and Bobbies: Police Authority in New York and London, 1830–1870*. Chicago: University of Chicago Press.

Moglen, Eben. 1994. "Taking the Fifth: Reconsidering the Origins of the Constitutional Privilege against Self-Incrimination." *Michigan Law Review* 92: 1086.

NAACP (National Association for the Advancement of Colored People). 1969. *Thirty Years of Lynching in the United States, 1889–1918*. 1919. Reprint, New York: Arno Press.

Nelson, William. 1975. *Americanization of the Common Law: The Impact of Legal Change on Massachusetts Society, 1760–1830*. Cambridge, Mass.: Harvard University Press.

"Note: Crimes—Newspaper Publication—Contempt." 1912. *Journal of the American Institute of Criminal Law and Criminology* 1: 774.

O'Conner, Richard. 1963. *Courtroom Warrior: The Combative Career of William Travers Jerome*. Boston: Little, Brown & Co.

Randel, William Peirce. 1965. *The Ku Klux Klan: A Century of Infamy.* Philadelphia: Chilton Books.

Rankin, Hugh F. 1965. *Criminal Trial Proceedings in the General Court of Colonial Virginia.* Charlottesville: University Press of Virginia.

Reid, John Philip. 1997. *Policing the Elephant: Crime, Punishment, and Social Behavior on the Overland Trail.* San Marino, Calif.: Huntington Library.

Richardson, James F. 1974. *Urban Police in the United States.* Port Washington, N.Y.: Kennikat Press.

Roberts, W. Lewis 1922. "The Unwritten Law." *Kentucky Law Journal* 10: 45.

Rothman, David J. 1971. *The Discovery of the Asylum: Social Order and Disorder in the New Republic.* Boston: Little, Brown & Co.

Schickel, Richard. 1985. *Intimate Strangers: The Culture of Celebrity.* Garden City, N.Y.: Doubleday.

Schneider, John C. 1980. *Detroit and the Problem of Order.* Lincoln: University of Nebraska Press.

Senkewicz, Robert D. 1985. *Vigilantes in Gold Rush San Francisco.* Stanford: Stanford University Press.

Smith, Joseph H., ed. 1961. *Colonial Justice in Western Massachusetts (1639–1702): The Pynchon Court Record.* Cambridge, Mass.: Harvard University Press.

Swanberg, W. A. 1956. *Sickles the Incredible.* New York: Scribners.

Tourgee, Albion W. 1880. *A Fool's Errand.* New York: Ford, Howard, & Hulbert.

Twain, Mark. 1972. *Roughing It.* 1871. Reprint, Berkeley: University of California Press.

Williams, Daniel E. 1986. " 'Behold a Tragic Scene Strangely Changed into a Theater of Mercy': The Structure and Significance of Criminal Conversion Narratives in Early New England." *American Quarterly* 38: 827.

———. 1992. *Pillars of Salt: An Anthology of Early American Criminal Narratives.* Madison, Wis.: Madison House.

Wisehart, M. K. 1922. *Criminal Justice in Cleveland.* Part 7: *Newspapers and Criminal Justice.* Cleveland: Cleveland Foundation.

Wolf, Marvin J., and Katherine Mader. 1986. *Fallen Angels: Chronicles of L.A. Crime and Mystery.* New York: Facts on File Publications.

Wright, George C. 1990. *Racial Violence in Kentucky, 1875–1940: Lynchings, Mob Rule, and Legal Lynchings.* Baton Rouge: Louisiana State University Press.

Chapter 3

Beyond the Law of Evidence: Facts and Inequality in Criminal Defense

Kenneth Mann

The criminal trial is in large part a process of image-making through the control of facts. Each of the parties seeks to present its own image of what "actually happened." Trials, of course, are not only about facts. Sometimes the facts are assumed, and the parties dispute only the legal consequences of those facts. Trials vary in the degree to which factual issues as opposed to legal issues predominate. In this chapter, I focus on the control of facts in criminal trials, and I view the trial as a process of image-making. In so doing, I seek to show how defense attorneys with a strong sense for the importance of factual detail and with sufficient resources to invest in the control of facts can create and change factual images through the trial process. This leads to the conclusion that variations in the availability of time for fact control create great inequalities in the criminal trial process.

To demonstrate these points, I discuss the facts and trial in an actual criminal case brought in the district court of Israel in 1996.[1] I focus on the trial activities of the defense attorney in defending his client, Mr. Daniel Coase, a retired general in the Israeli army who was accused of shooting his twenty-six-year-old neighbor.

The Shooting

The criminal charge against Daniel Coase was initially disclosed to the defense attorney in an indictment that charged Daniel with the shooting of Jonathan Shua. The indictment described the events as follows:

> On or about August 12, 1995, there occurred an argument between the defendant's twenty-five-year-old son, Avi Coase, and the neighbor's twenty-six-year-old son, Jonathan Shua, in connection with the parking arrangement in front of their adjacent homes. The argument ended in a fist fight between Avi and Jonathan. After Avi returned home, the defendant went out of his house, walked toward the adjacent Shua home, and when he saw Jonathan Shua, he pulled out a pistol that he had been carrying in a holster on his waist and shot Jonathan in the stomach, causing him serious bodily injury. The defendant emptied his pistol, wounding also Ms. Ronda Shua, the mother of Paul Shua, who was standing near and behind Paul Shua.

The defendant was charged with the crime of intentionally causing serious bodily injury in aggravated circumstances, under section 329 of the penal code, an offense bearing a sentence of up to twenty years in prison. As the defense attorney read the indictment, he learned additional facts from his prospective client, Daniel Coase.

Immediately following the shooting of Jonathan Shua, police arrived at the scene of the crime and arrested Daniel. The police interrogated Daniel, brought him before a magistrate's court judge, who remanded him into custody. During the same period, police investigators interrogated members of Daniel's and Jonathan's families, who had been witnesses to the shooting, and a neighbor who had witnessed the earlier fist fight between Jonathan and Daniel's son Avi. Two weeks after completion of the investigation, the court released Daniel from custody and put him under house arrest. The case was set for arraignment before a district court judge.

Defense Attorney Advice

In the period following his release from custody, Daniel's defense attorney recommended to him that he plead guilty. The attorney had by then obtained and studied all witness statements and documents in the police file.[2] He explained to Daniel that he could not persuade the prosecutor to reduce the charge, but that he could arrange for a beneficial sentencing agreement in the context of a plea bargain. Under the plea bargain, Daniel would plead guilty and receive a three and a half year prison term. The defense attorney also explained to Daniel that if he went to trial and was convicted, the judge would give him a sentence of between five and seven years.

Daniel, his wife, and his children consulted with friends, and friends of friends, about how to approach the matter of the pending trial. Daniel was not satisfied with the advice of his attorney. He believed that he was innocent. He decided to examine the possibility of going to trial with a different attorney.

After holding a series of meetings to search for trial representation, Daniel selected a new attorney to study the evidence and determine whether going to trial was an appropriate course of action. The new attorney had several meetings with Daniel and members of his family and consulted with private investigators. The attorney and Daniel reached the decision that Daniel would plead not guilty and that they would go to trial.

Prosecution Image

The prosecutor drew up the indictment creating the prosecutorial image of the event in question. This image of events portrayed a simple case of aggravated assault. In the frame of the indictment, the image presented to the judge was unidimensional; there were no ambiguities and no facts to indicate that the defendant might have acted to protect himself or someone else from death or serious injury. The indictment was void of any hint of complexity, and the facts were easy to understand and easy to classify. Any reader of the indictment would have little trouble summarizing the event in one sentence: "unlawful shooting of young man by neighbor."[3]

Pretrial Judicial Fact Assessment

The judge reacted negatively to the case during the initial hearing. It was not unusual in this court for the judge to disclose to the parties her assessment of the case rather than maintain a demeanor of judicial aloofness. In this system of criminal trials, judges often try to facilitate plea bargaining by admonishing defendants and defense attorneys about the difficulties in their cases, often implying that they should avoid a trial they have little or no chance of winning. The judge's initial negative reaction appeared to be based not only on her desire to bring about a plea of guilty, thus avoiding a trial, but also on her moral assessment that the event described in the indictment constituted a serious offense committed by the defendant.

Within the relevant communal setting of this case, carrying a concealed weapon is neither considered illegal nor viewed as deviant behavior. This is a community marked by unexpected terrorist attacks that pose a serious threat to human life. The judge could assume that the defendant was licensed to carry a weapon as protection against terrorism.

The judge's marked negative reaction to the indictment was based on the uncontested fact that the defendant had used the gun in the context of a dispute with a neighbor. There could be no presumed justification for this highly unusual use of a handgun. Given the widespread presence of handguns in the community, courts had set a policy of meting out heavy sentences against persons who used their weapons in domestic circumstances. The judge believed that this case exemplified the serious danger in giving handgun licenses to private citizens.[4] She assumed, from what she read in the indictment, that the defendant had suffered a breakdown of self-control, letting some kind of frustration bring him to a grossly irresponsible use of the gun, that could easily have led to the death of the young man who was shot. The judge openly challenged the defense's attorney: "Why conduct a trial in these circumstances?"

Defense Argument at Arraignment

Addressing the judge's expected negative comments and setting the stage for what was to come, the defense attorney gave notice to the court that he would argue that the shooting took place in circumstances of justified defense. This was quite surprising to the judge; this sort of plea seemed to be an unlikely explanation of what had occurred. Taking full advantage of his first opportunity to communicate an alternative image of the events, the defense attorney summarized the defense argument: After the fight between Avi and Jonathan, and after Avi had returned home and told Daniel about the fight, Daniel went outside to the front gate of his home to receive his daughter, who he feared would be angrily confronted by one of the Shuas, and at the very moment that he arrived at the gate, Jonathan charged at him and at his son Avi with a heavy plank, stuck with open nails on one end. Daniel then shot Jonathan in order to prevent him from killing Avi.

The judge was not impressed by the defense attorney's explanation. She sighed perceptibly, explaining in a short-tempered glance that she had serious doubts about the possibility of the defense attorney's proving circumstances of justification. The judge reemphasized that she would not be happy with what she called a "manufactured defense." The judge reinforced her view by explaining that the legal requirements of the defense were demanding. She told the defense attorney that he should study his options carefully before embarking on the trial.

Counter-Intuitive Factual Complexity

As I show in the following presentation of facts, what appeared to be an open-and-shut case of serious armed assault proved to be a substantially more complex event. Although not revealed in the indictment, the larger picture of this apparently simple case was composed of many additional facts. The image that the defense attorney would portray would be multilayered, rich with nuance, and in some respects highly ambiguous. The picture of the events in the indictment would be transformed substantially through the trial process. The trial would at least open the possibility that the defendant committed a justified act in shooting his neighbor.

Daniel Coase believed that he was innocent because he had acted to protect the life of his son in justified circumstances. The defense attorney agreed with Daniel. The defense attorney would have to convey to the judge what the defense believed to be the real picture of events. However, the defense attorney carefully warned the defendant that the task of persuading the judge would be difficult and that the odds of winning were substantially below 50 percent. The defendant insisted that he should be acquitted and that he would provide all of the necessary fees and costs to support the defense attorney in preparing and conducting the trial. He was willing to forgo the reduced sentencing that could be arranged through a plea bargain.

Image-Making Through Fact Control

How does the defense attorney conduct a criminal trial in this situation? Typically, a defense attorney makes procedural arguments—for instance, he or she may argue that the prosecution failed to disclose all witness statements. Typically, also, a defense attorney makes substantive arguments about criminal responsibility—for instance, about the legal standards for the defense of justification.

Another defense activity, typically engaged in but not typically written about, is what I call fact control. Defense attorneys attempt to create exculpatory defense images of the events in question by gathering and carefully presenting facts unknown to the prosecution, by confronting prosecution witnesses with facts unknown to them or hidden by them, and by preventing the prosecutor from introducing into evidence facts that might appear to be or actually be inculpatory. The defense attorneys present witnesses coached to avoid spontaneously volunteering inculpatory facts.[5] Similarly, defense attorneys affirmatively coach witnesses to testify in a predesigned order about certain facts known to them. They search widely for persons who can make observations and assessments that would otherwise remain unknown to the fact finder. Tightly controlled gathering, preparation, and presentation of facts constitute a principal means for creating in the mind of the decisionmaker the exculpatory defense image of the event in question.[6]

Here, I continue to use the concept of "image" to describe fact-related trial procedures.[7] An image is a decisionmaker's subjective construction of facts into an intelligible picture or story.[8] Essential to the concept of image is the axiom that the meaning or significance of any one fact is always dependent on other facts within the field of perception or on the absence of such other facts. There are two subsidiary rules to this axiom. The first is that the meaning of any one fact or any set of facts will change as additional facts are introduced into the arena in which the perception of fact occurs. The second is that the meaning of facts will depend on the preexisting reservoir of facts known by the person perceiving the facts. In relation to the trial process, the concept of image stresses the incremental and subjective nature of the fact-finding process. Parties acting in the criminal trial create images of the event in question by introducing and preventing the introduction of factual detail into the arena of decisionmaking. At the same time, the parties are acutely aware that the facts presented by them are given meaning by the larger set of fact patterns in the mental reservoir of the fact finder. Image construction emphasizes the interpretive role of the decisionmaker in assessing the facts introduced by the parties in the context of their own reservoir of culturally rooted fact patterns.[9] The concept of image also points to the distinctive tasks of attorneys at trials that rise from the notion that the subjective process of image construction is highly sensitive to changes in minute factual detail.

Understanding the presentation of facts as a means of controlling the image of events created in courtroom trials requires paying close attention to factual detail. Small changes in fact change the composite image of events communicated to a court. In many trials, the prosecutor and defense attorneys continuously alter the images of events presented to the court by continuously introducing new facts. This process is examined by Richard K. Sherwin in his interesting account of the production and impact of the movie *The Thin Blue Line*. Sherwin describes the importance of constructing familiar cultural images—what he terms "affirmative postmodernism"—in trial practice (Sherwin 1994, note 3). He writes that,

> Affirmative postmodernism [in trial litigation] employs postmodern story telling techniques, but unlike its skeptical cousin, it either closes around a coherent meaning or at least points to one. Thus, while it is postmodern in its use of popular cultural images and symbols, it does not employ these images and symbols as an insular or solely self-referential manner. . . . Persuasiveness here comes from the sudden power of an isolated phrase or image or type or from novel juxtapositions of familiar representations. [Sherwin 1994, note 3, 72–73]

In the description of the actual trial presented here, I draw on a postmodern idea of subjective image construction, but I downplay the import of cultural symbols and focus instead on the power of factual detail in producing variable understandings of events that are the focus of a trial. If we conceive of the trial as a montage of facts, Sherwin would emphasize the importance of an alternative script, an alternative culturally rooted story. In contrast, I point to the overwhelming power of isolated facts in changing the interpretive meaning of a picture, as if one small drop of paint could change the meaning of an entire composition. My concept of image-making is not radically subjectivist, for it admits to the existence of an objective event. The question of how much of the event is brought into the trial arena focuses on how attorneys act to control factual detail in the trial process.[10] This is not a portrait of how the law of evidence allows in certain facts and keeps out others, but rather of what attorneys do to control facts beyond what they can achieve by using the law of evidence. In this study, participant observation and other social science methodology allow us to deepen our understanding of the complexity of fact finding and the importance of professional resources for controlling facts in a criminal trial.

In the description of a real but disguised criminal trial that follows, I ask the reader to sustain attention to facts, as presented by the prosecution and defense, in spite of the burden of the detail, and to take account of his or her own processes of decisionmaking about the events in question.

Prosecution Testimony

I now describe what the court learned about the case from the prosecution witnesses. I do so by summarizing the witnesses' testimony. I do not present the questions asked by the attorney, even though they often contained an assertion of alternative facts, particularly the questions asked by the defense attorney while examining the prosecution witnesses. Although the fact finder learns about the defense image of the event from defense questions on cross-examination, as well as from answers to the questions, only the answers should count in supplying evidence on which the court can base its decision.

Paul Shua

The Witness   Paul Shua is approximately fifty years old. He works part-time managing the floor polishing company owned and operated by his two sons. His brother is a policeman. Paul's father is still living and shares the house with him. Paul is tall, thin, graying. He has a rough voice and tended to get heated up during his testimony.

The Testimony   Paul Shua testified that there had been a series of arguments with Daniel Coase about parking space and that Daniel had threatened the Shua family with violent reprisals. Paul said that Daniel could park in front of his house (Daniel's), but not in a manner that blocked the Shua family's only entrance to their house. Paul said that Daniel and Daniel's wife Miriam had persisted in obstructing the Shua's entry path. Paul also testified that he was present when Daniel told Ronda, Paul's wife, that he would "take care" of "putting an end" to the entire Shua family if they did not change their attitude to the parking problem. Paul admitted that on one occasion there had been an argument in front of their house (the Shua family's house) and that he had had to restrain his son Jonathan, because Jonathan "rightly" believed that Daniel was about to attack him. Paul said that Daniel's son Avi and Jonathan had had a fist fight, but that a fist fight was nothing out of the ordinary for boys their age. Paul provided considerable detail about bad language used by the defendant, including calling Paul's wife a prostitute, a pig, and a Mafia boss.

With respect to the day of the event, Paul testified that when he came out of his house, he saw Daniel with his pistol in his hand and that without any provocation Daniel shot at Ronda. Immediately thereafter, Jonathan came running to the scene to defend the family, picked up a stick, and charged at Daniel. When Jonathan came toward Daniel, Daniel shot him, from point-blank range, directly in the stomach.

Ronda Shua

The Witness Ronda is a heavy-set woman with a loud, squealing voice. She is the mother of five children. She is a housewife who takes care of four children. When not on the witness stand, she heckled the defendant and grunted at the judge.

The Testimony Ronda stated that she had been threatened numerous times by Daniel in arguments about parking. She also stated that she and Daniel had argued about an oil-burning heating unit that she had wanted to build, but that he had opposed due to the air pollution created by the burn-off of oil. She complained in her testimony that Daniel and Miriam Coase constantly disturbed them by parking directly across their front entrance. She reported that she had never threatened Daniel, that she and her husband had never had any trouble with any neighbors, and that she had tried to get the dispute with Daniel settled peacefully. She testified that when Avi and Jonathan had had a fist fight, she had intervened to separate them.

On the day of the shooting, Ronda explained that she was watching Daniel from her upstairs window and that when Daniel saw her he started swearing at her with the worst insults she had ever heard. Immediately thereafter, she and other members of her family went downstairs to try to resolve things with Daniel. She stated that as soon as they arrived in front of their house, Daniel pulled out his pistol and shot at her. She also testified that Jonathan came running, picked up a stick, and headed for Daniel. As Jonathan approached Daniel, Daniel shot, and Jonathan fell, severely wounded.

The foregoing testimony contradicted Ronda's statement to the police. Ronda was cross-examined by the defense attorney about why she had said in her out-of-court police statement that Daniel first shot her son Jonathan and then afterward shot her. Ronda explained that she had gotten confused when making her statement to the police, because she was groggy from the pain-killing drug she had been given at the hospital just before she gave her police statement.

Jonathan Shua

The Witness   Jonathan Shua is twenty-eight years old. He recently spent three years in the army and then set up a floor polishing business with his brother Eli. He is a large, imposing young man, who wears a religious headcover. He has a partial beard of tiny whiskers, wore jeans to court, and jumped around a lot on the witness stand.

The Testimony   Jonathan testified that there had been bitter arguments between his family and the Coase family about parking and that Daniel Coase had repeatedly threatened the Shua family with serious and violent actions. He admitted to having a fist fight with Avi, who had pushed him and knocked him down before he, Jonathan, had used any physical force.

On the day of the event and while walking toward his own apartment, which was about 100 meters away from his parents' home, Jonathan heard shouting and then gun shots. He stated that he immediately sprinted to the area in front of his house and saw Daniel standing with his gun in his hand. According to Jonathan, at the moment of his arrival on the scene he saw that his mother was wounded by gunshot. Jonathan stated to the police that he then picked up a stick and ran toward Daniel in order to stop him from further shooting. When he reached Daniel, Daniel raised his pistol and, from a standing position, shot directly into Jonathan's stomach. Jonathan fell wounded.

On cross-examination, while testifying that the defendant shot him when he, the defendant, was standing up and almost at point-blank, Jonathan pulled up his shirt and said "look here," showing that the bullet had gone through him at the same level on the front and back of his body. The naked eye could see that the entry point on Jonathan's stomach was at the same level as the exit point on his back.

The implication was that the defendant's version of the story could not be true. If in fact the defendant had been lying on the ground when he shot at Jonathan in the stomach and Jonathan had been standing, then the bullet would have taken an upward trajectory, creating an entry point on the stomach lower than the exit point on the back.

Eli Shua

The Witness Eli is Jonathan's younger brother. He works with Jonathan in the floor polishing company. Eli is tall and wiry. He is twenty-two years of age. He was nervous and stammered on the witness stand.

The Testimony Eli managed to report that he had had a loud and aggressive argument with Avi, after Avi came to his house, insulted his mother, and then left, slamming the door in Eli's face. Eli stated that on the day of shooting, he went downstairs to the front of his house with the rest of this family and saw Daniel pull the gun and first shoot his mother and then Jonathan.

The foregoing testimony contradicted Eli's statement to the police. On cross-examination, Eli was asked why he had stated in his police statement, as had his mother, that he saw Daniel shoot first at Jonathan and only after at his mother. He stated that he was confused due to over-excitement when he talked to the police and that after thinking of the matter for some months, he realized that he had been mistaken and that his courtroom testimony was correct.

Physical Findings from the Police Investigation

In addition to interviewing persons involved in the shooting and other witnesses to the event, the police collected physical evidence and examined expert findings. Among the relevant findings presented in testimony by police investigators as part of the prosecution's case-in-chief were the following:

- Jonathan's mother had been injured by bullet shrapnel, not by a full bullet.

- A two-by-four plank with closed (not open) nails on the end and an iron rod were found on the entrance path to the defendant's house.

- Medical reports showed serious bullet damage to Jonathan's stomach and intestines.

- Four bullet shells were found close to the front door of the Coase home.

Each of the prosecution witnesses was cross-examined at length about contradictions in his or her testimony as compared with out-of-court statements made to the police or with other facts relevant to the charges made and to the Shua family's testimony. The following statements were made by witnesses on cross-examination:

- Each of the Shua family witnesses denied having talked about his or her testimony with another member of the family before testifying in court, even though more than a year had passed between the event and the trial!

- In out-of-court statements, as indicated above, two of the Shua family members stated to the police that Daniel shot Ronda first and two said that Daniel shot Jonathan first. Each of the family members provided explanations for the apparent contradiction.

- Each of the family members was asked about serious disagreements with neighbors in the past and violence or threats of violence in which he or she had taken part. Each of the family members denied any background of serious disagreement or violence.

- After the initial cross-examination and motion of the defense attorney, the court made an on-site visit to the place where the shooting occurred. Each of the Shua family members was asked by the defense attorney to indicate exactly where he or she was standing when Daniel was shot. Each of the family members situated himself or herself at the beginning of the entry path to Daniel's house, just outside or just inside the entry gate, an area approximately 18 meters from the front door to Daniel's house.

- Jonathan's father testified that during an earlier argument over parking, Jonathan had come running up to protect his family and that he had physically restrained Jonathan while he threatened Avi. On cross-examination, Jonathan testified that he was not present at this earlier argument and thus could not have threatened anyone.

- The defense attorney knew that Daniel was going to testify that Eli also charged at him, that Jonathan was there with the plank, and that Eli assaulted him with a bent-iron rod. On cross-examination, Eli was questioned about this and denied it. Each of the Shua family members denied that Eli or anyone else used a bent rod; they persisted in calling the weapon a "wooden stick" rather than a metal rod.

At this intermediate point in the trial, we can see that the initial image of the case had been transformed through fact presentation. The defense attorney succeeded in bringing out contradictions between certain Shua family members' testimony and their out-of-court statements. In out-of-court statements, two said that Ronda was shot first, and two said that Jonathan was shot first. But in their courtroom testimony, they all said that Ronda was shot first. The Shuas claimed that Daniel shot because he wanted to get revenge for the fight between Jonathan and Avi and because he was angry about the parking impasse. They implied that Daniel was a frustrated former army general, who believed that only violence worked in situations of conflict.

Reinterpretation of the Initial Image

The criminal trial is a fact-finding forum in which live testimony may differ greatly from the distillation of events in an indictment and from the out-of-court statements made to police during the investigation.

An indictment necessarily constructs a summary picture of events. Even if an indictment is long and more than usually detailed, its function in the criminal trial requires that it convey clearly a moral and legal assessment of events. It must resolve ambiguities and conflicts in factual details. It must paint with a brush whose legal consequences are unmistakable.

The unmistakably clear image of events in an indictment will in some cases describe accurately the real event. But where the events in question are complex and rich in nuance, and where the correct interpretation is problematic, the indictment will necessarily distort reality and not be fully explanatory. If ambiguities and conflicts in facts are given full play, an indictment will fail to instruct the decisionmaker as to what the prosecution believes should be the final factual conclusion in the legal process. Some events are neat and simple, others are complex and ambiguous. The more complex the event, the more the indictment must distort the initial image of the events in question. The trial then has the potential to transform significantly the initial image.

In the testimony presented so far in the trail of Daniel Coase, it is now evident that the indictment obfuscated real factual complexity. Midway into the trial, the testimony overwhelmed the indictment. The indictment now appears thin, over-conclusive, over-concrete, even unfair to the defendant.

The trial image, as opposed to the indictment image, raises several difficult questions: Was Ronda actually shot by Daniel, given the fact that she was hit only by shrapnel? Did the defense attorney discredit Jonathan Shua's and Paul Shua's testimony on the critical issue of the circumstances of Daniel's shooting? Jonathan denied being present at a prior argument, while his father Paul testified that he had had to restrain Jonathan during that argument! Are these contradictions within the boundary of normal mistake? Could the fact finder now say that the correct image of events was that Daniel simply shot Jonathan out of anger and perhaps revenge? The defense attorney introduced the court to much of the defendant's version, in the questions that he asked of the prosecution witnesses, yet there was little factual proof of the defense claims. The prosecution called four eyewitnesses who provided an image of the event inculpatory of the defendant, as well as a theory of motive, although the reliability of their testimony was questionable. The image of action still tended to be inculpatory to the defendant, but the defense had not yet introduced its own testimony.

Defense Testimony

The defense attorney took part in the fact presentation procedure led by the prosecutor. During cross-examination, the defense attorney sought to undermine the validity of facts presented by the prosecution, as well as draw out facts favorable to the defense. In some criminal trials, almost all of the procedure of fact finding takes place during the case in chief, presented by the prosecutor. Defense attorneys often rely almost exclusively on cross-examination, adding only the defendant as a witness when the defense has its turn to rebut prosecution testimony. They restrict as much as possible their own presentation of witnesses, seeking not to inadvertently present damaging testimony. Of course, decisions about evidence presentation after the case in chief but before the defense opens its case depend greatly on the nature of the prosecution evidence. In this particular trial, the defense attorney had to present a large number of witnesses in order to attempt to establish the defense image of the events in question. The alternative image was not established either by undermining the validity of the facts presented by the prosecution witnesses or by drawing out from them new facts.

Daniel Coase

The Witness   Daniel owns and operates an open-air restaurant in a picturesque valley on the edge of Jerusalem, on a site that had once been an Arab village. He had been a commanding officer in the army and, after retiring, opened a restaurant, drawing many of the city's well-known personalities to his modest establishment. Daniel was divorced and remarried, the father of one son from his first marriage— a physician at a local hospital—and two sons and two daughters from his second marriage. The oldest son of his second marriage had also been a commanding officer and was then studying law. The remaining children are still in high school.

Daniel and his family moved into their new home about one year before the shooting, after being forced to leave their previous home under a court order to vacate the site to make way for a new highway. Their new home was adjacent to the Shua home, where Jonathan's mother, father, brother, and sister lived.

The Testimony   Daniel testified that shortly after the defendant and his family moved into their new home they were accosted verbally by their neighbors, the Shua family, who told them that they should know that they, the Coases, would not be allowed to park on the street, not even in front of their own house. The Shuas said that they needed all the parking space in front of the two houses. Daniel explained that this interchange surprised him greatly and led to a series of aggressive verbal conflicts between the two families, in which the Shuas insulted him, his wife, and children and threatened to remove them by force from the neighborhood.

Daniel also reported that he had had an earlier argument with Jonathan's mother over the Shua family's plan to build an oil-burning master heating unit exactly on the boundary between the two homes, which would include a chimney pointed toward the front door of the defendant's home.

The conflict got progressively worse, but Daniel testified that he understood from his son Avi that a few weeks prior to the shooting Avi had reached an agreement with the Shuas about the parking, in which Jonathan's mother and father had agreed to let the Coase family use one parking space some 30 meters from their house.

Daniel explained that on the day of the event, after Avi returned home physically beaten by Jonathan Shua, he—Daniel—went out to the front of his house to receive his daughter who was supposed to return by foot from the bus station. He stated that when he was outside in front of the house, the entire Shua family—Jonathan, Eli, and their mother and father—came outside and that Jonathan grabbed a large two-by-four plank with protruding nails on one end and charged at him, waving the plank in the air. During a period of less than a minute, Daniel called to Avi for help. Avi, who was already outside, came running. As Avi arrived, Daniel was moving backward, retreating toward his house while watching Jonathan. He then tripped and fell. As Avi bent over to assist Daniel, Daniel saw Jonathan raise the heavy plank high in the air, preparing instantaneously to chop heavily at Avi's head. At this very split second, Daniel drew his gun from his holster and shot directly into Jonathan's stomach. Jonathan fell on Avi, and Avi fell on Daniel. Daniel stated that he had no memory of what happened after shooting Jonathan, until the police arrived, handcuffed him, and took him to the police station.

Daniel testified that he always wore a gun in a holster underneath his shirt and that he had done so for years, since he opened the restaurant in the valley outside of the city.

Avi Coase

The Witness   Avi is twenty-five years old. He had been in an elite commando unit in the army. After serving for the regular period of three years, Avi went to London to attend law school. During his first year of law school, he was accepted into a special program to study international law. At the time of the incident, he was visiting home on a school break. Almost two years later when he testified, he had been studying in an exchange program in the United States and had traveled to Israel especially to be called as a defense witness.

The Testimony   Avi testified that four or five days before the shooting, Jonathan's younger brother, Eli, came to his house and demanded that Avi move the family car that was parked in front of the Shuas' house. Avi went out to see what he could do and found Eli taking air out of one of the tires of his father's—Daniel's—car. There followed a loud and bitterly aggressive argument over the parking spaces, which was joined by Jonathan's father and mother, who heard the boys yelling. During this verbal confrontation, Jonathan arrived, running at top speed, threateningly demanding to know who was attacking his mother and father, and boasting that he would kill anyone who touched his parents. Jonathan approached Avi aggressively, and during a moment when it looked as if Jonathan might physically attack Avi, Jonathan's father intervened and held him back. Daniel and his wife Miriam arrived on the scene and watched anxiously without intervening. As tempers heated and cooled, Avi asked that he and the Shuas enter the Shuas' house to discuss as he put it, *civilly*, the parking problem. When he entered the house, Avi asked Ronda Shua for a cup of Moroccan tea and Eli Shua for boxes of wooden matches. He used the matches as cars and, on the living room coffee table, created a model of how both families' cars might be parked in front of their two houses. An agreement was reached.

Avi went on to testify that the agreement was not kept by the Shuas. On the day of the incident, Avi's mother asked Avi to have the Shuas move one of their cars so that she could get close enough to the house to carry the groceries from the car. Avi went next door, and an argument followed, proving that the agreement had fully collapsed. As Avi left the house, Jonathan followed, jumped on Avi, and pulled him down to the ground while hitting him on the back. Eli's father followed and kicked Avi in the stomach. Avi scrambled out of reach and ran back to his house. Shortly thereafter, his father—Daniel—shouted desperately for help. Avi went quickly to his father. The shooting occurred.

Miriam Coase

The Witness   Miriam was born in England and emigrated to Israel in the 1950s. She had studied and earned a degree in chemistry and worked for many years as a lab technician in a university. After her husband, Daniel, left the army, they opened the restaurant together, and she left the university to work with him.

The Testimony   Miriam stated that she and the defendant had been completely overwhelmed by what had happened to them on arriving in the new neighborhood. Only shortly after their move, she re-alized that she would have difficulty finding an appropriate entrance path to their new home. The Coases' house and the Shuas' house were situated next to each other, with clearly separate entrances, yet Miriam claimed that Jonathan's family expanded their claim to ter-ritory quite far beyond their own boundary, parking their cars in ways that prevented her, Miriam, from getting close to the entrance to her own house with her car. A few months before the shooting, and only shortly after the Coases had moved into their house, the Shuas began building a new home for themselves across the street from the house where they were living. The building contractors brought in materials and created a large amount of waste product. Both the building materials and the waste product were thrown about, blocking the main entrance to the Coase family home.

Miriam testified that when her children went out at night, they had to take a flashlight in order to find their way through the building ma-terial and refuse. There had been several discussions with the Shua family about getting the path cleared away, but these had been un-successful. Miriam also testified that she and Daniel had decided to use a self-made dirt road to create an alternative entrance to their home that would allow them access without having to pass near the Shua house and without having to argue with them. The defense at-torney acted surprised by this story, asking Miriam why she would not go to the authorities in order to protect her right to enter her own home. All that Miriam could say was that she and her husband were afraid of the Shuas, particularly of Jonathan and his father. They had heard much about the Shuas from the neighbors, including stories about threats made against previous owners of their own house. They had been told that the Shuas intentionally opened their sewer-age pipes so that the sludge would flow into the yard of the previous owners of the Coases' house.

Sarah Coase

The Witness   Sarah, daughter of Daniel and Miriam, is a recent high school graduate.

The Testimony   Sarah gave an account of the background of the con-flict. She affirmed that she had to move in and out of their family house with a flashlight in order to find her way around refuse and building materials. She also affirmed that the Shua family cursed her and other Coase family members for no reason. She recounted an incident in which Eli intentionally burped loudly in her face. She also stated that her father had always worn the gun under his shirt.

Additional Circumstantial Evidence

As a result of study and planning, the defense attorney decided to introduce and make prominent a set of additional facts that he hoped and expected would alter the image of the events communicated to the court. These are what is called circumstantial evidence.

Circumstance: Place of Entry and Exit of Bullets

Jonathan Shua exposed his stomach during his testimony to demonstrate that the bullet entered through his stomach and exited through his back at the same level. As indicated, this created an inference that the defendant had shot while standing; if proved, it contradicted the defendant's version and undermined the defense's image of events.

Jonathan's testimony on the levels of the bullet wound opened a factual conflict that seriously weakened the defense case. The defense could not let this prosecution point go unchallenged. The first defense challenge to the inculpatory image of Daniel's physical position came in Jonathan's cross-examination, but little was achieved in eliminating the impression that the defendant must have been standing. The defendant's version was not yet made credible.

After studying the issue with the assistance of a pathologist expert in body injuries, the defense attorney learned that there was a distinct possibility that the real entry and exit levels on Jonathan's body had been distorted by the operations that Jonathan underwent to repair his stomach. The pathologist suggested that he might be able to show that the present entry point had been shifted upward by medical treatment. Before deciding to introduce testimony on this point, the defense pathologist would have to examine the medical records of the operation. He might also have to make a physical examination of Jonathan.

There were several possible trial complications that could result from the pathologist's testimony. Initial study of the medical records to determine the path of the bullet were inconclusive. The pathologist said that he could make an argument that the medical records indicated an original place of entry lower than the postoperative appearance of entry, but the ambiguity in the records left open a large measure of possible error. In considering whether to offer this testimony, the defense attorney had to take into account the possibility that if a defense expert testified, the prosecution might summon its own expert and introduce contradicting testimony. If the prosecution expert were to testify persuasively that the defense expert had drawn improper inferences, the expert defense testimony would detract in a serious way from the credibility of the defense image of events. It would also magnify the probative relevance of the body wounds, making them appear in the mind of the judge as highly important to the composite meaning of the image of the events.

The defense attorney concluded that the issue of the bullet trajectory would confuse the judge and deflect attention from facts that would be more persuasive for the defense image. The defense attorney preferred to emphasize inconsistencies in the prosecution witnesses' testimony as compared to out-of-court statements, as well as testimony not yet offered with respect to the previous violent conduct on the part of the Shua family. The defense attorney made a tentative decision not to present expert testimony on the effect of medical operations on the positions of the bullet wound.

The defense attorney's initial decision on this issue was then complicated by the following development. Subsequent to Jonathan's testimony, the prosecution decided to call the surgeon to introduce into evidence Jonathan's medical file, not to prove anything about the position of the bullet wounds, but to establish the seriousness of Jonathan's injury. This raised a problem. If the medical records in fact corroborated the argument that the bullet had entered and exited at the same level, then the prosecution could in its summation direct the court's attention to the medical records to support the inference that Daniel was standing when he shot Jonathan, not lying down, even though the prosecution had not asked for oral testimony on that issue. Thus, if the defense attorney did not cross-examine the surgeon on the issue of the level of the bullet's entry and exit, this could be understood as a waiver of an objection to the accuracy of the inference possibly to be found in the medical records. After considering this issue, the defense attorney decided that he would need to cross-examine the surgeon and at least raise the possibility that the place of the hole wounds on Jonathan's stomach and back side had been changed by surgical procedures.

Notwithstanding the foregoing, at the time of the surgeon's testimony, the defense attorney reconsidered and decided not to ask the surgeon whether the position of the entry and exit had been changed by medical operation. Without having obtained a persuasive expert opinion on this issue from an independent source, there was too great a risk that the surgeon would affirm the prosecution's version rather than the defense's version of the wounds on Jonathan's stomach and back. The defense attorney refrained from asking the surgeon questions about the possible distorting effects of the operations.

As it later turned out, the prosecution did not make a summation argument on this issue, probably because the prosecutor was not aware of the potentially probative strength of the inculpatory inference that possibly could be drawn from this issue.

During a period of weeks in which there was a delay between prosecution and defense witnesses, the defense attorney studied further the issue of entry and exit of the bullet through a photographic-assisted analysis of the supposed body positions of Daniel and Jonathan at the time of the shooting. The defense attorney had made videotaped photographs of various enactments of Jonathan's attack on the defendant and the defendant's shooting of Jonathan while a stand-in raised and swung the plank over Avi's head. The video tapes were made under the direction of the defendant and attorney, who attempted to recreate exactly the position of the parties when the shooting took place. Examination of the tapes showed that if the shooting had taken place when Jonathan was in a forward-running motion and swinging the plank at the same time, as Daniel had described in detail in his first verbal account of the incident to his attorney, the trunk of Jonathan's body would have been perpendicular to the defendant's outstretched hand while the defendant lay propped on the ground after falling. This picture of the event demonstrated that the bullet could go into the body at a place equidistant to the ground as compared to the place where it came out, as measured when the defendant stood upright, if the defendant shot from a position on the ground while Jonathan was bending over to strike Avi.

In order not to prod the prosecution into cross-examining the level of the bullet holes at the time the video was entered into evidence, the defense attorney sought to introduce the videotapes without making obvious that he was addressing the issue of the bullet's entry and exit point. To achieve this objective, the defense made still pictures from the video and had the defendant present them during his testimony, presumably for the purpose of demonstrating that the defendant was lying down. The defense attorney did not announce during admission into evidence that the picture was also intended to prove the angle of Jonathan's body and the trajectory of the bullet's passage through the body for the purpose of invalidating Jonathan's testimony that the shooting took place while the defendant was standing. The important inference could be drawn during summation.

In its summation argument, the prosecution did not address the issue of the level of entry of the bullets and the positioning of the parties by referring to the video. Thereafter, in its summation, the defense requested the judge to examine the pictures introduced into evidence in order to see that the position of the bullet wounds on Jonathan's body coincided with the defense image of the body positions at the time of the shooting.

Circumstance: Violent Character of the Shua Family

Daniel and Miriam emphasized repeatedly that neighbors and former residents of the neighborhood had complained bitterly about the threats directed at them by the Shuas. During the long period of pretrial preparation, the defense attorney hired private investigators to meet and talk with several persons who were said to have had serious problems with the Shua family in the past. Private investigators used undercover agents who collected information from former residents of the area. The private investigators learned that two prior occupants of Daniel's house had moved out because of intolerable relations with the Shua family. The investigators interviewed other persons, including a building contractor, a truck driver, and persons who had rented a room from the Shuas. In one case, the investigators used a disguise and recorded the conversation; in another instance, they conducted their interviews openly. Of the eight persons interviewed, three were called as defense witnesses. The following is a summary of the testimony of two of those witnesses.

Character Witness Number One   Dr. Amos Brand is a brain surgeon. He had been in an elite commando unit in the army. After the army, he entered medical school. When he received his first permanent hospital employment, he bought the house that he later sold to the Coases. Two years before the shooting incident, he went to the

United States for advanced training and rented the house to a young couple, one of whom is witness number two.

The Testimony   Dr. Amos Brand testified that the Shua family was grotesque. Immediately upon entering his new house, Paul Shua, from whom he had purchased the house, told him that he would not be allowed to park his car on the street near his house. During a very difficult confrontation, Paul pushed Dr. Brand in the chest and threatened to break open his head with a huge boulder that he held up high in the air. The witness added the following detail:

- Paul Shua intentionally did not have his cesspool wells cleaned and they ran over into his front yard—that is Dr. Brand's yard, later the defendant's yard. Dr. Brand stated that he and Paul argued about this issue, until Dr. Brand finally had to clear the Shua family's pool of sewerage himself.

- One day when Dr. Brand was working on his house with the assistance of day laborers, Ronda Shua called to her son Jonathan, who came out of his house at high speed and threatened Dr. Brand with fists clenched. The Shuas claimed that they were bothered by the noise made by the laborers working on Dr. Brand's house.

- Paul Shua tried to remove a fence that Dr. Brand erected on the boundary between them. Dr. Brand called the police for help. The police referred Dr. Brand to local headquarters to file a complaint. At police headquarters, Dr. Brand was told by the duty officer that the police had received many complaints about the Shua family, that they were well-known "troublemakers."

- On cross-examination by the prosecutor, Dr. Brand stated that he had told Daniel Coase when he sold the house to him that the neighbors were difficult and might cause problems.

Character Witness Number Two   Annette Cohen is a social worker and director of a nonprofit corporation that assists victims of cerebral palsy. Annette and her husband rented the house from Dr. Brand when he left for training in the United States.

The Testimony   Annette Cohen testified that the Shua family had, in her emotionally expressed words, tortured the Cohen family during the short period that the Cohens lived next to the Shuas. This figurative torture included the following:

- The Shuas would not allow the Cohens to park their car on the street in front of their house.

- The Shua children tried to kill the Cohens' dog by throwing him down a mountainside in a closed box. The Shuas killed their own dog and left its carcass on the Cohens' front porch.

- The youngest Shua child continually made pornographic telephone calls to the Cohen house during the Gulf War when the two families sat in their bomb shelters.

- During one incident, Paul Shua raised his fists and threatened Annette.

- Annette said that she had worked professionally in a shelter for battered mothers and that, although she had never been touched by any of the Shuas, she had been "battered" by them.

- Ronda Shua constantly yelled and screamed at her husband and children, calling them pigs and sons of bitches. Annette saw Ronda hitting her children with a broom.

The foregoing testimony was provided to establish two points: first, the Shuas were characterologically unreliable and thus lied on the witness stand, and, second, they tended to behave in the way that Daniel said Jonathan had behaved on the day of the event. The prosecutor objected to the admission of this testimony on the grounds that it was legally irrelevant, would confuse issues, and was scientifically not probative of the question of whether Jonathan attacked Avi on the day of the event. The judge, who revealed in her behavior a genuine interest in the testimony, complained to the defense attorney that he was "overdoing" and "pushing the court to the limit" but agreed to admit the testimony.

Circumstance: Eli's Presence on the Scene Holding a Bent Rod

In testimony, but not in his out-of-court statement, Daniel Coase stated that he was assaulted not only by Jonathan Shua but also by Eli Shua. Daniel testified that Eli Shua held a large, heavy bent-iron rod and that he thought he received a blow from the rod on his right arm. Daniel's daughter supported this testimony when she stated that her father complained of an injury to his arm in the courtroom during the initial arrest hearing.

Each of the Shua family members was questioned about the iron rod. Eli denied holding a rod or charging Daniel. Paul and Ronda denied that Eli charged with a rod; they said that only Jonathan charged, in self-defense, with a stick. Following up on this issue, and acting on a lead provided by the Coase family, investigators went to a local television station and found a tape of a midnight newscast on the night of the shooting in which Paul was recorded saying that "one of my sons took a bent-iron rod and charged at Daniel in order to protect the family from further injury."

Paul's out-of-court statement contradicted directly the oral testimony of Shua family members. This limited factual detail seemed to the defense attorney to carry strong discrediting weight, putting virtually all of the Shua family testimony in question. The prosecutor did not object to the admission of the television tape, did not request that it be shown in court (the defense submitted a written summary), and did not address the meaning or relevance of the television statement in her summation.

Circumstance: Four Shots

The indictment against Daniel stated that Daniel emptied his gun and that at least four bullets were fired. If this were true, it raised the distinct possibility that Daniel acted with disproportionate force. A finding of disproportionate use of force would prevent the court from accepting a justified-use-of-force defense, even if the first shot was justified. If the first shot was justified, but the second through fourth were not, Daniel would be convicted. His sentence would be mitigated because of the partial justification, but he could not be acquitted. But a greater problem lay in allowing the prosecution to show that Daniel fired intentionally not only the first shot, but also the second through fourth shots. The judge might find that the unjustified intentional firing of shots two through four constituted circumstantial evidence of unjustified firing of the first shot. This would lead the judge to convict Daniel of firing his gun, not recognizing any justification.

In their testimony, the Shua family claimed and the police findings at the scene indicated that the defendant shot four bullets, not just one. The prosecution argued, relying on this evidence, that the defendant either shot at least once before he was attacked by Jonathan or that he tried to hit a member of the Shua family who had not threatened him, arguably the mother. The mother was wounded, raising even another possibility: that the defendant would be acquitted of shooting Jonathan but convicted of intending to or actually causing serious bodily harm to the mother. The defense had to provide a noninculpatory explanation for the firing not only of one but of three additional bullets.

Daniel testified that his first shot was aimed at Jonathan and that thereafter he had no recollection whatsoever until he found himself back in his house with the police. How could the additional shots be explained? The defense attorney and the defendant agreed that it was plausible that the defendant panicked and continued to shoot without thinking. But a reasonable alternative image was that the defendant continued to intentionally shoot while aiming either at Jonathan or at other members of the Shua family.

In assessing this issue, the defense attorney decided that he would attempt to use a psychiatrist to support the inference that Daniel fired the additional shots out of panic, spontaneously, and without in-tending to hit anyone. The psychiatrist met with Daniel several times and determined that Daniel's own perception of himself at the time of the event was that he acted in defense of his son and that he fired only for this purpose. The psychiatrist believed that the lapse of memory of the three additional shots arose from a traumatic reaction to the first shot and that the three additional shots were most likely fired as an automatic response. The psychiatrist told the defense at-torney that he believed that the defendant did not form any specific intent after firing the first shot. The psychiatrist prepared an opinion stating that a trauma syndrome had overwhelmed the defendant on firing the first shot. He wrote that persons affected by the syndrome will often react automatically and without rational control. The psy-chiatrist emphasized that it was likely that Daniel was affected by this syndrome immediately after firing the first shot. The opinion was in-troduced into evidence.

The prosecutor strongly objected to the admission into evidence of the psychiatric opinion. She argued that the psychiatrist overstepped his professional role by drawing conclusions on the question of whether the defendant intended to fire shots three through four. She stated that the psychiatrist had to limit his opinion to an assessment of the defendant's psychological state at the time the shots were fired and that only the judge was authorized to draw conclusions on the issue of intent. In this context, argued the prosecutor, intent was a legal, not a psychological, issue. The prosecutor also objected on the grounds that the psychiatrist had not read the defendant's statements to the police immediately after the shooting, only the defendant's testimony at trial. The judge decided to accept provisionally the psychiatric opinion, putting off the final determination of admissibility to the end of the trial. The judge stated that she would give her decision on this matter within the final court judgment on the issue of guilt.

Circumstance: Situs of Bullet Shells

During pretrial disclosure, the defense attorney was given a police report that situated the bullet shells near the front door to the Coases' home. As circumstantial evidence, this would indicate that the shooting took place at or near the door. The prosecutor did not address this potential defense evidence in her case-in-chief. During testimony, each of the Shua family witnesses placed the situs of the shooting at the outer gate to the Coase plot. The outer gate lay some 18 meters from the front door to the home.

The defense attorney introduced expert ballistics testimony that supported the version of the facts presented by the Coases. Daniel, Miriam, and Avi Coase testified that the shooting took place near the door to the home, not near the outer gate. A strong defense point was made. The expert witness testified that the bullet shells could not have been jettisoned 18 meters and that unless they were kicked accidentally after landing on the ground, or were intentionally moved to the situs near the front door, the bullet shell landing points supported the version of the event presented by the Coase witnesses and contradicted the version presented by the Shua witnesses. A particularly strong detail of the expert opinion was the fact that one of the bullet shells landed in a flower pot near the front door to the house and therefore could not have been accidentally kicked to that position from an earlier situs at the outer gate, 18 meters away. The shots were fired near the front door, unless someone intentionally moved the bullet shells immediately after the shooting, before police investigators examined the scene and wrote their own ballistics report.

Image Construction in Criminal Trials

I have now come to the end of the detailed presentation of facts. At this point, the judge had two possible pictures to choose from. Either the defendant committed an unprovoked pistol attack on Jonathan and Ronda Shua, or the defendant's son Avi was brutally attacked by Jonathan Shua, with a wooden plank filled with upright nails, and the defendant acted in justified defense of his son. On the one hand, the judge had before her the image of a mature adult who lost control in an argument about a parking space. On the other hand, she had the image of an angry and violent young man brutally attacking the defendant's son and the defendant acting out of desperation to save his son's life. Facing the choice of contending images, factual detail came to take central importance; the judge would be strongly influenced by any small fact that revealed a fault in the image projected by either party. For example, the defendant said that he was attacked with a wooden plank with open nails sticking out at the end. A plank was found with bent-down closed nails. If the judge came to the conclusion that the defendant had lied about the nails, she might choose the prosecution image as determinative, even if every other piece of defense testimony seemed to fit. One small detail could in this respect construct or deconstruct the entire picture.

A professional judge, like any other recipient of information about an event in question, integrates the case-specific information with generalized assumptions about social life. The general field of pictures of events residing in human memory is a basis for interpreting case-specific facts through the use of imagination. The indictment in the case of Daniel Coase conveyed only a small amount of information: "defendant exits house and shoots neighbor," something like a newspaper headline. The text of the indictment allowed little flexibility of interpretation: moral and legal responsibility was placed squarely on Daniel Coase. This fit the reservoir of presumptions in the mind of the fact finder. But the indictment failed to address many critical details, such as the distance between the defendant and victim, the position of each of the players at the time of the shooting, the nature of the physical surrounding, motivational factors, the history of conflict between the two families, the entry and exit point of the bullets in the body of Jonathan, the situs of the bullet shells on the ground, and the prior bad acts of the Shua family. These additional facts would alter the image constructed by the judge.

The basic information of the indictment remained—the defendant exited the house and shot his neighbor—but the addition of the many surrounding facts created a distinctly different moral and legal conclusion, providing an entirely different understanding of the event. The reasonable alternative image was that of a father acting to save the life of his son.[11]

The real criminal case described here demonstrates that the criminal trial is a process of image construction in which the parties take turns putting pieces of the image in place, much like a puzzle. But unlike the usual puzzle, centrally important to the trial is that each piece of the puzzle, that is each fact, has potential multiple functions. A fact may confirm the prosecution image (witness A testifies that he heard Daniel say that he intended to shoot the next door neighbor) or defense image (witness B says that he heard Jonathan say that he tried to attack Daniel's son with a two-by-four with open nails on the end), or a fact presented by either of the sides may contradict the validity of another fact already presented by the opposite side (witness C testifies that witness A told him that he, witness A, lied to the court about what the defendant did). Each fact contains the power to transform the image describing the event displayed to the fact finder.

One can say, metaphorically, that the trial presupposes two artists taking turns using a brush to draw a preferred image of the event. In this process, the artist may choose either to add new color or to eliminate the color added by the opponent artist. Each stroke of the brush may change the social, moral, and legal meaning of the image. In assessing how the parties use their brushes, we should recall that the judge often begins with the general unspecified image: "defendant shoots neighbor."[12] The artists use their brushes to create the "real" meaning of the outline in the indictment.

At trial, a defense attorney's major efforts are invested in reducing and expanding the field of facts in the decisionmaking arena. Defense attorneys will coach witnesses not to "unnecessarily" volunteer certain facts, and they will object to the introduction by the prosecutor of other facts. At the same time, they will seek to introduce still additional facts, in order to alter the image of the events that has been drawn in the indictment presented by the prosecution. Controlled presentation of fact is at the center of defense practice in all criminal trials in which there are factual disputes.

Factual Detail and Time Consumption in Criminal Defense

Through a step by step review of fact presentation in this case study, I have sought to demonstrate that minute factual detail as well as facts unrelated directly to events that constitute the alleged offense have a determinative impact on the nature of the image of the events made for fact finders. The law of evidence sets a background structure to the discourse. Within that structure, the defense attorney can invest nearly boundless resources in the management of facts. This aspect of trial litigation requires a large investment of time.

The defense attorney in the case of Daniel Coase invested well over a hundred hours in preparing evidence and deciding how best to present facts that would prove that his client shot the victim in defense of his son. Fact preparation was a complex task whose most demanding aspect was the need to give careful attention to detail. It also required imagination, in order to project the potential implications for an image of the introduction or nonintroduction of each possibly relevant fact. And it required patience in order to think and rethink the puzzle of facts many times. Defense attorneys specialize at trial in giving careful attention to the sources of information, to details in the content and quality of the information collected, and to decisions about whether or not to present facts. Defense attorneys know that the prosecution is engaged in similar strategies of fact control and may give equal or more attention to detail.

The various component tasks of fact presentation require that the defense attorney invest large amounts of time in handling facts in different ways. Attorneys spend many hours meeting with clients and witnesses, pouring over factual details in documents, and conducting meetings dedicated to developing explanation, adding facts, pointing to resources, and deciding what to include and what to exclude. Highly motivated defense attorneys go home at night shuffling the facts in their head, talking about facts with their spouse, writing notes about facts, and processing facts in the half-aware disturbances of unsound sleep.

Daniel Coase paid the equivalent of $80,000 in fees and costs. The cost of trial preparation was relatively high because of the large amount of time invested in fact-related procedures, including financial resources needed for investigators, experts, and support staff.

This close-up focus on defense attorney activities, rather than on the professional status of the attorney and his or her hourly fee, should allow one to appreciate that the high cost of criminal trials is related to the weight given to time in the formula for assessing costs, more than the hourly rate. High cost in criminal trials is related directly to the large quantity of human resources, necessarily measured in time, that are needed for careful and intensive fact control, even in a case of comparatively simple factual issues, such as the case of Daniel Coase. If Daniel Coase had been charged with committing a fraud on the stock market, the amount of time needed for intensive fact litigation surely would have been many times greater. Proving factual reality is time-consuming.

Inequality in Criminal Defense

The large amount of time consumed in criminal trials means that only a small subgroup of the total population of defendants can afford to purchase enough time to conduct full-blown fact finding. Most trials are conducted with resources insufficient to exploit factual detail in full. Attorneys refrain from investing time in order to preserve a desired level of remuneration per unit of time. They forgo conducting meetings with clients, witnesses, investigators, and experts, and they limit the time invested in reading, assessing materials, and preparing facts. They also limit their willingness to think about facts, making a clearer division between work hours and leisure hours. Because most trials are underfunded, the potential in fact-finding procedures is systematically underexploited.

Variable funding of fact finding and chronic underfunding mean that the quality of criminal trial litigation is severely stratified. This view of the criminal trial focuses on the particular manner in which lack of resources affects equality: time limitations correlate directly with and limit the control of factual detail. With limitations on the ability to pay for time, defense attorneys will not use the private investigator, the expert in the performance of firearms, or the psychiatrist, and he or she will not meet repeatedly with the defendant. The point is not that the quality of the attorney is different, but that the time spent by attorneys whose resources are limited by the client's financial inability to pay will be limited, whatever their personal skills, and that this will limit their ability to control the image of the event in question.

The true extent of the problem of inadequate fact control is not confined to the small percentage of criminal cases that actually go to trial. Defense attorneys choose to forgo trials and plead guilty because their client lacks the resources to invest in fact control. But another reason for not going to trial is that many defense attorneys have never achieved or have lost the ability to identify factual ambiguity in the cases they handle, because they routinely represent clients with only modest resources. Systematic representation of poor or only moderately situated clients wears away and eventually destroys the attorney's capacity to see factual ambiguity. Other attorneys representing financially well-situated clients are able to achieve and maintain a more acute ability to identify potential factual ambiguity. Thus some or even many defendants "unjustifiably" plead guilty, not only because they lack the resources to mount a trial, but also because the defense attorney is not sufficiently sensitive to the presence of factual ambiguity.

The impact of limited resources on the ability of the attorney to conduct a trial varies greatly depending on the nature of the case. The pathological impact of underfunded fact finding is concentrated among cases in which there are factual bases for contending images. Certain cases are indeed open-and-shut-cases, particularly those in which the defendant makes a fully inculpatory confession. In such situations, limited resources cannot be said to limit the willingness of the defense attorney to conduct a fact control defense in a criminal trial. The choice to plead guilty is often simply dictated by the facts.

Inequality in the criminal trial system is thus highly concentrated in the population of cases bearing real factual ambiguities. Within this population of cases, lack of time results either in the choice to conduct an inadequate trial or the default choice to plea bargain. Accepting that the full-blown criminal trial must be a high-cost venture, inequality in funding results in inequality of opportunity to construct exculpatory images. In other words, inequality in resources creates inequality in the ability to exploit factual detail.

This analysis of criminal trials puts underfunded fact finding in perspective. At trial, resource limitations heavily stratify defense practice. Resource limitations create a large variation in the defense attorney's ability to do what is necessary to collect, prepare, and present facts. Underfunding means lack of fact control and limited leverage in image construction. The result is a highly variable ability to litigate factual disputes at trial, or, using the concept of image, a highly variable ability to make images. The adversarial system of criminal justice infrequently, relative to the large mass of cases, achieves full benefit of fact development. The gap between reality and the determination of judicial fact is then, at some immeasurable level, due to the lack of time for proper handling of facts.

Afterword

Months after this article was written, Daniel Coase was acquitted of all charges brought against him. In a seventy-page opinion, the judge found that the Shua family members were not truthful in their testimony before the court, that Daniel Coase's son, Avi, was attacked by Jonathan Shua, and that Daniel acted in justified defense of his son when he shot Jonathan.

The local prosecutor's office leaked strong criticism of the judge's opinion to a national newspaper, which published a critical article implying that the judge was misled by the defense attorney. The appellate staff in the national office of the state prosecutor studied the opinion during a forty-five-day appellate period.

No appeal was made by the state prosecutor, and thus the judgment of acquittal in the criminal case became final. Still pending is a civil suit for several million shekels that was filed by the Shua family against Daniel Coase during the proceedings in the criminal trial.

Notes

1. The names have been changed in order to protect the identity of the parties. The district court is the higher of two criminal courts in the State of Israel. It has jurisdiction over criminal offenses the punishment for which is at least eight years of imprisonment as well as several other special categories of offenses. A single professional judge sits in judgment on all cases, except for murder, rape, and a few of the most serious security offenses. In cases of serious security offenses, a panel of three professional judges sits in judgment. Criminal law and procedure were derived at their origin mainly from English law and continue to be developed following the model of the Anglo-American adversary system. Rules similar to the English rules of evidence control principles of admissibility. Except for the absence of juries, the trial procedure would be familiar to anyone with basic knowledge of Anglo-American criminal procedure.

2. The criminal procedure law of Israel has a strict rule of disclosure, requiring the prosecution immediately to make available to the defense attorney all witness statements and records of all actions taken, observations made, tests undertaken, and expert opinions received at each step of the police investigation.

3. Indictments are usually based on a strict causal model. They remove the "noise" in the background, meaning the discontinuities and ambiguities in a story of the event. In this sense, the indictment is like any other legal test. In some cases, the main job of the defense attorney is simply

to make that picture blurry, if you will, to deconstruct it. See Singer (1984), which describes the interaction between constructivist and deconstructivist perspectives with respect to legal text.

4. The question of how decisionmakers perceive danger, damage, and risk is, of course, intimately connected with community and culture. A classic work on this connection is Mary Douglas's *Risk and Blame:* "If you want to cast blame there are always loopholes for reading the evidence right" (Douglas 1994, 9).

5. "Inculpatory Facts" are facts that lead to indicate guilt, but they may falsely indicate guilt, so that coaching against unintended disclosure of inculpatory facts may tend to help create a true image of innocence.

6. In previous work, I examined the pretrial fact control strategies of defense attorneys. See Mann (1983). In this chapter, I look only at fact control during trial, the strategies being fundamentally different in orientation.

7. See Sherwin (1994), which describes the key role of the defense attorney in creating images and symbols that are easily integrated into cultural symbols.

8. The idea of the malleable image as a legal artifact has taken a central place in the debate over objectivity and postmodern constructivism in law and legal interpretation. Interpretation of factual images, as well as legal text, may be seen as particularly rule-bound or as reflecting more communal constructs of the truth. With respect to interpretations of legal texts, see Fiss (1982) and the reply (Fiss 1984).

9. See Pennington and Hastie (1991, 528): "A story is plausible to the extent that it corresponds to the decisionmaker's knowledge about what typically happens in the world and does not contradict that knowledge."

10. One could also focus on crime reporting variables, methods of investigation, testimonial readiness of citizens, and other factors that bear on the range of facts brought into the trial arena.

11. The burden of image-making and the strategy adopted by litigators in this process are deeply affected by the legal burden of persuasion. Theoretically, it is enough for the defense to prevent the prosecution from presenting facts—that is, from creating the prosecution image—thus relieving the defense from creating an image. However, one can also argue that the fact finder must always have some image of the defendant's actions in order to decide a case, even if that image is that the defendant must have been somewhere else doing something else.

12. For an assessment of analogous processes, see Moore (1987), which emphasizes the multiple potential frames of reference.

References

Douglas, Mary. 1994. *Risk and Blame: Essays in Cultural Theory.* London: Routledge.

Fiss, Owen. 1982. "Objectivity and Interpretation." *Stanford Law Review* 34(4): 739–63.

———. 1984. "Fish v. Fiss." *Stanford Law Review* 36(6): 1325–47.

Mann, Kenneth. 1983. *Defending White-Collar Crime: A Portrait of Attorneys at Work.* New Haven, Conn.: Yale University Press.

Moore, Albert J. 1987. "Trial by Schema: Cognitive Filters in the Courtroom." *UCLA Law Review* 37(2): 273–341.

Pennington, Nancy, and Reid Hastie. 1991. "A Cognitive Theory of Jury Decisionmaking: The Storey Model." *Cardozo Law Review* 13(2,3): 519–57.

Sherwin, Richard K. 1994. "Law Frames: Historical Truth and Narrative Necessity in a Criminal Case." *Stanford Law Review* 47(1): 39–83.

Singer, Joseph William. 1984. "The Player and the Cards: Nihilism and Legal Theory." *Yale Law Journal* 94(1): 1–70.

Part II
Barriers to Influence

Chapter 4

A Bad Press on Bad Lawyers: The Media Sees Research, Research Sees the Media

Deborah L. Rhode

Jokes about lawyers have become so common in American culture that there is now a recognized subspecialty in jokes about lawyers. A recent addition to this collection summarizes some of the sleaziest conduct that humorists attribute to the profession and then asks, "How many jokes about lawyers are there? Answer: One. The rest are all documented case histories."

For those of us who study the legal profession, the quip captures an unintended insight. It is dispiriting to note how readily folklore passes for fact in discussions about lawyers. On topics involving regulation of the legal profession, systematic research plays at best a walk-on role; skewed statistical sound bites and unrepresentative anecdotes are the main attraction.

Much of the reason involves the press. In American culture, the law and the media are inescapably intertwined. Apart from limited personal experience, most of what the public knows about the legal profession comes from the media (Garst 1996). The picture that emerges is inevitably incomplete. The way journalists frame their coverage helps reshape the legal world that they claim only to represent. What gets lost in translation also gets lost in public policy debates. As social science research consistently demonstrates, the media influence not only what we know but also what sense we make of that knowledge (Fiske 1994; Reeves and Campbell 1994; Hall 1977).

Although people are by no means passive, uncritical consumers, press coverage generally sets the agenda for public discussion (Fiske 1987; Price 1992; Qualter 1989; Shaw and Marlin 1992). Journalists' profiles of legal institutions affect attitudes, aspirations, and policy agendas. So too, the media are a primary means of ensuring public accountability of the legal profession (Hans 1990; Galanter forthcoming). The press not only evaluates lawyers' performance, it also creates pressures for other institutions to do so as well.

Yet the media's own performance in that evaluation process remains largely unexamined. We lack systematic research on journalists' use and abuse of research. On matters involving regulation of the legal profession, we know too little about a wide range of questions. What kinds of information does the press present or fail to present and what factors influence its choices? How do lawyers individually and collectively help shape media coverage? What effects do press portraits have on public attitudes and policy outcomes?

The premise of this chapter is that legal scholars need to pay more attention to such questions, both as researchers and as contributors to media discussions. Academics write mostly for one another and for others in their profession. Seldom do we consciously seek a mass audience, and rarely do we find one. Nor do we focus much scholarly attention on the media as a legal institution or on the processes that translate and transform the law in popular consciousness.

This insularity is one that we can ill afford. Policy agendas are more often set by media accounts than by scholarly journals. Many of these accounts are seriously distorted, and coverage of the legal profession is no exception. A large part of the reason involves the self-interest and structural pressures that constrain both journalists and the sources on which they primarily rely—lawyers and politicians.

This chapter attempts to place those constraints in sharper focus. To that end, it explores the ways in which concerns about profitability, convenience, and "fairness" systematically bias media coverage. Such concerns tend to skew stories in favor of spectacle. The dramatic and unusual, personalized, and polarized events receive undue attention. And the desire for "balance" too often yields uncritical presentation of competing partisan sources.

That is not to imply the existence of some single, objectively verifiable truths about the legal profession that the media fail to capture. Postmodernist theorists across a wide range of disciplines remind us that "reality" is constructed, not simply discovered; our views of the world are inevitably incomplete and filtered through our own experiences. But although all perspectives are partial, some are more coherent and respectful of available evidence than others. By those criteria, too much media coverage falls short. What often remain out of sight and out of mind are the undramatic problems, underlying causes, and complex tradeoffs that should inform policy debates. Only by gaining a richer understanding of the dynamics underlying media accounts are we likely to improve them.

Giving the Public What It Wants

> They've got us putting more and more fuzz and wuzz on the air . . . so as to compete not with other news programs but with entertainment programs, including those posing as news programs. [Dan Rather, quoted in Bennett 1996]

In an increasingly competitive media market, the line between news and entertainment increasingly blurs. Mass communication technologies, coupled with profit motives, have driven journalism toward what media theorist W. Lance Bennett (1996, 39) terms "lowest common denominator information." Serious news coverage struggles to survive among a widening range of livelier rivals: talk radio, tabloid trash, docudramas, *Court TV*, and journalistic roundtables. As a result, factual content often is dumbed down and spruced up in ways that preempt informed debate. Even the most conscientious journalists feel pressure to respond in kind, because circulation levels and consumer satisfaction surveys have assumed such importance in media markets. Widening audience appeal is critical not just to securing sales but also to attracting advertisers concerned with broad exposure (Baker 1994).

Yet giving the public what it wants poses obvious problems if, as Bennett claims, "most people really don't want more serious news even when they say they do" (Bennett 1996, 22–23). Americans seem to prefer what sociologist Murray Edelman has labeled "news as spectacle" (Edelman 1988). To gain widespread attention, the news must be "new." As a consequence, media coverage focuses on the aberrant, novel, or exceptionally dramatic event (Benedict 1992; Gans 1979; Peter Kann, "10 Disturbing Trends in U.S. Journalism,"

Editor and Publisher, October 9, 1994, p. 19). And "stories deficient in drama" sometimes "have drama grafted on" (Paletz and Entman 1981). Patterns that are more commonplace but also more significant drop out of view.

Such skewed coverage is typical on issues involving the legal profession. Attention centers on seemingly egregious proceedings: frivolous claims, excessive awards, and outrageous fees. In the picture that emerges, the system seems seriously askew, and attorneys appear intent on keeping it that way. The public sees mainly cases that are too big for courts, cases that are too small, and cases that never should have been cases at all.

In these accounts, "people are suing each other with abandon" (Jack Anderson, "U.S. Has Become a Nation of Lawsuits," *Washington Post,* January 25, 1985, p. B8; Bryan 1993; Galanter 1993a, 1994). A twenty-five-year-old victim of "improper parenting" seeks damages from his mother and father (Rhode and Luban 1995, 722). A customer having a "bad hair day" sues the beautician (Stossel 1996, transcript 69). A woman tries to dry her poodle in a microwave following a shampoo and demands compensation from the manufacturer for the unhappy outcome (Cramton 1996).

From these cases, the media constructs a culture of "hair-trigger" litigation and "legal hypochondria" (Rhode 1998). But in this construction, the line between fact and fiction is often fuzzy. Politicians are particularly likely to exercise poetic license, and their homespun homilies receive wide circulation. "Everyone is suing everyone," announces Kentucky Senator Mitch McConnell (McConnell 1986). According to California Governor Pete Wilson, the "lawyer's briefcase has become a weapon of terror" (Sullivan 1997, 43). Dan Quayle (1994, 283) replays similar themes with downhome details. In his portrait of a "crazily litigious country," a baseball crashes through a window, and "the 'victim' . . . sues the neighbor. Or the baseball's manufacturer. Or the glassmaker. Or usually all three."

Yet these aberrant, often embellished, accounts fail to establish that the United States has exceptional numbers of frivolous suits or that such cases occupy a substantial amount of judicial time. In many cultures, courts have long provided outlets for minor grievances, and American judges have broad power to sanction or summarily dismiss clearly meritless claims. If press profiles included some historical or cross-cultural comparisons, such as the Belgrade court that once coped with some 9,000 slander suits, then America's current collection of loony litigants might look less alarming (Galanter 1983; Friedman 1978).

Moreover, what qualifies as a frivolous claim depends on the eye of the beholder. Although a few commonly cited examples meet almost anyone's definition, the line between vindictiveness and vindication is sometimes difficult to draw. Sexual harassment claims were once routinely dismissed as matters beneath judicial notice. Among some courts and commentators, the situation has not significantly improved. Pundits like John Leo (1993, 20) and John McLaughlin (quoted in Epstein 1996) complain about the climate of "corporate McCarthyism," which allows radical feminists to "sue anybody about anything" (McMenamin 1997, 123). Some male judges similarly worry about the use of antidiscrimination law to redress the "petty slights of the hypersensitive" (Rhode 1997, 97–98). Yet only through the persistence of plaintiffs have Americans finally begun to recognize the real costs of harassment. Women pay the highest price in terms of direct economic and psychological injuries, but all of us pay more indirectly. Seldom do press accounts acknowledge that harassment costs the average Fortune 500 company more than $6 million annually in turnover, worker absences, and lost productivity (Segrave 1994).

So too, many of the media's favorite illustrations of trivial claims and outrageous verdicts rely on highly selective factual accounts. A textbook illustration involves a recent multimillion dollar punitive damages award against McDonald's for serving coffee at scalding temperatures. In most journalists' simplified moral universe, this case served as an all-purpose indictment of the legal profession and legal process; an avaricious lawyer parades a petty incident before an out-of-control jury and extracts an absurd recovery. Newspaper editorials, radio talk shows, and magazine commentaries replayed endless variations on the theme summarized by the national Chamber of Commerce: "Is it fair to get a couple of million dollars from a restaurant just because you spilled hot coffee on yourself?" (Chamber of Commerce, quoted in Nader and Smith 1996, 267).

On closer examination, that question is not self-evidently rhetorical. The plaintiff, a seventy-nine-year-old woman, suffered acutely painful third-degree burns from 180 degree coffee. She spent eight days in the hospital and returned again for skin grafts. Only after McDonald's refused to reimburse her medical expenses did she bring suit. At trial, jurors learned of 700 other burn cases involving McDonald's coffee during the preceding decade. Although medical experts had warned that such high temperatures were causing serious injuries, the corporation's safety consultant dismissed the number of complaints as "trivial." The jury's verdict of $2.3 million was not an arbitrary choice. Its punitive damages award represented two days of coffee sales revenues, and the judge reduced the judgment to $640,000. To avoid an appeal, the plaintiff then settled the case for a lower, undisclosed amount. As a result of this litigation, McDonald's posted warning signs and other fast-food chains adopted similar measures (Webb 1995, 32). Although evaluations of this outcome may vary, it was not the patently "ridiculous" travesty that media critics presented (Chamber of Commerce, quoted in Nader and Smith 1996; Press, Carroll, and Waldman 1995; Andrea Gerlin, "A Matter of Degree: How a Jury Decided That a Coffee Spill Is Worth 2.9 Million," *The Wall Street Journal*, September 1, 1994, p. A1; Morgan 1994).

Of course, to convince Americans that they are truly suffering from "hyperlexis," more than a few anecdotal illustrations are necessary. The public generally is reluctant to perceive problems as problems until they become crises (Bennett 1996). Accordingly, the press dutifully has discovered an "epidemic" of litigiousness (Budiansky 1995). As a consequence, America is suffering from an onslaught of mixed metaphors. Lawyers descend like a "plague of locusts" and bury the nation under an "avalanche" of lawsuits, creating a "bloodbath" for U.S. businesses and a social "epidemic of bubonic plague proportions" (Dee 1986, 23; Paul W. McCracken, "The Big Domestic Issue: Slow Growth," *The Wall Street Journal*, October 4, 1991, p. A14). For the last two decades, this crisis rhetoric has periodically resurfaced, along with the perennially popular claim that America is "the world's most litigious nation" (Leo 1995, 24).

Scholars have been debunking such assertions so often that it is startling to see how much bunk survives. Much of the media's "evidence" relies on statistical sleights of hand. Commentators point to dramatic growth in certain kinds of cases, such as product liability suits in federal courts (Dee 1986; Galanter 1986, 1996). But federal filings account for only 2 percent of American litigation. And tort claims, the lightning rod for most critics, did not increase over the past decade (Marc Galanter, "Pick a Number, Any Number," *Legal Times*, February 17, 1992, p. 26; Galanter 1996).

Moreover, experts generally agree that current litigation rates in the United States are not exceptionally high, either in comparison with prior eras or with many other Western industrial nations not known for contentiousness. Higher per capita rates of litigation occurred in previous centuries in some American jurisdictions. U.S. court filings now are in the same range as those in Canada, Australia, New Zealand, England, and Denmark (Galanter 1988; Rhode and Luban 1995; Friedman 1989).

Similar factual problems accompany the equally frequent assertion that America is awash in lawyers. Media accounts repeatedly and uncritically rely on assertions like Dan Quayle's claim that America has 70 percent of the world's attorneys. By contrast, informed estimates put the figure somewhere between a quarter and a third, which is roughly the United States's share of the world's combined gross national product (Marc Galanter, "Pick a Number, Any Number," *Legal Times*, February 17, 1992, p. 26; Galanter 1993a). Cross-cultural comparisons are also misleading because they fail to reveal the number of individuals in other countries who are not licensed members of the bar but who receive legal training and perform tasks that the United States reserves for lawyers.

Media commentators' endlessly favorable references to Japan are particularly in need of qualification. According to conventional accounts, this hypothesized haven of cooperation manages with less than 20,000 licensed lawyers, while America produces 36,000 new law graduates every year. Yet such comparisons overlook certain key facts. Many Japanese receive legal training in universities and provide legal services, but never obtain licenses to practice in court because bar exam pass rates are set at around 2 percent. Indeed, some Japanese commentators complain that their country produces too many legal advisors and that the rate is higher than in America. As one of these critics explains, Japan is experiencing "a massive diversion of younger talent into the world of law. Every year more than 38,000 youngsters graduate from law faculties in Japan as compared to 36,000 who graduate from U.S. law schools. Since the population of Japan is approximately half that of the United States, there are proportionately two times more law graduates produced in Japan" (Junjiro Tsubota, quoted in Galanter 1986, 13).

Yet to conclude that either country has too many attorneys requires more extended consideration than media sound bites supply. An informed answer would require analysis along several dimensions. Do contemporary lawyers perform socially valuable tasks in a cost-effective manner? Does the current distribution of legal services reflect public needs? What might we gain or lose with fewer lawyers and lawsuits?

On these questions, media discussion is infrequent and unsatisfying. Conventional analysis, such as it is, relies heavily on arguments by adjective or anecdote. One common strategy substitutes rhetorical flourish for factual support. The weaker the support, the stronger the adjectives. And the more prominent the source, the more widely the claims are circulated, irrespective of the evidence. The public hears endless replays of such exaggerated claims: Dan Quayle fulminating against "staggering expense and delay," George Bush denouncing procedures "torn from the pages of Kafka," and the former chair of the President's Council of Economic Advisors warning of "suffocating" effects on the economy (Quayle, quoted in David Margolick, "Address by Dan Quayle on Justice Proposals Irks Bar Association," *The New York Times*, August 14, 1991, p. A1; Paul W. McCracken, "The Big Domestic Issue: Slow Growth," *The Wall Street Journal*, October 4, 1991, p. A14; Bush 1992b).

Such vague generalities invite the bar to respond in kind. Lawyers are not shy about identifying "irresponsible" political grandstanding, "one-sided" or anecdotal media reporting, and the public misunderstandings that inevitably result. But polemical exchanges do little to correct those misperceptions or to address the media culture that encourages them (Pfander 1996).

Similar problems arise with the media's excessive reliance on arguments by anecdote. Homespun illustrations attract disproportionate journalistic attention because they play to the public interest in "human interest." The problem is not that journalists use anecdotes. So do responsible scholars. Specific illustrations often convey important information in ways that audiences are particularly likely to retain. The difficulty comes when anecdotes substitute for analysis and unrepresentative stories masquerade as reflective of broader trends. That problem is compounded by cognitive biases. Because vivid incidents are especially easy to recall, our tendency is to overestimate how frequently they occur (Saks 1992). When stories displace hard data on statistical trends, the audience can end up with highly distorted impressions.

Such distortions are all too common in an era marked by what Robert MacNeil terms "news as vaudeville"—an era where "bite sized is best" and "complexity must be avoided" (Postman 1985, 105; Bill Schmitt, "And Now, News for Scatterbrains," *Editor and Publisher*, August 17, 1996, p. 48). Because stories are easier to sell than statistics, coverage of the legal profession tends to be long on folklore and short on data.

John Stossel's 1996 ABC News Special *The Trouble with Lawyers* is a case study in the use and abuse of case studies. The program more than fulfilled its opening promise that "If you think there are too many lawyers making too much money off too many lawsuits, this program is for you" (Stossel 1996, transcript 4).

Throughout the broadcast, Stossel finessed the sticky question about what litigation rates actually are, whether they are growing, or how they compare with those in other eras or other nations. "But whatever the numbers are," he noted, "and they are hard to pin down, fear is up" (Stossel 1996, transcript 7). Because data are irrelevant and only perceptions matter, the viewer got lots of poignant illustrations of legal pathologies. First came the Arizona couple who "cooked thousands of free Thanksgiving dinners for the poor, until . . . someone got a stomach ache and threatened to sue" (Stossel 1996, transcript 7). Then followed the all-time favorite of politicians and pundits: the parents who "are afraid to coach Little League because they could get sued over a pop fly" (Stossel 1996, transcript 8; Bush 1992a).

Next came the obligatory references to seemingly unnecessary investments in product safety and unwarranted withdrawals of medically valuable products. Stossel, like other critics, was appalled that "every football helmet costs $100 more because of lawsuits" (Stossel 1996, transcript 6; Leo 1995, 24). The result, as he explained in a companion *Wall Street Journal* editorial, "is that some financially strapped schools don't have football programs. The kids play in the streets. Is that safer?" (John Stossel, "Protect Us from Legal Vultures," *The Wall Street Journal*, January 2, 1996, p. A8).

Similar questions surround the disappearance of hip replacement products and silicone breast implants. According to the ABC broadcast, these products are gone "not because they are unsafe" but because "lawyers get a few juries to send a message" (Stossel 1996, transcript 7). Apart from a perfunctory acknowledgment that some goods and services are dangerous and "some victims deserve compensation," no effort was made to weigh the gains or losses (Stossel 1996, transcript 7). Nor did anyone mention the lives saved because of helmet improvements or the factual disputes surrounding breast implants.

Instead, the broadcast shifted to safer ground: the greed of lawyers. Stossel began reasonably enough, by indicting the current tort system for its inefficiency. He even invoked some respected research, which finds that less than half of what tort defendants pay actually reaches victims; the rest goes for legal fees and court costs (Stossel 1996, transcript 8; Kakalik and Pace 1986). However, rather than discussing the complex causes of high transaction costs or the merits of alternative compensation structures, the program selectively zeroed in on a single target: greedy plaintiffs' lawyers and the contingent fee system that encourages them.

As is typical of anecdotal accounts of legal fees, Stossel relied heavily on the "some" construction (Leo 1995, 24). "What's not in doubt," Stossel gleefully asserted, "is that some lawyers are getting very rich." In just one year, "some made $10 million, $20 million, $40 million" (Stossel 1996, transcript 4). As to the logical next question, "how many exactly," or even approximately, Stossel was notably close-mouthed. The viewer heard nothing about average lawyers' incomes or about how contingent fee cases compare with hourly fee cases in terms of litigant costs and outcomes.

Instead, the broadcast produced a live exhibit, Joe Jamail, a self-proclaimed "King of Torts," who racked up $90 million in a single year. In the interview clips that ABC editors featured, Jamail was a walking advertisement for a program titled *The Trouble with Lawyers*. He came across as an arrogant, avaricious boor who "extorts" outrageous settlements just by warning an opponent that he is about to "kick your ass" (Stossel 1996, transcript 4). If the producer had wanted a thoughtful evaluation of the current tort system, Jamail was hardly adequate to the occasion. At one point Stossel asked, "How can it be a good system if most of the money [defendants pay] goes to you lawyers and not to these poor victims?" Jamail responded, "I don't know what price to put on justice" (Stossel 1996, transcript 8).

Price, however, was what especially interested Stossel. And he had plenty of other anecdotes ready at hand about overpriced lawyers.

One of his most effective vignettes relied on argument by autobiography, another time-honored technique in legal profession debates: Stossel had several "first-hand experiences" with lawyers. Unsurprisingly, none cast the profession in a favorable light, although facts omitted by the broadcast do not reflect all that well on Stossel either. One experience involved his suit against a wrestler who had slapped him in retaliation for an insulting interview comment. Stossel reportedly recovered $500,000, an amount that might appear a bit steep to someone truly concerned about litigiousness and excessive damage awards (Ken Hoffman, "Talking on the Radio and Making Some Airwaves," *Houston Chronicle*, January 3, 1996, p. 2).

This first-hand experience is not the one that got significant airtime. Instead, the broadcast highlighted a libel action against Stossel and ABC based on their exposé of unnecessary dentistry. By Stossel's account, the case turned on a relatively simple question about the accuracy of excerpts from a taped interview. But rather than just letting a jury watch the tape, the lawyers collected "thousands of documents" and spent three years "sending them back and forth." Although Stossel prevailed in court, he, and presumably any rational viewer, was disgusted by the "extravagant waste" (Stossel 1996, transcript 14–16).

Many lawyers were equally disgusted by Stossel's report, but for predictably different reasons. California State Bar President Jim Towery appeared on local television and wrote follow-up letters protesting the program's "distort[ed] reality" (Towery 1996, 6). Jamail was not exactly a representative member of the bar, Towery noted. Nor did the broadcast mention lawyers' constructive responses to the problems Stossel identified, such as use of less expensive alternative dispute-resolution techniques or pro bono contributions. "Consumers need a better understanding of their legal system," Towery concluded. "But this much ballyhooed program did little to educate in any constructive way" (Towery 1996, 9).

Well, no argument there. Yet too often, the organized bar's response does no better. When embattled lawyers meet their critics, the result is frequently a rhetorical standoff and policy stalemate. A case in point involves recent state and federal proposals to curb jury verdicts, lawyers' fees, and frivolous claims. The distortions that have emerged in an increasingly anecdotal and ad hominem debate have become news stories in themselves (Press, Carroll, and Waldman 1995, 32).

One of the nastier state skirmishes began during the early 1990s when a coalition of business groups formed East Texans Against Lawsuit Abuse. The coalition's public education initiatives included a television commercial chronicling a fictitious bank robbery. The thief, felled by tear gas in the money bags, sued the bank. "This [suit] would not have been prevented from being filed in Texas," a group leader explained (Kay Manning, "Lawyers Battle Legal Reform Effort," *Dallas Morning News*, November 8, 1992, p. A45). A spokesman for Texas Trial Lawyers offered the equally edifying response: "What [East Texans Against Lawsuit Abuse] is doing is an attack on democracy. There is nothing more democratic than a jury" (Kay Manning, "Lawyers Battle Legal Reform Effort," *Dallas Morning News,* November 8, 1992, p. A45).

Similar exchanges occurred during the 1996 campaigns over four California ballot initiatives. Three of these voter propositions were promoted by the Alliance to Revitalize California, an unusual consortium of Democratic consumer advocates, Republican politicians, and corporate executives. These voter propositions would have established no-fault auto insurance, required losing litigants in some law suits to pay their opponent's fees, and limited lawyers' contingency fees for cases that settle quickly. Opponents of these measures included the Consumer Attorneys of California (formerly the California Trial Lawyers Association), Ralph Nader, and various labor, senior citizens, and environmental organizations. A similar group of lawyers, consumers, and pension funds backed a fourth initiative that would have prohibited limits on attorneys' fees and made it easier to sue for securities fraud in California than in other states.

Press coverage of these measures was quickly eclipsed by paid media campaigns. The securities proposition alone was reportedly the most expensive ballot initiative campaign in history and cost the two sides more than $46 million (Jackson 1996, 72). Because facts about what the measures would accomplish were complex and contested, much of the media discussion focused on more entertaining issues— who was saying what about whom and who was paying for it.

This coverage of the paid coverage did little to advance debate, given how little substance emerged from the commercial messages. One typical advertisement of the Alliance to Revitalize California lambasted "fat cat" plaintiffs' lawyers living in the "lap of luxury" at the expense of taxpayers and consumers (Reuben 1996, 29).

California bar leaders denounced such "mean-spirited attacks" and then outspent their opponents three-to-one with more of the same (Towery, quoted in Hallye Jordan, "Lawyer Bashing Fuels Three Initiatives," *San Jose Mercury News*, March 21, 1996, p. A8). One commercial of the Consumer Attorneys of California featured a pack of hungry wolves with a voice-over message that "corporate wolves are hunting down contingent attorneys who protect retirees, small investors, and consumers. Under propositions 201 and 202, the corporate wolves will pay their lawyers unlimited fees and prevent Californians from fighting back against stock swindlers like Charles Keating, polluters, and manufacturers of defective products" (taped broadcast March 23, 1996; "Lawyer Lies," *The Wall Street Journal*, March 22, 1996, p. A12).

Another commercial of the Consumer Attorneys of California pictured convicted felon Charles Keating mutating into Alan Schugart, a key backer of the tort reform initiatives. The announcer noted that Mr. Schugart himself had been the subject of lawsuits and warned the viewer to "protect yourself from the next Charles Keating" ("Lawyer Lies," *The Wall Street Journal*, March 22, 1996, p. A12). Schugart, who had never been charged with any criminal offense, found the ad more than "mean-spirited." After he sued for libel, sponsors withdrew the commercial.

Such antics got plenty of unpaid airtime, but at the expense of in-depth reporting on the merits of the initiatives. Press coverage supplied a barrage of "proponents say X," "opponents say Y," but offered little analysis of their factual basis (Reynolds Holding, "Big Bucks Battle over Securities Fraud Propositions," *San Francisco Chronicle*, October 27, 1996, p. A8). Indeed, many reporters seemed disinclined to take either side seriously. The tone of some media accounts was reminiscent of a chaperon describing a fraternity food fight. The narrators seemed vaguely appalled that educated young adults were behaving this way but had little idea how it all started or what exactly to do about it. Such gaps in analysis are of particular concern in ballot initiative campaigns because voters rely almost entirely on the mass media for information about propositions (Schacter 1995).

The inadequate coverage on such issues may be partly attributable to the public's short attention span, but journalists' own self-interest also plays a role. As Lance Bennett puts it, "The news reflects what people prefer among those choices that [the media] find profitable and convenient to offer them" (Bennett 1996, 129). And these choices are all too limited.

Giving the Media What They Want

For even the most responsible journalists, various constraints of craft work against responsible journalism. Coverage of the legal profession is subject to the same pressures of time, resources, expertise, and "balance" that limit reporting on most topics. To survive in an increasingly competitive market, journalists need to match their rivals on a wide array of topics under tight deadlines and limited budgets (Benedict 1992; Bennett 1996; Peter Kann, "10 Disturbing Trends in U.S. Journalism," *Editor and Publisher*, October 9, 1994, p. 18). The typical generalist reporter often is not prepared to assess partisan claims on law-related issues. Short turnaround times prevent these journalists from contacting experts or reading relevant materials. When, as is frequently the case, the priority is getting the story out, rather than getting it right, a lot of corners get cut. As James Fallows notes, most media coverage is driven by the dynamic captured in a classic vaudeville act. A drunk searches for keys under a light post, not because that is where he lost them, but because that is where the light is (Fallows 1996).

One way that journalists cope with these constraints is to report assertions by a "newsworthy" but biased source without attempting to confirm their factual basis. For example, accounts of the California initiatives often offered unelaborated summaries of competing assertions. A typical *San Jose Mercury News* story reported, "Dan Wolf, Executive Director of Silicon Valley Citizens Against Lawsuit Abuse, claims frivolous lawsuits raise the price of consumer products and cost every Californian $1,200 a year. Sean Crowly, spokesman for Citizens' Retirement and Protection Security, responds that accounting firms 'basically bought themselves immunity in federal courts for fraud' by making large lobbying contributions and are now seeking total immunity in state courts as well" (Hallye Jordan, "New Fighting Flares in Lawsuit Wars," *San Jose Mercury News*, April 19, 1996, p. B3; Vidmar, this volume). The reader never learns where the $1,200 figure came from, whether respected researchers found it credible, and how disinterested experts evaluated the merits of the California securities initiative.

Debates about the state's no-fault-insurance proposal were equally unilluminating. A common media strategy was to report proponents' reliance on a Rand study suggesting that premiums would drop, coupled with opponents' references to contrary experience in other states. Rarely did reporters appear to have looked at the Rand study, discussed it with researchers, or talked to experts knowledgeable about state no-fault results.

Such uncritical reporting is partly responsible for the resilience of certain wildly implausible factoids. Marc Galanter's diligence in tracking down the origins of several common myths about litigiousness is instructive. For example, Dan Quayle was fond of trumpeting the estimate of the Council on Competitiveness that America spends some $300 billion annually on the direct and indirect costs of civil litigation. Prominent journalists repeatedly relied on this claim without making any apparent effort to confirm its plausibility. In fact, this figure came from *Forbes* magazine, which relied on an estimate of tort expenditures offered by commentator Peter Huber. Huber based his estimate partly on an undocumented conjecture by Robert Mallott, the chief executive officer of FMC, offered during a *Chief Executive* magazine roundtable discussion, and partly on one 1984 study of physicians' responses to malpractice liability. From this dubious foundation came Huber's generalization about all tort litigation and its extension by the Council on Competitiveness to all civil litigation (Galanter 1993a, 83–84).

Such fictionalized facts are partly responsible for widespread concerns about litigiousness. About three-quarters of surveyed Americans believe that litigation is damaging the country's economy, and about half of surveyed chief executive officers think that product liability suits have a major impact on their company's international competitiveness (Samborn 1993, 1; McGuire 1994; Galanter 1993a). Surveyed California business leaders repeatedly identify liability law as the factor most likely to hurt the state's business climate (Sullivan 1997).

It is, of course, unrealistic to expect that most journalists would have the time or stamina to track down the dubious pedigree of claims like Quayle's. But neither does it seem naive to hope that a few inquiring minds might consult with experts in the field or make passing reference to some of the systematic research on point.

Although we lack reliable estimates of the civil justice system's total cost, some informed estimates are available for the tort system.

These figures are substantially lower than Huber's and do not show a substantial effect on economic productivity (Galanter 1996; Litan 1991). For example, Robert Litan of the Brookings Institution estimates that tort liability could represent no more than 2 percent of the total cost of U.S. goods and services. As he notes, it is "highly unlikely" that liability expenditures on that order materially affect the competitiveness of American products (Litan 1991). So too, a Conference Board survey of risk managers from some 200 major corporations found that tort liability improved product safety and warning efforts without adversely affecting larger economic indicators such as gross revenues or market share (Weber 1987).

Such studies are not, to be sure, what journalists will stumble across in airport bookstores. But this kind of research is sufficiently well known among experts in the field to make it onto a careful journalist's radar screen. What prevents that from occurring is a media culture willing to settle for less.

Facts fall by the wayside even in newsrooms with the time and resources to do better. For example, John Leo, in a 1995 column in *U.S. News and World Report*, presents as an uncontested fact the claim by an obstetricians' association that more than 12 percent of New York doctors "have stopped delivering babies because of the cost of litigation" (Leo 1995, 24). Yet a review of malpractice research by the federal government's Office of Technology Assessment around the same time found no relation between increases in insurance premiums and withdrawal from obstetrics practice in New York (U.S. Office of Technology Assessment 1994).

Another notorious example of unnecessary shortcuts involves a *60 Minutes* exposé of an ostensibly outrageous award in an ostensibly frivolous case. After a ladder slipped while placed in horse manure, the injured plaintiff recovered $300,000, reportedly because the manufacturer had failed to warn about the perils of placing its product in such locations. This slip and fall had comic potential too good to be true. Or so editors might have discovered if anyone had bothered to look at the trial record. In fact, the ladder was defective, and the victim's fracture and cracked vertebrae caused permanent injury. When questioned about the failure to check the facts, news anchor Harry Reasoner denied the need to do so. After all, he noted, "we were only trying to present [this defendant's] perspective" (Reasoner, quoted in Brill and Lyons 1986, 1, 12).

Yet when journalists simplify a story to simplify their own investigation, they often miss what the real story should be. Coverage of bar disciplinary actions reveals countless missed opportunities. A typical illustration is a 1996 article in the *Phoenix New Times*. Under the headline, "The Living Lawyer Joke," the story began with a promising question: What do you call someone who allegedly forges signatures, takes clients for hundreds of thousands of dollars, lies to police, and helps burn down a building in an insurance scam? [Answer] Until recently, an attorney in good standing." The article recounted how "since 1989 [Ted] Segal's legal career has been accompanied by a litany of serious charges" but only in 1996 did the bar attempt to suspend his license (Terry Greene Sterling, "The Living Lawyer Joke," *Phoenix New Times*, September 26, 1996). Disciplinary officials declined to explain their delay because secrecy rules prevented such comments.

The article noted in passing that these same rules prevent anyone from learning of complaints against lawyers unless the bar takes public action and that proposals to end the secrecy policy were pending and open to public comment. This would have been an ideal occasion for a deeper probe into the problems with bar disciplinary processes and confidentiality rules. Information about where to file public comments would also have been useful. Instead, the reader got a 2,700-word blow-by-blow account of Segal's misdeeds, with no analysis of how such repeated abuses might be prevented.

A similar missed opportunity occurred in a *Portland Press Herald* report from around the same time. The story concerned a lawyer convicted of seven misdemeanors between 1992 and 1996, including criminal assault, trespass, and domestic violence (Andrew D. Russell, "Lawyer Faces Tampering Charge," *Portland Press Herald*, June 29, 1996, p. B1). When the lawyer allegedly tried to bribe his former girlfriend to drop one of the assault charges, the local district attorney notified the bar. A spokesman for its disciplinary board, citing confidentiality rules, refused to indicate whether an investigation was pending. He did, however, confirm that there was no record of prior discipline against the attorney and that "not all minor crimes are considered unethical conduct" (Foster 1996, quoted in Andrew D. Russell, "Lawyer Faces Tampering Charge," *Portland Press Herald*, June 29, 1996, p. B1). Again, this case could have been the springboard for broader questions about the adequacy of disciplinary processes, the crimes that should result in bar sanctions, and the role of secrecy procedures in preventing public accountability.

On the infrequent occasions when journalists have seized such opportunities, much of the coverage has been excellent. A series in the *San Francisco Examiner* during the mid-1980s involved more than 1,000 interviews and a review of 20,000 pages of documents concerning bar disciplinary processes. It triggered state legislative hearings and a major overhaul of the disciplinary system (Connie Kang and James Finefrock, "The Brotherhood: Justice for Lawyers," *San Francisco Examiner*, March 24–29, 1985). Yet all too often, the absence of any sustained media interest has undermined the influence of even the best reports. A trilogy of 1996 articles from the *Seattle Times* suggests the problem. The first in the series, a front-page feature, offered a promising title and an equally promising focus: "Lawyers Who Flouted Ethics Rules Escape Reprimand—Bar Association Inundated with Complaints, Some of Them Languish for Years" (Barbara Serrano, "Lawyers Who Flouted Ethics Rules Escape Reprimand," *Seattle Times*, March 31, 1996, p. A1). This story's centerpiece was a Seattle firm that, according to a former associate, committed repeated billing fraud by altering time records. Four years after the associate's well-documented complaint to disciplinary authorities, they still had not taken any action. The article then detailed the understaffing and mismanagement that were undermining the bar's enforcement efforts.

Yet the paper's follow-up articles on the case, buried in the second section, failed to pursue those themes. One short piece discussed a pending hearing. Another reported that a disciplinary board had rejected as too lenient the bar's proposed thirty-day suspension for one of the partners responsible for fraudulent bills (Barbara Serrano, "Bar Board Rejects 'Lenient' Penalty for Overbilling," *Seattle Times*, May 24, 1996, p. B6; Barbara Serrano, "Lawyers' Billing May Bring Sanctions," *Seattle Times*, August 9, 1996, p. B1). Both articles mentioned lengthy delays in enforcement processes, but only in passing. Neither discussed what efforts were or were not under way to correct the backlog, or whether such delays and inadequate sanctions were representative of broader problems.

Reporters who want to provide more informed coverage of law-related issues are constrained not just by time and resources but also by journalistic principles of fairness. Under conventional views, such principles require reporters to "gather as much information as they can while giving both sides equal time to register their comments and interpretations" (Bennett 1996, 143). Yet although presenting alternative views clearly serves some useful purposes, it by no means ensures adequate coverage and occasionally works against it. One obvious problem arises when journalists attempt to reduce complex issues to simple pro and con positions. Disproportionate airtime often goes to partisans at opposite poles of debate. Those with more complicated, nuanced positions drop by the wayside. Too much knowledge is a dangerous thing in mass media circles; commentary that resists simplistic sound bites frequently ends up on cutting room floors.

A related problem is that equal time does not necessarily yield equal information or an equal opportunity to present it. Much depends on the capabilities of the speakers and the familiarity of their positions. New ideas take more effort to communicate intelligibly than conventional clichés or polemical potshots (Bennett 1996). Balanced positions do not necessarily make for balanced messages if the reporter declines to fill in gaps or to add any critical analysis. Yet many journalists are reluctant to abandon a stance of apparent even-handedness, however misleading. Not only does it conform to accepted ethical standards of "objectivity," it is least likely to cause offense and to jeopardize circulation levels (Baker 1994). The paradox of current fairness norms is that the news can be biased "not in spite of, but precisely because of, the professional journalism standards intended to prevent bias" (Bennett 1996, 143).

The most serious distortions occur when the media offers a facade of fairness to mask what is essentially one-sided reporting. This approach, often promoted as "hard-hitting" investigative journalism, provides equal time for warring camps. But some participants are more equal than others. This was, of course, apparent in Stossel's ABC broadcast, which pitted Joe Jamiel against a Yale University law professor, John Langbein, who had the modest advantage of knowing what he was talking about.

Another broadcast as skewed as Stossel's was one I can recall from personal experience. In 1983, I was an assistant professor toiling on what was then an obscure issue, the unauthorized practice of law. My interest, which began at Yale University under Stanton Wheeler's guidance, had resulted in two extended empirical studies of the bar's efforts to police its own monopoly. In essence, these articles had concluded that lawyers' attempts to preempt their nonlawyer competitors often served the profession's interests at the expense of the public's. Although this conclusion had yet to become household knowledge, it had somehow come to the attention of *60 Minutes* researchers. They were preparing a story on the Florida bar's success in shutting down a divorce form preparation service. Its owner, Rosemary Furman, was a former legal secretary who had become something of a local folk hero. To many consumers, she was providing reasonably competent services at a fraction of the prices charged by lawyers. It was clear from my conversations with *60 Minutes* staff what role they had in mind for me. I was to claim that bar enforcement efforts were motivated solely by greed and that I had the data to prove it.

My view then—and now—was that money was a large part of the story, but that the victims and villains were less sharply drawn than the broadcast seemed prepared to acknowledge. Not surprisingly my carefully qualified interview with Mike Wallace did not survive the cut. Nor, apparently, did other interviews that offered a plausible factual basis for some unauthorized practice enforcement (William Cotterell, "Florida Bar, Wounded by Furman Case, Want to Drop Illegal Law Practice." *UPI State and Regional Wires*, December 29, 1984). Rather, "balance" was achieved via a representative of the Florida bar, who sounded like central casting's vision of greed personified.

The result of this bad press for the bar was not all bad. The issue got some national attention, Furman got a governor's pardon, and Florida citizens eventually got a simplified process for uncontested divorces (William Cotterell, "Florida Bar, Wounded by Furman Case, Want to Drop Illegal Law Practice." *UPI State and Regional Wires*, December 29, 1984; Rhode and Luban 1992; Rhode 1990).

But the program also missed an opportunity to educate the public, including lawyers, about the full range of consumer interests at issue and the merits of alternative policies for nonlawyer practice. Because gestures toward balance were such a sham, bar leaders could dismiss the broadcast as "wholly one-sided, biased, and totally misleading" (William Cotterell, "Florida Bar, Wounded by Furman Case, Want to Drop Illegal Law Practice." *UPI State and Regional Wires*, December 29, 1984). They then hired their own public relations consultant and developed a barrage of responses that were equally one-sided and misleading. It was not a recipe for informed policymaking, and recent debates on the issue have offered more of the same (Rhode 1996).

Giving the Public What It Needs

What ails the truth is that it is mainly uncomfortable and often dull. The human mind seeks something more amusing and caressing. [H. L. Mencken quoted in Cross 1983, 49]

Laments about the news are, of course, nothing new. But their relevance should not be discounted, particularly on issues involving the legal profession. Misleading media coverage distorts decisions across a wide range of litigation, business, and policymaking contexts.

Part of the problem begins with the media's disproportionate coverage of certain kinds of cases. Recent surveys find that press accounts significantly overrepresent product liability and medical malpractice litigation (Garber 1996). Disproportionate attention also focuses on successful claims and large awards of punitive damages. One study concluded that plaintiffs' awards were four to five times larger in cases profiled in the media than in actual trials (Bailis and MacCoun 1996).

This skewed emphasis reflects not only public preferences but also biases in journalists' conventional sources. Plaintiffs' lawyers have an obvious interest in publicizing large victories rather than humiliating losses. As a result, victories are overrepresented in national jury verdict publications and press releases that rely on attorney reports (Galanter 1993b, 85). Not only are large tort victories more often reported, they also are more readily recalled than cases with more typical facts. As noted earlier, when events are especially vivid, people tend to overestimate their frequency (Tversky and Kahneman 1974, 1973).

The combined effect of selective reporting and selective recall leads to misperceptions of the likelihood of large verdicts, particularly in tort contexts. Even relatively well-informed individuals, including doctors, lawyers, legislators, and insurance adjusters, overestimate the frequency of litigation, the likelihood of plaintiffs' verdicts, and the size of judicial awards (Songer 1988; Galanter 1993b).

In fact, punitive damages are quite infrequent. Rarer still are the "staggering" awards in tort and discrimination cases that invite so much media criticism (Sullivan 1997, 43). Plaintiffs recover punitive

damages in only 2 to 3 percent of product liability and medical malpractice cases, a fact that commentators almost never mention (Nader
and Smith 1996; Moller 1996; Andrew Blum, "Study Finds Punitives
Are Small, Rare." *National Law Journal*, July 1, 1996, p. A6). Such
damages are less common in these contexts than in commercial litigation, which attracts no comparable concern among leading critics.

Moreover, tort awards are by no means as arbitrary and unpredictable as media commentators often contend. The typical amount
is modest and strongly correlated with the level of compensatory
damages (Eisenberg et al. 1997; Galanter 1996). Contrary to widespread assumptions, jury decisions are not biased against corporations with deep pockets. Nor are these verdicts out of line with the
judgments of other decisionmakers, such as judges and physicians
who evaluate the same facts (Galanter 1996).

Over time, the press and public's inflated assessments of liability
risks can significantly distort litigation outcomes. Mock juror studies
indicate that erroneous beliefs about the frequency of large verdicts
affect the damages that people are willing to grant (Greene,
Goodman, and Loftus 1991). Ironically enough, although most individuals agree that the press tends to exaggerate awards, they continue to rely on media accounts in concluding that awards are too
high (Greene, Goodman, and Loftus 1991). A belief that runaway
verdicts are common can also skew behavior by lawyers and litigants.
A few highly publicized recoveries, however aberrant, spawn unap-
pealing offspring. Particularly when media profiles are as distorted as
in the McDonald's case, they have inspired some ludicrous claims. It
is hard to work up much sympathy for the customers who recently
sought $5 million dollars for injuries inflicted by a McDonald's em-
ployee, who allegedly insulted them and doused them with mustard
("Adding Condiment to Injury" 1996; Webb 1995).

Media accounts that exaggerate liability risks affect potential defendants as well as plaintiffs. Concerns about frivolous litigation may
contribute to defensive medicine and withdrawal of goods and services. However, the causal relationships are difficult to gauge, and
the adverse effects are frequently exaggerated. Some defensive medicine is not particularly expensive or self-evidently excessive.
Examples include greater use of informed consent forms, more detailed explanations to patients, and more frequent consultations with
other doctors (Conlin 1993). Although other measures are more

costly, the U.S. Office of Technology Assessment has estimated that "a relatively small proportion of all diagnostic procedures—certainly less than 8 percent overall—is performed primarily due to conscious concern about malpractice liability risk" (U.S. Office of Technology Assessment 1994, 74). Yet whatever the exact magnitude of unnecessary procedures, everyone would benefit if physicians had more realistic perceptions of liability exposure (Galanter 1993b; Bailis and MacCoun 1996; Conlin 1993, 30).

Reliable data concerning product withdrawal are even harder to obtain. Nor is the public well served by one-sided polemics like the editorial in the *Wall Street Journal* aptly titled "Lawyers May Kill My Daughter." It lambastes the potential withdrawal of silicone products following breast implant litigation but fails to acknowledge the uncertainties about safety that prompted such decisions (Linda Ranson, "Lawyers May Kill My Daughter," *The Wall Street Journal*, March 29, 1996, p. A16). In one of the few studies on point, almost half of chief executive officers reported that they had discontinued product lines because of liability concerns (Galanter 1993b). Whether those reports are accurate and whether they represent reasonable concessions to safety are open to question. What is not in dispute is the desirability of accurate risk assessments and the inadequate factual basis for many current business decisions about tort liability (Galanter 1993b; Saks 1992; Thompson 1997).

Similar inadequacies confront policymakers. Most recent proposals for litigation reform rest on premises encouraged by media accounts: that people sue too often and win too much, that frivolous claims are clogging the courts, and that damage awards are out of control. Such assumptions underpin proposed legislation that would cap damages and require losing litigants to pay their opponents' legal costs (U.S. Congress 1995a, 1995b, 1995c). Yet virtually all systematic research makes clear that the most pervasive problem with the American tort system is undercompensation, not overcompensation, of victims. And recent reform proposals would compound that injustice.

To begin with, a large proportion of individuals who have legitimate claims never file suit because they lack adequate information or legal resources. For example, Rand researchers have found that only 2 to 3 percent of accident victims sue (Hensler et al. 1991). In another study of some 30,000 New York hospital records, only about 12 percent of patients who sustained injuries from negligent medical care brought malpractice actions, and only half of those received compensation (Harvard Medical Practice Study 1990; Saks 1992; Jost 1993; Abel 1987). Among those who do file claims, the most seriously injured victims are grossly undercompensated, while those with less severe injuries and modest economic losses are sometimes overcompensated. For example, one study of Florida medical malpractice cases found that, overall, plaintiffs recovered just over half their costs. Those with the least serious injuries received three times their estimated losses, while some of the most seriously injured parties received only a third (Sloan and van Wert 1991). Similar patterns hold for automobile and airline accident victims (Galanter 1996). And in cases attracting the most adverse media comment—those involving large product liability awards—surveyed plaintiffs with claims higher than $1 million recovered only a small fraction of their losses (Viscusi 1989; Saks 1992; Vidmar, this volume).

The media's failure to focus on undercompensation of victims distorts policy discussion. Limiting damages would strike hardest at those with the greatest losses, who do not receive excessive remedies under the current system. Requiring unsuccessful litigants to pay their adversaries' legal fees might reduce overcompensation, but at the cost of discouraging meritorious as well as frivolous claims. Those most likely to suffer would not be corporations that can absorb risks of dubious proceedings as a tax deductible business expense. The real losers would be people of moderate means, including those with strong claims but no ability to risk substantial liability to their opponents (Kritzer 1995; Rowe 1995).

Media commentators who advocate fee-shifting initiatives often fail to discuss this problem. Instead, they present "loser-pay" systems as the norm for other Western industrialized nations (Stossel 1996, transcript 24). But what commentators almost never acknowledge is that those countries typically have more comprehensive legal assistance, social welfare, and medical insurance programs. Such programs cushion the deterrent effects of fee shifting by reducing reliance on the tort system (Pfenningstorf and Gifford 1991; Kagan 1994; Kritzer 1995).

Similar inadequacies arise in most media coverage of lawyer regulation. Commentators generally are long on diagnosis of the problem and extremely short on solutions. Sweeping reforms are summarily prescribed with no discussion of their likely adverse effects.

Research on how such proposed alternatives work in practice rarely makes an appearance.

For example, press accounts advocating fee-shifting policies almost never acknowledge Florida's unsuccessful experience. After five years, the state abolished its loser-pays system in medical malpractice cases. Although the threat of additional legal fees did somewhat reduce the number of malpractice cases filed, it also increased the number that went to trial. Plaintiffs fought harder because the stakes were higher. And because a significant number of losing plaintiffs had insufficient assets to pay opponents' costs, defendants' overall expenses were higher. Whether comparable results would occur in other litigation contexts or whether they would be avoidable under more carefully designed systems are questions subject to debate. But that debate is too often missing in press accounts, and it is essential for rational policy choices (compare Stossel 1996, transcript 24, with Kritzer 1995; Rowe 1995; Snyder and Hughes 1990).

Responsibility for such gaps in media coverage does not lie solely with the media. We lack adequate data on many issues that should be central to our reform agenda (Saks 1992; Thompson 1997; Galanter 1993b). As Law Professor Peter Shuck also notes, the legal profession "has failed to educate the public about the complexity of the systems in which we live. We have a number of different goals . . . and we can't realize all our ideals at the same time or to the same extent" (quoted in Samborn 1995, 73). Tinkering with just one aspect of a complex regulatory structure can create as many difficulties as it solves. Yet the research community has made far too little effort to communicate the complexity of the tradeoffs involved.

For many scholars, outreach to the press is an unwelcome add-on to life. Educating reporters can be a time-consuming and sometimes thankless enterprise. Reporters frequently call at inconvenient times, get our comments wrong, or, worse still, fail to mention them at all. Writing our own editorials or letters to the editor does not help our tenure files and is viewed as faintly déclassé by many colleagues. Although most of us might enjoy the illusions of influence that sometimes accompany media recognition, few of us are willing to undertake the awkward self-promotion that such a status requires. Even when a rare opportunity for glory comes unsolicited, it often carries significant limitations. For example, commentators on the O. J. Simpson trial frequently received introductions such as, "in the ten seconds remaining, what does [this] acquittal . . . tell us about justice?" (Levenson 1997).

There are no simple solutions to any of this. Given the prevailing incentive structures for both researchers and reporters, they seem destined to talk past each other much of the time. But at least some improvement at the margins seems possible.

One strategy is to make the press a more sophisticated consumer of claims about the legal system and the legal profession. We could support more short courses or graduate programs for journalists in law schools, as well as more guest lectures or classes on law and social research methods for students in journalism schools. Systematic efforts to monitor and correct press oversights also would help. Groups like Fairness and Accuracy in Reporting have made a difference by publicizing examples of biased coverage. Journalists need more institutions that review coverage of the legal profession, that demand critical scrutiny of partisan reports, and that encourage greater use of independent experts.

A related strategy is to make lawyers and legal academics more sophisticated participants in media discussions. Presenting research in ways that are intelligible and interesting to the general public is an acquired skill and one that too few of us have absorbed by osmosis (Levy and Robinson 1986). It would, of course, aid the communication effort if our profession had more reliable research to communicate. Our knowledge base is embarrassingly thin on many issues involving regulation of lawyers and the performance of the civil justice system (Galanter et al. 1994, 185, 229–30).

That will change only if we do more to support the kind of research that this volume honors. "People may expect too much of journalism," claims commentator Lewis Lapham. "Not only do they expect it to be entertaining, they expect it to be true" (quoted in Bennett 1996, 117). My expectations are more modest. I do not believe that there is some unmediated Truth out there waiting to be captured. But I do believe that some accounts are closer to ascertainable facts than others. And just as I expect the media to pay attention to credible research, I expect researchers to do more to make that possible.

References

Abel, Richard L. 1987. "The Real Tort Crisis: Too Few Claims." *Ohio State Law Journal* 48(2): 443.

"Adding Condiment to Injury." 1996. *California Lawyer* 16(December): 29.

Bailis, Daniel S., and Robert J. MacCoun. 1996. "Estimating Liability Risks with the Media as Your Guide: A Content Analysis of Media Coverage of Tort Litigation." *Law and Human Behavior* 20(4): 419, 426.

Baker, C. Edwin. 1994. *Advertising and a Democratic Press*. Princeton, N.J.: Princeton University Press.

Benedict, Helen. 1992. *Virgin or Vamp*. New York: Oxford University Press.

Bennett, W. Lance. 1996. *News: The Politics of Illusion*. 3d ed. New York: Longman.

Brill, Steven, and James Lyons. 1986. "The Not-So-Simple Crisis." *American Lawyer* (May): 1, 12.

Bryan, Penelope Eileen. 1993. "Toward Deconstructing the Deconstruction of Law and Lawyers." *Denver University Law Review* 71(1): 161, 165.

Budiansky, Stephen. 1995. "How Lawyers Abuse the Law." *U.S. News and World Report*, January 30, 1995, pp. 50, 56.

Bush, George. 1992a. "Acceptance Speech at the 1992 Republican National Convention." Quoted in *Tasseled Loafers. Report from the Institute for Philosophy and Public Policy*, edited by David Luban. Institute for Philosophy and Public Policy. College Park, Md.: Institute for Philosophy and Public Policy.

———. 1992b. "Remarks to the American Business Conference." *Washington D.C. Federal News Service*, April 7, 1992.

Conlin, Roxanne Barton. 1993. "Doctors' Liability Considered." *National Law Journal*, August 2, 1993, pp. 23, 30.

Cramton, Roger. 1996. "What Do Lawyer Jokes Tell Us about Lawyers and Lawyering." *Cornell Law Forum*, July 7, 1996.

Cross, Donna Woolfolk. 1983. *MediaSpeak*. New York: Coward–McCann.

Dee, Robert. 1986. "Blood Bath." *Enterprise* 10(March/April): 23.

Edelman, Murray. 1988. *Constructing the Political Spectacle*. Chicago: University of Chicago Press.

Eisenberg, Theodore, John Goerdt, Brian Ostrom, David Rothman, and Martin T. Wells. 1997. "The Predictability of Punitive Damages." *Journal of Legal Studies* 26: 623.

Epstein, Deborah. 1996. "Can a Dumb Ass Woman Achieve Equality in the Workplace? Running the Gauntlet of Hostile Environment Harassing Speech." *Georgetown Law Journal* 84(3): 399, 408.

Fallows, James. 1996. *Breaking the News*. New York: Pantheon.

Fiske, John. 1987. *Television Culture*. New York: Methuen.

———. 1994. *Media Matters: Everyday Culture and Political Change*. Minneapolis: University of Minnesota Press.

Foster, John P. 1996. Quoted in Russell, "Lawyer Faces Tampering Charge." *Portland Press Herald*, June 29, 1996, p. B1.

Friedman, Lawrence M. 1978. "Access to Justice: Social and Historical Context." In *Access to Justice*, vol. 2, edited by Mauro Cappelletti and John Weisner. Milan: Giuffee.

————. 1989. "Litigation and Society." *Annual Review of Sociology* 15(1): 17.

Galanter, Marc. 1983. "Reading the Landscape of Disputes: What We Know and Don't Know (and Think We Know) about Our Allegedly Contentious and Litigious Society." *UCLA Law Review* 31(4): 56, note 238.

————. 1986. "The Day after the Litigation Explosion." *Maryland Law Review* 46(1): 3.

————. 1988. "The Life and Times of the Big Six: Or the Federal Courts Since the Good Old Days." *Wisconsin Law Review* 1988(6): 921–54.

————. 1993a. "News from Nowhere: The Debased Debate on Civil Justice." *Denver University Law Review* 71(1): 77–103.

————. 1993b. "The Regulatory Function of the Civil Jury." In *Verdict: Assessing the Civil Jury System,* edited by Robert E. Litan. Washington, D.C.: Brookings Institution.

————. 1994. "Predators and Parasites: Lawyer-Bashing and Civil Justice." *Georgia Law Review* 28(3): 633.

————. 1996. "Real World Torts: An Antidote to Anecdote." *Maryland Law Review* 55(4): 1093–160.

————. Forthcoming. *The Media as a Legal Institution.* Unpublished manuscript. Madison, Wisc.

Galanter, Marc, Bryant Garth, Deborah Hensler, and Frances Kahn Zemans. 1994. "Viewpoint: How to Improve Civil Justice Policy." *Judicature* 77(January/February): 185, 229–30.

Gans, Herbert. 1979. *Deciding What's News: A Study of CBS Evening News, NBC Nightly News, Newsweek, and Time.* New York: Pantheon.

Garber, Steven. 1996. "Punitive Damages and Business Decision Making: A Tale of Two Industries." Paper presented to the National Conference on the Future of Punitive Damages, Madison, Wisc. (October 25–27, 1996).

Garst, Karen. 1996. "Reporting on Surveys, Part II." *Oregon State Bar Bulletin* 57(December): 39.

Greene, Edith, Jane Goodman, and Elizabeth F. Loftus. 1991. "Jurors' Attitudes about Civil Litigation and the Size of Damage Awards." *American University Law Review* 40(2): 805–20.

Hall, Stuart. 1977. "Culture, Media, and the 'Ideological Effect.' " In *Mass Communication and Society,* edited by James Curran, Michael Gurevitch, and Janet Woolacott. London: Edward Arnold.

Hans, Valerie P. 1990. "Law and the Media: An Overview and Introduction." *Law and Human Behavior* 14(5): 399–407.

Harvard Medical Practice Study. 1990. "Patients, Doctors, and Lawyers: Medical Injury, Malpractice Litigation, and Patient Compensation in New York: The Report of the Harvard Medical Practice Study to the State of New York." Report commissioned by the Department of Health of New York. Cambridge, Mass.: President and Fellows of Harvard College.

Hensler, Deborah R., M. S. Marquis, A. F. Abrahmse, S. H. Berry, P. A. Ebner, E. Lewis, E. A. Lind, R. J. MacCoun, W.G. Manning, J. A. Rogowski,

M. E. Vaiana. 1991. *Compensation for Accidental Injuries in the United States.* Santa Monica, Calif.: Rand Corporation Institute for Civil Justice.

Jackson, David S. 1996. "Litigation Valley." *Time*, November 4, 1996, p.72.

Jost, Kenneth. 1993. "Still Warring over Medical Malpractice: Time for Something Better." *American Bar Association Journal* 79(May): 68.

Kagan, Robert A. 1994. "Do Lawyers Cause Adversarial Legalism? A Preliminary Inquiry." *Law and Social Inquiry* 19(1): 1–62.

Kakalik, James S., and Nicholas M. Pace. 1986. *Costs and Compensation Paid in Tort Litigation.* Santa Monica, Calif.: Rand Corporation Institute for Civil Justice.

Kritzer, Herbert M. 1995. Prepared statement, Hearings before the Subcommittee on Courts and Intellectual Property of the Committee on the Judiciary, House of Representatives, 104th cong, 1st sess, February 6, 1995.

Leo, John. 1993. "An Empty Ruling on Harassment." *U.S. News and World Report*, November 29, 1993, p. 20.

———. 1995. "The World's Most Litigious Nation." *U.S. News and World Report*, May 22, 1995, p. 24.

Levenson, Laurie L. 1997. "TV, or not TV." *California Lawyer* 17(July): 96.

Levy, Mark R., and John P. Robinson. 1986. "The 'Huh?' Factor: Untangling TV News; TV Viewers Miss the Point of Most Major Stories." *Columbia Journalism Review* July/August: 48.

Litan, Robert E. 1991. "The Liability Explosion and American Trade Performance: Myths and Realities." In *Tort Law and the Public Interest: Competition, Innovation, and Consumer Welfare*, edited by Peter H. Schuck. New York: Norton.

Luban, David, ed. 1992. *Tasseled Loafers.* Report from the Institute for Philosophy and Public Policy (summer/fall). College Park, Md.: Institute for Philosophy and Public Policy.

McConnell, Mitch. 1986. *Congressional Record* S948–49. Daily edition, February 4, 1986.

McGuire, Patrick E. 1994. *The Impact of Product Liability.* Report 908. New York: Conference Board.

McMenamin, Brigid. 1997. "Un-Natural Justice." *Forbes*, May 5, 1997, p. 123.

Moller, Erik. 1996. *Trends in Civil Jury Verdicts Since 1985.* Santa Monica, Calif.: Rand Corporation Institute for Civil Justice.

Morgan, S. Reed. 1994. Letter to the editor: Verdict Against McDonald's Is Fully Justified, *National Law Journal*, October 24, 1994, p. A20.

Nader, Ralph, and Wesley J. Smith. 1996. *No Contest: Corporate Lawyers and the Perversion of Justice in America.* New York: Random House.

Paletz, David L., and Robert M. Entman. 1981. *Media Power Politics.* New York: Free Press.

Pfander, James E. 1996. "Allerton House 1996: Measuring the Tension between Lawyers and the Press." *Illinois Bar Journal* 84(10): 576–77.

Pfenningstorf, Werner, and Donald G. Gifford. 1991. *A Comparative Study of Liability Law and Compensation Schemes in Ten Countries and the United States,* edited by Donald G. Gifford and William M. Richman. Oak Brook, Ill.: Insurance Research Council.

Postman, Neil. 1985. *Amusing Ourselves to Death.* New York: Penguin.

Press, Aric, Ginny Carroll, and Steven Waldman. 1995. "Are Lawyers Burning America?" *Newsweek,* March 20, 1995, p. 32.

Price, Vincent. 1992. *Public Opinion.* Newbury Park, Calif.: Sage Publications.

Qualter, Terence H. 1989. "The Role of the Mass Media in Limiting the Public Agenda." In *Manipulating Public Opinion: Essays in Public Opinion as a Dependent Variable,* edited by Michael Margolis and Gary A. Mauser. Pacific Grove, Calif.: Brooks/Cole Publishing Co.

Quayle, Dan. 1994. *Standing Firm: A Vice Presidential Memoir.* New York: Harper Collins Publishers.

Reeves, Jimmie L., and Richard Campbell. 1994. *Cracked Coverage: Television News, The Anti-Cocaine Crusade, and the Reagan Legacy.* Durham, N.C.: Duke University Press.

Reuben, Richard C. 1996. "Fee Caps: An Issue That Won't Go Away." *American Bar Association Journal* 82(May): 29.

Rhode, Deborah L. 1986. "The Rhetoric of Professional Reform." *Maryland Law Review* 45(2): 274–77.

———. 1990. "The Delivery of Legal Services by Non-Lawyers." *Georgetown Journal of Legal Ethics* 4(2): 209–33.

———. 1996. "Professionalism in Perspective: Alternative Approaches to Non-Lawyer Practice." *New York University Review of Law and Social Change* 23(3): 101.

———. 1997. *Speaking of Sex.* Cambridge, Mass.: Harvard University Press.

———. 1998. "Too Much Law/Too Little Justice: Too Much Rhetoric/Too Little Reform." *Georgetown Journal of Legal Ethics.*

Rhode, Deborah L., and David Luban. 1992. *Legal Ethics.* 1st ed. New York: Foundation Press.

———. 1995. *Legal Ethics.* 2d ed. New York: Foundation Press.

Rowe, Thomas D. 1995. Prepared statement, Hearings before the Subcommittee on Courts and Intellectual Property of the Committee on the Judiciary, House of Representatives, 104th cong, 1st sess, February 6, 1995.

Saks, Michael J. 1992. "Do We Really Know Anything about the Behavior of the Tort Litigation System—and Why Not?" *University of Pennsylvania Law Review* 140(4): 1147, 1161.

Samborn, Hope Viner. 1995. "Public Discontent: The Debate Goes Beyond Tort Law: It's about Lawyers." *American Bar Association Journal* 81(August): 70, 73.

Samborn, Randall. 1993. "Anti-Lawyer Attitude Up." *National Law Journal,* August 9, 1993, p. 1.

Schacter, Jane S. 1995. "The Pursuit of 'Popular Intent': Interpretive Dilemmas in Direct Democracy." *Yale Law Journal* 105(1): 107–76.

Segrave, Kerry. 1994. *The Sexual Harassment of Women in the Workplace, 1600–1993.* Jefferson, N.C.: McFarland.

Shaw, Donald L., and Sharman E. Marlin. 1992. "The Function of Mass Media Agenda Setting." *Journalism Quarterly* 69: 902.

Sloan, Frank A., and Stephen S. van Wert. 1991. "Cost and Compensation of Injuries in Medical Malpractice." *Law and Contemporary Problems* 54(1, 2): 131–68.

Snyder, Edward A., and James W. Hughes. 1990. "The English Rule in Allocating Legal Costs: Evidence Confronts Theory." *Journal of Law, Economics, and Organization* 6: 345, 362.

Songer, Donald R. 1988. "Tort Reform in South Carolina: The Effect of Empirical Research on Elite Perceptions Concerning Jury Verdicts." *South Carolina Law Review* 39(3): 585.

Stossel, John. 1996. *The Trouble with Lawyers.* ABC News Special, January 2, 1996.

Sullivan, John. 1997. "Ridiculous Unjustified Suits Are Bringing Down State's Economy." *San Jose and Silicon Valley Business Journal* 15(2, May 12–18): 43.

Thompson, Mark. 1997. "Letting the Air Out of Tort Reform." *American Bar Association Journal* 83(May): 68–69.

Towery, James E. 1996. "State Bar President Chastises ABC News." *California Bar Journal* (February): 6.

Tversky, Amos, and Daniel Kahneman. "Availability: A Heuristic for Judging Frequency and Probability." *Cognitive Psychology* 5(2): 207–32.

———. 1973. 1974. "Judgment under Uncertainty: Heuristics and Biases." *Science* 185: 1124.

U.S. Congress. 1995a. 104th session. The Attorney Accountability Act, H. R. 988.

———. 1995b. 104th session. The Common Sense Legal Reform Act, H. R. 10.

———. 1995c. 104th session. The Lawsuit Reform Act of 1995, S. 300.

U.S. Office of Technology Assessment. 1994. *Defensive Medicine and Medical Malpractice* 103(July): 56, 71.

Viscusi, W. Kip. 1989. "Toward a Diminished Role for Tort Liability: Social Insurance, Government Regulation, and Contemporary Risks to Health and Safety." *Yale Journal on Regulation* 6(1): 65–107.

Webb, Cindy. 1995. "Boiling Mad." *Business Week,* August 21, 1995, p. 32.

Weber, Nathan. 1987. *Product Liability: The Corporate Response.* Report 893. New York: The Conference Board.

Chapter 5

Maps, Gaps, Sociolegal Scholarship, and the Tort Reform Debate

Neil Vidmar

This chapter is about mapping the tort system and a body of empirical knowledge that has only developed over the past dozen years. Stan Wheeler was among the first to draw attention to the need for systematic information if we are to understand the legal system and develop rational policies rather than rely on anecdotes and intuition. In the early 1970s, Wheeler spelled out the concept of legal indicators and proposed collecting standardized data on variables such as litigation filing patterns, disposition patterns, legal manpower resources, and public knowledge and attitudes about the legal system (Wheeler 1971; see also Hensler 1994). He was slightly ahead of his time, but he inspired many scholars who are today contributing to his basic ideas. This leads to a second historical note.

Almost a decade after Austin Sarat and I shared an office during our 1973 to 1974 academic year as Russell Sage Fellows under Wheeler's mentoring, Sarat wrote an article criticizing the failure of sociolegal research to have an impact on legal policy (Sarat 1985). Risking the hazard of oversimplifying, let me summarize the essence of his thesis.

Sarat asserted that the bulk of sociolegal research was driven by an instrumentalist perspective and directed at legal effectiveness. In essence, research focused on the "gaps" between the identified goals of legal policies and the actual results produced by those policies. Research was driven by selective searching of areas where gaps might be found. In large part, Sarat argued, this was because sociolegal scholars could thereby assert the importance of their research endeavors and stake a claim to an independent area of legal scholarship. And, indeed, this selective investigation of likely gaps between policy goals and actual outcomes produced hundreds of studies in different substantive areas concluding that, for instance, legal rules were continually evaded, rights were not achieved, reforms were ineffective, and noncompliance characterized court orders.

Sarat also pointed out, however, a contradiction between "gap" researchers' widespread conclusion that "nothing works" and their ultimate faith in the potential of law to correct societal ills and injustice. In fact, many of their conclusions called for more and better law, rather than less law. To remedy this ideological malaise, Sarat called for sociolegal scholars to recognize the obvious fact that, on the whole, law is effective. He urged scholars to shift their orientation from the preoccupation with gaps. Instead, they should describe normal patterns of law and consider gaps in proper perspective with effective law. Whatever the merits of Sarat's assessment of the state of sociolegal scholarship in the mid-1980s, in many ways empirical research over the past decade has produced a sizable corpus of the type of scholarship that Sarat was advocating. Moreover, in some areas it has the potential to have the impact on legal policy that Sarat thought was lacking.

In this chapter, I focus on the tort system, with particular emphasis on medical malpractice litigation. I emphasize medical malpractice because it is an area that contains the largest and best body of findings about the tort system and because I have been conducting research on the topic for more than a decade. I offer a selective overview, not a comprehensive treatment of the literature. My goal is to demonstrate that, at least in this area, gap strategy has been replaced by "map" strategy and that the emerging map begins to provide grounds for making informed policy choices.

Tort System Debate: Circa 1985 to the Present

While research on the tort system provides an opportunity to assess what empirical scholarship can tell us about the normal patterns of legal institutions as well as the gaps, it also raises some important questions about Sarat's critique. Sarat's analysis assumed that there was consensus about legal goals and definitions of effectiveness. He also appeared to assume that sociolegal scholarship was inherently biased against the legal status quo. Before turning to empirical data, I provide some background that bears on these issues.

Critics of the System

Sarat's article was published just as the tort reform movement of the 1980s was beginning to build momentum. In 1975 liability insurers raised rates dramatically or stopped coverage altogether for certain activities, including health care. This set off a series of reforms in various states that were intended to make coverage available (see Bovbjerg 1989; Daniels and Martin 1995; Danzon 1985, 1990; Schuck 1993). The reforms had various foci and goals but included measures aimed at the number of lawsuits, the size of recoveries, the plaintiff's costs of winning, and the functioning and costs of the judicial process. Whether these reforms were successful or whether the crisis eased for other reasons is still a matter of debate (Bovbjerg 1989). However, beginning in about 1985, insurance companies, facing declining profits, again abruptly and dramatically raised premiums for liability insurance, particularly for medical negligence. This led to a renewed tort reform debate that continues to this day. An amalgam of interest groups, including insurers, manufacturers, and medical interests, alleged that the costs of health care services and manufactured products were becoming more expensive or unavailable and that manufacturers had lost their competitive edge with respect to the rest of the world (see Daniels and Martin 1995).

Although claims of the adverse impact on society were supported primarily by anecdotal examples and misleading statistics produced by vested interest groups rather than by systematic research (Daniels and Martin 1995; Galanter 1996), the reality is that the cost or unavailability of insurance caused hardships. Naturally, the concerns evoked a need to explain the crisis. Although there were a number of possible causes, including a natural downturn in the financial cycle or insurance company misjudgments of their investments, insurance companies, business leaders, and medical interests quickly centered attention on the tort system. As Daniels and Martin (1995) have documented, these interest groups quickly politicized the issues by labeling them as a crisis brought about by the tort system. Juries and plaintiff trial lawyers were singled out as particular culprits. Juries were said to favor the plaintiff and to be incompetent, capricious, and prone to give awards that ignored the laws of liability and the evidence on damages. Plaintiff lawyers were portrayed as avaricious predators who generated unfair and frivolous lawsuits and led juries astray with emotional appeals and the use of hired-gun experts who expounded specious theories of science and medicine.

Product liability and medical malpractice lawsuits were the two most prominent areas of concern. With regard to the latter, juries were said to biased against doctors, swayed by sympathy toward injured patients, confused by hired-gun experts, and prone to award excessive amounts to plaintiffs for pain and suffering and to levy unjustified and exorbitant punitive damages. These jury outcomes were said to fuel frivolous litigation and to cause doctors and their insurers to settle both meritorious and nonmeritorious suits out of fear that a jury would award many times more if the case went to trial (see, for example, President's Council on Competitiveness 1991). These facts, it was alleged, required insurers to increase liability premiums, and those costs ultimately had to be passed on to patients. Moreover, the fear of lawsuits caused doctors to practice "defensive medicine," which was defined as ordering unnecessary tests and procedures in order to protect against unwarranted claims of negligence in future lawsuits. The costs of defensive medicine also raised the costs to patients. (For general reviews of these claims, see Daniels and Martin 1995; Vidmar 1995). Although the main aim of the tort system is to provide compensation, some legal theorizing also considered its potential to deter negligent behavior by imposing costs on wrongdoers (see Schwartz 1994). Tort reform advocates variously ignored, dismissed, or treated deterrence as needing modification.

Considerable amounts of publicity and lobbying efforts were bankrolled by the allied tort reform groups. With only weak organized resistance by trial lawyers and public interest groups, the reform movement had a substantial degree of success. Before the decade passed, many states adopted measures intended to ameliorate the perceived problems. These changes included limits on jury awards, mandatory offsets of collateral benefits, limits on lawyers' contingency fees, restrictive statutes of limitations, periodic payment schedules, and procedural devices such as pretrial screening panels and mandatory arbitration or mediation.

The tort reform movement continued into the 1990s, and its impetus has not been spent as we approach the end of that decade. The issue is still discussed in congress. State legislatures continue to implement reforms intended to alleviate the perceived problems.

Most of the private sector advocates of tort reform remain strongly supportive of the fault principle embodied in the common law tort system. A clear example is contained in the preamble to the 1995 Illinois tort reform bill (Illinois Public Act 89-7), which specifically endorsed the fault principle in conjunction with a number of reform measures:

> It is the public policy of this state that liability should not be imposed absent fault on the part of the defendant. The State is concerned with evolutions in tort law that erode the fault principle . . . It is the public policy of this State to reject tort theorists who would use tort doctrine as a system of socialized compensation insurance.

Concern with fault probably reflects a philosophy of personal responsibility and a limitation of government in public life, but it also reflects a concern with economic costs. By imposing high entry and transaction costs on plaintiffs, the tort system can deter claims. Critics of the tort reform movement have argued that the real goal of tort reform is simply to increase the barriers to entry and recovery, thereby reducing economic costs to defendants irrespective of the merits of the plaintiff's claims (see Bovbjerg 1989).

Other critics, many residing in academic institutions, criticize the tort system on many of the same grounds as those in the tort reform movement (for example, Studdert et al. 1997; Sugarman 1985; Weiler 1991; Weiler et al. 1993). They too argue that the jury system is capricious and irrational and that transaction costs are much too high. They also question the alleged deterrent effect of tort law. However, their focus is on the transaction costs of the system and on the persons who, they allege, do not receive compensation or are inadequately compensated under a tort regime. Their goal is to provide a system that will compensate more people, more evenly, and with fewer transaction costs. In this view, the problem is to reduce the barriers to access and to transfer the transaction costs into more compensation that is spread as evenly as possible over claimants. To effect this goal, these authors advocate a "no-fault system" along the lines of worker compensation systems.

Although the tort reform movement and the no-fault advocates are the most easily categorized critics of the present system, there are other categories of critics as well. These include academics who would retain the tort system but propose revising litigation procedures in order to streamline the dispute resolution process, increase reliability, and reduce transaction costs (Strier 1994). In the area of medical malpractice, a committee of the American Medical Association (AMA/Specialty Society Medical Liability Project 1988; Johnson et al. 1989) proposed moving all malpractice cases out of the tort system and into an arbitration procedure in which decisions on liability would be based around a fault principle but procedures would be streamlined and the decision on liability would be made by a panel of doctors and lawyers rather than a jury. The rationale for the AMA proposal was based on the same criticisms of the tort system voiced in the tort reform movement generally.

Advocates for the System

There are a substantial number of supporters of the present tort system among the practicing bar and in academic institutions (for example, Miller 1994; Thompson 1997; Rustad 1994; Koenig and Rustad 1995). At the beginning of the tort reform movement, those supporting the current system were put on the defensive in the debate. In part, this was because they were defending the status quo and, in part, because the plaintiff bar itself was charged with making excess profit from the tort system. The organized plaintiff's bar subsequently lobbied vigorously against the tort reform efforts by arguing that the criticisms of the system were false and that whatever inefficiencies existed in the system were due to obstructionist tactics by defendants. Defenders of the system further argue that the barriers to entry and recovery deny recovery to many injured parties; if anything, barriers should be lowered. These advocates also assert that the concept of fault, and especially the remedy of punitive damages, serves as a deterrent to negligence.

Overlapping Perspectives, Values, and Factual Assertions

The various perspectives on the tort system overlap in interesting ways. Thus, reformers who favor the fault-based approach and advocates of no-fault each assert that both liability and damages are unfairly and unreliably decided by juries and that transaction costs are too high. However, whereas the tort reformers ignore the problem of undercompensated and uncompensated parties, no-fault advocates are particularly concerned with the failure to compensate. No-fault critics and tort system supporters argue that barriers to entry and recovery are too high and that many injured persons are prevented from seeking compensation, while no-fault critics blame the problem on inherent inefficiencies and flaws in the concept of tort law.

The divergence in the philosophies of groups wanting reforms raises one of the issues ignored in Sarat's analyses of gap research, namely whether consensus can be achieved on the goals that law is intended to serve. Are the goals to accelerate the process and lower transaction costs? Are they to compensate the largest number of injured persons or to limit the number of persons seeking access? Is deterrence of negligent behavior an important goal? The question of effectiveness of a system depends on the values one assigns to these criteria. The goals may sometimes be incompatible. Alternatively, the tort system may be more efficacious in achieving some goals than others. In any event, it is important to recognize that the debate revolves around a series of factual assertions about the behavior of the tort system. These assertions offer conflicting conclusions about what the tort system actually does.

An Emerging Map of the Tort System

Tort reform advocates have generated a number of claims about the behavior of the system. Most of the evidence used to support those claims, however, is scientifically questionable (for example, see Daniels and Martin 1995; Galanter 1996; Saks 1992; Sanders and Joyce 1990; Vidmar 1993, 1994b, 1995). One source of evidence was based on anecdotes: some of which were not representative of tort cases, and some of which have been proven to be false.

Other claims were bolstered by suspect data. For instance, a report by the U.S. Department of Justice (1986) Tort Policy Working Group is a heavily cited study. The report was based on filings in federal courts. It concluded that there was considerable growth in the number of tort filings and verdicts in favor or plaintiffs and that there was increasing uncertainty in the outcomes of tort cases. Its summary conclusion was that "Developments in tort law are a major cause of the sharp [liability insurance] premiums increases." However, the report failed to take notice of the fact that federal courts handle only 5 percent of nationwide tort litigation and, moreover, that federal cases are probably an unrepresentative sample of all tort cases (Sanders and Joyce 1990; Galanter 1996; Saks 1992). Further, the report did not consider base rates, which could considerably alter the interpretation of the data. For example, if more people were injured as a result of negligence at time two as compared to time one, the percentage increase in filings could be ascribed to injury rates rather than to increased litigiousness. Other problems with the report's conclusions were also ignored.

The Rand Corporation's Institute for Civil Justice (ICJ) also began producing a series of reports based on verdicts rendered by juries in California jurisdictions and Cook County, Illinois (Peterson 1987). Those reports purported to show a dramatic increase in plaintiff win rates and damage awards over a twenty-five-year period, beginning in 1960. Despite some qualifications to their conclusions, the ICJ studies pictured a tort system in need of serious correction. Flaws in the ICJ studies were noted as early as 1986 but were not fully exposed or widely recognized until the mid-1990s (Vidmar 1994b; Hensler 1993, 1994).

Sociolegal scholars had little initial impact on the highly charged political and policy debates for a couple of reasons. First, the few scientific critiques of the various claims were published in relatively obscure scholarly journals. Second, and perhaps more important, there were few systematic empirical studies of the tort system. Thus, the view of a poorly performing tort system was shaped by questionable evidence that painted it as chaotic, biased, and unreliable. The claims, nevertheless, became widely shared by legislators and other policymakers, journalists, and the general public (see Daniels and Martin 1995; Galanter 1993).

The assertions made by tort reform advocates did encourage scholars from many disciplines to undertake empirical research. As a result, an empirical map of the tort system is beginning to emerge. The largest corpus of findings involves the area of medical negligence. This area also has the clearest markers against which to compare the performance of the tort system.

Jury Performance and Behavior

Although trial is one of the last stages in the litigation process, it makes sense to begin with jury decisions because there is fairly wide consensus that trial outcomes provide the markers against which settlements are reached. Moreover, the tort debate involves claims that erratic, incompetent, and biased jury verdicts fuel the tort crisis by encouraging unwarranted lawsuits that raise expectations about easy plaintiff wins and high payoffs (see Ostrom, Rottman, and Goerdt 1996).

The increase in the number of civil court cases brought to trial has been ascribed to jury trials (see Galanter 1993). Moreover, the tort debate has created a public impression that malpractice, product liability, and mass toxic torts account for a large share of the civil court docket. In reality, jury trials account for less than 3 percent of dispositions in state general jurisdiction courts (Ostrom, Rottman, and Goerdt 1996). The bulk of these trials involve "ordinary litigation" arising from automobile accident and premises liability injuries. Medical negligence cases constitute about 11 percent of jury trials compared to product liability, with 3 percent, and mass toxic torts, with about 2 percent. Moreover, although the trials in medical negligence cases typically appear to last longer than other trials, the average duration is short. In North Carolina, for example, medical negligence trials average less than five days (Vidmar et al. 1992).

Considering all tort cases, plaintiffs win on the issue of liability about 49 percent of the time (Ostrom, Rottman, and Goerdt 1996). However, win rates vary substantially by the type of case. In medical malpractice cases nationwide, plaintiffs prevail at trial only about 30 percent of the time (Vidmar 1995; Ostrom, Rottman, and Goerdt 1996) compared to product liability cases with a win rate of about 40 percent, automobile negligence cases of about 60 percent, and toxic substance cases of about 70 percent.

Many cautions must be exercised in interpreting the trends in verdicts over time (Vidmar 1994b). Some current data suggest that the plaintiff win rates in tort trials generally may have declined slightly in the 1990s. However, Eisenberg et al. (1996) found no evidence for either a decline or an increase. In any event, plaintiff win rates in medical negligence cases certainly do not appear to be increasing (Vidmar 1998).

The finding that plaintiffs prevail in malpractice trials at the low rate of 30 percent would appear to contradict the claim that juries are biased in favor of plaintiffs, but it is not persuasive. In theory, for example, one could argue that doctors deserved to prevail in all of the cases and, thus, that the verdicts were in error 30 percent of the time (see Saks 1992; Vidmar 1993).

Because trials involve contested versions of facts, there can be no "correct" verdict in the absolute sense, only a comparison of the verdict against some chosen criterion (see Kalven and Zeisel 1966; Vidmar 1993). One such criterion was suggested by the Physician Payment Review Commission (1992), which asserted that juries decide cases differently than doctors would, presumably because doctors are more capable of understanding the technical evidence and because they are unlikely to be misled by false theories about improper medical care (or by improper sympathies for patients). However, several studies (Taragin et al. 1992; Sloan et al. 1993; Farber and White 1991) have compared liability verdicts brought by juries to independent assessments of negligence made by physicians. Contradicting the AMA hypothesis, there was a high correspondence between the verdicts and the doctors' judgments. Furthermore, the verdicts were not related to the seriousness of the plaintiffs' injuries, contradicting the assertion that juries decide liability out of sympathy for the plaintiff rather than according to legal rules (see Vidmar 1995 for further discussion).

Supporting these findings, surveys have found that trial judges conclude that juries are generally competent (Sentell 1991). Systematic interviews with actual jurors and findings from simulation experiments with jurors show that jurors are skeptical of experts and that they also scrutinize the motives of plaintiffs in seeking compensation at trial (Hans 1996; Vidmar 1995, 1998).

There is emerging evidence that juries apply stricter standards of liability against defendants that are business corporations or other commercial enterprises than against individual defendants or not-for-profit corporate entities (Hans 1996; Hamilton and Sanders 1996; MacCoun 1996). If subsequent research confirms these findings, policy debate will have to revolve around the question of whether it is acceptable to have a "reasonable corporation" as opposed to a "reasonable person" standard. In the health provider arena, some research has found that hospitals are more likely than doctors to prevail at trial (see Vidmar 1998). However, this result could be due to case selection or other factors. The more important test may appear in instances where health maintenance organizations (HMOs) are sued for negligence rather than, or in addition to, physicians. There is a clear gap of data, but the issue has been noted by scholars.

An accumulating body of data about jury damage awards overall tends to show a system that is far more rational than has been claimed (see Vidmar 1998). Ostrom, Rottman, and Goerdt (1996) concluded that for all torts combined, the median jury award in state courts in 1992 was around $50,000 and the mean was $455,000. When very large outlier awards were excluded from the data, the mean award was about $160,000. However, there were major differences when the data were disaggregated by type of case. The median award for automobile accident and premises liability cases was $29,000 and $57,000, respectively. In contrast, medical malpractice, product liability, and toxic substance torts all had medians exceeding $100,000. In fact, one in every four medical malpractice awards in their data set exceeded $1 million.

Amounts of awards, in and of themselves, tell us nothing about their reasonableness (see, for example, Saks 1992). In addition, the differences may be a result of differing patterns of litigation (Vidmar 1994b). The economic losses due to past and future medical costs and lost income have been documented to be extremely high for some injuries (see Sloan et al. 1993; Vidmar 1995). Bovbjerg, Sloan, and Blumstein (1989) found that the magnitude of total awards in a sample of tort cases was positively correlated with the seriousness of injury, except that injuries resulting in death received considerably less, on average, than grave injuries in which the plaintiff survived. Taragin et al. (1992) reported a similar positive correlation between jury verdicts and severity of injury in their sample of New Jersey malpractice cases.

Despite the positive correlation between severity of injury and payment, Bovbjerg et al. (1991) noted that within categories of severity of injury, there was considerable variability of awards. They speculated that a principal reason may have been variability across juries. There are other plausible explanations, however, including variability in the amount and quality of evidence on damages that was presented at trial. Such variability could reflect differences in the decisions made by lawyers regarding the evidence presented at trial (see Vidmar 1993, 1995) as well as true differences in economic loss.

Consistent with this last hypothesis, Sloan et al. (1993) conducted systematic assessments of economic losses in a sample of Florida cases involving claims of medical negligence occurring in birth-related and emergency room incidents. Even though the authors cautioned that their assessment procedures probably underestimated losses, severely injured parties frequently incurred economic losses exceeding $1 million. The data also demonstrated that there was great variability in economic loss among persons who suffered injuries similar in severity. This latter finding strongly suggests that a significant portion of the variability in jury awards may reflect actual economic loss rather than jury caprice or incompetence.

Research on actual jury awards by different authors (see Vidmar, Gross, and Rose 1998 for a review) indicates that the general damages portion of jury awards (often called the "noneconomic portion of awards" or just "pain and suffering") equals or exceeds 50 percent of the total award. However, more careful analysis of these awards indicates that they contain compensation for elements such as disfigurement, loss of consortium, and loss of parental guidance that have very arguable economic consequences (Vidmar, Gross, and Rose 1998). Hence, the tendency to label all damages that are not special damages as "pain and suffering" is misleading (see Bovbjerg, Sloan, and Blumstein 1989; Johnson et al. 1989). Moreover, the research also indicates that these awards are also directly related to the seriousness of the injury suffered by the plaintiff. Within categories of serious injury, there is some degree of variability, however. This may be due to unreliability of the jury, as some critics have suggested, but an equally plausible explanation is that the jurors are responding to differences in the quality and quantity of suffering by the plaintiff (see Wissler et al. 1997; Vidmar, Gross, and Rose 1998). Moreover, when juries render large awards, the amounts are frequently subjected to judicial adjustments before judgment or to post-trial settlement agreements that drastically reduce the awards, especially the general damages portion (Vidmar, Gross, and Rose 1998).

Although several studies have shown that plaintiffs are more likely to receive higher awards, on average, when the defendant is a business rather than an individual (Ostrom, Rottman, and Goerdt

1996; Bovbjerg et al. 1991; Peterson 1987), this finding cannot rule out the possibility that the cases were selected or litigated differently (Vidmar 1993, 1994a, 1994b; Danzon 1985; Saks 1992). Furthermore, experimental studies that controlled for these confounding variables tended to find no support for the hypothesis that juries award more when the defendant has "deep pockets" (Vidmar 1993; MacCoun 1996; Hans 1996; also see Vidmar 1998).

Another claim is that juries are less reliable than judges would be in awarding amounts for pain and suffering. Judges are alleged to be more reliable because of their knowledge of amounts awarded in comparable cases and because their legal training and institutional restraints make them less susceptible to emotional appeals (see Vidmar and Rice 1993). In contrast to these claims, experimental research comparing jury awards with awards rendered by former judges and senior lawyers concludes that, through the process of combining individual judgments over twelve persons, juries will, on average, award about the same amount as a judge deciding alone; aggregated across cases the jury awards will be less variable, that is more reliable, than a judge's (Vidmar and Rice 1993; Vidmar 1995).

Research studies have also produced a profile bearing on the claims that punitive damages are levied frequently and that they are typically excessive. Daniels and Martin (1990, 1995), Eisenberg et al. (1996), Peterson, Sarma, and Shanley (1987), Koenig and Rustad (1995), and Ostrom, Rottman, and Goerdt (1996) have demonstrated that these awards are infrequent, primarily given in lawsuits involving breach of contract and bad faith rather than torts, and that the amounts awarded in tort cases typically are modest in comparison to compensatory damages. Even though much of the public debate about punitive damages has centered around product liability cases, these awards occur in fewer than 7 percent of toxic substance torts and around 2 percent of other product liability trials. Punitive damages occur in less than 3 percent of medical malpractice cases when the plaintiff prevails (or less than 1 percent of all cases tried). Moreover, closer examination indicates that many malpractice cases involve claims of egregious negligent conduct (Koenig and Rustadt 1995).

As already mentioned, jury verdicts are frequently adjusted downward as a result of the trial judge exercising a common law or statutory right to reduce awards, of post-verdict settlement negotiations, or of reductions on appeal. Studies indicate that adjustments are most common in cases involving large awards (Broeder 1986). For instance, Vidmar, Gross, and Rose (1998) found that some of the largest awards in New York that made nationwide headlines ultimately settled for well under 10 percent of the award.

This overview of research about the malpractice jury ignores some complexities and complications in research findings. Nevertheless, the overwhelming majority of empirical research studies present a portrait of jury behavior that shows a malpractice jury system operating at a reasonably rational level. Widespread claims regarding the gaps between legal policy goals and performance are greatly exaggerated. Indeed, the research evidence lends little support to the view that randomly chosen judges could do the job better. This does not mean that the jury is a perfect institution, but sociolegal research suggests that procedural innovations in jury trials could enhance its performance (see Munsterman, Hannaford, and Whitehead 1997).

The Settlement Process

Although the studies of juries indicate that claims about their rampant incompetence and misbehavior are in error, these misconceptions may induce defendants to make unwarranted settlements or, at least, to drive the costs of settlements upward. In other words, a false perception of the jury's shadow could have as much impact as a true shadow. The research evidence, although incomplete, appears inconsistent with the false shadow hypothesis. As a starting point, consider that of the total number of formal malpractice lawsuits, roughly 50 percent result in a payment to the plaintiff before trial, about 10 percent proceed to trial, and the remaining approximately 40 percent eventuate in no payment to the plaintiff (Vidmar 1995; Danzon 1985; Taragin et al. 1992).

Taragin et al. (1992) studied settlement practices in a sample of 8,231 closed claims in the files of a New Jersey liability insurer. Some of the cases were settled before a formal lawsuit was filed. A payment to the claimant was made in 43 percent of all cases. Whenever an incident comes to the attention of this insurer, a nondiscoverable review of the incident is made by other physicians to determine whether negligence occurred. In 25 percent of the cases, the reviews yielded an assessment of "indefensible"—that is, it is likely there was negligence—and in 62 percent of the cases the assessment was of no negligence; in an additional 13 percent of cases, negligence was unclear. A payment to the patient was made in 21 percent of cases considered defensible, in 91 percent of cases considered indefensible, and in 59 percent of cases considered to be unclear. It should be noted, however, that the assessments were made shortly after the incident occurred and that information that turned up later in the case might have changed those assessments (see Sloan et al. 1993; Vidmar 1995). Of the cases where payment was made, 52 percent of the time the amount was under $50,000; the payment exceeded $200,000 in only 15 percent of cases. The amount of the payment was closely correlated with the severity of injury.

Using data sets from hospital insurer files, Farber and White (1991) and Sloan and Hsieh (1990) drew similar conclusions. Interviews with liability insurers (Vidmar 1995) yielded comments that were consistent with these hard data: insurers are unlikely to settle if they believe negligence did not occur. In short, payments to plaintiffs appear to be based on defendant assessments of liability.

As to the amount of settlements, the data suggest that, on average, claimants who settle do so at a substantial discount of the potential jury award and that the compensation is uneven. Danzon (1985) studied a sample of closed claims in California and concluded that the amounts claimants received were substantially discounted. Sloan et al. (1993) conducted a systematic economic analysis of claimant losses in a sample of Florida cases. Plaintiffs who settled received, on average, only about half of their actual economic loss. However, they also found that patients with large losses were compensated at proportionately lower rates than those with relatively smaller losses.

In summary, settlement compensation in the tort system appears to be driven more by assessments of fault than any other factor. Settlements involve a substantial discount of actual projected losses. Compensation is uneven with regard to seriousness of injury: persons with relatively less serious injuries are overcompensated.

Frivolous Litigation

Claims about frivolous litigation have also punctuated the policy debates about tort reform. The topic is, of course, closely tied to the settlement issue. The claim that frivolous litigation is encouraged by the tort system is based on two interrelated assertions. The first is that the premises of big payoffs at trial encourage lawyers and their clients to file lawsuits without sufficient screening or evaluation in the hope that an errant jury verdict will compensate for many losing cases. The second is that cases with expectations of smaller payouts are encouraged because liability insurers will make modest payments even to undeserving plaintiffs to avoid the transaction costs associated with litigation. In the area of medical malpractice, fuel for this speculation has come from the finding that between 35 and 40 percent of lawsuits are eventually dropped voluntarily by plaintiffs or removed from the system by summary judgments or other procedural rulings (see Farber and White 1991; also Vidmar 1995).

Research findings challenge these claims. As described, defendants and their insurers settle cases primarily on the basis of their own assessments of negligence. Several studies further indicate that the primary reason for the high failure rate is that lawsuits have to be filed in order for plaintiff lawyers to assess whether negligence occurred (see Vidmar 1995; Farber and White 1994; Sloan and Hsieh 1990). By filing suit, the plaintiff can obtain the medical records, depositions, and other evidence to determine if the case is meritorious. Indeed, an analysis of liability insurer records from a sample of closed claims documented the fact that in the early stages of litigation, defendants themselves are often unsure as to whether negligence occurred (Vidmar 1995). Sometimes the answer becomes clear only many months into the litigation process. At this point, after evidence develops indicating that there was no provable negligence or that the costs of litigation will exceed the potential payoff, the lawsuit is often dropped.

Kritzer's (1997) study of plaintiff screening of malpractice cases supports these findings. Kritzer draws attention to the fact that almost all plaintiff lawyers work on a contingency fee basis and in most cases bear the expenses of experts and other costs if there is no recovery (see also Gross and Syverud 1991; McClellan 1993). Consequently, Kritzer argues, plaintiff lawyers screen cases as carefully as possible even before lawsuits are filed. Drawing on studies conducted two decades apart, Kritzer concluded that lawyer screening results in the rejection of as many as nine out of ten malpractice cases. Kritzer's finding receives support from the finding of Sloan et al. (1993) that even plaintiffs who eventually prevailed with their claim often had great difficulty getting a lawyer to take their case (see also Sloan and Hsieh 1990).

The Lawsuit Winnowing Process: A Summary

The data bearing on jury trial verdicts, settlement, and frivolous litigation strongly suggest that the traditional tort system is in fact relatively effective in screening out nonmeritorious cases (see Bovbjerg 1992; Gross and Syverud 1996). At the same time, there appears to be little question that the transaction cost in time, money, and emotional toll on the parties is very high. Cases often take many months, sometimes years, to resolve (see Vidmar et al. 1992). However, some of these costs may be inherent in the very nature of the cases (see Vidmar 1995) rather than an inherent failure of the tort system. Attempts at alternate screening mechanisms have also proved to be costly and slow. The data gathered to date also do not address the issue of false negatives, that is, cases in which the plaintiff should have prevailed but did not because of the inability to obtain experts or other evidence, the cost of litigation, or the unreliability of decisionmaking at any stage in the litigation process (see Saks 1992).

Settlements Outside the Tort System

A certain percentage of claims are settled informally without a lawsuit. Nevertheless, the claims and subsequent settlements take place in the shadow of the tort system. These claims are settled by various procedures, including bilateral negotiations, arbitration, and other forms of alternative dispute resolution (Bovbjerg 1989, 1991, 1992, 1993; Vidmar and Rice 1991). Data on the precise number of cases settled in this manner are sparse. The closed claim files of liability insurers contain this information, but most research published to date has not disaggregated the data in this way.

Sloan and Hsieh (1990) examined 6,612 claims closed in Florida between October 1985 and April 1988. They reported that 16.5 percent of claims were closed before a lawsuit was filed. Of these cases, the plaintiff received payment 80 percent of the time. The average indemnity was $38,000 in 1987 dollars, but there was substantial variability according to severity of the injuries. Minor injuries averaged $5,000 per case, but total permanent disability averaged $297,000, and death of a patient averaged $144,000. The Taragin et al. (1992) study of 8,231 closed claims in New Jersey allows an additional estimate. Approximately 8.5 percent of incidents resulting in injury to a patient were settled outside of a formal lawsuit. Their data do not report the amounts of these settlements.

Equitable Compensation in the Tort Regime

An important policy question revolves around the percentage of patients suffering negligent injuries who actually receive compensation. This is the baseline issue, the denominator against which the effectiveness of the tort system as a compensation mechanism may be assessed (see Saks 1992; Felstiner, Abel, and Sarat 1980–81; Kritzer et al. 1991). Many advocates of tort reform have focused on alleged deficiencies in the ability of tort law to screen lawsuits properly but have devoted little attention to uncompensated injuries. In contrast, advocates of no-fault compensation schemes, while critical of the efficiency and fairness of the system, argue that it compensates only a small percentage of injured persons: in short, they claim that there is a "gap" in compensation delivery.

The first step in analyzing these claims is to determine the incidence of injury. Several studies have investigated the problem by having physicians and other health care providers examine hospital records to identify negligent iatrogenic injuries. Hospital record databases ignore injuries that may occur in individual doctor's offices or clinics and, thus, provide a conservative estimate of negligent injuries.

A seminal study by the U.S. Department of Health, Education, and Welfare in 1972 concluded that the rate of negligent injury was, at minimum, 218 injuries per 10,000 patients (see Saks 1992, 1994). A 1977 study by California medical groups concluded that 79 negligent injuries occurred for every 10,000 patients (see Saks 1992, 1994).

The most comprehensive study, however, was conducted by the Harvard School of Public Health and involved a random sample of 31,000 patients hospitalized in New York State in 1984 (Weiler et al. 1993). Teams of medical experts reviewed the hospital records of each of these patients. The study concluded that one of every one hundred patients suffered an injury that was legally actionable. An estimated 57 percent of the injuries resulted in minimal and transient disability, but 14 percent of the time the adverse event caused death; approximately 10 percent of the incidents resulted in hospitalization

for more than six months, with 7 of that 10 percent suffering a permanent disability.

Research by Lori Andrews (1993) extends our knowledge of negligent error rates even further. Andrews and her researchers conducted an observational study of health care workers in the surgical
ward of a Chicago area hospital. Over the nine-month duration of
the study, more than 1,000 patients were treated. Treatment errors
were defined as those identified by the health providers in their communications with other health providers during work rounds or in
clinical meetings. Andrews reported that at least one treatment error
was identified for 44 percent of the patients. For 9 percent of patients,
more than five errors were identified. On average, four errors
occurred per patient, and for 14 percent of them, the error was
defined by the health care workers as having caused "serious injury"
(such as temporary or permanent disability or death).

Andrews's figures are obviously higher than the 3.7 percent serious error rate that was uncovered by the Harvard study. However,
Andrews's study offers an explanation for the discrepancy, namely
that many of the errors were never recorded in the patients' records,
nor were current reports filed with the hospital administration.
Andrews concluded that, typically, the health professionals took
actions to correct the errors. She also suggested that it may be presumed that the patient was never told of the error and "was led to
believe that the subsequent treatment was necessitated by his or her
original condition." It is likely that the patient was subsequently
billed for the corrective treatment.

The Andrews study provides additional insights about responses
to errors. In the health care providers' clinical meetings, blame for
errors was seldom assigned to the highest ranking physicians. Blame
was assigned less frequently when the errors caused serious as
opposed to minor or no injury. Second, among the identified errors,
only 32 percent were related to surgery per se; the remainder
involved monitoring and daily care. Additional analyses revealed
that although 38 percent of errors were caused by individuals, significant numbers of errors were related to communication problems
between health care providers or to administrative deficiencies of the
hospital, such as unavailability of equipment or inadequate staffing.

The Andrews study leads to the plausible hypothesis that despite
its sampling rigor, the Harvard study's reliance on patient records

underestimated rates of negligent error. This is not to imply that all of the injuries identified in the Andrews study would be considered legally negligent; some iatrogenic injuries are actuarially expected even under medically acceptable standards of care. Nevertheless, because many of the errors identified by Andrews never made it into hospital records, it is reasonable to hypothesize that reliance on hospital records alone underestimates legally actionable errors.

From the baseline of injury, the next issue is the number of patients who file claims for injuries, who they are, and what barriers they face. The Harvard study provides the best data (Weiler et al. 1993). The authors of that study traced claims that resulted from the injuries. They concluded that for every 7.6 negligent injuries, only one claim was filed. Of course, many of the injuries were minor and patients might not be expected to make claims. However, even among patients under seventy years of age who suffered serious injuries, only two claims were filed for every five injuries. Some claims were made in instances in which, the Harvard team concluded, no negligence had occurred (either no injury had occurred, or the injury was not caused by negligence). Put another way, the issue can be viewed in comparative terms of false negatives and false positives. Considering the data in this way, Saks (1994) concluded that for every invalid claim filed against a doctor or hospital, seven valid claims were not made. The Harvard group of researchers concluded as follows: although the tort system for medical malpractice "does in fact operate erratically, it hardly operates excessively" (Weiler et al. 1993, 73).

Other research has investigated who sues and why. Working from the Harvard data set, Burstin et al. (1993) examined the widely held belief of health care providers that poor patients are more likely to sue than persons who are higher on the socioeconomic scale. This belief of doctors allegedly creates fears of poor patients and increases barriers to treatment of medically indigent patients. In fact, after controlling for severity of injury, Burstin et al. found that poor patients, uninsured patients, and elderly patients were *less* likely to sue health care providers.

May and Stengel (1990) found that persons who do file lawsuits are more likely to seek input from friends and relatives, lawyer acquaintances, and others. Persons low on the socioeconomic ladder have many fewer of these societal resources that help to identify negligent injuries and successfully pursue them (Burstin et al. 1993; Felstiner, Abel, and Sarat 1980–81; Galanter 1983).

The research findings indicate that, on the whole, the tort system is relatively effective in weeding out nonmeritorious lawsuits and providing compensation that is not irrational and biased as many critics have claimed. At the same time, the system produces substantial inequity. Persons with less serious injuries are compensated proportionately more than those with more serious injuries. Additionally, it appears that, especially among plaintiffs who opt for settlement rather than trial, compensation is substantially less than actual economic loss. The findings also indicate that the tort litigation process is typically both lengthy and expensive and extracts psychological tolls on both plaintiffs and defendants.

Perhaps most important, the research findings indicate that only a small percentage of negligently injured persons actually make claims and are compensated for their injuries. We do not have reliable information on why this gap exists. It may be that some injuries are partially compensated through other sources, such as medical and disability insurance. It may be that some injured parties accept the injury as part of the fate that befell them in requiring medical treatment in the first place (Lloyd-Bostock 1991). Or it may be that the substantial barriers to accessing the tort system prevent injured parties from receiving just compensation. More research mapping is needed on these issues.

Tort Reforms: Assessment Research

Beginning with the 1975 liability insurance crisis and continuing through the 1980s and 1990s, various states passed tort reform measures directed at medical malpractice litigation (as well as other areas of tort law). Sanders and Joyce (1990) and other authors (Galanter 1993, 1996; Saks 1992; Daniels and Martin 1995; Vidmar et al. 1992) have observed that these reforms were passed largely on the basis of anecdotes and unsubstantiated assertions rather than empirical evidence of a crisis, reasoned consideration about the cause of the crisis, if it existed, and the potential impact of the reforms on other parts of the tort system.

The reforms varied from state to state and typically included a mix of the following measures: pretrial screening panels, mandatory mediation of malpractice claims, statutory limits (or "caps") on pain and suffering damages or even the total amount of the compensatory award, abolition of punitive damages, restrictions on lawyer contingency fees, and modifications of the doctrine of joint and several liability.

Legislators assumed that the reforms would have a number of broad-ranging salutary effects (Bovbjerg 1989, 1991, 1992, 1993). The incidence of nonmeritorious, or frivolous, litigation would be reduced, as would the overall incidence of malpractice claims. The aggregated magnitude of compensation payouts would be reduced, particularly as a result of the reduction of "excess" awards in cases involving serious injury. The number of medically unwarranted defensive medicine measures would be reduced, as the fear of litigation receded because doctors would no longer order unnecessary and expensive tests or undertake other measures solely as precautions in the event of a lawsuit. Liability premiums would stabilize or decline as the costs of indemnity and litigation transaction costs declined. The trend of obstetricians unwilling to practice in rural communities would be slowed or reversed because the reductions in malpractice premiums would make practice in these areas more attractive.

Two characteristics of these reforms and the alleged benefits that would flow from them deserve repeating. The reform efforts generally ignored other possible causes of the perceived problems. Second, with few exceptions, they were implemented without rejecting the fault principle that underlies tort law. In other words, most legislative enactments were intended to curb perceived problems with tort law, not to abolish the fault-based system nor to remove major barriers to access to that system. As described earlier, the 1995 tort reform measure passed by the Illinois legislature made this commitment to the tort system explicit.

Research on Alternative Dispute Resolution

One of the earliest attempts to deal with the perceived malpractice crisis was the development of pretrial screening panels (Bovbjerg 1989; Goldschmidt 1991). The theory behind these panels was that many malpractice claims were nonmeritorious and that many meritorious cases could be settled early without formal litigation. Depending on the state, claimants were encouraged or required to submit their claim to a panel composed of doctors, lawyers, and citizens for evaluation before becoming a formal legal claim.

In almost all instances, the concept of a screening panel failed and was abandoned. Research evaluating the effectiveness of the panels is not scientifically rigorous, but it does reveal a number of flaws in the concept of screening. Often the panels were dominated by doctors and perceived to be biased in favor of defendants, causing plaintiffs to reject their findings and recommendations. In some instances, claimants simply refused to participate, while in others, the panels may have increased the number of legal claims because some plaintiff lawyers used the panels to screen their cases for evaluative purposes rather than hiring and paying their own screening experts. Some of the cases brought before panels were tenuous on the issue of liability or had sufficiently small ad damnums that would otherwise have discouraged the lawyers from investing time and money in screening. The panels, however, reduced their screening costs. For the most part, however, the screening panels only added another costly hurdle for both sides in the litigation process (see Goldschmidt 1991; Macchiaroli 1990).

A number of health maintenance organizations encouraged arbitration or made it compulsory as part of their contract with the patients. In a review of arbitration procedures, Danzon (1986; see also Brady and Cubanske 1993; Nichols 1986) concluded that arbitration apparently increased the frequency of claims but reduced the overall average magnitude of the claims. Subsequently, a number of health maintenance organizations abandoned arbitration clauses on the grounds that defendants fared better in jury trials (see Vidmar 1995). However, in the 1990s many HMOs introduced mandatory arbitration clauses as part of their contracts with the insured. No research evidence of their impact is known at this time (see Rolph, Moller, and Rolph 1997).

Vidmar and Rice (1991) described an unusual form of voluntary arbitration that was successful in resolving malpractice disputes. The procedure, called a "jury-determined settlement," uses a panel of jurors rather than a single arbitrator or panel of arbitrators to decide the case. The "trial" involves an abbreviated presentation of the case over one or two days. It is different from a "summary jury" trial in several ways. The procedure is developed and managed by the litigants themselves rather than a trial judge. That is, the parties negotiate the time limits and rules of evidence that will be followed, and they jointly agree on an experienced lawyer to be the judge. Unlike a summary jury trial used in most courts, the jury's verdict is binding rather than advisory. In some instances, the parties develop a "high-low" agreement whereby the plaintiff receives some indemnity even if the jury rules in favor of the doctor, but the doctor pays no more than some set figure even if the jury award exceeds that amount. Although it is a promising technique for some cases, the effectiveness of the jury-determined settlement procedure has not been rigorously assessed, largely because it has not been used with sufficient frequency.

The State of Wisconsin enacted a mandatory mediation statute for malpractice cases in 1986 that replaced a system of mandatory screening panels. The statute called for a three-person mediation panel consisting of a lawyer, as chair, a physician or health care professional with some expertise in the area of the claim, and a member of the public appointed from a panel of persons chosen by the governor. In a preliminary assessment of the effects of the statute, Meschievitz (1991, 1994) concluded that the mediation panels differed greatly from what is typically known as mediation. In fact, despite their name, the composition and operation of the panels resemble the old patient composition panels that they replaced. The panelists have little or no mediation training, and if a settlement is not reached in the session, the panel is free to advise the parties of the projected outcome if the case proceeds to trial. Meschievitz concluded that the process as implemented allowed little direct party participation. She further concluded that the process resulted in few settlements and did little to promote harmony or to facilitate joint resolution of problems.

Michigan's mediation process also appears to differ from traditional conceptions of mediation. The mediation panel is composed of three lawyers and two health care professionals, one chosen by each party. No witnesses are permitted, and each party is allowed only fifteen minutes to present its case; the panel recommends awards. Simmons's (1996) study of the process and outcomes of these panels found that mediation awards were generally higher than settlement and trial awards but that defendants rejected mediation awards more often than plaintiffs. He concluded that if Michigan's mediation process is to work more effectively, it will have to be restructured.

A number of states have passed statutes mandating or encouraging mediation that more closely comports with traditional definitions of mediation (see Metzloff, Peeples, and Harris 1997; Dauer and Marcus 1997). However, despite the formal descriptions, in practice the process tends to have few of the characteristics associated with a process of true mediation.

Another attempt to expedite malpractice litigation and reduce its cost involved vesting the court with responsibility for singling out malpractice cases for special judicial conferences and expedited calendars. A study of a statute in North Carolina that sought to close most malpractice cases within a year indicated how badly it failed (Vidmar et al. 1992). In many of the counties in the state, court personnel viewed the procedures as impractical and failed to implement them properly. In one large county, a sincere attempt at implementation conflicted with other court procedural rules and actually slowed the pace of malpractice litigation. Analysis of the underlying bases of resistance to the statute revealed that the preparation of malpractice cases for both sides and the discovery process were too complex and involved to be treated fairly with the expedited procedure mandated by the statute. Therefore, defense and plaintiff lawyers, judges, and other court personnel found ways to avoid implementation.

Forms of alternative dispute resolution that attempt to force parties to resolve their malpractice dispute through formal screening or other intervention procedures have shown little success and have sometimes produced results that are counter to the intentions behind the development procedures. However, procedures that are voluntary and allow parties to control the settlement may, in some instances, result in settlements that are more satisfactory to the parties. Substantially more research is needed to document these possible effects.

Changes in Tort Laws

A central question in mapping the tort system involves the impact that changes in tort law itself have on human and economic behavior. This complex question raises incredibly difficult problems for empirical sociolegal research, but even here some rudimentary findings provoke thought about policy decisions.

Beginning in 1975 and extending to the present time, various state legislatures have passed a plethora of statutes intended to affect medical malpractice litigation. At the risk of oversimplification, the goal is to reduce the cost and increase the availability of health care (see Bovbjerg 1989 for a review). As described, the philosophy behind almost all of the reforms remains loyal to the fault principle embodied in tort law. Few of the reforms seek to reduce the incidence of negligent medical treatment—that is, deterrence. Instead, they are directed toward reducing access to the tort system rather than toward ensuring compensation for all persons injured through medical negligence. Zuckerman, Bovbjerg, and Sloan (1990) summarized how cost reduction is expected to be achieved: (1) by reducing the frequency of claims, (2) by lowering the amounts that claimants can recover, and (3) by curbing the costs of the legal process. The system-level impact of such changes would be reflected in several ways. Doctors, having less fear of lawsuits, would reduce the use of unnecessary medical procedures—that is, stop practicing defensive medicine. The indemnity and transaction costs of liability insurers would be reduced, allowing them to lower insurance premiums. The effects of lower premiums would be passed on to doctors and their patients. The lower costs would encourage doctors to practice in areas that would otherwise be financially and psychologically prohibitive. A primary target is obstetrical practice, where it is said that doctors do not want to practice because of the costs of liability insurance and the fear of ruinous lawsuits.

The most serious effort to assess the theory behind the tort reform movement was undertaken by Zuckerman, Bovbjerg, and Sloan (1990) (see also Rosenblatt, Whelan, and Hart 1990; Rosenblatt et al. 1991). They attempted to measure the effects of tort reforms on insurance premiums in all fifty states in a thirteen-year period from 1974 through 1986. Their time-series analysis considered eleven categories of tort reforms: total limits (caps) on physician liability, caps on noneconomic damages, mandatory collateral offset rules, permissive collateral offset rules, rules on costs that are awardable, general statutes of limitations, statutes of limitations for children, length of discovery periods, pretrial screening panels, the allowing of arbitration agreements, and controls on attorney fees. Additional variables were considered in their regression equations to control for exogenous factors that might affect insurer losses. In addition to the main dependent variable of the level of insurance premiums, they included measures of the amount paid per claim and the frequency of claims.

Zuckerman, Bovbjerg, and Sloan (1990) concluded that the only reforms that lowered premiums were limits on the total economic and noneconomic awards that could be awarded to claimants and reductions in the amount of time that plaintiffs have to initiate claims. Caps on noneconomic, or pain and suffering, awards, by far the most popular tort reform measure, had no significant effect on premiums. However, the researchers found only a weak link between premiums and the frequency of claims and the amount of indemnities paid. The lack of a strong relationship between these variables is problematic because claim frequency and indemnity payouts are posited to be central causal factors in the reduction of premiums. It could be that the measures of claim frequency and award were flawed, but the other possibility is that the study did not sufficiently control for exogenous variables that influence the cost of liability insurance premiums.

Viscusi and Born (1995) conducted a study of the impact of tort reforms in Michigan and Wisconsin on medical insurers' profitability for the years 1984 to 1991. They also conducted a secondary study on a national sample of insurers. In 1986 Michigan passed a number of tort reforms that included a cap of $225,000 for noneconomic damages in medical malpractice cases. The cap did not apply to wrongful death actions or cases involving injuries to the reproductive system or loss of vital bodily functions. Wisconsin also enacted tort reforms in 1986 but placed a cap of $1 million on the total award—that is, economic as well as noneconomic damages. Viscusi and Born's primary dependent variable was the liability insurers' "loss ratio," a measure of profitability. Those authors concluded that damage caps were the most influential reform affecting profitability. However, they also observed that the reforms were not uniform across the entire insurance market and that, in fact, the greatest effects of the reforms were produced for the least profitable insurers.

The Viscusi and Born study has a number of significant limitations. The first is that it did not address the question of whether the increased profitability resulted in lower premiums. The second is that it did not control for rates of claims, severity of injuries, or declines in awards or settlements—the crucial variables that are hypothesized to be affected by the reforms. The authors also acknowledged that changes in underwriting practices and shifts in interest rates might have affected profitability and that a comparative analysis of loss ratios between malpractice insurers and a control group of automobile insurers was problematic because very different market factors influence profitability for the two types of insurers. Finally, some of the projected long-term effects predicted from their equation models "appear to be implausibly large" (Viscusi and Born 1995, 18), a conclusion that also raises questions about the short-term effects noted in the study.

A study by Kinney et al. (1991) (Gronfein and Kinney 1991) examined the effects of tort reform in Indiana, a state that in 1975 enacted what has been described as the most comprehensive and restrictive tort reform in the country. Indiana's legislation placed a cap on the total economic and noneconomic award for malpractice at $500,000, a figure that was raised to $750,000 in 1990. The legislation also included a number of other controls on the litigation process, including preliminary screening by a medical review panel and a patient compensation fund to pay claims exceeding $100,000. Finally, it placed a limit of 15 percent on the amount of lawyer contingency fees.

Kinney and her colleagues found that during the 1980s Indiana experienced increases in the frequency of claims that were similar to national trends. (Even before the tort reforms, Indiana's annual frequency of claims was lower than that of most states.) The severity of claims also increased substantially over time, a trend similar to national trends. A comparison of Indiana with the demographically similar states of Michigan and Ohio, neither of which had damage caps during the three-year period covered by the study, yielded a result exactly opposite to what would be expected if the reforms were effective: on average the amount of indemnity paid to Indiana claimants with injuries exceeding $100,000 was substantially higher than those in comparison states. Indiana's payment was 39.6 percent higher than Michigan's and 33.5 percent higher than Ohio's.

Kinney, Gronfein, and Gannon (1991) also reported that the financial solvency of the patient compensation fund was a persistent concern from its inception and that attempts to keep it solvent required a surcharge of 125 percent on a doctor's liability premium. Although medical liability premiums were lower in Indiana than in Michigan and Ohio, surcharges on the premiums of obstetrician/gynecologists and neurosurgeons in Indianapolis made their effective insurance costs just slightly lower than those of comparable specialists in Cincinnati and Cleveland, but substantially lower than those of specialists in Kalamazoo and Detroit. However, the Indiana doctors received complete malpractice protection, whereas the Ohio doctors did not.

Spurr and Simmons (1996) analyzed the amount of recovery by plaintiffs in a sample of more than 20,000 Michigan malpractice cases closed between 1978 and 1990. During this period, Michigan passed a number of measures intended to correct perceived advantages of plaintiffs in malpractice litigation, including the mandatory "mediation panels" discussed above but also a series of other reforms. They concluded that although some individual tort reform measures did not produce the intended effects, there were cumulative effects. After the reforms, there was an increased probability that claims would be abandoned rather than settled. Moreover, cases settled for substantially less than would be expected at trial. The hypothesis advanced to explain this finding was that because plaintiffs are more risk-averse than defendants, the latter are advantaged in the bargaining process.

In a recent study, Kessler and McClellan (1997) concluded that states with liability reforms that directly reduced the malpractice pressure on doctors experienced lower growth rates in malpractice claims and in insurance premiums. These findings are not consistent with earlier findings but cannot be dismissed.

Research on the relationship between medical malpractice litigation and healthcare tends to indicate that it has little impact on physician's income (see Budetti 1992). This suggests that the claim that liability premiums drive doctors out of practice needs close scrutiny.

Another rationale for the tort system is that by imposing fault on persons who act negligently, the system deters negligent behavior (see Schwartz 1994). This is a difficult question to investigate empirically because of the complex factors driving human behavior and also because of value judgments on what constitutes the appropriate amount of deterrence, if deterrence actually occurs. For instance, in the area of medical negligence, many health care providers and their organizations have claimed that doctors are so fearful of lawsuits that they prescribe medical procedures and tests that provide little or no benefit to patients. Their primary purpose is to protect against a charge of negligence, and the consequence is that the cost of health care is driven upward. The basic problem in studying deterrence is reaching agreement on what is *appropriate* defensive medicine—that is, taking steps beneficial to patients—and what is *inappropriate* defensive medicine—that is, wasting resources. In reviewing the data from a series of studies, Schwartz (1994) concluded that the threat of lawsuits has encouraged hospitals and professional groups to adopt risk management programs and reduced the actual number of malpractice incidents and the amount of harm that results from incidents when they do occur.

A recent study by Kessler and McClellan (1996) attempted to study the effects of tort reform on the variable of "defensive medicine" and drew a conclusion partially contradicting Schwartz's conclusion. Kessler and McClellan defined "defensive medicine" as the use of medical tests and procedures that are unnecessary in contrast to procedures that actuarially promote better outcomes for patients. Their hypothesis was that the enactment of tort reforms would reduce physicians' fear of lawsuits and thus encourage them to avoid treatments that do not have worthwhile medical benefits. If this phenomenon in fact occurred, it should be reflected in lower medical costs.

To test the hypothesis, Kessler and McClellan examined nationwide Medicare payments for elderly patients admitted to a hospital with a new primary diagnosis of a heart disease, either myocardial infarction or ischemic heart disease. Amounts of Medicare payments in the years 1984, 1987, and 1990 were compared across states according to the degree and type of tort reforms. The authors also controlled for a number of demographic and other variables that might account for differences across states. In addition to Medicare payments, the authors included the important variable of mortality rates. Their reasoning was that if Medicare expenditures were lower in tort reform states but there was no difference in mortality rates, this would reflect a drop in defensive medicine.

The regression analyses conducted by Kessler and McClellan appear to support their hypothesis. They concluded that malpractice reforms that directly reduce provider liability reduce medical expenditures between 5 and 9 percent without any substantial effects on mortality rates. The Kessler and McClellan study is well reasoned and contains a number of control variables, but the results will have to be replicated before any conclusions can be drawn. The study has a number of limitations. The most major limitation is that the sample only dealt with elderly patients with heart disease. It is not clear that the results would have any generalizability. Moreover, this population poses a possible significant methodological problem, namely a ceiling effect on the mortality variable. Mortality rates for elderly patients with heart disease are very high, and thus the variance on the mortality variable may be quite restricted. If this is the case, then we would not expect to obtain significant differences between states regardless of the presence or absence of tort reforms. Finally, Kessler and McClellan observed that the results they found were ephemeral: after a five-year period following tort reform, the differences in Medicare payments disappeared. This finding raises the possibility that the effects were temporary and due to short-term psychological reactions.

In a subsequent study, Kessler and McClellan (1997) concluded that doctors who had a malpractice claim filed against them were more likely to report changes in the way they practiced medicine than doctors who had not had such an experience. They speculated that reforms of liability laws affect physicians' attitudes, which in turn affects their behavior, but the precise effects could not be determined from their research.

Many advocates of tort reform who still favor the fault principle have cited Indiana as an ideal instance of tort reform, as exemplified by the legislative history and assertions in the Illinois Tort Reform Act of 1995 (Illinois Public Act 89-7). However, Kinney et al.'s (1991) study of the actual process of malpractice litigation in Indiana indicated that the reforms seriously eroded the fault principle. Recall that a central part of the reforms was the establishment of a patient compensation fund for claims exceeding $100,000. Kinney et al. found that health care insurers and defendants chose not to seriously contest claims with damages near or exceeding the $100,000 limit. In a word, there is little incentive to devote time and finances to contest claims that will be paid by the patient compensation fund. Kinney et al. summarized their findings as follows:

> Indiana's malpractice reforms operate in a unique fashion that softens the expected impact of these reforms and actually results in a compensation scheme that is more generous in several respects than the common law tort system. . . . [T]he factors that influence the final

payment of claims in the common law tort system, such as, what a jury will find on liability or the future expenses involved in pressing a claim through trial, are not considered in the claimant's compensation. In these respects, Indiana's system is similar to no-fault compensation systems that pay claims more efficiently with little regard to fault. [Kinney et al. 1991, 1303]

The Kinney et al. research clearly points to the complexity of the legal system and the unexpected effects of legal reforms. It has the potential to provide important guidance to policy decisionmakers.

Summary and Perspective on Maps and Gaps

This selective overview of research on medical malpractice litigation shows that a useful, though still crude and incomplete, map of an important and controversial component of the tort system has begun to emerge over the past fifteen years. Strikingly, it contradicts some of the most widely held public and professional beliefs about the tort system. To wit, once cases enter, the tort system appears to be relatively effective in weeding out nonmeritorious cases. Within limits, the tort system provides compensation with more rationality than many critics have charged. It discourages frivolous lawsuits. There is some evidence that it deters negligent behavior. At the same time, persons with less serious injuries tend to be compensated at proportionately higher rates than persons with more serious injuries. Besides, there are major barriers to the tort system. Many injured persons do not receive compensation. Research on other areas in the tort system is less developed but what does exist appears generally consistent with the research on medical malpractice (see Eisenberg et al. 1996; Galanter 1996; Gross and Syverud 1991, 1996; Hensler 1993; Ostrom, Rottman, and Goerdt 1996; Saks 1992).

The research on the tort system, therefore, appears to be consistent with the goals set forth in Stan Wheeler's seminal paper on "legal indicators" and on Sarat's call for research that documents routine behavior of the legal system as well as inconsistencies and gaps. However, as pointed out at the beginning of this chapter, the question of "effectiveness" involves multiple criteria and value judgments about these criteria. In some instances, one definition of effectiveness is irrelevant to that of another. Other criteria may be diametrically opposed. In the most obvious example, some persons favor raising barriers to recovery, while others favor lowering them. Empirical sociolegal research cannot resolve these value disputes, but it can set terms around which the dialogue must center and focus policymakers on the real issues.

The other issue discussed by Sarat, and one that often occupies the discussions of sociolegal scholars, is whether anyone in a position to make policy listens. There are, of course, the striking examples in which courts have rejected solid social science findings, misinterpreted them, defined them as irrelevant, or, perhaps even worse, ignored them altogether (Sarat 1985).

This is not always the case. In *Best v. Taylor Machine* (179 Ill. 2d 367, 689 N.E. 2d 1057 [1997]), the Illinois supreme court ruled that the Civil Justice Reform Act of 1995 (Illinois Public Act 89-7) was unconstitutional. As part of its reasoning, the court cited affidavits by Marc Galanter, Stephen Daniels, Joanne Martin, and myself that discussed research findings contradicting empirical assertions in the legislative record associated with passage of act.

Most of the time, however, impact is less direct. Empirical research on the tort system has had some success in causing both traditional legal scholars and interest groups to back away from some of their unsubstantiated claims about the tort system. Some serious journalists, who ultimately have influence with the public and with legislators, have also begun to show more balanced reporting of the issues, particularly with respect to unfounded claims about the tort system that they used to accept uncritically on a regular basis (Vidmar 1995).

We should not be too optimistic about the immediate impact of sociolegal research on policymakers, and perhaps this is a good thing. After all, as is apparent from this overview, even within a narrow area of tort law, such as medical malpractice, the issues are complex. They change over time because laws change and social, psychological, and organizational behaviors change, sometimes even as we are studying a phenomenon. And even within a single time frame, studies frequently contradict one another because researchers' methodologies or data sets produce different results. However, this is a general problem with any scientific enterprise (see Jasanoff 1995). Scientific discoveries in physics, chemistry, medicine, and astronomy, to take a few examples, frequently emerge from conflicting studies conducted by many researchers over years and even decades. Why should sociolegal research be any different? It is imperative to take a long view and not anguish over impact.

In any event, it is safe to say that considerable progress has been made toward understanding the behavior of the tort system. Much of the progress has been the result of sociolegal studies that map the routine activities as well as the gaps.

References

AMA (American Medical Association)/Specialty Society Medical Liability Project. 1988. *A Proposed Alternative to the Civil Justice System for Resolving Medical Liability Disputes: A Fault-based Administrative System.* Chicago: American Medical Association.

Andrews, Lori B. 1993. "Medical Error and Patient Claiming in a Hospital Setting." American Bar Foundation Working Paper 9316. Chicago: American Bar Foundation.

Bovbjerg, Randall, 1989. "Legislation on Medical Malpractice: Further Developments and a Preliminary Report Card." *University of California, Davis, Law Review* 22: 499–556.

———. 1991. "Lessons for Tort Reform from Indiana." *Journal of Health Politics, Policy, and Law* 16: 465–83.

———. 1992. "Medical Malpractice: Folklore, Facts, and the Future." *Annals of Internal Medicine* 117: 788–90.

———. 1993. "Medical Malpractice: Research and Reform." *Virginia Law Review* 79: 2155–208.

Bovbjerg, Randall, Frank Sloan, and James Blumstein. 1989. "Valuing Life and Limb in Tort: Scheduling 'Pain and Suffering.' " *Northwestern Law Review* 83: 908–76.

Bovbjerg, Randall, Frank Sloan, Avi Dor, and Chee Hsieh. 1991. "Juries and Justice: Are Malpractice and Other Personal Injuries Created Equal?" *Law and Contemporary Problems* 54: 5–42.

Brady, Michael, and Peter Cubanske. 1993. "The Judicial Arbitration System: Its Promise and Its Shortcomings." *For the Defense* (August): 29–31.

Broeder, Ivy, 1986. "Characteristics of the Million Dollar Awards: Jury Verdicts and Final Disbursements." *The Justice System Journal* 11: 349–59.

Budetti, Peter. 1992. "Malpractice and Access to Health Care. *St. Louis University Law Journal* 36: 879–96.

Burstin, Helen, William Johnson, Stuart Lipsitz, and Troyen Brennan. 1993. "Do the Poor Sue More?" *Journal of the American Medical Association* 270: 1697–741.

Daniels, Stephen, and Joanne Martin. 1990. "Myth and Reality in Punitive Damages." *Minnesota Law Review* 75: 1–64.

———. 1995. *Civil Juries and the Politics of Reform.* Evanston, Ill.: Northwestern University Press.

Danzon, Patricia A. 1985. *Medical Malpractice: Theory, Evidence, and Public Policy.* Cambridge, Mass.: Harvard University Press.

———. 1986. "The Frequency and Severity of Medical Malpractice Claims: New Evidences." *Law and Contemporary Problems* 49: 57–84.

———.1990. "The 'Crisis' in Medical Malpractice: A Comparison of Trends in the United States, Canada, the United Kingdom, and Australia." *Law, Medicine, and Health Care* 18: 48–57.

Dauer, Edward, and Leonard Marcus. 1997. "Adapting Mediation to Link Resolution of Medical Malpractice Disputes with Health Care Quality Improvement." *Law and Contemporary Problems* 60: 185–218.

Eisenberg, Theodore, John Goerdt, Brian Ostrum, and David Rottman. 1996. "Litigation Outcomes in State and Federal Courts: A Statistical Portrait." *Seattle University Law Review* 19: 433–53.

Farber, Henry, and Michelle White. 1991. "Medical Malpractice: An Empirical Examination of the Litigation Process." *The Rand Journal of Economics* 22: 199–217.

———. 1994. "A Comparison of Formal and Informal Dispute Resolution in Medical Malpractice." *Journal of Legal Studies* 23: 777–806.

Felstiner, William, Richard Abel, and Austin Sarat. 1980–81. "The Emergence and Transformation of Disputes: Naming, Blaming, and Claiming." *Law and Society Review* 15: 631–54.

Galanter, Marc. 1974. "Why the 'Haves' Come Out Ahead: Speculations on the Limits of Legal Change." *Law and Society Review* 9: 95–160.

———. 1983. "Reading the Landscape of Disputes: What We Know and Don't Know (and Think We Know) about Our Allegedly Contentious and Litigious Society." *UCLA Law Review* 31: 4–71.

———. 1993. "News from Nowhere: The Debased Debate on Civil Justice." *Denver University of Law Review* 71: 77–113.

———. 1996. "Real World Torts: An Antidote to Anecdote." *Maryland Law Review* 55: 1093–160.

Goldschmidt, Jona. 1991. "Where Have All the Panels Gone? A History of the Arizona Medical Liability Review Panel." *Arizona State Law Review* 23: 1013–109.

Gronfein, William, and Eleanor Kinney. 1991. "Controlling Large Malpractice Claims: The Unexpected Impact of Damage Caps." *Journal of Health Politics, Policy, and Law* 16: 441–64.

Gross, Samuel, and Kent Syverud. 1991. "Getting to No: A Study of Settlement Negotiations and the Selection of Cases for Trial." *Michigan Law Review* 90: 319–93.

———. 1996. "Don't Try: Civil Jury Verdicts in a System Geared to Settlement." *UCLA Law Review* 44: 1–64.

Hamilton, Lee, and Joseph Sanders. 1996. "Corporate Crime through Citizens' Eyes: Stratification and Responsibility in the United States, Russia, and Japan." *Law and Society Review* 30: 513–48.

Hans, Valerie. 1996. "The Contested Role of the Civil Jury in Business Litigation." *Judicature* 242–48.

Hensler, Deborah. 1993. "Reading the Tort Litigation Tea Leaves: What's Going on in the Civil Liability System?" *The Justice System Journal* 16: 139–54.

———. 1994. "Why We Don't Know More about the Civil Justice System and What We Could Do about It." *USC Law* (fall): 10–15.

Jasanoff, Sheila. 1995. *Science at the Bar.* Cambridge, Mass.: Harvard University Press.

Johnson, Kirk, Carter Phillips, David Orentlicher, and Martin Hatlie. 1989. "AMA Report 1989. A Fault-Based Administrative Alternative for Resolving Medical Malpractice Claims." *Vanderbilt Law Review* 42: 1365–406.

Kalven, Harry, and Hans Zeisel. 1966. *The American Jury.* Boston: Little, Brown & Co.

Kessler, Daniel, and Mark McClellan. 1996. "Do Doctors Practice Defensive Medicine?" *Quarterly Journal of Economics* 111: 353–90.

———. 1997. "The Effects of Malpractice Pressure and Liability Reforms on Physicians' Perceptions of Medicare." *Law and Contemporary Problems* 60: 81–106.

Kinney, Eleanor, William Gronfein, and Thomas Gannon. 1991. "Indiana's Medical Malpractice Act: Results of a Three-Year Study." *Indiana Law Review* 24: 1275–307.

Koenig, Thomas, and Michael Rustad. 1995. "His and Her Tort Reform: Gender Injustice in Disguise." *Washington Law Review* 70: 1–90.

Kritzer, Herbert. 1997. "The Wages of Risk: The Returns of Contingency Fee Legal Practice." *DePaul Law Review* 47: 267–320.

Kritzer, Herbert, William A. Bogart, and Neil Vidmar. 1991. "The Aftermath of Injury: Cultural Factors in Compensation Seeking in Canada and the United States." *Law and Society Review* 25: 499–543.

Lloyd-Bostock, Sally. 1991. "Propensity to Sue in England and the United States of America: The Role of the Attribution Process." *Journal of Law and Society* 18: 428–30.

Macchiaroli, Jean. 1990. "Medical Malpractice Screening Panels: Proposed Legislation to Cure Judicial Ills." *George Washington Law Review* 58: 181–260.

MacCoun, Robert. 1996. "Differential Treatment of Corporate Defendants by Juries: An Examination of the Deep Pockets Hypothesis." *Law and Society Review* 30: 121–61.

May, Marlynn, and David Stengel. 1990. "Who Sues Their Doctors? How Patients Handle Medical Grievances." *Law and Society Review* 24: 105–20.

McClellan, Frank M. 1993. *Medical Malpractice: Law, Tactics, and Evidence.* Philadelphia: Temple University Press.

Meschievitz, Catherine. 1991. "Mediation and Medical Malpractice: Problems with Definition and Implementation." *Law and Contemporary Problems* 54: 195–216.

———. 1994. "Efficacious or Precautious? Comments on the Processing and Resolution of Medical Malpractice Claims in the United States." *Annals of Health Law* 3: 123–38.

Metzloff, Thomas, Ralph Peeples, and Catherine Harris. 1997. "Empirical Perspectives on Mediation and Malpractice." *Law and Contemporary Problems* 60: 107–52.

Miller, Richard. 1994. "Tort Law and Power: A Policy-Oriented Analysis." *Suffolk University Law Review* 28: 1069–97.

Munsterman, G. Thomas, Paula Hannaford, and G. Marc Whitehead, eds. 1997. *Jury Trial Innovations.* Williamsburg, Va.: National Center for State Courts.

Nichols, Terry. 1986. "The Technical and Conceptual Flaws of Medical Malpractice Arbitration." *St. Louis Law Review* 30: 571–631.

Ostrom, Brian, David Rottman, and John Goerdt. 1996. "A Step above Anecdote: A Profile of the Civil Jury in the 1990s." *Judicature* 233–241.

Peterson, Mark A. 1987. *Civil Juries in the 1980s: Trends in Jury Trials and Verdicts in California and Cook County, Illinois.* Santa Monica, Calif.: Rand Corporation.

Peterson, Mark, Syam Sarma, and Michael Shanley. 1987. *Punitive Damages: Empirical Findings.* Santa Monica, Calif.: Rand Corporation.

Physician Payment Review Commission. 1992. *Annual Report to Congress, 1992.* Washington, D.C.: Physician Payment Review Commission.

President's Council on Competitiveness. 1991. *A Report from the President's Council on Competitiveness: Agenda for Civil Justice Reform in America.* Washington, D.C.: President's Council on Competitiveness.

Rolph, Elizabeth, Erick Moller, and John Rolph. 1997. "Arbitration Agreement in Health Care: Myths and Reality" *Law and Contemporary Problems* 60: 153–84.

Rosenblatt, Roger, Randall Bovbjerg, Amanda Whelan, Laura-Mae Baldwin, Gary Hart, and Constance Ling. 1991. "Tort Reform and the Obstetrics Access Crisis: The Case of the WAMI States." *Western Journal of Medicine* 154: 693–96.

Rosenblatt, Roger, Amanda Whelan, and Gary Hart. 1990. "Obstetric Practice Patterns in Washington State after Tort Reform: Has the Problem Been Solved?" *Obstetrics and Gynecology* 76: 1105–10.

Rustad, Michael. 1994. "The Jurisprudence of Hope: Preserving Humanism in Tort Law." *Suffolk University Law Review* 28: 1099–162.

Rustad, Michael, and Thomas Koenig. 1995 "Reconceptualizing Punitive Damages in Medical Malpractice: Targeting Amoral Corporations, Not Moral Monsters." *Rutgers Law Review* 47: 975–1083.

Saks, Michael. 1992. "Do We Really Know Anything about the Behavior of the Tort Litigation System—and Why Not?" *University of Pennsylvania Law Review* 140: 1147–292.

———. 1994. "Medical Malpractice: Facing Real Problems and Finding Real Solutions." *William and Mary Law Review* 35: 693–726.

Sanders, Joseph, and Craig Joyce. 1990. "'Off to the Races': The 1980's Tort Crisis and the Law Reform Process." *Houston Law Review* 27: 207–95.

Sarat, Austin. 1985. "Legal Effectiveness and Social Studies of Law: On the Unfortunate Persistence of a Research Tradition." *Legal Studies Forum* 9: 23–31.

Schuck, Peter H. 1993. "Mapping the Debate on Jury Reform." In *Verdict: Assessing the Civil Jury System,* edited by Robert Litan. Washington, D.C.: Brookings Institution.

Schwartz, Gary. 1994. "Reality in the Economic Analyses of Tort Law: Does Tort Law Really Deter?" *UCLA Law Review* 42: 377–444.

Sentell, R. Perry, Jr. 1991. "The Georgia Jury and Negligence: The View from the Bench." *Georgia Law Review* 26: 85–178.

Simmons, Walter. 1996. "An Economic Analysis of Mandatory Mediation and the Disposition of Medical Malpractice Claims." *Journal of Legal Economics* (fall): 41–75.

Sloan, Frank, Penny Githens, Ellen Clayton, Gerald Hickson, Douglas Gentile, and David Parlett. 1993. *Suing for Medical Malpractice.* Chicago: University of Chicago Press.

Sloan, Frank, and Chee Rhuey Hsieh. 1990. "Variability in Medical Malpractice Payments: Is the Compensation Fair?" *Law and Society Review* 24: 601–50.

Spurr, Stephen, and Walter Simmons. 1996. "Medical Malpractice in Michigan: An Economic Analysis." *Journal of Health Politics, Policy, and Law* 21: 315–46.

Strier, Franklin. 1994. *Reconstructing Justice: An Agenda for Trial Reform.* Chicago: University of Chicago Press.

Studdert, David, Eric Thomas, Brett Zbar, Joseph Newhouse, Paul Weiter, Jonathan Bayuk, and Troyen Brennan. 1997. "Can the United States Afford a 'No Fault' System of Compensation for Medical Injury?" *Law and Contemporary Problems* 60: 1–34.

Sugarman, Stephen. 1985. "Doing away with Tort Law." *California Law Review* 73: 555.

———. 1987. "Taking Advantage of the Torts Crisis." *Ohio State Law Journal* 48: 328.

Taragin, Mark, Laura Willett, Adam Wilzek, Richard Trout, and Jeffrey Carson. 1992. "The Influence of Standard of Care and Severity of Injury on the Resolution of Medical Malpractice Claims." *Annals of Internal Medicine* 117: 780–84.

Thompson, Mark. 1997. "Letting the Air out of Tort Reform." *American Bar Association Journal* 83: 64–68.

U.S. Department of Justice. 1986. *Report of the Tort Policy Working Group on the Causes, Extent, and Policy Implications of the Current Crisis in Insurance Availability and Affordability*. Washington, D.C.: U.S. Department of Justice.

Vidmar, Neil. 1993. "Empirical Evidence on the 'Deep Pockets' Hypothesis: Jury Awards for Pain and Suffering in Medical Malpractice Cases." *Duke Law Journal* 43: 217–66.

———. 1994a. "Are Juries Competent to Decide Liability in Tort Cases Involving Scientific/Medical Issues? Some Data From Medical Malpractice." *Emory Law Journal* 43: 885–911.

———. 1994b. "Making Inferences about Jury Behavior from Jury Verdict Statistics: Cautions about the Lorelei's Lied." *Law and Human Behavior* 18: 599–617.

———. 1995. *Medical Malpractice and the American Jury: Confronting the Myths about Jury Incompetence, Deep Pockets, and Outrageous Damage Awards*. Ann Arbor: University of Michigan Press.

———. 1998. "The Performance of the American Civil Jury: An Empirical Perspective." *University of Arizona Law Review* 40: 849–99.

Vidmar, Neil, Laura Donnelly, Thomas Metzloff, and David Warren. 1992. *An Empirical Examination of a Legislated Procedural Reform: Court-based Management of Medical Malpractice Litigation*. Durham, N.C.: Private Adjudication Center, Duke University School of Law. January.

Vidmar, Neil, Felicia Gross, and Mary Rose. 1998. "Jury Awards for Medical Malpractice and Post-Verdict Adjustment of Those Awards." *DePaul Law Review* 48: 265–99.

Vidmar, Neil, and Jeffrey Rice. 1991. "Jury-determined Settlements and Summary Jury Trials: Observations about Alternative Dispute Resolution in an Adversary Culture." *Florida State University Law Review* 19: 89–103.

———. 1993. "Assessments of Noneconomic Damage Awards in Medical Negligence: A Comparison of Jurors with Legal Professionals." *Iowa Law Review* 78: 883–911.

Viscusi, W. Kip, and Patricia Born. 1995. "Medical Malpractice Insurance in the Wake of Liability Reform." *Journal of Legal Studies* 24: 463–90.

Weiler, Paul. 1991. *Medical Malpractice on Trial*. Cambridge, Mass.: Harvard University Press.

Weiler, Paul, Howard Hiatt, Joseph Newhouse, Troyen Brennan, and Lucian Leap. 1993. *A Measure of Malpractice: Medical Injury, Malpractice Litigation, and Patient Compensation*. Cambridge, Mass.: Harvard University Press.

Wheeler, Stanton. 1971. "Notes on Legal Indicators." Report presented at the Social Science Research Council meetings. Unpublished report.

Wissler, Roselle, David Evans, Alan Hart, Marian Morry, and Michael Saks. 1997. "Explaining 'Pain and Suffering' Awards: The Role of Injury Characteristics and Fault Attributions." *Law and Human Behavior* 21: 181–208.

Zuckerman, Stephen, Randall Bovbjerg, and Frank Sloan. 1990. "Effects of Tort Reforms and Other Factors in Medical Malpractice Insurance Premiums." *Inquiry* 27: 167–82.

Chapter 6

Hunting for Bias: Notes on the Evolution of Strategies for Documenting Invidious Discrimination

Jack Katz

Since the 1950s, academic research has increasingly sought to document the reach of invidious discrimination in U.S. society. As a quick
indicator of the scale of change, we can take an electronic look at the
annual increases since the mid-1970s of the research literature on
bias. A search, conducted in mid-1998, of the title word "bias" in
Sociological Abstracts produced five articles for 1972, ten for 1976, sixteen for 1985, twenty-five for 1990, and thirty-six for 1995.[1] The increase in numbers is less revealing about the dynamics of social
thought than is the expansion of targets. What has expanded are the
background variables of interest (not only gender but also sexual orientation, not only race but ever new varieties of ethnic identity,
newly defined disabilities of many sorts, and so forth) as well as the
terrain on which they may be influential. Now bias is hunted, not
only in employment decisions, criminal justice decisionmaking, news
broadcasts, apartment renting, and real estate mortgage lending but
also in the interaction that takes place in college classrooms; in the
selection of research subjects for health studies; in the casual comments made by judges, employers, and virtually anyone with power;
in the location of hazardous waste facilities; and in the use of nursing homes, social security, or any publicly funded service.

Outside the field of sampling methodology, the hunt for bias
began in earnest only after the opening created by the civil rights

and related social movements of the 1960s. When, in the early 1970s, the "Watergate" scandals stimulated accusations of social class bias in the administration of criminal justice, an additional group of researchers joined the more general hunt for biases of political and ascribed status.[2]

Research seeking to document bias is a movement that has come to distinguish social thought in the last quarter of this century, but it is a movement that has not generated a collective self-awareness among those who study different institutional domains. It should now be useful to appreciate research on bias as a general wave in the history of ideas and to explore several issues about it. I first differentiate three major ways of hunting for bias that have been pursued in a range of social fields and institutions. Next, in the three sections that comprise the bulk of this essay, I describe the characteristic methodological problems that have pestered and provoked the evolution of each research strategy.

Finally, I address the natural history of bias hunting. As increasingly sophisticated methods for documenting bias have brought responsive transformations in social organizations and popular culture, there has been a patterned progression from the first to the second to the third hunting strategy, in one institutional setting after another. In this evolution, the version of evil constructed by bias researchers has been radically transformed in a direction that threatens to undermine the moral fervor of the hunt.

Three Conceptions of Bias

Wherever it is sought, both academic research and popular culture understand bias in one or another of three ways: as personal psychological prejudice, as disproportionate organizational outcomes, and as systematic imbalances in pressures on decisionmakers. These constitute three contrasting ontologies of bias, three understandings of where and how bias exists. The first two are well known in legal, popular, and research cultures; the third is a familiar form of popular cynicism but has developed with less fanfare in social research.

The three strategies of hunting for bias sometimes converge, but they often produce very different results. In the employment area, for example, an interview study may successfully hunt out hidden prejudices by asking employers to comment on their attitudes toward employment applications that vary by race. But an outcome study may show that a disfavored group is, in any case, disproportionately *over*represented in the ranks of those employed by the prejudiced employer. And a study of the interaction processes through which the employer in fact makes hiring decisions may explain why (see Waldinger 1997). The employer may be prejudiced to hire Asians rather than Latinos, but he may never get to make a decision on Asian applicants because Latinos fill job openings before he knows that vacancies exist. This occurs because Raul only informs the employer that he is leaving his job after he has lined up his cousin, Luis, as a replacement. Presented with a problem that was solved before he confronted it, the employer is tempted to disregard his prejudices because, if he goes to the trouble of advertising and recruiting Asians and they do not turn out to be better employees than Latinos, he will have been a fool three times over, first for losing the opportunity to allow Raul to solve his immediate problem without cost, second for hiring an undesirable employee that he now will find costly to dismiss, and third for taking the risk of alienating Raul and his circle or at least for sacrificing an opportunity to underwrite his relationship with them.

Consider also the varying pictures of bias that the three strategies may provide when applied to news media coverage of environmental issues. A content analysis of news shows may reveal that the comparative ratios of positive and critical items in the editorial language used by broadcasters favor environmental groups over their industry targets, suggesting a "liberal" bias among news workers. But an outcome analysis may show that, somehow, corporate spokespeople get more airtime than do environmental advocates (Danielian 1994). And a study of the practical construction of news programs is likely to show that editors and producers more regularly and more diffusely anticipate how corporate sponsors, as compared to environmental activists, may react to news broadcasts.

The three strategies may also lead in different directions when they are used to hunt for bias in the administration of criminal justice. Observers may code police personnel as expressing racist attitudes toward African American juveniles. An outcome study may show that the race ratios in juvenile arrest statistics reflect the race ratios in victim complaints. And studies of how court personnel arrange punitive and rehabilitative treatments with residential placement officials are likely to find that courts find it substantially easier to negotiate understandings that place white, as compared with black, delinquents in minimally restrictive supervisory facilities.

Of course, the findings of the three strategies for documenting bias may converge, but it is characteristic of the hunt for bias that a given study will pursue one or the other, but not all three, and hence will never confront the possibility of divergent outcomes. Hunters of bias as personal prejudice tend to be researchers who devise survey research questions. Bias is often documented in organizational outcomes by researchers who analyze statistics produced by others. And bias as differential pressures on decisionmakers is typically the province of ethnographers. In a way, the isolated pursuit of each hunting strategy speaks to the segregation of groups of social researchers, a division that is in the first instance methodological rather than self-consciously moral or political. As these examples show, it is not clear that each strategy has a consistent ideological undertone, at least not in terms of left and right, liberal and conservative, critical and quiescent. Indeed, the literature is replete with findings that appear to surprise and even disappoint the researchers themselves.

Spoiled Psyches

A generation before the civil rights successes of the 1960s, what came to be targeted as bias was studied primarily as a matter of personally held prejudice. When the existence of bias was de jure, a matter of group pride, and explicit in the social practices often referenced as "Jim Crow," social researchers still hunted bias, because not everyone embraced, or equally embraced, cultures of prejudice. But with prejudice so openly trumpeted, researchers, in order to warrant their efforts, had to probe the subtleties of personal attitudes and the features of individually held stereotypes in order to find something that, having been hidden, could be revealed.[3]

In this period, psychologists and survey researchers led the way. Posing questions to respondents, university researchers might vary the settings in which fictional blacks were placed in order to elicit evidence of bias. If more positive opinions were expressed about blacks who were described in a nonstereotypical black setting or in a more elevated social status, the researcher could take for granted that prejudice accounted for the more negative opinions of blacks described in a lower status (Westie 1953) and in a more stereotypical setting (Riddleberger and Motz 1957). In surveys, predefined indicators of biased attitudes were administered to large populations, usually with disturbing results (Selznick and Steinberg 1969).

Sociologists with a flair for investigative innovation marked out the field. Playing off of informal "stooge" experiments (or "auditing" studies), they might match black and white restaurant customers to see if they received differentially respectful treatment (Selltiz 1955). Or they might craft variations in applicants' biographies and mail them according to quasi-experimental design procedures in order to see how employers would respond to varying indications of applicants' criminal records (Schwartz and Skolnick 1964).

On the ethnographic side of research before the 1970s, investigators rarely adopted participant observer roles as members of dominant groups in order to document the workings of prejudice. Instead they either came as outsiders or passed as members of groups victimized by prejudice in order to write narratives in which they documented the socially pervasive and personally intimate reach of biased customs (Griffin 1961). In the innocent (unsuspecting) times before the civil rights era, student ethnographers could readily document expressions of racial prejudice among officials. Police in northern cities seemed to assume that anyone, or at least any white researcher who hung around them for a while, would sympathetically understand their symbolic and physical violence against blacks (Westley 1953).

A long history of "whites only" signs, law school entrance criteria that rejected female applicants out of hand, and formal newspaper affiliations with political parties created warrants for a generation of researchers who could expect to bag abundant evidence of abiding prejudice just under the surface of recently adopted masks of equal treatment. Although other methods for hunting bias have become more prominent in the past twenty-five years, the hunt for signs of personally held, invidious stereotypes remains vigorous. Despite the fact that overt discrimination is now taboo, researchers still can make major trappings of explicit prejudice. Thus in their recent research on racial discrimination in employment, Kirschenman and Neckerman (1991) interviewed Chicago-area employers and found them egregiously using invidious racial stereotyping. Similarly, in recent studies of juvenile criminal justice processes, researchers found police, prosecutors, judges, and social workers using stereotypes about the black family in order to justify less favorable treatments for African American juvenile defendants, even without evidence that the specific youths in question were in fact members of families that fit the stereotypes (Frazier and Bishop 1995).

If the outlawing of explicit prejudice has not pushed the use of invidious stereotypes into private reserves that social research cannot penetrate, still there is reason to believe that bias, as a psychological disposition, has become a more closely held matter. Accordingly, after the 1960s academic researchers and lay interpreters of popular culture began searching for new ways of revealing hidden psychological bias. Survey researchers began looking for race prejudice that hides behind respondents' overt affirmation of principles of equal justice but that may be elicited by asking about their support for the government's implementation of abstract values (Sears, Hensler, and Speer 1979).

As sanctions for discrimination were developed, researchers could expect that the evil they hunted would change form. If prejudice must be exercised under greater cover, then the prejudiced decision-maker is likely to search for new, more indirect indicators of whether people fit into favored or disfavored categories. If, for example, employment applications must not ask directly for racial identifiers, then race-prejudiced employers need to develop a folk understanding of the relationship between race and biographical matters that legitimately can be requested of applicants, such as residential address. Similarly, with the news media under pressure to justify the identification of race when reporting crime, bias hunters have reason to suspect that news readers and news writers have begun a silent collaboration to settle on new conventions to convey and recognize racial identity. As a result, one direction in the hunt for psychological bias that has emerged since the 1960s is the detection and documentation of its folk-recognized handles or "code language." (On perhaps the most famous instance in recent political history—the "Willie Horton" phenomenon—see Feagin and Vera 1995, 114–24.)

An evolving part of this symbolism of evil is the development of res ipsa loquitur indicators of personal prejudice. Certain pejorative terms for indicating people's ascriptive characteristics—"nigger" being the most prominent, "queer" and "PMSing" being perhaps the most recently condemned—have, since the 1960s, come to be understood as possessing a negative sacred force so destructive that their expression creates a virtually unrebuttable sign of prejudice when used by people to describe other kinds of people. In popular culture, symbolic indicators of personal prejudice are now treated as so diabolical that they cannot be used safely in many situations in which they were used casually before the 1960s. The hunt for bias as personal prejudice proceeds in tandem with popular cultural codings of the evil. As the eponymously named Earl Butz unwittingly demonstrated more than twenty years ago, joking by an official at the expense of an ascriptively designated group can now let loose spirits of humor that may quickly turn self-destructive if the audience is expanded to include representatives of the "others" who are being ridiculed.[4] Social researchers follow a parallel logic of presumptive damnation, for example by coding as sexist broadcasters' descriptions of female athletes as "girls" (Sabo and Jansen 1992).[5]

The hunt persists for indicators of prejudice that are still emitted by the unwary. For example, U.S.-born Asian American university students often spice autobiographical statements in their graduate school applications with indignant recollections of remarks such as "How well you speak English!" or "You don't have any accent," which they offer up as obvious indicators of racial prejudice. And researchers, somewhat paradoxically using their own stereotypes with some success, search for overt expressions of invidious stereotypes in what they presume have been backwaters to progress. Criminal justice researchers must look for the old ways in increasingly out of the way locations, such as in rural and small town courts as compared to large urban jurisdictions (Feld 1995).

Obstacles to Trapping Bias in Psyches

Personal prejudice, conceived as a stained state of mind, a spoiled quality of character, a perverse outlook, a corrupted predisposition, or a hostile set of attitudes, calls the bias hunter to an essentially hermeneutic task. One serious problem with discerning the spirit behind an expression is that of determining what Erving Goffman (1974) has called the "frame" and the "key" of an expression. (Currently, analysts of "postmodern" life address these issues as matters of "irony.") A judge in open court refers to a litigant before him as a "nigger." The local district attorney quickly demands that the judge be removed from the bench. But the judge does not step down. Instead he contacts friends in the local civil rights organizations in which he has long been active, and they help to create a setting in which he can get a hearing for his version of the event, which is that he was mocking the racist perspective of a litigant in the case before him.[6]

Social research is not exempt from similar risks of imputing prejudice in circumstances where an expression may be heard in a different key by interviewer and interviewee or by third parties to the interview who may come on it later. Do we understand Mark Fuhrman's use of "nigger," in an interview with an aspiring script writer, as motivated by racist passions, as a private joke about what Fuhrman took to be the interviewer's prejudices about white L.A. policemen, or as an unsolicited audition, an effort to enact a screen-worthy racist cop?[7] Without a clear understanding of the frame (the interaction context) and the key (the nature of personal involvement) in which an expression is uttered, the analyst lacks a firm basis for imputing prejudice to an interviewee.

In social research today, there is often an awkward struggle as interviewees, anticipating that their opinions might be construed as racist, try to work out a key to share with an interviewer. One can detect an unsuccessful effort by interviewee and interviewer to establish a common key in the following passage from a much-cited study that attributes "racism or discrimination as a significant cause [of blacks'] disproportionate representation" among the jobless. The interviewee is described as a suburban drug store manager.

Interviewee: It's unfortunate, but, in my business I think overall [black men] tend to be known to be dishonest. I think that's too bad, but that's the image they have.

Interviewer: So you think it's an image problem?

Interviewee: Yeah, a dishonest, an image problem of being dishonest men and lazy. They're known to be lazy. They are [laughs]. I hate to tell you, but it's all an image though. Whether they are or not, I don't know, but it's an image that is perceived.

Interviewer: I see. How do you think that image was developed?

Interviewee: Go look in the jails [laughs]. [Kirschenman and Neckerman 1991, 221]

Any uncertainty in the interpretation of what this transaction means about the interviewee's racial attitudes, such as precisely why he is laughing, apparently is to be resolved by the reader joining with the authors in silently snickering contempt.[8] But in order to understand this employer's laugh as evidence of racism, one must presume the existence of the employer's racism that the data are supposed to demonstrate.

Where the issues of frame and key are not in doubt, the effort to establish bias may falter on the need to impute a broader substantive context in order to understand whether res ipsa loquitur indicators of prejudice are indicating favorable or unfavorable attitudes. If black athletes are more often described by sportscasters as "naturally talented," is that an insulting imputation of biological predetermination to nonintellectual careers or a metaphor expressing aesthetic dimensions in observed performance (Sabo and Jansen 1992)? When judges use terms of endearment to address female attorneys, are they imposing gender-specific obstacles, offering opportunities for adversarial maneuvering, or enacting innocent rituals such as the still-acceptable gender references "Mr." and "Ms." (Riger et al. 1995)? There is a difference in treatment, but what the difference means, indeed whether such expressions even raise a prima facie case of prejudice, depends on whether one assumes that consequential practices are nonrandomly related to the difference in expressions.

The problem of how to read such expressions is one that distinctively haunts the search for bias in the form of psychological prejudice, as opposed to studies of bias either as differential outcomes or as nonparallel pressures anticipated by decisionmakers. The other two methods of hunting for bias are not faultless, but neither do they play so closely with the lid of this particular Pandora's box. For even when prejudice is established, it is another matter to demonstrate that the personal outlooks of decisionmakers play a significant role in influencing the distribution of rewards and penalties to cases. What may be at stake may be only the appearance of unjust treatment. Only in some institutional arenas, such as the administration of criminal justice, do such limited findings reliably constitute grounds for objection.

The Moral Career of Stalking Prejudice

One of the virtues of the search for bias in the form either of outcomes or of pressures in the social context of decisionmaking is the relative impersonality of the inquiry. Bias in the form of prejudice targets individuals, and because of the characterological understanding of prejudice, reforms tend to address individual personality in a deep way. When, for example, students of bias in juvenile justice interpret the interview responses of court personnel as racist, they may recommend not only sensitivity or "diversity training" programs but also personally focused review procedures (Frazier and Bishop 1995). Triggered by the charges of coworkers and observers that casual expressions by criminal justice personnel are racist, such review procedures carry implications for the tenor of everyday work life that will be chilling for some civil libertarians.

Another problem for researchers who would document bias as a form of personal prejudice has developed in part from the very success of bias hunters in introducing bias as an interpretive category in popular culture. In a number of extraordinarily publicized cases, symbols of prejudice have been taken as sufficient to justify remedial action without the outraged audience receiving a full airing of the defense. In the O. J. Simpson case, the prosecution abandoned Mark Fuhrman after he was shown to have made apparently racist remarks of a sort that he had denied having made; no contextual account of the remarks was developed. In 1995, ATF (federal alcohol, tobacco and firearms) agents were sanctioned when a videotape of their annual social affair displayed racist signs; the sanctions were geared in part to overcome the agency's initial failure to treat the charges with sufficient concern (Michael Abramowitz, "Early 'Roundup' Allegations Were Ignored by ATF Officials," *Washington Post*, July 22, 1995, p. A1, col. 4). The Texaco corporation recently issued an apology and settled a pending multimillion dollar claim shortly after the broadcast of an audio recording of executives' seemingly racist conversations.

The very speed at which controversies like the Texaco matter are settled deprives researchers of the evidence on contextual meaning that a vigorous defense would provide. On closer listening, it appeared that the Texaco executives had not used the word "nigger," as originally reported, and that another phrase that initially seemed to reek of prejudice (a reference to "black jelly beans") was a reference to a metaphor used by a human relations consultant employed by the corporation (Kelly 1996). The incident less clearly demonstrates that large corporations are racist than that their concerns about public image overwhelm their interests in creating a clear public record on the question of whether they are racist.

Such public events, by promoting a widespread understanding that allegations of racist attitudes can be explosively powerful, have far-reaching consequences for researchers who would hunt for bias in the form of personal prejudice. Prejudice is flagged with increasing ease even as resources for its documentation become more restricted. Recall the uneasy character of the interview noted above, in which a drug store manager varied the tone of his comments on blacks as potential employees. The more successful the indictment of prejudice through charges aired in public discourse, the more difficult it is to interpret research interviews that seek to gather high-quality, original data on the matter.

Additional obstacles for documenting bias in the form of personal prejudice have been mounting as research practices have become more sophisticated. For decades, only whites were asked about their views of blacks, and surveys that showed a high percentage of whites agreeing with negative views of blacks (as lazy, irresponsible, prone to violence, complaining, boastful) were readily taken as shocking proof of racism. But in a recent, leading survey that included black views, the percentage of blacks agreeing with negative views of blacks exceeded the levels reached by white respondents. Sniderman and Piazza (1993, 45) comment on results from the 1991 National Race Survey (which interviewed 1,744 whites and 182 blacks):

> Whenever there is a statistically significant difference between the views of blacks and whites, it *always* takes the form of blacks expressing a more negative evaluation of other blacks than do whites.

What if everyone is prejudiced? For social researchers, such findings challenge the process of characterizing some people as "not prejudiced" and, hence, what it can mean to be prejudiced. Similarly, if black employers have views of black job applicants that are similar to those of white employers, does that not bear on the understanding that the latter's views are racist (Wilson 1996)?

The interpretation of prejudice has become more problematic, not only because of increases in popular motivations for making charges of traditional forms of prejudice but also because of an enlarged understanding of what people can be prejudiced about. A recent study of a focus group discussion conducted in Los Angeles shows Latino, Chinese, Korean, and black participants all understanding that prejudiced attitudes impair their job chances. It also found "Anglo" women seeing that, with regard to promotions, "it's the boys' club" that determines who moves up. And "Anglo" men, lacking ethnic and gender bases for seeing themselves victimized, had no difficulty finding that prejudice hurt their chances because they lacked a kinship bond of the kind that is acquired through one's educational experience.

> I don't know if I want to clarify it in terms of an ethnic group. I would say, you know, maybe that it's all the same fraternity or something like that. Or went to the same school together. [Bobo et al. 1995, 75]

At some point, the proliferation of symbols that people are willing to read as indicia of prejudice forces research on personal prejudice to take on hermeneutic burdens that would make a literary critic jealous.

Further complicating the interpretation of expressions of prejudice are the new ascriptive rules of deixis that have developed for distinguishing ironic and other uses of denigrating terms. "Nigger," pronounced by blacks, is now presumptively understood as an ironic usage, while its use by nonblacks is presumptively treated as strictly liable. It now takes substantial argumentation to offer an ironic reading of defamatory racial and gender terms when they are used by people who lack the biological bona fides to put a self-effacing gloss on them. A sharp split between a richly nuanced and a straight, serious reading of the same expressions, depending on whether the defamatory term is self-indicating or not, has become familiar in American popular culture.

This split has been institutionalized commercially by the development of a segregated culture market in which ascriptively licensed merchants, such as "rap" singers of popular music and autobiographical performance artists, sell ritualized expressions of prejudice to the masses, sometimes with fabulous success. The public sensitivities developed since the civil rights era have been exploited to create a series of monopolies for ascriptive groups (ascriptive by ethnicity, gender, sexual persuasion, disability, and so forth) over an emotionally supercharged part of the national cultural marketplace. But if public discourse can sustain an increasingly clean line between subtle and simple readings of expressions of personal bias, academic researchers find this hermeneutic schizophrenia increasingly difficult to manage.

Students of bias-as-prejudice understand that there are interpretive dangers in their methods, even if they do not fully acknowledge them. Study after study begins by claiming, in its title and opening paragraphs, to document prejudice as a feature of personal psyche, but in the quick of the hunt the search almost always becomes a study of *perceptions* of prejudice. Researchers of prejudice appear to know that they cannot in the end finesse the challenge that called them to the hunt. They often slide between, on the one hand, careful descriptions of their findings, which are the perceptions of one set of people that another set is prejudiced and, on the other, groundless claims of having bagged the evil itself. Authors of studies on prejudice often try to let passages such as the following slip by, but some necks will snap in the reading:

> Presence of Bias [a category used in the author's analysis] refers to the belief in the presence of discrimination. Women in this study perceived more bias than men, and lawyers perceived more than judges. Identifying the extent of discrimination may be the first step in correcting the problem of gender bias. [Riger et al. 1995, 478]

Given the challenges of documenting prejudice in a historical epoch when prejudice is no longer proud of itself, those who would rely on perceptions of bias to establish psychological prejudice risk discovering, at the end of the chase, that they have been playing a virtual reality game.

To review, the documentation of personal prejudice has developed through three historical stages of research. From the 1940s to 1970, social psychological research was inspired by a definition of the prejudiced person as one who held negative racial ideas that were resistant to factual argumentation. The image of the biased person as a nonrational, emotionally governed, thick-headed sort was popularized in application to anti-Semitism (see, for example, Allport 1954; Selznick and Steinberg 1969).

This first stage of research began to be overtaken by methodological critiques and historical changes in the 1970s. Critical voices began to shake the faith that the line between fact and fantasy, or emotion and reason, was as bright as the early researchers had assumed. What level of proof should be necessary to discount assertions that Jews were clannish and tricky in business (Seeman 1981)? At the same time there was a major downward shift in respondents' declarations of prejudiced principles or "overt" racism. Whites dramatically stopped expressing views of inherent black inferiority and began embracing the ideal of desegregation (Schuman, Steeh, and Bobo 1988). A new generation of research would have to find prejudice in more subtle forms if it was to find major groupings of prejudiced psyches.

Accordingly, in the 1970s the documentation of personal prejudice entered a second stage by introducing a metaphysical distinction, one between what people *say* they believe about race relations and what they *really* believe. If respondents no longer voiced favorable views about the maintenance of racial barriers and segregation, they could still be considered racist if they opposed the implementation of programs to redress the inequalities that had been imposed on blacks (Sears, Hensler, and Speer 1979). Implementation—practical government actions to promote equality—was real stuff; ideals and principles were something else, something morally and psychologically less weighty. Now evil intent and spoiled personality could be scientifically found behind the opposition to progressive policies.

By the 1990s, both the straightforward interpretation of individuals' characterizations of racial groups as indicating prejudice and the metaphysical interpretation of conservative policy views as indicating prejudice were seen to be on shaky grounds. Some governmental efforts toward equal treatment, such as busing, had long been opposed by whites at levels so high (near 90 percent) as to make questionable the reading of policy views as signs of prejudice. But now opposition to busing began growing to substantial levels among blacks. As whites' negative statements about blacks continued to decline, and as whites' support for egalitarian and integration ideals continued to increase, a new generation of bias hunters began to question the logic of the earlier metaphysical distinction (Bobo 1983).

Advances in methodological sophistication created a new dilemma to confound the documentation of personal prejudice. In "experiments" that varied the order in which survey questions were put to respondents, it was found that people who voiced their views of blacks before they were asked for their views on affirmative action were *more positive* about blacks than were people who were first asked their opinion on affirmative action and then asked for their views on blacks. Racial hostility explained little of the variance in opposition to affirmative action, in part because that opposition was so intense and widespread; but asking about the issue of affirmative action significantly increased the expression of interracial hostility (Sniderman and Piazza 1993). Social survey researchers have reason to question their contribution to popular culture if, by hunting bias enthusiastically, they are stirring the dogs of prejudice to leap out of subconscious caves.

Experiments within surveys (randomly assigning to respondents questions that differ in strategic ways) have improved the ability to ferret out a significant level of prejudice in the forms of personal dislike and prosegregation sentiment, and to show that such traditional racism is still biasing views against pro-black policies (Schuman and Bobo 1988). But for over twenty years the big game in the survey hunt has been "new," "subtle," or "symbolic" racism (Sears et al. 1997), a target pursued in a way that is circular, logically and perhaps empirically. Respondents' views on race issues (for example, believing that most blacks on welfare could get along without it or that the position of most blacks has improved in recent years) are used to impute "symbolic racism," which is then used to explain views on (other) racial issues (for example, busing and affirmative action). Neither empirical grounds nor explicit definitional criteria justify labeling the independent variable as "racism." Thus, ironically, the effort to demonstrate underlying bias in the form of irrational prejudice at most can show rational consistency in overt policy views. (Compare, the argument by Sniderman and Tetlock 1986.)

More subtly, these bias hunters disregard that white opposition to race-specific policies may itself increasingly be in opposition to imputations of racism. The reseachers imagine that when people are polled, the questions elicit buried or covert thoughts and feelings about stereotypical blacks. But perhaps "symbolic racists" are in a different discourse, one directed at advocates, whatever their race, who would arbitrarily denigrate people as racist. As culture wars have exploded in the twenty years in which "symbolic racism" has been hunted, the survey researcher's shotgun has become so bent around that it risks hitting, not racist respondents but respondents' opposition to a perceived mass of racial moralists consisting of politicians, culture commentators, and social scientists who would impute the powerfully insulting term, racism, without a demonstrable warrant.

Attacked both as a politicized corruption of scientific research (Tetlock 1994) and as politically naive for failing to recognize the ubiquitous interpenetration of racial and social views (Bobo 1998), some advocates have retreated from "symbolic racism" to "racial resentment" (Kinder and Sanders 1996), and some leading survey researchers carefully avoid provocative terminology altogether, preferring neutral language about "racial attitudes" (Schuman et al. 1997). The central finding on "symbolic racism," that a large segment of the white population has views on race issues that are, presumably, offensive to most blacks as well as independent from both the liberal-conservative split and from overt expressions of racism, remains robust. But "symbolic racism" researchers have not explored the context and meaning of respondents' expressions sufficiently to determine whether that body of opinion should be denigrated as racist and dismissed, or explored as an outlook in contemporary culture wars with historically emergent meanings for its adherents. (The possibility that the same race questions change their meaning over time is noted in Schuman et al. 1997, 193, 327). Significantly, when researchers look for "subtle prejudice" they typically exclude "minority" respondents (for example, Meertens and Pettigrew 1997), a move that conveniently sidesteps the challenges that would be posed by the substantial proportions of minority respondents who share some of the responses that are systematically labeled "racist" when attributed to whites (Schuman et al. 1997, 251, 257, 308). Imputing "racism" or "prejudice" without an evidentiary base of the traditional anti-black affect and prosegregation sort and without explaining what "racism" means when the label is stampled on views shared by whites and at least a significant minority of blacks, increasingly seems to be an outworn rhetorical strategy that risks intimidating discussion and hindering research progress.

The certainty with which social researchers originally took for granted statements about blacks and Jews as indicating prejudice has been deeply shaken. When respondents do not agree to characterize themselves as racist, bias hunters are hard-pressed to find the methodological authority with which to confer the label. If, to boot, survey researchers intensify intergroup hostilities by searching for psychological bias by asking questions about controversial public policies, what is left to call hunters to the chase?

Organizational Outcomes

The normative theories for independently condemning bias as personal prejudice and as organizational outcomes have been discussed for thirty years now, perhaps most elaborately in the context of race and employment opportunities (for example, Fiss 1971). It is now widely taken for granted that, without any evidence about what decisionmakers in the system think or how they make decisions, researchers can document bias by showing that:

- Arbitrators' outcomes favor employees over employers (Bingham 1995).

- The news media broadcast the comments of noncandidates in presidential campaigns disproportionately from the liberal side (Lowry 1995).

- The sons of well-educated and occupationally elite fathers were underrepresented among Vietnam-era soldiers (Wilson 1995).

- A lower percentage of female than male students speak up in university classes (for a review of several studies, see Brady and Eisler 1995).

- A higher percentage of black than white juveniles are detained after arrest (studies cited in the following section).

If a question is raised as to how the biased outcomes are produced, the researcher can, without fixing blame on personnel of the organizations studied, point in one of at least two directions. First, one can indicate the organization's role in giving institutional form and specific personal impact to prejudices that operate outside a decisionmaker's jurisdiction. For example, if blacks are incarcerated in disproportion to their representation in the general population, but in proportion to their representation among arrests, one may still treat the imprisonment decision as racist by suggesting that judges carry forward the racism that governs the decision to arrest or, even without alleging prejudice among police, by suggesting that racial bias in employment opportunities explains racial differences in criminal conduct. Judges, in this view, unwittingly join forces with the racism that persists somewhere outside the criminal justice system.

Second, one may invoke understandings of deeply institutional-ized cultures of prejudice to rebut claims that differential outcomes equitably reflect differential performance. In this manner, one may dismiss evidence that women fare less well in promotions in sales jobs because they are less "aggressive." One may argue that "aggres-siveness" has become part of a gratuitous general conception of sales work, a culture shared by men and many unenlightened women (Eichner 1988).

For many bias hunters, the methodological issue is solely a tech-nical matter of comparing two definitions of a population, the one generated by the possibly biased institution and another generated by independent, morally neutral criteria. The model for this method-ology is the long history of research on sampling bias. The definition of a population produced through a given sampling procedure, say a telephone sample survey of residents, is compared with a door-to-door census in a small geographic area or perhaps with a mail sam-ple survey. The results of the telephone sampling procedure will be "corrected" by the results of the independent census or sampling pro-cedure, either on the presumption that the census is more accurate or on the view that neither the telephone nor the mail sample is more correct but that a weighted average of their findings is more likely to be near the true distribution of population than is either sample considered alone.

Similar weighting techniques for correcting organizational biases have been proposed in various institutional areas. "Affirmative ac-tion" is understood by some of its proponents as a correctional weighting procedure for employment opportunities, independent of any proof of personal bias against qualified applicants by employers, on the view that the principle taken from the Declaration of Independence, that "all men are created equal," provides a morally binding, irreducible, independent measure of the population picture that organizational action should, in a scaled down version, repro-duce. If applicants are not equally qualified, the principle of equal human worth, or competency in an existential sense, means that bias must have operated somewhere in the background, and there is no need to specify where, how, or by whom. To insist that the victims carry the burden of proving how bias was operationalized by social machinery is, in this view, to compound historically rooted injustice or, in a resonant contemporary phrase, to blame the victim.

Obstacles for Capturing Bias in Organizational Outcomes

The strategy of studying outcomes to establish bias faces a distinctive series of interpretive problems. One of the virtues of a conception of bias as a matter of personal prejudice is that, given a common cultural history in a society, one would expect prejudices to run consistently in a given direction through a multistage person-processing system, for example against rather than for blacks, all the way from hiring through the various stages of promotion in an employment career, and for rather than against white-collar defendants over the stages of criminal case careers. But outcome studies, once they begin to get even moderately complicated in modeling organizational processes, describe outcomes at successive stages of case or career processing, and the outcomes often are not consistent in the direction of advantage they describe. Barriers to employment at one stage may be reversed by affirmative action at another.

In a frustrating paradox for those who hunt bias in outcomes, bias appears to be systematically less visible in the final stages of case processing and career development where decisions are themselves more visible. This paradox is captured by the image of gender and ethnic "glass ceilings" in occupational careers. Since most organizations have fewer positions at the top of their hierarchies, the "n" of employment decisions becomes smaller at higher levels. Employment decisions at the top will be relatively more visible because they generate a relatively small database and because decisions on top jobs get unusual attention from internal and external audiences. But the inputs to employment decisions at the top, and thus the workings of any bias that may be present, are less visible because they are more idiosyncratic, making it harder to compare candidates. "Leadership" requirements are in a sense systematically invisible because they are about the ability to respond to unprecedented circumstances—the unknown. It is easier to write a job description for the work demands of the past than for those of the future.

The paradox of lesser visibility of bias in outcomes later on in employment careers has a parallel in the processes of criminal sentencing in juvenile (Dannefer and Schutt 1982), death penalty (Baldus, Pulaski, and Woodworth 1990), and white-collar cases (Wheeler, Weisbud, and Bode 1982). Let us assume that in the early stages of official action to create criminal cases, biased processes of sifting evidence give white and high-status defendants disproportionate opportunities to escape punishment. (This is, in fact, so, as I argue later, because bias in the earliest stages of white-collar, as opposed to street crime, case-making is more often a matter of unrecorded shifts in the direction and intensity of a suspicious gaze.) At later stages of decisionmaking, white-collar crime law enforcement officials respond to "cases," that is, to a formally documented pool of matters: arrests, referrals from investigating agencies, dossiers summarizing grand jury inquiries, and so forth. A bias toward capturing white-collar crimes early in the process would tend to make the cases addressed by officials at later stages especially egregious offenses. Officials at later stages will then seem to be exercising a neutral or even reverse-bias treatment of a class of suspects that was handled with special lenience at earlier stages (Berk and Ray 1982). Thus at the stages of case processing where the data for outcome studies are most "hard" (accessible, formally equivalent, and routinely and reliably produced), bias is likely to be least in evidence or, worse, to be systematically misleading. Put in other words, the most methodologically defensible outcome studies of bias in criminal justice administration are themselves biased against documenting bias accurately.

Another common methodological problem arises from the failure of organizations to specify formally the contingencies of their decisionmaking. "Comparable worth" and other studies of bias in employment generally begin by contrasting how two groups are distributed in applicant pools and how they are represented in job offers, promotions, or wage and benefit rates. Researchers then investigate whether differences in group outcomes may be explained by differences in the work that group members do or by the qualifications that they possess. But employers are not necessarily able to state, with a formality that would facilitate social research on bias, the considerations they use in sifting job applications. Outcome studies often reach a kind of standoff in which researchers, having demonstrated group differences in rewards that cannot be explained by existing, legitimate, measurable differences among members, confront employers who in effect will not reorganize their decisionmaking routines to produce data on as-yet unmeasured differences unless researchers can make not doing so very costly. But the bias hunter's ability to increase the pressure on employers hinges on the credibility of the case about bias that can be made with existing data. The debate here runs into a cul de sac over the question, who has the burden of coming forward with improved data, the social researcher or the employer? From the side of the social researcher, it is tempting to expect work organizations to reconstitute their operations so that they could be more easily studied. From the side of the employer, changes in operating or even documentation procedures might be appropriate if existing practices are biased, but that is the very matter at issue.

A similar problem haunts outcome studies of bias in all institutional settings. Social researchers typically come to the organizational targets of their inquiries relatively ignorant of traditional local procedures and culture. The measures of outcome that researchers devise often initially show bias, but they also show signs of artificiality. Thus a highly systematic study of news broadcasts may show a bias in favor of industry representatives, as opposed to consumer or environmental groups, in measures of spokespeople given airtime (Danielian 1994). But the initial posture of news stories involving industry and consumer/environmental conflicts is almost always critical of industry rather than of consumer/environmental groups. It is the forest cutting, air polluting, or oil spilling activities of industry, not the employment practices or tax filing status of advocacy groups, that are typically the premise of the story. Thus it is not clear that a balance of spokespeople—that is, industry's equal right to defend itself—is a sensible measure of equality. Social researchers are themselves biased to ignore the issue of the framing of news stories. What determines which stories do and do not become news in the first place is a trickier matter to quantify than is interest group representation in stories that are broadcast.

A similar issue—whether the hunted or the hunter has the burden of coming forward with readily measurable evidence that would rule out hypotheses rival to an explanation of bias—arises in the analysis of outcomes in death penalty cases. Existing studies indicate that there may be racial bias in the greater likelihood of a death sentence for the killers of whites. In resisting being swayed by such proof, courts have explained that "there are, in fact, no exact duplicates in capital crimes and capital defendants"; that is, decisionmakers may have been responding to nonracial aspects of cases that escaped the researcher's best efforts at measurement. Consider the following argument, which is intended to restore force to a showing of outcome bias in the face of such a defense.

Of course, if that conclusion is correct, it casts doubt on nearly every statistical study that is offered to establish a relationship in the real world. For example, studies that explore the relationship between smoking and heart disease control for a number of variables that might explain the relationship—age, blood pressure, diabetes, and obesity, for example—but inevitably they do not consider every factor that could possibly influence the health of each particular person. [White 1991, 154]

There is, however, a key difference between the two contexts for assessing bias, one that judges are not likely to miss even if social researchers and death penalty critics would prefer to ignore it. There are numerous reasons why, with respect to obtaining better measurable evidence of causation, it makes sense to impose a burden of coming forward with alternative explanations on tobacco companies but not on the prosecution in death penalty cases. With regard both to smokers' deaths and jury decisions, we would improve our understanding of the relevance and weight of causal influences if we had a more detailed record of causal processes. Tobacco companies could obtain additional data and offer their rival hypotheses as to what factors other than tobacco cause the greater mortality of smokers, in contrast to matched groups of nonsmokers, while still making cigarettes in the same way. But the additional data that the prosecution would need to demonstrate nonracial influences on jury decisionmaking is of a different nature. Research progress in this arena is likely to depend on transforming implicit processes of small group interaction into explicit forms of self-examination. It is not clear that juries could take on the burden of, in effect, explaining their decisions while remaining juries. Judges seem to be resisting what they hear as demands that they make legal proceedings into adjuncts of research projects that hunt for bias.[9]

Several other methodological challenges confronted by researchers of bias in organizational outcomes are specific to particular institutions. Employment is a highly differentiated social institution, as compared to the centralization of the criminal justice system and the relative concentration of the news media. If outcome studies document bias in one employment sector, they may document offsetting biases in another. This complexity is not abstract; it is the reality of contemporary American socioeconomic life. Thus in Los Angeles, there is ethnic bias in employment in the garment industry, in favor of Latinos; in public employment, in favor of African Americans; in white-collar Hollywood, in favor of Jews; and in nursing and other hospital employment, in favor of Filipinos (Waldinger 1997).

Shall we ignore the overall picture and undertake affirmative action in order to give blacks a proper representative presence in furniture manufacturing jobs and to boost Latinos to the advantages that blacks now enjoy in recruitment to public employment? Shall we aim for a society in which there is no bias in any employment sector or for one in which every group has the opportunity to discriminate within an equally prosperous zone (Glazer 1987)? Hunters of bias in organizational outcomes consistently find bias execrable in any employment area in which it is documented; but is such a stance more practical or morally superior to promoting a societal structure of offsetting biases?

The difficulty of these normative questions has methodological parallels. If we complete an analysis of bias in newspapers and major broadcast news programs, we may consider that we have covered the field because we tend to equate "the press" with these forms of dissemination, and "the press" has constitutional significance as a category. But why should we consider that a study of bias in manufacturing employment is complete before a study of bias in hospital employment has been conducted? "Manufacturing" is separate from the "health sector" and from "public employment" in various senses, but none justifies putting boundaries on the reach of social research.

If bias hunters first look at the "bottom line" of the distribution of income in different population groups, and then only look for employment bias to account for a given group's underrepresentation in income data, they may implicitly sanction biases that overrepresent the same group in other institutional sectors. And if the "bottom line" of outcomes does not show inequality, should that undermine the search for biased outcomes in particular employment sectors? The issue is not hypothetical. Over the past twenty years in Los Angeles, black working women have obtained and held parity with white working women with respect to median annual earnings (Waldinger and Bozorgmehr 1996). Does that dispose of the issue or leave the proper measure of income (such as range and standard deviations rather than just medians) as the sole remaining issue for investigation?

The administration of criminal justice presents special problems for capturing bias in outcomes. There is the problem of a lack of an authoritative independent touchstone for assessing organizational outcomes. In the employment area, for example, the success of unusually inclusive firms in a given sector may be cited to indict relatively exclusive firms. It is, however, a tricky matter to compare criminal justice results across jurisdictions and argue, for example, that a higher proportion of white people convicted in cities indicates that there is an inequitable failure to prosecute white criminals in small towns (Feld 1995).

The problem is not that the state, through police action, provides the only reliable definition of the distribution of crime. For thirty years, it has been possible to use victim surveys to check suspicions of bias in police action against independent measures of criminality. (Twenty-year-old findings that racial distributions in police arrests roughly paralleled racial distributions in victimization surveys have not been overturned; see Hindelang 1981.) The study of white-collar crime has highlighted a more intractable problem in developing independent benchmarks for the measurement of social class equity in criminal law enforcement. For most white-collar crimes, criminality does not take a situation-specific form that would allow disinterested stranger-observers to make authoritative reports of crime. Instead if criminal intent exists, it will have been diffused through a large set of routine practices, each of which may appear normal when viewed alone. When a parking meter attendant takes a bribe, there is a specific situation for the quid pro quo that an observer or undercover agent might efficiently put into evidence; when a president takes a bribe, the quid pro quo may be diffused over years of elaborate policymaking. Victimization surveys can be used to check for race, geography, and sex biases in police arrests with respect to common crimes, but not for biases that might let white-collar criminals off the hook.

Adding to the relative invisibility of white-collar crimes, common crimes disproportionately produce presumptive evidence of criminality—brutalized bodies, broken door jambs, and stashes of contraband—that enable law enforcement officials routinely to establish that crimes have occurred even without knowing the identity of the criminals. In contrast, when political corruption cases fail, they often end with protestations that not only is the accused innocent but no crime ever occurred. The very practice of street crimes often entails creating clear evidence that a crime is occurring. In order to rob someone, it helps to convince the victim quickly and unambiguously that he or she is being robbed. When defrauding an investor, on the other hand, it is helpful to steal a little from a lot of people, not to answer the phone too often, and to exercise the right of all innocent Americans to go bankrupt. When owners want to torch a building, they can arrange to have fires spring out of apparently negligent maintenance; without such an insider's advantage, an arsonist is more likely to leave evidence that enables fire inspectors to make presumptive conclusions that a "suspicious fire" has occurred (Goetz 1997).

Researchers who would find social class bias in the outcomes of criminal justice processing therefore must choose between the horns of the following dilemma. If they hunt for outcome bias by using victim allegations of criminality as the touchstone for measuring the evenhandedness of law enforcement response, they risk becoming the prisoner of partisan conflicts and of paranoid claims that attribute personal miseries to business and governmental conspiracies. If, however, they insist on authoritative evidence for allegations of victimization before finding bias, their procedures for documenting bias will be systematically biased against perceiving white-collar criminality and in favor of depicting street crimes.

Perhaps most troublesome to the logic of proving class bias in criminal processing is a rarely materialized but significant possibility: the prosecution of white-collar crimes can undermine the state of criminal law in a way that the prosecution of common crimes generally cannot. Vilhelm Aubert long ago identified this problem in a study of political negotiations over the criminalization of unpaid employment tax obligations in middle-class Norwegian households (Aubert 1952). Many criminal prohibitions of business and political practices were created on an understanding that they would not be broadly and vigorously enforced, an understanding reflected in limited appropriations for enforcement mechanisms. An increase in the successful prosecution of robberies and homicides is not likely to result in a movement to reduce the reach of criminal law enforcement, but a dramatic increase in tax fraud prosecution might, a sudden surge in the prosecution of international business bribery already did, and a large-scale prosecution of presidential campaign contributors and recipients very well may.

There are, then, distinctive problems of metaphysics and of political philosophy in hunting for independent measures with which to assess social class bias in the outcomes of criminal law enforcement proceedings. These were glossed with élan by Edwin Sutherland (1940), who described corporations as guilty of crimes on the basis of records of civil enforcement actions by government agencies. But since Sutherland's expressly socialist-inspired work on white-collar crime, these problems have haunted less politically committed white-collar crime bias hunters.

Because many criminal prohibitions of white-collar occupational conduct only exist to the extent that they are not enforced, *the hunt for social class bias in outcomes is itself biased against perceiving a bias in favor of white-collar criminals*. Those who would assert social class bias in law enforcement outcomes are in the uncomfortable position of waiting until cases conclude for authoritative proof of criminality to emerge. Gaps between cases that are effectively prosecuted and white-collar crimes that escape punishment appear with great regularity, but only retrospectively. By the time these bias hunters come face-to-face with their prey, hunting season is officially over.

The Natural History of Research on Bias in Outcomes

As with researchers who would document bias in personal psyches, cultural changes since the 1960s have significantly changed the research field that is encountered by researchers who would find bias in organizational outcomes. The historical experience in death penalty research represents a general pattern of continuing evolution in various institutional areas. Beginning with *Furman v. Georgia* in 1972, (408 U.S. 238) the U.S. Supreme Court made a series of decisions in response to charges that state systems of capital punishment are racist and arbitrary. It is arguable that the effects of reform have been to diminish but also to obscure the influence of bias in the administration of death penalties. Juries are now less likely to express racial prejudice unambiguously because they are more likely to have black members. And by blocking the death penalty for the rape of an adult woman, the Supreme Court also blocked the continued production of what had been the strongest evidence of racial bias in capital punishment (White 1991, 135–63).

A novel, unanticipated upshot of making bias less visible in the outcomes of criminal justice administration has been the emergence of a conflictual and silent discourse, carried on at the tacit level of practical action more than through explicit statements, of cross-cutting charges of bias in system outcomes. In 1992, an all-white jury acquitted Los Angeles policemen of allegations of aggression against black suspects, and then race riots were the response to what was seen widely as a biased case outcome.[10] For two days, live television coverage showed blacks and masses of immigrant Latinos looting stores. In California, verdicts in the O. J. Simpson and Reginald Denny cases were widely perceived among the white population as controlled by black jurors who, it was presumed, acted in a biased manner.[11] The O. J. Simpson verdict was especially controversial. Black college students were shown on television celebrating the acquittal, while many white citizens understood the jury to be treating the trial as a kind of negative affirmative action case in which facts specific to a black candidate who was qualified for conviction were overlooked in favor of redressing racial bias in the outcomes of routine criminal cases. In the aftermath of the riots and the controversial verdicts, California voters passed statewide voter initiatives that limited the ability of illegal immigrants to obtain public services, that increased criminal penalties (a "three strikes" law), and that ended affirmative action by state agencies.

What role did a perception of bias in the routine workings of the criminal justice system play in producing the verdicts in the Denny and Simpson cases? What role did the riots and the controversial verdicts play in contributing to passage of voter initiatives that were hostile to minorities? When the most critical arenas for assessing bias move into the jury room and the voting booth, bias becomes especially difficult to document, given the rules of institutional secrecy surrounding both processes as well as the historical uniqueness of votes on statewide propositions and of verdicts on particular cases. This paradoxical history (in which allegations of racial bias are, in a vociferous if inarticulate fashion, addressed to secret government processes) is summed up in two new, disturbing challenges for research on bias. One is symbolized by public assertions, some offered by University of California research professors, that the state's governor was racist because he backed anti-immigrant and anti–affirmative action voter initiatives. The hunt for bias in the outcomes of voting processes is here thrown back to a rhetoric alleging personal prejudice. The other challenge is symbolized by accumulating journalistic and anecdotal evidence that black jurors across the country, believing that correction is needed for the criminal justice system's biased outcomes, are refusing to base their judgments on evidence of individual guilt and are producing a record number of hung juries (Rosen 1997). The century draws toward a close with cross-cutting and perhaps unprecedentedly strong beliefs that racial bias rules the populist lawmaking and criminal punishment institutions of democratic government and with social researchers more confounded than ever in their attempts to find a neutral methodology to establish bias in organizational outcomes.

Unequal Pressures on Decisionmakers

A third strategy of investigation, although well represented in research studies, has yet to be appreciated as a distinct way of documenting bias. (See, for example, the review of studies of bias in Harris and Hill 1986.) As with the hunt for biased psyches, the focus here shifts back to specific individuals. However, the focus is on patterns that characterize how power wielders interact with others in their routine work practices, not on their personalities. More specifically, the focus is on actions taken toward the decisionmaker by others. Bias in this perspective is a matter of an imbalance in the pressures that an empowered person has reason to anticipate.

In Gary Becker's (1957) economics of discrimination, this perspective comes to life when the costs to an employer of not discriminating (such as reduced cooperation from an existing, prejudiced workforce) are set against the opportunity cost of lost profits that is entailed if discrimination is abandoned, the labor pool expands and wages fall.[12] If Becker's model does not deny that personal psychological prejudice is rampant, it does deny that one need be concerned to establish whether or not the employer-decisionmaker is him- or herself prejudiced. It is, in any case, much less clear how to reduce psychological pressures to discriminate than how to increase the cost of discrimination. One makes markets more competitive, for example by reducing trade barriers so that southern U.S. manufacturers must compete with foreign suppliers of substitute products.

Various research methodologies, but especially ethnographic research, tend to produce a similar perspective on bias, although they usually do so without guidance by theory or self-consciousness about the effort. Implicitly, they describe relative pressures against active and passive errors. To the extent that people are concerned about making errors at work, their concerns take the form of either apprehensions that someone will say that they have bungled a task they attempted or anxieties that someone will charge that they failed to take on challenges that a more competent employee would have perceived and seized. When researchers become curious as to *how* organizations shape the fates of the people they process as news subjects, applicants and employees, service clients, or criminal suspects, they naturally develop materials for documenting an appreciation of bias in the interaction context of work. A similar curiosity is stimulated when researchers who have constructed statistical descriptions of outcomes at several stages of people processing attempt to make sense of inconsistent indications of the direction of bias.

Difficulties for Documenting Bias in Its Interaction Context: The Case of Class Bias in Criminal Justice

A focus on differential social class treatment by the criminal justice system reveals multiple analytical problems for hunting for bias in the constellation of pressures surrounding decisionmaking. In this institutional context it is relatively obvious that one cannot conclude the hunt by comparing how a given organization handles different types of people or cases. A similar point holds but is more difficult to see when bias is sought in employment, broadcasting, and other institutional contexts.

There is a range of social class statuses within the pool of suspects addressed by any law enforcement agency, but these differences are relatively small compared with the pools of suspects formed by the state and federal systems in the United States. Thus one of the initial problems confronted by the effort to document social class bias in law enforcement is that the researcher must comprehend and develop a common language to talk across systematically divided organizational worlds.

The challenge is made geometric by the multiplicity of cultural worlds that constitute the system of federal law enforcement, which in recent history has included postal inspectors, ATF agents, the Secret Service, the Federal Bureau of Investigation, the Securities and Exchange Commission (SEC), treasury agents, wildlife protection personnel, customs officers, specialized drug enforcement units that are mobilized and put to rest from time to time, and so forth. In contrast, local police and sheriff departments relate to city- and county-level prosecution offices within a relatively homogenous cultural world and within a relatively simple set of interorganizational relations. If common and white-collar crime defendants are as apples to oranges, the researcher must compare how relatively simple and extremely complex social machines try to peel and crush them.

Although there are relatively tight organizational relationships between the police agencies and prosecution offices that handle the bulk of cases dealing with common crimes, the agencies that must cooperate to make federal cases against white-collar crimes are "loosely coupled" (see the application of this concept to criminal justice in Hagan 1989).[13] As a result, a comparative study of common crime and white-collar crime law enforcement must contain two methodologically different studies. The researcher can construct an atemporal model of the ideal typical functioning of the common crime enforcement system (see, for example, Rosett and Cressey 1976). But in order to document the social realities on the side of white-collar crime enforcement, the researcher must track a series of mini–social movements in which investigative agencies push prosecutors into action and prosecutors hustle agencies to get the resources necessary to make cases.

If the documentation of multiagency, intralaw enforcement pressures presents a substantial practical challenge to hunters of bias in criminal justice administration, the mobilization of pressures by audiences outside law enforcement creates substantial problems of another methodological order of difficulty. The series of scandals known as "Watergate" presented great opportunities for documenting class bias in law enforcement, but these research opportunities were so great as to caution severely against generalizing research findings.[14]

What should we make of such historically heightened social pressures on prosecutors not to make the passive error of failing to pursue cases of white-collar crime that ought to be brought to justice? Do they show that the enforcement system is usually biased against common criminals and away from aggressive responses to white-collar crime? Or do they show that law enforcement is moving in the opposite direction?

This methodological problem—that the data sets for analyzing social class bias in criminal justice processing only become richly available in historically unrepresentative times—would be more manageable if criminal justice processes in the 1980s had returned to their pre-Watergate status. But what happened was more complex. Subsequent scandals have reignited mini-waves of law enforcement against particular forms of white-collar crime. A prime example is the massive enforcement effort against fraud in the savings and loan industry (Pontell, Calavita, and Tillman 1994). The savings and loan enforcement experience and smaller-scale affairs such as Orange County's bankruptcy indicate another methodologically troublesome pattern. Unpredictable economic recessions bring business failures, which then predictably bring massive pressures from victims for governmental redress, in turn bringing even more predictable demands from legislators for investigations and prosecutions that will flesh out a moralized account of the victimization. Starts of economic hysteria and fits of morally indignant investigation systematically pattern the law enforcement effort against white-collar crime.

The methodological upshot of these fluctuations in enforcement effort is that hunters for social class bias will find a relatively stable target when examining the pressures on law enforcement against common crime but must describe a more jittery phenomenon when they try to analyze law enforcement against white-collar crime. Even though the system of pressures for and against the enforcement of white-collar crime law cannot be captured and confined, there surely is a beast out there that leaves a historical trail. The researcher must pursue that most elusive target of inquiry, a trajectory of historical development.

The Reversal of Bias in the Institutional Career of Case Processing

There is plentiful evidence that social class, considered as a matter of an individual's financial and social resources, systematically affects the fates of criminal cases (for an exceptionally useful study of the advantages that white-collar crime suspects receive from their defense counsel, see Mann 1985). When we define white-collar crimes by whether or not holding a position of trust is a distinctive resource for committing crime, there is additional plentiful evidence that social class, independent of one's financial resources, systematically affects the treatment that cases receive. However white-collar cases are defined, the different treatment they receive itself differs by the stage of case processing.

In the early stages of case development, it is easier for enforcement officials to let high-status people go and harder for officials to bring charges against them, as compared to the situation of low-status suspects. At the time that the prosecutor must decide whether to bring an indictment, common criminals, as compared to white-collar criminals, generally have relatively few resources with which to protest their innocence. In addition, the victims of common crimes are likely to be more actively and authoritatively pressing for prosecution than are the victims of white-collar crimes such as political corruption, price fixing, and inside trading. (As noted earlier, victims of white-collar crime often do not suspect that they are crime victims until a criminal case is well under way.) With respect to white-collar as opposed to common crimes, it is relatively easy for a prosecutor to avoid *even deciding* whether or not to prosecute (Katz 1979).

In the juvenile justice system, suspects with high personal status also have recurrent, significant advantages. Middle-class juveniles enjoy such advantages when they are stopped by the police, brought to police stations for processing and investigation, considered for deferral from formal charging, sentenced to types of punishment, and sent to detention facilities (Leonard, Pope, and Feyerherm 1992). Juveniles from well-to-do families have greater resources to hire lawyers who will argue that errors are being made if cases are handled aggressively. They also have family resources that make it easy for enforcement officials to dispose of cases in ways that are less harsh for the accused. In order to get formal charging deferred, middle-class families may offer to arrange for private therapy, pay tuition at special schools, and transfer an adolescent to the home of a respectable relative. The more desirable treatment facilities are likely to "cream" the applicant pool. Even the fact that the juvenile has a privately retained lawyer will sometimes indicate to judicial personnel that the family is committed to the youth's future and that the process has in a material sense already been a punishment (Feeley 1979).

Middle-class juveniles appear to receive more personally palatable treatment than do lower-class juveniles essentially because they can facilitate the interests of the enforcement system in pursuing diversionary and rehabilitative as opposed to individual justice goals. Poor juveniles generally have fewer resources for writing compelling essays that might get them admitted to desirable treatment facilities, for arriving at interviews with admission officials with their supportive parents on hand, and for locating relatives who, without themselves displaying multiple social problems to investigating social workers, could offer alternative residential placement. Comparing those who get sentences of confinement, poor (and black) juveniles more often get sent to impersonal, institutional facilities (Leonard, Pope, and Feyerherm 1992).

The flexible administrative framework of juvenile justice was historically based on an understanding of the need to rescue the urban immigrant poor from beginning careers in crime (Platt 1969). A richness of opportunities was created to avoid the "last resort" (Emerson 1981) of a presumably alienating period of detention. That this historical background has come to give advantages to suburban middle-class youths of native-born parents only adds irony to the injustice of social class inequalities in the enforcement system.

The substantive interests of regulatory agencies in promoting social justice inadvertently confer similar advantages on white-collar crime defendants. If securities or banking investigators approach organizations suspected of fraud with the sole intent of making a criminal case, they are likely to proceed in ways that will bring loud protests from persons other than the target. (On the following, see Shapiro 1985; Pontell, Calavita, and Tillman 1994.) Some victims will pursue civil remedies, which may be more difficult to mount if civil discovery becomes clouded by a pending criminal investigation; courts may effectively block civil recovery if a criminal action is filed. Some investors will not yet have lost money but will certainly lose if the suspect institution goes bankrupt after being criminally charged. Interest group observers may argue persuasively to legislators that the industry as a whole would have better protection if oversight agencies would give priority to widespread compliance rather than to isolated criminal prosecutions. By restraining its ability to develop criminal cases, an oversight agency has a powerful tool with which to induce cooperation in the implementation of old and in the development of new regulations. Anticipating how these third parties may respond, the agency develops an acute self-consciousness about the costs entailed, should it move ahead with criminal prosecution.

In contrast, the police may have a great variety of noncriminal law enforcement functions to perform (Bittner 1979), but when they arrest an adult for a common crime such as robbery or car theft, they are rarely interested in a multiplex relationship aimed at reconstructing the suspect's life in the community, much less the lives of people similarly situated.

Goals of social justice produce advantages for people of high status in the early stages of both the administration of juvenile justice and the regulation of white-collar occupational deviance. In both areas, legality, or the goal of treating alike cases that are similar from the standpoint of the suspect's culpability and without considering the consequences of prosecution for third parties, is compromised because of mandates to protect the weak. Regulatory agencies that oversee businesses generally profess the goal of making investment and consumer markets equally secure for participants whatever their social status, a service that the smaller investor and consumer especially needs. As a general matter, the bigger the business firm, the greater the number of consumers and investors it serves, and the more significant the protection that an oversight agency can obtain by forgoing criminal law enforcement in favor of modified business practices.

Later in the administrative careers of common and white-collar criminal cases, the imbalance of advantages generally diminishes and in some respects reverses. In many district attorneys' offices, plea bargaining that reduces or dismisses an official charge is closely supervised and regulated in contrast to the discretion exercised by police on the streets and in the stationhouse.[15] There is a concern for the appearance that the record will have for journalists and political opponents, both as to the conviction rate and as to the criteria for downscaling charges. In effect, at this point in its development, the process of handling a case creates records that make it feasible for new types of outside audiences subsequently to review administrative action, and that possibility, by way of anticipation, enters the immediate interaction context of decisionmaking. To the limited extent that middle-class juvenile or adult defendants are part of the pool of those charged by city and county prosecutors, advantages they enjoyed earlier in case-processing history are likely to diminish. Indeed, the demand by the U.S. electorate in recent years to create greater vigilance against the error of not punishing the guilty has led to a series of mandatory sentencing and virtually mandatory charging laws that increasingly specify the outcomes a prosecutor must seek.

When enforcement agencies address white-collar crimes, a reversal of bias develops near the stage of bringing formal charges. Resources aiding the making of criminal cases routinely turn up unexpectedly in white-collar crime investigations. In order to figure out how criminality was arranged and how high culpability reaches, investigators commonly need the cooperation of insiders. The probing that is necessary to document the culpability of a given white-collar criminal is likely to turn up numerous crimes committed by others.

Moreover, when investigative agencies are highly selective and engage in substantial case preparation before referring cases for prosecution, they are likely to develop relationships with prosecution offices that bring them high rates of case acceptance.

The reversal of an earlier bias in favor of white-collar crime suspects occurs in part because prosecutors believe that this pattern is generally understood to exist.[16] When investigative agencies and prosecutors decide to commit themselves to "make" cases of white-collar crime, they often target individuals and organizations, allowing the charges to take whatever fortuitous forms they may. Often charges are brought under such substantively uninformative and morally uninspiring rubrics as making "false declarations" to the government. What becomes key for the prosecutor is the construction of a melodrama in which "the capacity of law enforcement" triumphs over the toughest obstacles and brings down the most powerful operator in the criminally stained institutional area. To the prosecutor in the federal system, these symbols make sense; he or she presumes that there is a professional audience—in federal law enforcement communities, on the local federal bench, in the local bar—that will appreciate the significance of the case in these terms. Thus it is common to find prosecutors boasting of having successfully brought the "first" case of a given type, as if someone is keeping count.[17]

The upshot of this law enforcement culture is that, when prosecutors are assessing a well-developed investigative file, a suspect's high social status becomes a heavy disadvantage. Only a handful, or perhaps only one senator, party boss, brokerage house, or Fortune 500 executive may be convicted, but if the convicted felon stood at the head of a vast hierarchy of power, it is presumed that his fall will help jar the lower levels of the institution into submission to government authority. And the more prestigious the opposing counsel, the greater the satisfactions of a conviction for the prosecutors involved.

By the time the criminal justice process works its way to sentencing, the biases that earlier on favored criminals of higher social status seem to have vanished almost completely (Wheeler, Weisburd, and Bode 1982). There are several ways of understanding this surprising finding (Wheeler, Mann and Sarat 1988). If white-collar criminals enjoy comparatively greater powers to discourage prosecution, then those relatively few who become white-collar convicts must be an especially egregious lot, compared to common criminals who have less means to resist being swept up in the criminal justice process and carried on to its end.[18] And independent of what they find when they look at the particularities of the individuals before them, judges often understand that a white-collar criminal is likely to have gotten away with many other offenses and that the defendant up for sentencing must stand for many who will never be brought into the system.

Legality Versus Equality

The hunt for bias in the form of differential pressures on decision-makers produces a vivid awareness of the tensions between legality and social class equality. The tensions in the processing of criminal cases have three critical parallels with the search for gender and race inequalities in employment settings. First, concerns for legality treat bias at each stage of an occupational history as problematic, ignoring reversals and the possible cancelling effects of biases at later stages. At any stage of decisionmaking, an imbalance in the pressures to hire or advance candidates due to their ascriptive attributes is objectionable. But when bias at any stage becomes objectionable, institutions are deprived of tools for correcting historically received patterns of social justice or group inequalities. Legality, when applied too strictly, undermines objectives of righting historical injustices. The furor over affirmative action essentially reduces to a conflict between proponents of legality and proponents of social justice.

Hunters for bias in employment face a second challenge on the issue of whether they should seek evidence of bias across-the-board or only in organizations in which historically disadvantaged groups fare poorly. For example, social justice concerns could justify limiting bias research to the underrepresentation of blacks in construction, without considering the overrepresentation of blacks in public employment. But concerns for legality, or the evenhanded administration of power over individuals, respect no such limits.

Third, the hunt for bias in the social interaction context of decisionmaking raises civil liberties concerns about the pursuit for civil rights. When the investigating gaze turns toward the ways that audiences facilitate or resist a decisionmaker's choice of alternatives, research crosses over organizational boundaries and enters the informal lives of individuals and communities. The investigative reach extends to the personal biographical and often kinship-based processes through which ethnic and gender-based communities alert and aid their members to job opportunities in different parts of the economy. At this point, not only civil liberties agencies concerned about the freedom of expression, association, and privacy but also ethnic and gender associations are likely to see a trespass and rise to oppose the hunt. They can anticipate that stripped of practical value for influencing the distribution of employment opportunities through informal socialization, gender cultures, kinship ties, and ethnic affiliations would diminish in strength.[19]

Bias Research and the Fate of Righteousness

It is not too much to state that bias hunting has been the major innovation by American academic social research in the effort to unveil and describe the distribution of evil in society in the late twentieth century. Researchers working on race prejudice in the 1940s and 1950s had Hitler in mind as they sought to document anti-Semitism and keep racism from slipping underground. In the 1960s, research on bias, responding to the civil rights movement, shifted its concerns from Jews to blacks, then expanded the hunt to cover women and numerous other historical victims of bias. In the United States, the Watergate incident made the issue of social class bias in criminal justice processes—an issue that had been alive for a relatively few Marxist scholars—relevant to a far larger, institutionally better established, and politically rather bland community of law-and-society academic researchers.

One way to highlight the distinctive nature of bias hunting as a form of social research is to note that questions of explanation have been marginal to the movement. Even though explanation was a major concern in the fields of criminology and social stratification in the postwar period from, roughly, 1945 to 1975, explanation was not the central focus in studies of personal prejudice. The focus was less on the "why" of prejudice than on its reality, "nature," and social distribution, all three being questions whose answers could motivate and guide remedial efforts. When researchers began to search for bias in organizational outcomes, questions of why organizations would be biased were largely moot. If researchers could show that capital punishment was biased against blacks, or employment in academia was biased against women, or news coverage was biased in favor of corporations, it would be more or less obvious "why" that was the case. Virtually no one asked just whose prejudice, from just what epoch in history, and just how irrational hostilities had caused the biased outcomes; generalities about historical oppression, cultures of discrimination, lack of education, and social psychological research on the relationship of intergroup contact to intergroup prejudice were generally sufficient. It was a measure of the general respect accorded the evil of bias that it could be taken essentially as its own cause and explanation.

It has been the work of the third strand in the movement—that of hunting for bias in the interaction context of decisionmaking—that has smuggled the explanatory issue back onto the research agenda. But as researchers began to document how and why people get treated differently in the everyday workings of organizational processes, the moral thrust of their research began to run into new obstacles. Numerous patterns of tension between moral fervor and grounded explanation have been growing in the hunt for bias.

For one thing, the very success of early efforts to document bias has led to institutional changes that have diminished the moral appeal of attacks on persisting patterns of bias. The case against racial differences in the administration of capital punishment was at its height when the problem was that white murderers would escape death while equivalent black murderers would be executed. But reforms made in the wake of such evidence have produced a much less direct, much less inspiring critique of current race differences in the official administration of death. Now the problem is often posed as one of executing murderers of whites in cases like those in which murderers of blacks are not executed. To satisfy that complaint, we might logically execute both more blacks and more whites who murder blacks. The humanistic sensibilities that oppose capital punishment are no longer in a natural alliance with the moral forces against racism.

Second, the study of outcome bias at successive stages in the movement of cases through organizational systems has produced a much more sophisticated picture of how people processing works in various institutional settings, enabling us to appreciate that bias at an early stage often will be taken into account by decisionmakers at later stages. The picture that emerges is less unidirectional in the group advantages it describes. And at the late stages of processing, such as in sentencing, where decisionmaking is most visible, the appearance of bias is harder to make out. To adapt a pun that Susan Shapiro (1985, 214) used to good effect in describing her study of the SEC's processing of cases against big and small securities law violators, by the time researchers follow sets of cases through tortuous organizational processing trails, there is not much morally inspiring light at the end of the funnel.

Third, social research has interacted with popular culture in ways that threaten to dampen enthusiasm among the hunters. Researchers now may be surprised to find themselves among the hunted, for example when a staff turns on its leaders to allege bias in the administration of a research project that seeks to document bias (Schuman et al. 1983). And, despite a decline in the overt embrace of racial bias by whites, black Americans have become less positive in reviewing progress in civil rights:

> There has been a continuing decline in black beliefs that a lot of progress has been made in civil rights, with only 19 percent choosing that alternative in 1986. [Schuman, Steeh, and Bobo 1988, xiv]

Perhaps this decline in faith honors past progress and recognizes that further advances have become more difficult. Perhaps it discounts American culture's integration goals as hypocritical. In either case, progress in race relations has enabled a black middle class to expand significantly in the past twenty-five years, especially through avenues of public employment, and this has made it more difficult to document morally inspiring patterns of discrimination. The example of upper-middle-class African Americans competing against working-class Hispanic and Asian Americans for state university admissions did not loom on the horizon when the season for hunting bias was inaugurated with great fanfare in the 1960s.

Finally and most interesting for the history of social thought, research results have made the moral cosmology that was the original foundation of bias hunting increasingly untenable. An effort to document the existence and social distribution of evil is also an effort to document who in society is good. It is striking to recall that the search for bias in the psyches of the general U.S. population emerged in the wake of World War II as a liberal parallel to another lively hunt to differentiate good people from evil people, the conservative hunt for communists in symbolically powerful institutions of American society. But if moralized beliefs about personal character were originally appealing across the political spectrum for impassioned if ideologically opposite reasons, by the 1960s the lines of division no longer could be drawn as clearly.

It became clear that organizational biases run in different directions, not only when cases are traced through different stages of institutional processing, but also when the research gaze moves from institution to institution. It is increasingly appreciated that the state would have to intrude intimately into family and ethnic network relationships in order to free employment sectors from bias across-the-board. Bias research has now spewed up the prospect that we may not want to have a ubiquitously good society, in the sense of one that provides equal opportunity in each social institution, considered separately. What is more likely is that contemporary multiethnic societies will thrive on a range of domains of competing discriminations, with perhaps only exceptional institutions, such as university faculties and news broadcasting staffs, modeling the earlier ideal of a representative social composition. As surveys show, Americans like to see themselves as devoted to integration. The American political economy appears to have found that the efficient way to serve that desire is to dedicate a small number of high-profile, showcase institutions to depict an inspiring collective self-portrait, but not to burden the whole society with a thoroughgoing reconstruction.

The moral anthropology that originally fueled bias hunting is also being challenged. It is no longer taken for granted that fact and fantasy, truth and prejudice, biased and unbiased people can be disentangled methodologically. It turns out that evidence of prejudice by members of one group about members of another will only seem obvious if researchers stay away from learning what the latter think about their own kind. Because of the emergence since the 1960s of public relations arms for virtually all victim groups, it is now almost impossible to study victims close up without undermining their public images and producing fuel for "blaming the victim" (Katz 1997).

Bias research began with the sensible conviction that, in effect, once we figured out who the Nazis were and how to get rid of them, it would be time enough to figure out why they existed. Now it increasingly appears that we cannot first get the facts on bias straight while treating the social processes that produce bias as matters of secondary concern. How much bias exists cannot be established without understanding how people find out about and are recruited to jobs, how criminal justice personnel sequentially interact with juveniles and their families, and how respondents understand discourse as they speak with interviewers. For the social research community, the major challenge now is to accept that bias can only be described as well as it can be thoroughly and contextually explained.

I thank Bob Kagan, Donald Horowitz, and Melvin Seeman for patient critiques of earlier drafts, and an anonymous reviewer, solicited by the editors of this volume, for providing exceptionally painstaking comments. This chapter was first delivered as a talk at Lund University, Sweden, and then at the spring 1997 conference honoring Stanton Wheeler at Yale law school. Questions by participants at both sessions were very helpful.

Notes

1. Some of the expansion may be explained by the proliferation of journals in social science and the addition of publication sources to the database, but twenty-two of the thirty-six sources of the 1,995 articles on bias were publishing in 1972. The count grossly underrepresents the relevant research literature because it ignores all but sociological publications, picks up only articles with "bias" in the title (rather than "prejudice," "discrimination," and so forth), and ignores articles that treat the subject of bias in their text but do not use the word itself in their title.

2. Perhaps it is time to rethink the distinction between ascribed and achieved status, but if so, this is not the place. I just note that sexual orientation may be considered an ascribed characteristic because, like age, even though it may change over time and in some sense be acquired after birth, it is generally understood as having become ineluctable at some relatively early point in one's sexual biography, even if for some people it remains imaginatively and spontaneously flexible.

3. See Burstein (1994, ch. 1), for a quick refresher on how prominent and unashamed were racial, ethnic, and gender restrictions on employment.

4. "In 1976 Earl Butz, a former Purdue University dean, was forced to resign his position as secretary of agriculture after making racially offensive comments. Joking about what Republicans should offer black Americans, he stated that all a black man wants is 'loose shoes,' warm toilet facilities, and sex" (Feagin and Vera 1995, 111).

5. Broadcasters now refer to fourteen-year-old female figure skaters as "women," a practice that, in guarding against offending feminist viewers, runs the apparently minor risk of offending advocates of a protected childhood.

6. A court commissioner found himself in this dilemma in Los Angeles in the mid-1980s. See the *Los Angeles Times*, August 30, 1987, issue 106, sec. V, p. 4, col. 1.

7. In the highly publicized murder trial of O. J. Simpson, Mark Fuhrman was a Los Angeles police detective whose testimony against Simpson was impeached by revelations that, some years before, he had used racially derogatory language in a private interview.

8. Ironically, laughter is always an effort to transcend what is perceived as two inconsistent perspectives (Katz 1996). It is not inconceivable that the interviewee's laughter was not aimed at blacks but rather was part of an effort to resolve his apparently uneasy relationship with the interviewer.

9. In a quite different context, that of the allegedly biased actions of a public housing authority in disproportionately rejecting the defenses against eviction of one ethnic group, Richard Lempert has recently shown that the rhetoric of bias, or seemingly value-neutral argumentation about discrimination, resolves into a power struggle between cultures (Lempert and Monsma 1994).

10. This was a new pattern in the American history of race riots. Early in the century, for example, in Chicago in 1919, race riots emerged out of direct physical conflicts between whites and blacks. In the 1960s, for example, in the 1965 Los Angeles riots that began in the Watts neighborhood, anarchy emerged directly out of police stops of blacks. In the 1980s and 1990s, race riots have typically started only after juries (in Florida as well as in California) have acquitted policemen who were criminally prosecuted for actions against blacks.

11. A videotape frequently aired during the riots that erupted following the acquittal of Los Angeles policemen for beating Rodney King showed Reginald Denny, a white truck driver, being pulled out of his truck without provocation and being kicked and beaten in a seemingly joyous manner by several black males. The assailants, although convicted, were acquitted of charges carrying severe penalties.

12. In the employment context, bias is said to be "rational" when managers dispassionately anticipate the personal prejudices of their superiors or their organization's clients. For an application to gender bias, see Larwood, Szwajkowski, and Rose (1988).

13. Within federal criminal law enforcement, referral and acceptance relationships among agencies are subject to constant policy negotiations (Rabin 1972). Such negotiations are critical for understanding the pressures anticipated by a decisionmaker if he or she goes ahead or fails to proceed with a case. Some agencies, like the SEC and the tax division of the Justice Department, have unusually high rates of success when referring their cases for prosecution at U.S. attorney's offices. Others, such as federal welfare agencies, are known to refer cases of client fraud in order to get rejections that will enable them to export responsibilities

while clearing their internal books. Some agencies, before contacting a prosecutor's office, work their cases up much more than do others. There is no simple way to summarize the overall mix of pressures that other enforcement agencies bring to bear on U.S. attorneys. One must trace interorganizational relations to understand which agencies are likely to cite a prosecutor as having erred for not proceeding with a case and which agencies will not care.

14. In the immediate wake of Watergate, prosecutions of white-collar crime reached into business, political, and even university communities in a multitude of unprecedented ways. In domino-like fashion, the exposure of the president to criminal investigation exposed to prosecution a series of lower institutional authorities (Katz 1980). Watergate inspired regulatory officials to take extraordinarily aggressive postures in developing and pressuring prosecutors to institute cases of fraud and corruption, and vice versa. Unprecedented investigative initiatives, plus a succession of scandalous revelations in the mass media, brought whistle-blowers out at federal and state levels across the country.

15. "To enforce internal office control, all D.A.s [district attorneys] in Los Angeles were required to fill out an 'alibi sheet' for any case lost at trial or dismissed, to explain why they think it was lost. Records were also kept by supervisors in the D.A.'s office on charge reductions and other plea bargains negotiated by each deputy, in order to ensure some accountability. One D.A. explained: 'The head of trials never gets mad if you lose a case. That could happen to anyone. But you'll really get burned if you make a [nontrial] disposition when you shouldn't have. In other words, when you go beyond your authority you'll get reprimanded, but not when you make an error'" (Mather 1979, 18).

16. I draw here on my observational study of the federal prosecutor's office in the Eastern District of New York (Katz 1979).

17. Academics will recognize this rhetorical form as one that is common in discussions on cases of promotion. There is no need to scale down the magnitude of one's enthusiasm to the narrowness of the type of conviction or of the academic field in which one claims to be "first."

18. Examining SEC decisions to prosecute, Susan Shapiro found an overrepresentation both of suspects high in organizational status and of isolated low-status suspects (Shapiro 1985, 208–11).

19. In the early 1970s, Chicago's Mayor Daley responded to news reports that he had given the city's insurance business to one of his sons with words to the effect that what good is a father if he can't help his children? It is easy to ridicule such a response when the issue is nepotism by a high public official. When, however, the focus is on workers at low levels in private industry, another range of concerns comes into play, namely the value of enabling adults to link their younger generation kin

to the job world, thereby underwriting family authority and limiting delinquency in at-risk communities.

References

Allport, Gordon. 1954. *The Nature of Prejudice*. Cambridge, Mass.: Addison-Wesley.

Aubert, Vilhelm. 1952. "White-Collar Crime and Social Structure." *American Journal of Sociology* 58(November): 263–71.

Baldus, David C., Charles A. Pulaski, and George P. Woodworth. 1990. *Equal Justice and the Death Penalty*. Boston: Northeastern University Press.

Becker, Gary S. 1957. *The Economics of Discrimination*. Chicago: University of Chicago.

Berk, Richard A., and Subhash C. Ray. 1982. "Selection Biases in Sociological Data." *Social Science Research* 11(4): 352–98.

Bingham, Lisa B. 1995. "Is There a Bias in Arbitration of Nonunion Employment Disputes? An Analysis of Actual Cases and Outcomes." *International Journal of Conflict Management* 6(4): 6.

Bittner, Egon. 1979. *The Functions of the Police in Modern Society*. Cambridge, Mass.: Oelgesclager, Gunn, and Hain.

Bobo, Lawrence. 1983. "Whites' Opposition to Busing: Symbolic Racism or Realistic Group Conflict?" *Journal of Personality and Social Psychology* 45(6): 1196–210.

———. 1998. "Race, Interests, and Beliefs about Affirmative Action." *American Behavior Scientist* 41(7):985–1003.

Bobo, Lawrence, and Vincent L. Hutchings. 1996. "Perceptions of Racial Group Competition: Extending Blumer's Theory of Group Position to a Multiracial Social Context." *American Sociological Review* 61(6):951–72.

Bobo, Lawrence, Camille L. Zubrinsky, Jr., James H. Johnson, and Melvin L. Oliver. 1995. "Work Orientation, Job Discrimination, and Ethnicity: A Focus Group Perspective." *Research in the Sociology of Work* 5(5): 45–85.

Brady, Kristine L., and Richard M. Eisler. 1995. "Gender Bias in the College Classroom: A Critical Review of the Literature and Implications for Future Research." *Journal of Research and Development in Education* 29(1): 19–21.

Burstein, Paul. 1994. *Equal Employment Opportunity: Labor Market Discrimination and Public Policy*. Hawthorne, N.Y.: Aldine de Gruyter.

Danielian, Lucig H. 1994. "The Heavenly Chorus: Interest Group Voice on TV News." *American Journal of Political Science* 38(4): 1056–78.

Dannefer, Dale, and R. K. Schutt. 1982. "Race and Juvenile Justice Processing in Court and Police Agencies." *American Journal of Sociology* 87(3): 1113–32.

Eichner, Maxine N. 1988. "Getting Women Work That Isn't Women's Work: Challenging Gender Bias in the Workplace under Title VII." *Yale Law Journal* 97(June): 1397–417.

Emerson, Robert M. 1981. "On Last Resorts." *American Journal of Sociology* 87(1): 1–22.

Feagin, Joe R., and Hernán Vera. 1995. *White Racism: The Basics*. New York: Routledge.

Feeley, Malcolm. 1979. *The Process Is the Punishment: Handling Cases in a Lower Criminal Court*. New York: Russell Sage Foundation.

Feld, Barry C. 1995. "The Social Context of Juvenile Justice Administration: Racial Disparities in an Urban Juvenile Court." In *Minorities in Juvenile Justice*, edited by Kimberly Kempf Leonard, Carl E. Pope, and William H. Feyerherm, pp. 66–97. Thousand Oaks, Calif.: Sage Publications.

Fiss, Owen. 1971. "A Theory of Fair Employment Laws." *University of Chicago Law Review* 38(2): 235–314.

Frazier, Charles E., and Donna M. Bishop. 1995. "Reflections on Race Effects in Juvenile Justice." In *Minorities in Juvenile Justice*, edited by Kimberly Kempf Leonard, Carl E. Pope, and William H. Feyerhorn, pp. 16–46. Thousand Oaks, Calif.: Sage Publications.

Glazer, Nathan. 1987. *Affirmative Discrimination: Ethnic Inequality and Public Policy*. Cambridge, Mass.: Harvard University Press.

Goetz, Barry. 1997. "Organization as Class-Bias in Local Law Enforcement: Arson-for-Profit as a 'Non-Issue.' " *Law and Society Review* 31(3): 557–87.

Goffman, Erving. 1974. *Frame Analysis: An Essay on the Organization of Experience*. Cambridge, Mass.: Harvard University Press.

Griffin, John Howard. 1961. *Black Like Me*. Boston: Houghton Mifflin.

Hagan, John. 1989. "Why Is There So Little Criminal Justice Theory? Neglected Macro- and Micro-Level Links between Organization and Power." *Journal of Research in Crime and Delinquency* 26(May): 116–35.

Harris, Anthony R., and Gary D. Hill. 1986. "Bias in Status Processing Decisions." In *Rationality and Collective Belief*, edited by Anthony R. Harris, pp. 1–80. Norwood, N.J.: Ablex.

Hindelang, Michael J. 1981. "Variations in Sex-Race-Age-Specific Incidence Rates of Offending." *American Sociological Review* 46(4): 461–74.

Katz, Jack. 1979. "Legality and Equality: Plea Bargaining in the Prosecution of White-Collar and Common Crimes." *Law and Society Review* 13(Winter): 431–59.

———. 1980. "The Social Movement against White-Collar Crime." In *Criminology Review Yearbook*, vol. 2, edited by Egon Bittner and Sheldon Messinger, pp. 161–84. Beverly Hills, Calif.: Sage Publications.

———. 1996. "Families and Funny Mirrors: A Study of the Social Construction and Personal Embodiment of Humor." *American Journal of Sociology* 101(5): 1194–237.

———. 1997. "Ethnography's Warrants." *Sociological Methods and Research* 25(4): 391–423.

Kelly, Michael. 1996. "The Script." *The New Republic* 215(24): 6.

Kinder, Donald R., and Lynn M. Sanders. 1996. *Divided by Color: Racial Politics and Democratic Ideals*. Chicago: University of Chicago Press.

Kirschenman, Joleen, and Kathryn Neckerman. 1991. " 'We'd Love to Hire Them, But . . .': The Meaning of Race for Employers." In *The Urban Underclass*, edited by Christopher Jencks and Paul E. Peterson. Washington, D.C.: Brookings Institute.

Larwood, Laurie, Eugene Szwajkowski, and Suzanna Rose. 1988. "When Discrimination Makes 'Sense': The Rational Bias Theory." *Women and Work* 3: 265–88.

Lempert, Richard, and Karl Monsma. 1994. "Cultural Differences and Discrimination: Samoans before a Public Housing Eviction Board." *American Sociological Review* 59(6): 890–910.

Leonard, Kimberly Kempf, Carl E. Pope, and William H. Feyerherm. 1992. *Minorities and the Juvenile Justice System*. Thousand Oaks, Calif.: Sage Publications.

Lowry, Dennis T. 1995. "The Sound Bites, the Biters, and the Bitten: An Analysis of Network TV News Bias in Campaign '92." *Journalism and Mass Communication Quarterly* 71(1): 33–44.

Mann, Kenneth. 1985. *Defending White-Collar Crime*. New Haven, Conn.: Yale University Press.

Mather, Lynn. 1979. *Plea Bargaining or Trial?* Lexington, Mass.: Lexington Books.

Meertens, Roel W., and Thomas F. Pettigrew. 1997. "Is Subtle Prejudice Really Prejudice?" *Public Opinion Quarterly* 61(1): 54–71.

Platt, Anthony M. 1969. *The Child Savers: The Invention of Delinquency*. Chicago: University of Chicago Press.

Pontell, Henry, Kitty Calavita, and Robert Tillman. 1994. "Corporate Crime and Criminal Justice System Capacity: Government Response to Financial Institution Fraud." *Justice Quarterly* 11(3): 383–410.

Rabin, Robert L. 1972. "Agency Criminal Referrals in the Federal System: An Empirical Study of Prosecutorial Discretion." *Stanford Law Review* 24(June): 1036–91.

Riddleberger, Alice B., and Annabelle B. Motz. 1957. "Prejudice and Perception." *American Journal of Sociology* 62(5): 498–503.

Riger, Stephanie, Pennie Foster-Fishman, Julie Nelson-Kuna, and Barbara Curan. 1995. "Gender Bias in Courtroom Dynamics." *Law and Human Behavior* 19(5): 465–80.

Rosen, Jeffrey. 1997. "One Angry Woman: The Dramatic Rise of the Holdout Juror." *The New Yorker*, 73 (February/March): 53–64.

Rosett, Arthur I., and Donald R. Cressey. 1976. *Justice by Consent: Plea Bargains in the American Courthouse*. Philadelphia: Lippincott.

Sabo, Donald, and Sue Curry Jansen. 1992. "Images of Men in Sport Media: The Social Reproduction of Gender Order." In *Men, Masculinity, and the Media*, edited by Steve Craig. Newbury Park, Calif.: Sage Publications.

Schuman, Howard, and Lawrence Bobo. 1988 "Survey-Based Experiments on White Racial Attitudes Toward Residential Integration." *American Journal of Sociology* 94(20): 273–99.

Schuman, Howard, Eleanor Singer, Rebecca Donovan, and Claire Selltiz. 1983. "Discriminatory Behavior in New York Restaurants: 1950 and 1981." *Social Indicators Research* 13(1): 69–83.

Schuman, Howard, Charlotte Steeh, and Lawrence Bobo. 1988. *Racial Attitudes in America: Trends and Interpretations*. Cambridge, Mass.: Harvard University Press.

Schuman, Howard, Charlotte Steeh, Lawrence Bobo, and Maria Krysan. 1997. *Racial Attitudes in America*. 2d ed. Cambridge, Mass.: Harvard University Press.

Schwartz, Richard D., and Jerome H. Skolnick. 1964. "Two Studies of Legal Stigma." In *The Other Side*, edited by Howard S. Becker, pp. 103–17. New York: The Free Press.

Sears, David O., Carl P. Hensler, and Leslie K. Speer. 1979. "Whites' Opposition to 'Busing': Self-Interest or Symbolic Politics?" *American Political Science Review* 73(2): 369–84.

Sears, David O., Colette van Laar, Mary Carrillo, and Rick Kosterman. 1997. "Is it Really Racism?: The Origins of White Americans' Opposition to Race-Targeted Policies." *Public Opinion Quarterly* 61(1): 16–53.

Seeman, Melvin. 1981. "Intergroup Relations." In *Social Psychology*, edited by Morris Rosenberg and Ralph H. Turner, pp. 378–410. New York: Basic Books.

Selltiz, Claire. 1955. "The Use of Survey Methods in a Citizens Campaign against Discrimination." *Human Organization* 14(3): 19–25.

Selznick, Gertrude Jaeger, and Stephen Steinberg. 1969. *The Tenacity of Prejudice*. New York: Harper & Row.

Shapiro, Susan. 1985. "The Road Not Taken: The Elusive Path to Criminal Prosecution for White-Collar Offenders." *Law and Society Review* 19(2): 179–217.

Sniderman, Paul M., and Thomas Piazza. 1993. *The Scar of Race*. Cambridge, Mass.: Harvard University Press.

Sniderman, Paul M., and Philip E. Tetlock. 1986. "Symbolic Racism: Problems of Motive Attribution in Political Analysis." *Journal of Social Issues* 42(2): 129–50.

Sutherland, Edwin H. 1940. "White-Collar Criminality." *American Sociological Review* 5(February): 1–12.

Tetlock, Philip E. 1994. "Political Psychology of Politicized Psychology: Is the Road to Scientific Hell Paved with Good Intentions?" *Political Psychology* 15(3): 509–29.

Waldinger, Roger. 1997. "Black/Immigrant Competition Re-Assessed: New Evidence from Los Angeles." *Sociological Perspectives* 4013(Fall): 365–86.

Waldinger, Roger, and Mehdi Bozorgmehr. 1996. *Ethnic Los Angeles*. New York: Russell Sage Foundation.

Westie, Frank R. 1953. "A Technique for the Measurement of Race Attitudes." *American Sociological Review* 18(1): 73–78.

Westley, William A. 1953. "Violence and the Police." *American Journal of Sociology* 59(July): 34–41.

Wheeler, Stanton, Kenneth Mann, and Austin Sarat. 1988. *Sitting in Judgment: The Sentencing of White-Collar Criminals.* New Haven, Conn.: Yale University.

Wheeler, Stanton, David Weisburd, and Nancy Bode. 1982. "Sentencing the White-Collar Offender: Rhetoric and Reality." *American Sociological Review* 47(October): 641–59.

White, Welsh S. 1991. *The Death Penalty in the Nineties: An Examination of the Modern System of Capital Punishment.* Ann Arbor: University of Michigan Press.

Wilson, Thomas C. 1995. "Vietnam-Era Military Service: A Test of the Class-Bias Thesis." *Armed Forces and Society* 21(Spring): 461–71.

Wilson, William J. 1996. *When Work Disappears: The World of the New Urban Poor.* New York: Knopf.

Chapter 7

Good for What Purpose? Social Science, Race, and Proportionality Review in New Jersey

David Weisburd

Social scientists stood for many years on the sidelines of the law, calling for courts to make greater use of social science evidence in decisionmaking. The initial references to social science in court opinions in the first half of our century were scarce and often prefaced with cautions noting that social science facts were not legal facts as they were conventionally understood in the law (Monahan and Walker 1988). In part, it was that social science did not constitute a traditional source of evidence in the law that inhibited its use. But it is likely that the scarcity of social science in the law related as much to the growing pains of social science as to any inherent conflict between social science and the law. The idea that social science was science in the traditional sense was yet to be established, and the notion that social science facts could be relied on as were facts in more traditional areas of science was still a matter of debate (see Cairns 1935). In some sense, for social scientists, the acceptance of social science in the law was part of a larger struggle to gain acceptance of social science in the academy and outside it.

Looking at law, as an example, it would appear as if social scientists have reason to be pleased with their efforts over the past half century. Although many are concerned with how judges have used social science evidence or their methods of evaluating such evidence (see Diamond 1989; Saks 1974; Zeisel and Diamond 1974), social science has become a substantive actor in the courts (Loh 1984). In education (see *Brown v. Board of Education,* 347 U.S. 483 [1954]; Clark 1959; Rosen 1972), discussion of jury size (*Apodaca v. Oregon,* 406 U.S. 404 [1972]; *Ballew v. Georgia,* 435 U.S. 223 [1978]; *Colgrove v. Battin,* 413 U.S. 149 [1973]; *Johnson v. Louisiana,* 406 U.S. 356 [1972]; *Williams v. Florida,* 399 U.S. 78 [1970]; see also Lermack 1979), death penalty cases (Baldus, Woodworth, and Pulaski 1990), and a host of other areas of the law, social scientists and social science evidence have been cited and discussed, and in many cases social science has been a central issue in deciding the outcomes of cases. Even though it is argued that social science has served more often than not as window dressing to bolster positions that judges have already taken (Zeisel and Diamond 1974), the very fact that judges see fit to support their arguments with social science says much about the acceptance of our discipline in the courts and in the wider culture.

Having achieved some measure of success in establishing social science as a tool in the law, social scientists have begun to focus greater attention on factors that continue to hinder the integration of social science in legal settings. More often than not, scholars refer to the weakness of the social science evidence that has been used in the courts. There is a long history of criticism, for example, of the strength of the methods used in specific studies related to desegregation of schools or changes in jury size (for example, Rosen 1972). Social science found in the law often fails to meet basic research standards, a fact that has important implications for the future role of social science in the law. Shari Diamond argues, for example, in regard to the use of psychological research in the courts: "If psychologists do not ensure that the quality of the social science research presented to the courts is high, we risk not only bad decisions on these topics, but also a reduced willingness to seriously consider social science data in other areas" (Diamond 1989, 250).

The resistance of judges and lawyers more generally to social science and the continuing social science illiteracy of legal actors are factors often mentioned in discussion of the difficulties social science has faced in legal settings. Many courts are still unwilling to seriously consider social science evidence, and the idea that social science can establish facts in the law is still a matter of debate in many courts (see *Lockhart v. McCree,* 476 U.S. 162 [1986]; *McClesky v. Kemp,* 481 U.S. 279 [1987]). But even where courts have been more open to using social science evidence, they often do so in a simplistic and unsophisticated way. In this regard, scholars have long criticized the fact that judges and lawyers who argue in their courts have little training in the social sciences (see Horowitz 1977; Lermack 1979; Sperlich 1980).

A resistant and unprepared legal community and social science that fails to meet basic standards have certainly hindered the development of social science in the courts. But can we assume that overcoming these barriers would enable social science to be smoothly integrated into legal decisionmaking? This is the central question we will address in examining the New Jersey supreme court's deliberations concerning race and the death penalty. In New Jersey, the court began with a considerable degree of enthusiasm and respect for the social science method and the opportunities that it presented for informing legal decisionmaking. The court not only commissioned a large social science study of proportionality review but also justified its use of social science with intelligence and sophistication. The social science evidence presented to the court was brought by an established and respected scholar and evidenced a high degree of sophistication. Nonetheless, in the end the New Jersey supreme court was frustrated and confused by social science and may yet reject the social science method altogether in its current consideration of race disparities in death sentencing.

In following the New Jersey example, I focus on the difficulties faced by the court in defining the limitations of the social science evidence brought before it to establish facts in the legal process. The first section of the chapter describes the social science methods presented to the court, its reactions to them generally, and its deliberations concerning the question of race biases. I then detail the specific methodological choices made in developing these methods and the way they were presented to and understood by the court. The discussion here focuses both on the failure of social scientists to provide clear guidelines for establishing how social science evidence can be used and on the weaknesses of the adversarial process in defining the utility of social science facts. In the section that follows I describe how the courts lost confidence in social science over time, as it was presented with growing evidence of the limitations of the methods that it had earlier justified. In concluding, I suggest that the New Jersey court, social scientists, and experts in the case focused their attention primarily on the traditional problem of distinguishing between "good research and bad." They neglected what may be a more perplexing question in advancing the use of social science in the law, that of defining "good for what purpose."

Race and Proportionality Review of the Death Penalty in New Jersey

The court in New Jersey opened the door to social science research in response to a legislative provision for proportionality review of the death penalty. Such a review was intended to establish whether a death sentence imposed in a particular case was "disproportionate to the penalty imposed in [other] similar cases, considering both the crime and the defendant" (N.J.S.A. 2C:11-3e). While the legislature mandated proportionality review, in New Jersey, as in most other states, the court itself was given the task of defining how proportionality would be assessed.

Simply defined, a proportionality review examines a case that results in a death penalty sentence and compares it with similar cases. Death sentences in this context are proportional if other similar cases have led to death penalty sentences. Cases are disproportionate if other similar cases did not result in a death sentence. Proportionality review, as such, is not special to New Jersey. Indeed, the majority of states that reintroduced death penalty statutes over the past twenty years have established some type of proportionality review of death penalty sentencing to meet the standards suggested by the U.S. Supreme Court in *Gregg v. Georgia,* 428 U.S. 143 (1976). However, the supreme court of New Jersey took a broader and more empirically based approach to proportionality review than most other state courts. In good part, what sets the New Jersey court apart from others is its reliance on sophisticated social science methods in the proportionality review process. In this, as Leigh Bienen notes in a recent review of proportionality review, the "Supreme Court of New Jersey is the exception" (Bienen 1996, 134).

In *State of New Jersey v. Ramseur* (106 N.J. 123 [1987]) in 1987, the court upheld the constitutionality of the New Jersey death penalty statute. But in so doing, it emphasized that the proportionality review process was to be an "important procedural mechanism to safeguard against the arbitrary and capricious imposition" of death penalty sentencing (*State v. Ramseur* [1987], 328). In this context, the court established at the outset that its system of proportionality review would not rely merely on traditional legal review but would seek a broader approach involving criminal justice experts as well as experts from "disciplines outside the law" (*State v. Ramseur* [1987], 328). In an order issued on July 29, 1988, the court appointed Professor David Baldus of the University of Iowa Law School as special master to "assist" the court in developing such a system. Professor Baldus was a well-known proponent of social science applications in the law and had recently completed a major empirical study of the death penalty in Georgia (Baldus, Woodworth, and Pulaski 1990).

The special master's task was to "produce a database and files sufficient to enable the supreme court to conduct proportionality reviews as required by statute" (*State v. Ramseur* [1987]). He was authorized to collect such data "as may be needed" and was provided with both the assistance of staff of the Administrative Office of the Courts and a significant budget by the court. The special master was also asked to recommend a system of proportionality review that would meet strong objective standards. The court described its general philosophy in *State of New Jersey v. Marshall*, 130 N.J. 109 (1992), the first death penalty case that used the new system:

> Although we recognize that proportionality is not a scientific determination, we have attempted to make our determinations as precise in terms of their bases and reasoning and as objective as possible. We have used scientific and statistical measures, when helpful, although we recognize that a value judgment is built into practically every measurement. A life is at stake, and although some degree of subjective value judgment may be required, we have attempted to make those judgments explicit so that they can be analyzed and tested against whatever objective measurements are applicable. [*State v. Marshall* (1992), 120]

The methodology recommended to the court was developed by the special master over a three-year period in what came to be known as the proportionality review project (Baldus and Woodworth 1993). Details of the methodology used were presented to the court in a final report prepared for the appeal of Robert Marshall's death sentence in 1991 (Baldus 1991a, see also 1991b). In that report, the special master described the proportionality review project and applied the procedures developed to the Marshall case.

The special master provided the court with a database including 246 cases and more than 400 measures that detailed the social and criminal backgrounds of offenders, their victims, the context of their crimes, and the various procedural and legal issues that were seen as relevant to death penalty cases (see Baldus 1991a). The offenders included in the database were drawn from all adult homicide cases processed in New Jersey after August 6, 1982, when the new statute began to be applied. The cases, in turn, were divided into two "universes." The first included only those cases in which there was a capital murder conviction. These 132 cases all advanced to a penalty trial in which a jury decided whether to impose a death sentence or not. The remaining 114 cases were deemed "clearly death eligible" based on facts of the case but were not capital murder cases and thus did not lead to a penalty trial (Baldus 1991a, 4–10). Only 39 of the total of 246 cases included in the database resulted in a death sentence.

The special master also provided the court with three distinct quantitative methods for assessing proportionality. Each was based on defining the "blameworthiness" or "culpability" of defendants. In the first, defined as the "salient factors" method, the cases were sorted by specific characteristics of the cases, for example, those cases with multiple victims or involving prior murders. The disadvantage of this approach, as noted by the special master, is that "there are often too few comparable cases to support a confident judgment about how prosecutors and jurors are likely to charge and sentence similar cases in the long run" (Baldus 1991a, 85). The second method, the "numerical preponderance test," provided a stronger numerical basis for comparison but relied simply on a counting of statutory aggravating and mitigating circumstances associated with the case. Here a death sentence could be compared with other cases in the database in which there were a similar number of mitigating and aggravating circumstances. The drawback of this method was that it "assumes an equal weight for all aggravating and mitigating circumstances" (Baldus 1991a, 92).

To solve this problem in a way that also allowed comparison of many cases simultaneously, the special master developed a third method based on "logistic multiple regression analyses." Using this technique, the special master was "able to rank-order the cases according to overall defendant culpability, as measured by the presence or absence in the cases of factors that appear to influence prosecutorial and jury decisionmaking" (Baldus 1991a, 93). A case that led to a death penalty could thus be compared with cases of similar culpability as defined by the statistical models estimated. The special master noted that the three alternative methods of assessing culpability could serve "as a cross-check on the results of each" and "that one's confidence in the ultimate conclusion in a given case will often depend on the consistency or inconsistency of results produced by the alternative methods" (Baldus 1991a, 80). Nonetheless, his choice of placing the multiple regression method after the other two, and his implication that it solved the weaknesses of the prior methods, implied that it would provide the most reliable system for assessing proportionality. Overall this seems to have been the understanding of the court (*State v. DiFrisco* 142 N.J. 148 [1995], 178).

This third method, which the court called an "index-of-outcomes test" (*State v. Marshall* [1992], 147), had important implications for the question of race and death penalty sentencing. Using the salient factors method or the numerical preponderance test, the court did not have to consider extra-legal factors. But in developing the index-of-outcomes test, the special master recommended that the court consider not only aggravating and mitigating factors as defined by statute but also other factors that were found to influence death penalty outcomes. The court was provided with a series of statistical models on which to base its decisions, from a model that included only statutory and aggravating circumstances to one that added only legitimate legal factors to one that added additionally extra-legal variables such as race and socioeconomic status.

Although, as the special master noted in his report, the supreme court "did not request the proportionality review project to undertake an analysis of arbitrariness and discrimination in New Jersey's capital charging and sentencing system" (Baldus 1991a, 100). The development of the final set of regression models including extra-legal factors inevitably led to an assessment of the impacts of race on death penalty sentencing. In some sense, it is surprising that neither the court nor the state expected the special master to examine such questions, since his previous work outlined his view that it was necessary to include extra-legal factors in developing a proportionality system (see Baldus, Woodworth, and Pulaski 1990). Explaining why his report discussed possible race effects in death penalty sentencing, the special master explained:

We were asked . . . to develop a reliable database with which the parties could address those issues [arbitrariness and discrimination] if they choose to do so. Moreover, in the development of the statistically based indices described earlier in this section, we included race variables in the culpability models to ensure that variables for legitimate case characteristics were not carrying any possible race effects. It was in the course of this work that we observed the race effects reported in this section. [Baldus 1991a, 101]

The main race finding was produced in a logistic regression model examining death penalty decisions in penalty trials.[1] The model included the sixteen statutorily defined aggravating and mitigating circumstances plus eleven other nonstatutory factors that were defined as conceptually or statistically important. The nonstatutory factors included the defendant's gender, four variables relating to the socioeconomic status of the defendant, and the race of the defendant and the victim. In this regression, race of defendant was a strongly significant factor ($p < 0.008$), with African American defendants more likely to be given a death penalty than other defendants. A weaker, but still statistically significant, finding was found in a similar analysis that examined which cases advanced to a penalty trial. Here however, it was not the race of offender, but the race of victim that was statistically significant ($p < 0.01$). In this case, defendants who killed white victims were found more likely to receive a death sentence.

The special master also presented the court with two additional analyses in which the proportion of cases with African American defendants or white victims receiving the death penalty was provided across four broad levels of culpability. The cases in each culpability level were again determined by the outcomes of logistic multiple regression analyses, although these models did not include the race factors. Defendants who gained a probability of a death sentence in the models below 0.25 were placed in culpability level one, those with a probability score between 0.25 and 0.50 were placed in level two, those with a probability score of between 0.50 and 0.75 were placed in level three, and finally those with a score above 0.75 were placed in level four. The special master argued that the data "suggest that, on average, after controlling for the aggravation level of the cases, African American defendants may have a 19 percentage point higher risk ($p = 0.0001$) of receiving a death sentence than do other defendants" (Baldus 1991a, 102). Regarding white victims in the analysis of cases that advanced to penalty trials, the data suggest that "on average, cases with a white victim may have a 14 percentage point or higher risk of advancing to a penalty trial than do other cases" (Baldus 1991a, 103).

Looking at the New Jersey supreme court's overall response to the social science evidence presented by the special master in *State v. Marshall* (1992) it is clear that the court continued to support the application of social science methods to legal decisionmaking. The court used all three of the proportionality methods suggested by the special master in reviewing Marshall's appeal of his death sentence. Its detailed description of the social science methods employed, and its direct use of the special master's tables and arguments, suggests the extent of the court's optimism that social science could improve legal decisionmaking. The court did not reject the traditional legal "precedent-seeking approach" but rather placed it side-by-side with the statistical methods suggested by the special master. The elevation of social science evidence to this status was no small achievement and stands in stark contrast to the status of social science evidence in earlier decades and in many other courts. Moreover, the court's description of the social science method was both sophisticated and clear. Note, for example, the court's description of the index-of-outcomes test or multiple regression approach:

> Recall that this measure looks not only at the "salient factors," or the "number of factors," but at all of the facts and all of the cases to determine a pattern of capital sentencing. In this process we have spread all of the index cards on the table and have sought to identify the characteristics common to the cases in terms of their degree of blameworthiness as perceived by prosecutors and juries. . . . Under the index-of-outcomes analysis, using the expanded indices that include nonstatutory factors, the predicted probability of a death sentence in Robert Marshall's case is 0.50 among all penalty trial cases. The master cautions, however, that that estimate is quite unstable because of the small number of c(4)(e) cases.[2] The predicted probability of death for Marshall's case among all death-eligible cases is 0.17. Here again, the master cautions that that estimate is uncertain because of the small sample number. [*State v. Marshall* (1992), 172–73]

Although the court essentially accepted the quantitative proportionality review process suggested by the special master, it did not accept as conclusive the evidence of race discrimination in sentencing. In *State v. Marshall*, the defendant raised a structural challenge to the death penalty based on the special master's findings regarding race and death penalty sentencing. In response, the court agreed that discrimination was an important factor in proportionality review. Indeed, it distanced itself from the U.S. Supreme Court's decision in *McCleskey v. Kemp* (1987, 279) that "apparent disparities in sentencing are an inevitable part of our criminal justice system." The court stated the following:

> New Jersey's history and traditions would never countenance racial disparity in capital sentencing. As a people, we are uniquely committed to the elimination of racial discrimination. All of our institutions reflect that commitment. We were among the first of the states that enacted civil rights law. . . . As a court, we have repeatedly emphasized our special commitment to equality in the administration of justice. . . . Hence, were we to believe that the race of the victim and race of the defendant played a significant part in capital-sentencing decisions in New Jersey, we would seek corrective measures, and if that failed we could not, consistent with our state's policy, tolerate discrimination that threatened the foundation of our system of law. [*State v. Marshall* (1992), 207, 209]

Nonetheless, the court concluded that "[we] do not find, . . . in this case, evidence of constitutionally significant race-based disparities in sentencing" (*State v. Marshall* [1992], 210).

The court did not directly challenge the findings of the special master. Indeed, in contrast to discussion of the outcomes of the three quantitative proportionality methods as applied to Marshall, which included detailed descriptions of the statistical data, the court did not explain or present the basic empirical findings regarding race that were discussed in the special master's report. Rather, the court responded primarily to assertions made by the public defender's office, which represented Marshall, based on "extrapolation of the master's figures." Overall, the court concluded that the race effect was neither consistent enough nor strong enough to meet a standard suggested in the dissenting opinion of Justice Brennan that the "statistical evidence relentlessly documents" a race effect (*McCleskey v. Kemp* [1987], 328). In the case of race of victim, the court noted that the impacts were not found in penalty trial decisions. In the case of race of defendant, the effects of race were not found to apply to cases that were decided after 1987, when the application of the statute was "more clearly defined" (*State v. Marshall* [1992], 213).

The court also suggested that it would require analyses that examined a "more extensive set of relationships between the statistical variables," such as those "presented to the McCleskey court" to come to a definitive conclusion. The analyses provided so far were seen as too preliminary. Citing the special master's final report in support of its position, the court noted that the special master did not find such results to be conclusive:

> Because discrimination was not the primary mandate in this project, we consider these results to be strictly preliminary. More work will be required to determine if they persist under closer scrutiny and alternative analyses, to determine, for example, whether they are statistical artifacts or flukes, and to assess their legal and practical significance. [*State v. Marshall* (1992), 211. Cited from Baldus 1991a, 101]

The Index-of-Outcomes Approach: Social Science Choices and Legal Dilemmas

The description of proportionality review so far suggests a smooth integration of social science into legal decisionmaking in New Jersey. The court began with an interest in integrating social science methods into its deliberations and followed up this interest by appointing a special master with an established reputation to identify how social science could be used in the proportionality review process. The special master created an elaborate database for the court that would form the basis for identifying and comparing relevant cases. The special master also suggested a series of methods, culminating in the index-of-outcomes approach, which relied on these data to come to decisions about proportionality review in specific cases. The court itself reviewed this evidence carefully and intelligently in the first case in which proportionality was relevant. It is no wonder in this context that Bienen describes proportionality review in New Jersey as a "live experiment in the use of social science data by a court" (Bienen 1996, 265). However, a closer review of the methodology used to create the index-of-outcomes approach illustrates concerns that plagued the court in its deliberations in later death penalty appeals.

Although strongly advocating the index-of-outcomes approach, the special master cautioned the court about specific problems in applying it to the Marshall case. He noted the "general uncertainty" of many of the predictions of culpability it produced and impressed on the court, as evidenced in its discussion in Marshall, the particular uncertainty of the estimates gained regarding Robert Marshall per se (Baldus 1991a, 96). Nonetheless, the special master told the court that the index-of-outcomes method was solid and conformed to basic social science standards.

There was, in one sense, very good reason for the confidence showed by the special master in the Marshall report. His point of departure for the index-of-outcomes approach, a multivariate regression, represented a significant advance over the run-of-the-mill proportionality studies used as evidence in many other courts. As noted, a multivariate approach in principle allowed the comparison of a large number of cases on a similar scale (a flaw noted in the salient factors test) and also provided a basic method for distinguishing the impacts of different statutory and aggravating factors on sentencing decisions (a solution to the problems encountered in the numerical preponderance test).

Nonetheless, the use of a multivariate approach included a very basic statistical assumption that was to create significant problems for carrying out the index-of-outcomes test in New Jersey. All relevant predictors (in this case, predictors of the death penalty decision) must be included in the statistical models that are estimated.[3] If an important predictor is left out, the specific predictions of culpability provided by the index-of-outcomes test would likely be biased. Such bias would fundamentally challenge the validity of the models used to rank-order individual cases for proportionality review. If the excluded predictor was statistically related or correlated in some way to a factor included in the model (for example, race or a statutory aggravating or mitigating factor), then the measurement of the included factor would also be biased—a fact that has important implications for evaluating the relationship between race and the death penalty. Indeed, the special master stumbled on the race effect primarily because of a reverse concern: "We included race variables in the culpability models to ensure that variables for legitimate case characteristics were not carrying any possible race effects" (Baldus 1991a, 100). Put in the language of social science, race was included in the model because it was a potentially important predictor and as such was a necessary factor for correctly specifying the statistical model estimated.

The first problem for the special master was to choose the variables to be included in a correctly specified model. This choice is always a difficult one for social scientists and becomes more difficult the less developed theory is in a particular area of research. The special master began with a baseline of the sixteen aggravating and mitigating circumstances defined by statute. These were factors that juries were legally required to consider, and thus it made good sense to include them in the model. He then added variables for the defendant's and victim's race, the defendant's gender, and the socioeconomic status of the defendant and the victim. Although not stated directly, the special master clearly defined these as conceptually important variables that must be recognized in the models. For the final set of variables to be included, he employed a statistical "screening" technique over which there is strong debate, but that was commonly used by social scientists at the time.[4]

Having defined the relevant variables in the model, the special master was confronted with another problem, which related to their inclusion in logistic regression analyses: "The first issue was how to include in a model all of the statutory aggravating and mitigating circumstances, let alone any other factors, with such a small sample of cases and especially only 39 death sentence cases" (Baldus 1991c, 1, 9). The statistical problem is that multivariate regression requires variability in the measures examined in order to disentangle their effects in a model. This applies both to the dependent variable, in this case the death penalty decision, as well as to the individual predictors or independent variables included in the model. As the number of relevant independent variables increases, the variability or split of scores in the dependent variable is divided up into smaller and smaller pieces. Similarly, if a specific independent variable includes little variability in a sample, it becomes difficult to disentangle its interrelationships with other independent variables and the dependent variable. For example, if gender is included in a regression analysis, but almost all the subjects of a study are men, there is little variability in our measurement of gender.

In the index-of-outcomes test, the special master was confronted with both of these potential problems. In order to assess what he de-

fined as all relevant predictors, he was required to include a very
large number of independent variables relative to the variability or
split in death penalty sentencing. Only thirty-nine of the cases resulted in a death sentence. Even if the special master had included
only the statutory factors, sixteen independent variables remained in
the analysis. Although there is no hard-and-fast rule about the number of independent variables that may be included in any specific
model, it is generally noted that models should be reviewed for problems of instability when there are fewer than ten cases in the less-
frequent category (a death verdict in this example) for each of the
independent variables. That threshold would have required a minimum of 160 death sentences rather than the thirty-nine present in
the Marshall case.

Similarly, the special master was faced with relevant factors that
included little variability in their measurement in the database. For
example, only three defendants were classified as having either a pe-
cuniary motive or a victim who was a public servant—both statutory
aggravating factors. The split, accordingly, for these factors in the
penalty trial analyses was only 3 of 132. It is a very controversial
choice in social science to include factors that have so little variation.
However, in the end the question is not whether a large number of
predictors are included, or whether such predictors have little variation, but rather the degree to which their inclusion affects the stability of the overall model or specific estimates within it.

The first indication of instability in the models came when the special master attempted to estimate them using logistic regression techniques. In statistical terms, these models failed to reach "convergence," meaning that a mathematical solution that would provide
stable and reliable regression estimates could not be reached. This left
the special master with two choices. He could reduce the number of
variables in the models by excluding statistically problematic ones, or
he could try to find a different statistical technique that would allow
estimation of the models. The special master rejected the former option, noting in his report and technical appendix the importance of
including all relevant factors even if they led to estimation problems.
For example, in explaining the "general uncertainty of many of the
predictions" produced by the index-of-outcomes method, he wrote,
"This uncertainty is a price we pay for our desire not to omit from the
models any case characteristic that may be important" (Baldus 1991a,

96). Regarding the inclusion of variables that have very little variation, he commented, "It is statistically impossible to explain the dispositions [of cases like these] without including those factors in the model" (Baldus 1991c, 8).

Having rejected the option of a reduced model, the special master identified a technique that was "capable of estimating regression coefficients with the same properties as logistic regression coefficients" but could "handle a much larger number of independent variables" (Baldus 1991c, 1). He used discriminant analysis as a first step in developing logistic regression analyses. In using this alternative technique, he was sensitive to the possibility that the estimates gained would be seen as inferior to those that would have been generated in the "preferred" simple logistic regression method (Baldus 1991c, 1).[5] Nonetheless, according to the special master, the discriminant-based logistic regression approach provided estimates very similar to those that would be gained in a simple logistic regression:

> We tested the comparability of the results from the two procedures [simple logistic and discriminant-based logistic models] with small models that both methods could handle. The results were comparable, and the discriminant analysis showed no signs of bias or tendency toward misspecifications. [Baldus 1991c, 1]

Whatever argument might be made in defense of the technique used, the models as presented to the court in the Marshall case included a substantial degree of instability or, as the special master defined it, "uncertainty." Such instability is not surprising, given the number and type of variables included in the models. Moreover, the use of discriminant procedures did not purge the models of the problems that caused lack of convergence in the first place. It merely allowed estimation of coefficients even though such problems were present.

Instability is most strongly reflected in the predicted probabilities of receiving a death sentence that were produced from these models.[6] Such predictions were used to assess the culpability of individual defendants, with those more likely to receive a death penalty (based on the models) defined as more culpable. The special master commented on the "general uncertainty of many of the predictions" in his final report (Baldus 1991a, 96). However, the extent of this uncertainty is best illustrated in examining 95 percent confidence intervals around culpability estimates for individual defendants. A confidence interval in this case provides a basic method for assessing how stable the estimates gained are for each specific defendant. The tighter the interval, the more stable the estimate. The larger the interval, the less confidence we can put in the specific result. A 95 percent confidence interval is commonly used in social science and is also commonly applied to public opinion polls, where the upper and lower limits are referred to as the margin of error of the poll. In statistical terms, the interval can be defined as the range of values within which we are fairly confident that the population (as opposed to the sample) estimate may be found. As indicated in figure 7.1, presented by the special master for post-1983 penalty trial cases, many of the confidence intervals are as large as, or close to, 100 percent. Few of these intervals are below 10 or 20 percent. It is clear from these estimates that a considerable degree of caution should be used in interpreting the culpability estimates produced by the index-of-outcomes approach.

As this discussion suggests, the special master did not claim either in his report or in his technical appendix that the index-of-outcomes approach was developed without cost. He noted the choices he made regarding specification of the model and the difficulties of including such a large number of factors (some that occur infrequently) in analyses with small samples. He also described a number of diagnostic methods used to assess the implications of decisions made in developing the models. Nonetheless, his report focused more on defending his method as good social science than on defining its limitations. He assured the court that with this method "we were able to rank-order the cases according to overall defendant culpability, as measured by the presence or absence in the cases of factors that appear to influence prosecutorial and jury decisionmaking" (Baldus 1991a, 93). Moreover, notwithstanding the cautions provided, he concludes that "the resulting statistical model conformed to what one would expect from jurors who attempted to base their decisions on a balancing of aggravating and mitigating circumstances" (Baldus 1991a, 94).

For its part, the court expressed confidence in the approach developed by the special master in the Marshall case. Its understanding appeared to be that the index-of-outcomes method was reliable overall and that its weaknesses were related to the specific circumstances of the Marshall case. The court, following the special master, did not state that the method overall evidenced significant instability, but

Figure 7.1   Predicted Death Sentence Rates for Penalty Trial Cases, 1983 to 1991

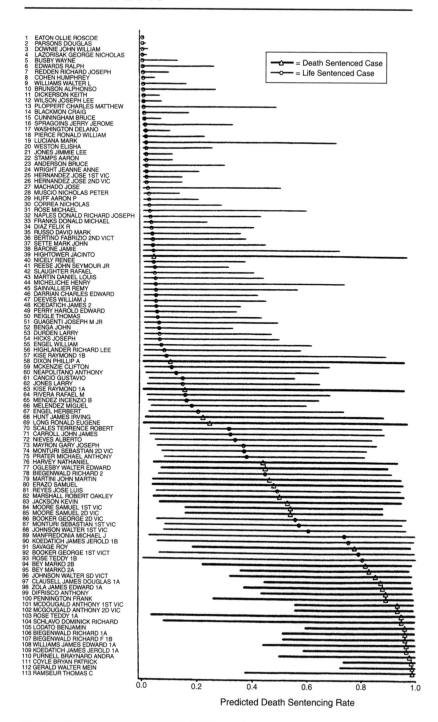

Predicted Death Sentencing Rate

Source: Baldus 1991a, fig 2.
Notes: The cases are sorted down the page by the predicted probability of a death sentence.
       The length of the line for each case represents 95 percent confidence limits for each prediction.

rather that the estimates associated with the Marshall case were "unstable" because of the small number of other cases that, like Marshall, involved a contract killing. Similarly, as cited, the court included the caution of the special master that his analyses of race and the death penalty were "preliminary." However, the court appeared to assume that if a larger and more consistent effect were found (across analyses), it could indeed rely on the index-of-outcomes method.

The adversarial process did little to aid the court in defining the limitations associated with the index-of-outcomes approach. The public defender's office became a strong proponent of the methods of the special master, arguing as one would expect, that his findings regarding a race effect were strong and persuasive. The state, not surprisingly, told the court that the special master's approach was flawed to such a great degree that it should be replaced. In response to the special master's report, the state enlisted its own expert, Herbert Weisberg, who not only challenged the special master's approach but also suggested an alternative approach based solely on aggravating factors. Weisberg commented in regard to the logistic multiple regressions underlying the index-of-outcomes method:

> The special master adopts an "everything but the kitchen sink" approach for his principal statistical models. To the lay observer, the highly elaborate statistical manipulations involving the "logistic regression" models may be impressive. However, the Baldus approach runs counter to good statistical practice. The models include far too many potentially predictive independent variables, including many that are not statistically significant. [Weisberg 1991, 13]

The court, however, did not find Weisberg's arguments persuasive. Weisberg's solution was not, in the court's opinion, an improvement over the special master's approach. The exclusion of mitigating factors was found "especially problematic" (*State v. Marshall* [1992], 165). The court also noted that the alternative approach suggested by Weisberg did not remedy the problem of a small sample from which to make proportionality comparisons. Clearly, the court saw Weisberg's warning (which it cited) that "an attempt to push statistical analysis beyond a more limited role may simply open the door to methodological controversy that will ultimately frustrate and confuse the court" as part of the usual rhetoric that accompanies the adversarial process. As it commented in its opinion, "Any statistical method can be found to be subject to improvements" (*State v. Marshall* [1992], 165).

We should not take the court's approach as naive. The important issue here is not one of basic standards of social science. Social scientists might debate the choices made by the special master, but his overall approach was very much within the social science tradition at the time. Indeed, he described his development of the index-of-outcomes models in an article appearing in *Chance*, a peer-reviewed publication of the American Statistical Association, dedicated to new directions in statistics and computing (see Baldus and Woodworth 1993). Herbert Weisberg also presented his view of proportionality review in an article appearing in the same issue of *Chance*, in which his criticisms of the special master appear considerably milder than those provided in his report to the court (Weisberg 1993). Indeed, his criticisms sound more like the court defined them in its decision in Marshall, as part of a debate among experts who respect each other's methods:

> I agree with Baldus and Woodworth on the general role of statistics in proportionality review. Statistical measures of case similarity can be helpful in guiding the court's focus to presumptively similar cases. . . . Moreover, we concur that alternative classification schemes may prove useful because there can be no single demonstrably "correct" approach.
>
> We have a somewhat different perspective, however, on the kinds of data and analyses that will be most useful for these purposes. Because the classes of presumptively similar cases provide only a starting point for further analysis, we downplay the importance of complex multivariate models and extremely comprehensive data.
>
> Baldus and Woodworth (1993) were motivated in part by the idea of creating the "capacity to monitor the state's death sentence system as a whole." We share the attorney general's concerns, however, that the data developed may not be well suited to investigating broader issues such as an alleged arbitrariness or discrimination in prosecutorial and jury decisionmaking. (Weisberg 1993, 24)

Post-Marshall: The Failure to Meet "Relentless" Criteria

Although the court noted in Marshall that proportionality is "not a scientific determination" and looked to use scientific and statistical measures "when helpful" (*State v. Marshall* [1992], 120), we might suspect that the justices were becoming increasingly skeptical of the index-of-outcomes approach as they noted in each subsequent case the instability of estimates of culpability. They might have asked: if the method was a solid one, and the instability in the Marshall case was a consequence of the specific characteristics of that case, why then do we find similar problems in each subsequent case? It is not difficult to imagine, for example, the justices' growing discomfort as they sought to explain the confidence intervals surrounding estimates of culpability for the three subsequent proportionality reviews, the cases of Marco Bey, John Martini, and Anthony DiFrisco:

> We find that the predicted probability of a death sentence in his case is seventy-six percent among all penalty-trial cases, with a lower limit of thirteen percent and upper limit of ninety-nine percent. [*State of New Jersey v. Bey*, 129 N.J. 557 (1992)]

> Defendant has a predicted probability of eighty-eight percent with a probability range containing a lower limit of twenty-five percent and an upper limit of ninety-five percent. [*State of New Jersey v. Martini*, 139 N.J. 3 (1994)]

> Defendant has a predicted probability of receiving a death sentence of seventy-four percent, with a probability range containing a lower limit of twenty-nine percent and an upper limit of ninety-five percent. [*State of New Jersey v. DiFrisco*, 142 N.J. 148 (1995)]

It is likely that confidence in the index-of-outcomes approach was also challenged as a result of a caution made to the court in the Martini case by the Administrative Office of the Courts (AOC). With the end of the special master's tenure in *State v. Bey* (1992), the AOC became solely responsible for producing analyses for proportionality review. After conducting an internal review of the index-of-outcomes approach, the AOC advised the court that "while the regression models generate a statistic which purports to estimate the 'predicted probability of a death sentence' in individual cases, our view is that little substantive reliance should be given to this statistic at this time" (McCarthy 1995).[7] Nonetheless, the AOC noted that the index-of-outcomes approach provided a "useful" method for comparing groups of cases at similar culpability levels. In *State v. DiFrisco* (1995) the court placed its discussion of the AOC's caution after its review of these broad culpability levels, noting that the "AOC again urges caution in relying on the results of those regression analyses" (*State v. DiFrisco* [1995], 178). It seems reasonable to conclude from this that the court's confidence in the index-of-outcomes approach was challenged not just in terms of individual probability estimates but in use of the regression approach more generally.

Although the court was beginning to display increasing concern over the index-of-outcomes approach, in the three subsequent proportionality review cases it did not have to confront the question of whether a more consistent and stronger race finding would lead to "relentless" evidence of a race effect as it was defined in the Marshall case. In the proportionality review conducted for *State v. Bey*, race was found to be statistically significant in only one of the models the AOC presented to the court. In the next two cases, Martini and DiFrisco, the effects of race were not found to be statistically significant in any of the models estimated. In *State of New Jersey v. Harris*, 141 N.J. 525 (1995), however, which followed DiFrisco in 1995, the index-of-outcomes approach yielded a more challenging set of findings, which appeared to be based on a more solid statistical foundation.

In the Harris case, the AOC found that a number of the statistical models included in the index-of-outcomes approach "converged" using simple logistic regression procedures. Lack of convergence, as noted earlier, was one of the indicators of instability in the regression models initially estimated by the special master. Lack of convergence of the models, in turn, led the special master to develop a controversial alternative estimating technique (the discriminant-based approach). The models could now be estimated using simple logistic regression procedures. Convergence of the logistic regression models, however, did not mean that the methodology developed by the special master had reached a high level of statistical reliability. The AOC's own analyses of the models suggested that they continued to be plagued by problems of instability:

> The addition of cases over time to the proportionality review sample has had a positive impact upon the stability of the models estimated. As evidenced both by conversion of specific models in the Harris case, and the settling of some of the unstable factors, the models presently estimated provide greater stability than those originally estimated by the special master. There is also evidence of stability in the magnitude of the coefficients across cases and across models. Nonetheless, the confidence intervals that surround the culpability indexes derived

from the models have remained large, and estimates of culpability across the models developed by the special master within a specific case are often very inconsistent. Using current models . . . the estimates gained are unstable both within and across models. [Weisburd 1995c, 6–7]

Nonetheless, in the case of a race of defendant effect, the convergence of the models appeared to have very important implications.

Comparing the "preferred" logistic regression approach with the discriminant-based method originally developed by the special master, the AOC found that the former analyses "hid" a finding that race significantly affects the likelihood that an offender will receive a death sentence (see Weisburd 1995a, 1995b). The special master had estimated various regression models each including somewhat different variables, both for the penalty trial and larger universes examined (see Baldus 1991a). For example, the special master provided models that included only statutory factors, as well as models that included both statutory and extra-legal variables. Race was included in four models that were estimated by the AOC for *State v. Harris*. In both models that examined the smaller penalty trial universe (which now included 145 cases and 43 death sentences), the models overall converged, and race was found to be statistically significant at the 0.05 significance threshold. Statistical convergence was achieved in only one of two models estimated for the larger death-eligible universe of cases (which now included 341 cases), and the effect of race was significant at the 0.10 threshold. These results overall suggested that African American defendants (as contrasted with all other defendants) were significantly more likely to receive a death penalty sentence. In contrast, race did not achieve statistical significance in any of the four models when the discriminant based procedures were applied to these data.

The size of these effects also raised important questions. Reporting the estimated probability of receiving a death sentence (based on logistic regression models and assuming that the defendant would otherwise have a 50/50 chance of being sentenced to death), the AOC found that the absolute difference between African Americans and others ranged between 20 and 40 percent (Weisburd 1995b). This means—for example, in the case of the largest effect—that when non–African American defendants have a 50 percent expected prob-

ability of receiving a death sentence, similar African American defendants have a 90 percent probability. The public defender's office,
using another estimate of size of effect, the odds ratio, reported that
the odds of African Americans being sentenced to death as opposed
to others range between two to one and eleven to one (AOC report
for State v. Harris [1995]). As a statistical consultant to the AOC, I
concluded more generally in a report based on these data:[8]

> Taken together, these analyses suggest strong and consistent biases in
> the application of death sentencing in New Jersey. Nonetheless, they
> are based on an initial analysis of prejudicial factors in the context of
> schedules developed for defining culpability for individual defendants
> for proportionality review. A full examination of these issues, which
> would begin with the goal of identifying the impacts of prejudicial fac-
> tors per se, is warranted given these findings (Weisburd 1995b).

In response to the race findings reported by the AOC, the state and
the public defender's office once again provided the court with completely opposing positions regarding the index-of-outcomes method.
The public defender's office claimed that the AOC report, combined
with additional analyses conducted using similar methods, provided
relentless and conclusive evidence of prejudice in death penalty sentencing. In contrast, the attorney general challenged the index-of-
outcomes approach even more furiously than it had in earlier cases.
The state's brief argued that "the models simply do not measure what
they purport to measure and cannot be utilized to prove racial discrimination" (Poritz 1996, 16).

The court did not rule on the race effect in *State v. Harris* (1995), in
part because of Harris's untimely death. However, with similar race
findings produced in the next proportionality review, conducted for
State of New Jersey v. Loftin, 146 N.J. 295 (1996), the court took an action that reflected its growing confusion and frustration with the
index-of-outcomes findings. It appointed a new special master "to
conduct a review, perform analyses, and make findings and recommendations relating to defendant's race as a possible factor in the decisions of juries to impose the death penalty" (Cohen 1997, 1). In this
case, the special master appointed was a well-respected retired New
Jersey appellate judge, Richard S. Cohen. He was given twelve weeks
to come to a conclusion and was aided in his efforts by a distinguished
professor emeritus of statistics from Princeton University, John Tukey.

The statistical assessments that form the basis for the report's conclusions follow earlier critiques of the index-of-outcomes approach. The special master and the statistical consultant noted that too many variables are included in the models estimated and that the continued instability of the models (as indicated by the still large confidence intervals of estimates) make both the culpability estimates provided for proportionality and the "odds ratios" presented by the public defender's office unreliable. In the main statistical analyses, the report asked whether the race finding provided by the index-of-outcomes approach allows a "relentless conclusion" regarding a race effect. The report concluded:

> The "relentless conclusion" is that, so far as these analyses go, there is no definite evidence of racial bias in penalty trials. Since the other analyses usually considered include far too many factors to be trusted, we must conclude that *there is no relentless evidence of bias in penalty trials.* [emphasis added] [Tukey 1997, 10]

In some sense, the approach taken by the new special master and his consultant reflects a kind of "Coney Island mirror" to that originally proposed by the special master in the Marshall case. Professor Baldus told the court that the cost of leaving out important variables could be so great that it was necessary to tolerate and overcome estimation problems that resulted. Judge Cohen and Professor Tukey took the position that the instability caused by including too many variables was so great that it was necessary to reduce their number. Three new models, each including race of defendant, were estimated, each including fewer than ten factors. The factors represented either a variable, such as an aggravating factor, or simple combinations of variables that were related in a similar way to receipt of a death penalty. The first two models included only race and statutory factors. In the first, the statutory factors were pooled to create two independent variables (all aggravating factors; all mitigating factors). In the second, the statutory factors were combined to create six independent variables. A third model added a single extra-legal variable and a factor combining six other extra-legal variables. The report did not explain the method for identifying which variables should be included in the model nor the criteria that were used for combining variables, except to note that "Examination of the number of occurrences of each statutory factor with some attention to estimated coefficients in available (nonparsimonious [AOC models]) analyses led to models one and two, using only statutory cases." The third model "including extra-statutory factors that seem to be predominant was suggested by John P. McCarthy of the AOC" (Tukey 1997, 7).

From a statistical perspective, the models presented in the report do not provide more reliable estimates of the race effect than those developed using the models suggested by Baldus. They simply "trade off" the problem of model instability for that of model misspecification. Misspecification in this case results either from the exclusion of relevant extra-legal factors or from measurement error produced from simply combining factors. This decision is particularly consequential for identifying a race effect. Multivariate models provide improved estimates over simple bivariate analyses, because they allow the researcher to control for biases introduced by other measures. The method used in the report would likely increase the effects of a factor that was overestimated in the bivariate case and decrease the impact of one that was underestimated (as is the case with race and the death penalty).[9] Not surprisingly, the first two models including only statutory factors and three and seven variables do not find a significant race effect. The third model, which includes a larger number of control variables, shows a statistically significant effect using one of two estimating procedures.[10]

Based on the statistical critiques raised in the report, Judge Cohen argued that the system of proportionality review developed by Baldus "reveals serious flaws when diverted to the task of providing reliable evidence relating to the race question."[11] He continued:

> One of the flaws is that there is such an excess of factors compared to the number of death verdicts as to cripple the system's predictive capacities. Another is that the ambiguities involved in some of the data selections and codings discourage reliance on precise outcomes. This is not criticism of the data selection and coding decisions made on these matters, but only recognition that the decisions . . . raise questions about predictive capacity. It is worthy of note that two out of the three of Dr. Tukey's models, . . . all designed to rid the study of the excess of factors, showed much less race effect. [Cohen 1997, 42]

But the special master did not simply challenge the race findings in the index-of-outcomes approach. In the tone of the report, it is clear that Judge Cohen doubted the reliability of the index-of-outcomes approach more generally. He had "substantial doubts about the accuracy of the culpability ratings" and recommended that the court "disregard" the odds ratios produced by the public defender's office as "unsupported and misleading." He described the methods used by the special master in the Marshall case as "tainted ground," noting that many of the criticisms brought by John Rolph, the state's expert, are "supported by my own findings."

Conclusions

The introduction of social science in the proportionality review process initiated by the New Jersey supreme court appears to conform to the requirements that most observers set for smooth integration of social science and the law. The court began with a considerable degree of respect for the social science method and justified its use with sophistication and intelligence. The social science evidence commissioned was developed by a leading scholar with an established reputation for conducting proportionality research. The evidence brought to the court was sophisticated and met basic social science standards. However, what began as an optimistic experiment in social science became yet another example of the confusion and frustration that often surround the use of social science in the courts. What went wrong, and what can we learn from the New Jersey case about the integration of social science in the courts?

Social scientists must think purposefully about the audience for their work and how that audience will read and apply social science evidence. The problem of social science in the law is often phrased in terms of "good" research and "bad." However, it may in the long term be more important for courts and social scientists to consider "good for what purpose." In social science we might applaud a researcher who finds elegant statistical methods for overcoming difficult estimation problems, even though we recognize that those solutions also have statistical costs. We are, in turn, most interested in work that pushes methods and data to their limits and that assesses how such decisions are likely to influence outcomes. In the case of proportionality review of the death penalty in New Jersey, the special master in the Marshall case was too concerned with defending his work to other researchers and scholars and not concerned enough with defining the limits of that research in the legal context.

He identified the index-of-outcomes approach as the best of a series of alternative methods for using social science to assess the proportionality of death penalty cases. He advised the court that his methods were "good enough." But his defense of his approach, presented in a technical appendix, was addressed primarily to the question of whether his approach was good enough for social science. The report of the special master in the Loftin case argued that the index-of-outcomes approach was not good enough, in this case, meaning not good enough to show a "relentless conclusion" of a race effect.

The supreme court of New Jersey has yet to rule on the race findings. Nonetheless, it seems unlikely given the special master's report in the Loftin case that it will conclude that relentless evidence of a race effect has been "proved" in the index-of-outcomes analyses. The court may as well take this opportunity to reassess the use of sophisticated social science methods more generally in the proportionality review process. A new chief justice now sits on the bench. She will likely want to place her own imprint on how the court will use social science data. I suspect in this context that the social science method will not fare well in the court's review. The index-of-outcomes approach, which was presented as the strongest method of proportionality review in Marshall, is now strongly criticized not only by the state but by a special master of the court.

Had proportionality review begun with the question of "good enough for what purpose," our story might have been very different. In most social science research, there are significant limitations that will impact on its use in legal settings. Although those limitations will vary from project to project, a trait of our methods is that they will always include a degree of uncertainty. Had the number of cases been larger in the Marshall review, for example, other limitations to the methods employed might have taken a more central place in the debates over proportionality review.[12] The problems associated with the models developed in the Marshall review suggest a high degree of caution, but they do not preclude the court from drawing conclusions from them. The special master in the Loftin case suggests such a conclusion: "Despite the undependability of the statistical evidence, it is troubling that so much of it tends in the same direction" (Cohen 1997, 43). The index-of-outcomes approach issues a warning to the court, not a definitive conclusion. The special masters in the Marshall and Loftin cases, and the court, should not have expected any more than this from the outset. The problem in some sense is that they did.

Notes

1. Analyses were conducted both for cases that led to death penalty trials and for the larger universe of death-eligible cases as defined by the special master.

2. The statutory aggravating circumstance of a contract killing.

3. For a more detailed discussion of this problem, see Weisburd (1998, ch. 15).

4. The special master examined the remaining factors in the database to identify which variables showed "a residual relationship with the dependent variable that was statistically significant at the 0.10 level or beyond and showed a nonperverse relationship" (Baldus 1991c, 3). For those that met this criteria, the special master used a factor analysis method to cluster into single factors related variables to be included in the index-of-outcomes models. Although such screening methods are commonly used in social science (often in so-called stepwise regressions), they can lead to serious misspecification errors. As an example, one statistician took a random set of numbers and created a database with fifty variables and one hundred cases (Freedman 1983). Using a technique similar to that employed by the special master, Freedman found that six of the variables were significantly ($p < 0.05$) and strongly related to the outcome measures after the statistical manipulations were employed. Because the statistical criteria used are based on a probabilistic model, conducting analyses over a large number of trials (as was done by the special master) is likely, just by chance, to produce factors that reach a specific statistical threshold.

5. One objection not noted by the special master is that discriminant analysis (in contrast to logistic regression) requires that all independent variables examined be interval level (that they have a real scale, for example, age or income). The models developed by the special master include primarily categorical or yes/no variables.

6. Another indication of instability is found in the unusually large size of a number of the coefficients gained in the discriminant-based logistic regression procedures. One of the measures, police officer victim, for example, has a coefficient of thirteen in one of the models estimated, which would imply that the odds of being sentenced to death are 400,000 times higher in those cases in which a public official is killed (Baldus 1991c, 8). Such an interpretation is very hard to believe, as suggested by the special master in his technical appendix. But it is important to stress that there are a number of less dramatic but still unusually large coefficients in the models estimated. Given the problems already noted, it is likely that such estimates are inflated and cannot be relied on as solid indicators of variable effects. The special master did

not address the issue of inflated coefficients directly in his report to the court, but he did devote considerable attention to this question in his technical appendix. Noting that some "statisticians urge caution in interpreting significant coefficients" when dealing with factors that occur infrequently, he described a series of diagnostic procedures that were used to assess the overall stability of his findings. These included examination of the models in the context of "bootstrap" procedures (citing Efron 1982) and "standard regression diagnostics" for multicollinearity. The bootstrapping procedures suggested that the race effect (among others) was solid, but that the "statistical significance of the 4D and 4H factors may be due to an unusual configuration of case characteristics in the data set" (Baldus 1991c, 8). Nonetheless, Baldus argued for the continued inclusion of such rare factors in the model on the basis that "it is statistically impossible to explain the dispositions of those six cases with 4D or 4H without including those factors in the model." In regard to multicollinearity, he "saw no evidence of multicollinearity to a degree that would threaten the validity of the results" (Baldus 1991c, 9).

7. My own involvement in proportionality review came during the Martini case. As a consultant to the AOC, I suggested that the court be cautioned directly about the instability of the index-of-outcomes approach.

8. The importance of race of victim and socioeconomic status were also examined. Although evidence of bias was found for these factors, the results were not as strong nor as consistent as the race of defendant effect (see Weisburd 1995b).

9. In general, researchers are concerned that the impacts of an effect may be inflated in simple bivariate analyses, because a variable is "picking up" the impacts of other measures. For example, in examining the relationship between race and criminality, failure to include factors such as socioeconomic status or education would lead the researcher to overestimate the impacts of race. In the case of race and the death penalty in New Jersey, precisely the opposite type of concern was raised (Weisburd 1995b). Control variables increase the impacts of race (as compared with the simple bivariate case). They correct for a negative rather than a positive bias, and thus the exclusion of specific factors or mistakes in their measurement would be likely to decrease the race effect.

10. In assessing the effects of race, Tukey also wanted to provide a measure of the statistical significance of the factors different from that provided in the packaged regression programs. To do this, he used a method called "jackknifing," which is based on drawing samples from the database being analyzed. He did not assume that jackknifing produces a better result than the traditional maximum likelihood estimates provided in the packaged SAS computer program used by the AOC. However, following the argument of relentless documentation, he argued that the

race effect should remain statistically significant irrespective of the technique used.

11. His concerns were reinforced by a small study conducted as part of his review, which asked selected New Jersey judges to rank actual cases in regard to their culpability. The index-of-outcomes approach suggested that while African Americans received the death penalty only slightly more often than others, their cases were overall less culpable than those of other defendants. In contrast, selected judges rated cases with African American defendants similarly to cases with white (including Hispanic) defendants when presented with actual scenarios with race of the defendant removed. This finding does not necessarily challenge the race findings reported by the AOC, which suggest that African American defendants are less culpable only on specific factors that are found to have strong and significant effects on death penalty juries.

12. For example, the methods used by the special master to define relevant variables to include in regression models are controversial. Moreover, as Farrington (1983) notes, criminological studies that employ regression methods may always be criticized on the basis that they have failed to include some important confounding factor.

References

Baldus, David C. 1991a. "Death Penalty Proportionality Review Project. Final Report to the New Jersey Supreme Court." Trenton, N.J.

———. 1991b. "Death Penalty Proportionality Review Project: A Report to the New Jersey Supreme Court." Trenton, N.J.

———. 1991c. "Methodology Appendix." In "Death Penalty Proportionality Review Project: Final Report to the Supreme Court—Appendices and Tables." Trenton, N.J.

Baldus, David C., and G. G. Woodworth. 1993. "Proportionality: The View of the Special Master." *Chance* 6(3): 9–17.

Baldus, David C., G. G. Woodworth, and C. A. Pulaski, Jr. 1990. *Equal Justice and the Death Penalty: A Legal and Empirical Analysis.* Boston: Northeastern University Press.

Bienen, Leigh B. 1996. "The Proportionality Review of Capital Cases by State High Courts after Gregg: On the Appearance of Justice." *Journal of Criminal Law and Criminology* 87 (Fall): 130–314.

Cairns, H. 1935. *Law and the Social Sciences.* New York: Harcourt, Brace.

Clark, Kenneth B. 1959. "The Desegregation Cases: Criticism of the Social Scientist's Role." *Villanova Law Review* 5 (Winter): 224–40.

Cohen, R. S. 1997. "Report to the New Jersey Supreme Court." Trenton, N.J.

Diamond, Shari S. 1989. "Using Psychology to Control Law: From Deceptive Advertising to Criminal Sentencing." *Law and Human Behavior* 13(3): 239–52.

Efron, B. 1982. "The Jacknife, the Bootstrap, and Other Resampling Plans." Society for Industrial and Applied Mathematics, Philadelphia.

Farrington, David P. 1983. "Randomized Experiments on Crime and Justice." In *Crime and Justice: An Annual Review of Research*, edited by Michael Tonry and Norval Morris. Chicago: University of Chicago Press.

Freedman, David A. 1983. "A Note on Screening Regression Equations." *The American Statistician* 37(2): 152–55.

Horowitz, D. L. 1977. *The Courts and Social Policy*. Washington, D.C.: Brookings Institution.

Lermack, Paul. 1979. "No Right Number? Social Science Research and the Jury Cases." *New York University Law Review* 54 (5): 951–76.

Loh, W. D. 1984. *Social Research in the Judicial Process: Cases, Readings, and Text.* New York: Russell Sage Foundation.

McCarthy, J. P., Jr. 1995. "Re: *State v. John Martini*: Proportionality Review." Memo to Stephen W. Townsend, clerk of the supreme court. Trenton, N.J.

Monahan, John, and Laurens Walker. 1988. "Social Science Research in Law: A New Paradigm." *American Psychologist* 43 (6): 465–72.

Poritz, D. T. 1996. "Brief on Behalf of the Attorney General—Amicus Curiae: *State of New Jersey v. Joseph Harris*." Trenton, N.J.

Rosen, P. 1972. *The Supreme Court and Social Science*. Urbana, Ill.: University of Illinois Press.

Saks, M. J. 1974. "Ignorance of Science Is No Excuse." *Trial* 10 (6): 18–20.

Sperlich, P. W. 1980. "Social Science Evidence and the Courts: Reaching Beyond the Adversary Process." *Judicature* 63 (6): 262–79.

Tukey, J. W. 1997. "Report to the Special Master." In "Report to the New Jersey Supreme Court," by R. S. Cohen. Trenton, N.J.

Weisburd, David. 1995a. "Re: Comparison of Logistic Regression and Discriminant Analysis (First Step) Results." Memorandum to John P. McCarthy, Jr., assistant director, Administrative Office of the Courts. Trenton, N.J.

———. 1995b. "Re: Prejudicial Factors in Death Sentencing." Memorandum to John P. McCarthy, Jr., assistant director, Administrative Office of the Courts. Trenton, N.J.

———. 1995c. "Re: Stability of the Models." Memorandum to John P. McCarthy, Jr., assistant director, Administrative Office of the Courts. Trenton, N.J.

———. 1998. *Statistics in Criminal Justice*. Belmont: Wadsworth.

Weisberg, Herbert I. 1991. "Proportionality Review of Death Sentences in New Jersey: An Independent Analysis of Data on Capital Charging and Sentencing." Trenton, N.J.

———. 1993. "Proportionality: An Alternative View." *Chance* 6(3): 18–24.

Zeisel, Hans, and Shari S. Diamond. 1974. " 'Convincing Empirical Evidence' on the Six Member Jury." *University of Chicago Law Review* 41(2): 281–95.

Part III

Law and the Reordering of Social Relations

Boundary Work: Levels of Analysis, the Macro-Micro Link, and the Social Control of Organizations

Diane Vaughan

Much theory and research asserts that the violative behavior of organizations cannot be explained solely by the actions of their individual agents but is explained more accurately as a predictable and systematic product of certain characteristics of organizational systems: industries, professions, professional networks, the workplace (Abolafia 1997; Baker and Faulkner 1993; Braithwaite 1984; Calavita, Pontell, and Tillman 1997; Coffee 1977, 1981; Coleman 1987; Cullen, Maakestad, and Cavender 1987; Ewick 1981; Finney and Lesieur 1982; Fleisher, Goff, and Tollison 1992; Geis 1967; Gross 1978; Hawkins 1984; Kramer 1992; Leonard and Weber 1970; Passas 1990; Reed and Yeager 1996; Reichman 1992, 1993; Reiss 1966; Shapiro 1984, 1987; Simpson 1986; Stone 1975; Sutherland 1949; Vaughan 1982, 1996, 1999; Wheeler and Rothman 1982; Yeager 1991). Nonetheless, the legal and administrative apparatus for the social control of organizations has lagged behind in acknowledging the socially organized causes of organizational misconduct as targets for regulatory attention, emphasizing instead strategies for control embedded in an ideology of individual causation.[1]

Kagan and Scholz (1984) state that the leading causal explanation of violations by business firms is the "amoral calculator model," which focuses on individuals who calculate the costs and benefits of illegal action on the organization's behalf. Punishment, long the strategy of choice for street crime, is considered an important tool for the social control of organizations because of institutionalized beliefs that the cause of both types of offenses is the same: agency, free will, and rational choice.[2] A deterrent approach is a natural consequence of this causal understanding. Often, the strategy for controlling organizational misconduct has been punishment, either for the organization, the individuals identified as responsible, or both. Despite a variety of regulatory approaches (see, for example, Ayres and Braithwaite 1992; Bardach and Kagan 1982), punishment often is prioritized and sometimes is combined with other strategies, such as a compliance approach, where the threat of sanctions against the organization is used as leverage to assure that compliance is obtained (see Braithwaite 1985; Hawkins 1983; Schlegel 1990). Frequently, however, the organization as a locus of wrongdoing is left out of the social control strategy. This is so not just for the violations of business firms that Kagan and Scholz address. It is also the response to misconduct in and by different kinds of organizations. In violations by agents of social control, fraud, and falsification in science, or malfeasance in the professions, the tendency is to identify the individual "bad apple" in order to redress social harm with punitive sanctions.

However, the legal and regulatory priority given to the deterrent effects of punishment for the social control of organizations rests more on untested assumptions about how decisions to violate are made than on research generated by sociolegal scholars that investigates these decisions. Ironically and unfortunately, in fact, several major research projects on "white-collar" and other forms of organizational misconduct may have had the unintended consequence of supporting an amoral calculator model by inference rather than data. Quantitative research using organizations as the unit of analysis (usually corporations) has repeatedly identified a correlation between competitive pressures from the environment and violative behavior (for example, Sutherland 1949; Simpson 1986; Clinard and Yeager 1980; Staw and Swajkowski 1975). The conclusion (either explicit or implicit) is that these competitive pressures affect the decision to violate in organizations, so that when an organization experiences structural strain to achieve its goals, individuals acting in their organizational roles may weigh the costs and benefits of their actions, choosing to violate laws and rules in pursuit of organizational goals. The data for these studies are macro level, however, and do not permit any empirical examination of how responsible individuals made the decision to violate. Lack of micro-level data notwithstanding, the consistent relationship between competitive pressures and violations has led to a rational choice explanation of organizational misconduct that leads incontrovertibly to an emphasis on deterrent strategies of social control.

Individuals act as agents for organizations and are responsible for illegalities, but alternative explanations of how decisions to violate are made suggest that a deterrent approach may not go far enough toward the effective social control of organizations. First, Kagan and Scholz (1984) point out that violative behavior also occurs for reasons that do not fit an amoral calculator model: individuals in organizations violate laws and rules sometimes from misunderstanding or lack of attention to regulatory requirements; sometimes they violate out of principled disagreement with legal and regulatory standards. Second, organization theory undermines an amoral calculator explanation, demonstrating that aspects of organization and environment shape choices so that neither decisions nor outcomes conform to the instrumental and calculated cost-benefit analysis that the amoral calculator model posits. The weighing of costs and benefits occurs, but individual choice is constrained by institutional and organizational forces (see, for example, Powell and DiMaggio 1991; Zucker 1977; March and Simon 1958; Weick 1979, 1995). Third, sociological theory contradicts the decontextualized rational choice model that underlies a legalistic deterrent approach, emphasizing that decisions are rational within situational contexts (Vaughan 1998, 1999). History, structure, culture, organizations, and routine interaction are crucial in shaping interpretation, meaning, and action at the local level.

No doubt there are many reasons why the legal and administrative apparatus has continued to prioritize a punitive stance over others that target the socially organized aspects of this form of illegality (see, for example, Stone 1975). However, at least in part, the legal and regulatory response may reflect the failure of sociolegal research to make a convincing case. In the absence of data showing how decisions to violate are made, gaps in knowledge remain that have real consequences for the social control of organizations. In this essay, I take the position that charting the course of sociolegal scholarship into the twenty-first century should necessarily include research on decisions to violate in formal organizations (nonprofits, firms, government, industries, and professional associations) and that this research should be conceptualized with a sensitivity to and a striving for designs that merge macro and micro levels of analysis.

To support this argument, I first analyze the historic trajectory of competing causal theories, showing that beneath the substantive differences is an unresolved and unarticulated debate about what level of analysis is appropriate for causal explanations. This covert debate points out the legitimacy of all levels of analysis, reinforcing the importance of each level and the need to integrate them in theory and research that connect macro and micro aspects of social life. Second, based on research on the 1986 space shuttle *Challenger* tragedy (Vaughan 1996), I show how qualitative research designed to bridge macro and micro levels of analysis gives new insight into decision-making in organizations. The *Challenger* case shows how deviance became normal at the National Aeronautics and Space Administration (NASA). The findings contradict rational actor models, showing how social context affected preference formation and therefore choice. Both the debate about covert levels of analysis and the *Challenger* case support the position that a deterrent approach does not go far enough toward effective control of organizational misconduct. Finally, I suggest an agenda for sociolegal research that emphasizes boundary work as a means of designing studies that examine the macro-micro connection in decisions to violate.

The Covert Levels of Analysis Debate

Developing theory that links macro and micro levels of analysis appears as a logical resolution to what has, to date, been a misunderstood pattern in the historic chronology of explanatory theories of both individual and organizational crime and deviance. The chronologies of both have been typified by shifts in the dominant paradigms. Because the pattern is more obvious in theories attempting to explain individual crime and deviance than in theories about organizational misconduct, the former are the best starting point for this discussion. Hirschi (1989, 37–38) observed that the shifts in theorizing the causes of individual deviance and crime indicate an oppositional tradition of denying an established perspective and substituting a new one, therefore giving the impression of progress. The historic shifts are indisputable. However, the oppositional element Hirschi noted in this evolutionary path is perhaps more accurately read as an ongoing and unresolved debate about the appropriate level of explanation. A quick and cursory discussion, a vast oversimplification due to limitations of space, nonetheless shows an ongoing contest between individualistic, social psychological, and structural explanations.[3]

In eighteenth- and nineteenth-century Europe, theorists as diverse as Beccaria, Lombroso, and Freud lodged the causes of crime and deviance in the individual. European individualism took a back seat as American sociology tackled the problem. Structural explanations (Merton, Cloward and Ohlin, Shaw, and McKay) became the dominant paradigm from the 1930s through the 1950s. Although the theories of European individualism and American structural sociology did not die out, social psychological theories—learning theory, control theory, labeling theory—became the dominant paradigm from the 1960s through the early 1970s. Subsequently, theory through the mid-1980s was marked not by a single dominant paradigm, but by two competing ones that located the explanation of crime and deviance at completely different levels of analysis: the structural, deterministic Marxist theory and a return to the free will, rational choice, deterrence perspective of Beccaria. Since the mid-1980s, the theoretical terrain has been dominated not by any one outstanding paradigm, but by multiple theories that, by virtue of the different positions they represent on the levels of analysis issue, draw attention to the lack of resolution in the historic debate.

Viewed against this history and the unarticulated debate about levels of analysis, current attempts to elaborate theory by merging macro and micro levels of analysis take on significance. Beginning in the mid-1980s, scholars theorizing about the causes of individual deviance and crime began to consider the possibility of theoretical integration. Verifying the extensiveness of this activity and simultaneously reifying it, Hirschi (1989, 39) called it the "integrationist movement," identifying proponents as "integrationists." Theoretical integration formulates linkages among different theoretical arguments (Liska, Krohn, and Messner 1989, 2). The fact that theoretical integration has been raised as a strategy worthy of consideration suggests an optimistic view about the status of causal theories of deviance and crime—particularly if we define theory consistent with the positivist model of the scientific process—a set of testable, interrelated propositions that explain some activity, event, or circumstance. From this perspective, the call for theoretical integration suggests that individual theories have attained sufficient rigor and explanatory power, such that refinement by integrating propositions from one with the propositions from another is a logical next step.

Practice, however, seems to be based on a less optimistic assessment of the status of causal theory: a keen awareness of its limitations and underdeveloped aspects. Although discussions of both the pros and cons and the possible methods of achieving integration have been extensive (for a review, see Liska, Krohn, and Messner 1989, 5–17), they have, for the most part, been at an abstract level. Practice centers not on theory integration, but on theory elaboration: strategies for fully developing existing theories by supplementing aspects of one theory with aspects of another that fill gaps in the first (Liska, Krohn, and Messner 1989, 16–17; Thornberry 1989; Vaughan 1992). The quantitative, positivistic approach that merges propositions for testing purposes is a road infrequently taken. Two strategies for theory elaboration have appeared. One draws together theories at the same level of analysis (see, for example, Akers 1985; Gottfredson and Hirschi 1990; Passas 1990). The other combines levels of analysis to elaborate theory, so that a macro-level theory is supplemented by a micro-level component or vice versa (see Short 1989; Agnew 1992).

Causal theories of organizational misconduct have followed the evolutionary pattern of theories of individual crime and deviance, but in a limited, less obvious way. A chronological history shows fewer competing theories—Sutherland's learning theory, Marxist theory, Mertonian theory, and more recently, rational choice/deterrence theory—and, with the possible exception of learning theory, none of them can legitimately be called a dominant paradigm that held sway over even a decade. This difference occurs, at least in part, because many of the extant theories that so readily applied to a variety of types of crime and deviance did not apply to high-status offending: labeling theory, ecological theory, subcultural theory. Unlike Mertonian theory, none of these others was importable either directly or with modification. Nonetheless, the trajectory of causal theories of organizational misconduct over time shows the same lack of resolution about levels of analysis: some locate cause in the individual, some in the social psychological, and some in structural sources.

Research on organizational misconduct has reflected—and even paralleled—the debate among causal theorists about covert levels of analysis. Systematically, researchers have been working at all levels of analysis since Sutherland's (1940) presidential address before the American Sociological Association calling for attention to white-collar crime. Research quite naturally included multiple levels of analysis from the beginning because white-collar offenses occurred in formal organizations and industries. However, Sutherland's own writing produced empirical work that explored different levels of analysis. First, his conceptualization included the individual, the social psychological, and the structural levels of analysis: his white-collar concept focused attention on individuals, learning theory incorporated both social psychological and structural conditions, and the units of analysis were formal organizations and their violations within the context of industries and a larger competitive structure. His data did not clearly articulate the link between all these components, but the conceptual basis was there for a theory elaborative strategy merging levels of analysis. Second, his conceptual definition was controversial and ambiguous, thereby freeing researchers to carve out new territory in their empirical work.

Sutherland conceptualized white-collar crime as offenses by individuals of high social status acting in their organizational roles. His attention to the individual offender generated controversy about what he had left out: scholars argued about whether the violative behavior in question should be defined as organizational, occupational, or economic crime (for details of these various positions, see Shapiro 1980; Wheeler 1983; Geis 1996). The debate remained unresolved. Geis (1992), among others, wrote eloquently and despairingly about the difficulties that Sutherland's definition created and how research had stalled while scholars concentrated on improving the conceptual definition. The same issues were being debated as recently as June 1996 at a conference designed to investigate the definitional question (Helmkamp, Ball, and Townsend 1996). No resolution. But this ongoing debate must be seen as a continuation of the covert debate about causal theories and levels of analysis: the main sticking point in the disagreement over conceptual definition was (and is) whether these offenses are to be treated as offenses by individuals of a particular social class, by organizations, or by occupation. Because of the unsettled definitional debate and Sutherland's identification of the relevance of individual, social psychological, and structural levels of analysis, research proceeded at all levels of analysis.

Considering that formal and complex organizations are the units of analysis, it is somewhat surprising that the macro-micro connection (receiving major attention by general social theorists as well as specialists in individual crime and deviance) has *not* become a central controversy in professional discourse about organizational misconduct.[4] The reason the covert levels of analysis debate is important to acknowledge—and the reason it has gone unresolved—is because it affirms that *all levels of analysis apply.* The research conducted since Sutherland drew attention to the problem in 1940 validates the legitimacy of each level of analysis, thus substantiating the importance of making macro-micro connections.

The Connection Between Cause and Control

Whatever the difficulty of conducting research into causal mechanisms, we live in a world filled with social problems that the state, political parties, voluntary associations, and citizens' groups are trying to solve. People will—and must—act. A deeper look at the historic trajectory of theories of cause in individual crime and deviance shows that each theory of cause has logically implied a particular strategy of control that targets the causal elements identified in the theory. Recall, for example, that the free will, rational choice model of Beccaria resulted in attempts to rationalize the criminal justice system so that an appropriate system of punishments would manipulate an individual's weighing of costs and benefits of particular acts. Similarly, the response to the social disorganization theory of crime causation was a crime control strategy that included organizing inner-city life (the Chicago Area Project); the appropriate strategy for control implied by labeling theory was radical nonintervention (the deinstitutionalization movement). The fact that Marxist theory and deterrence theory were competing paradigms during the 1970s takes on new significance when their contrasting implications for reducing crime are viewed as central to that competition. The levels of analysis debate is not just a theoretical exercise: it has both practical and political implications for social control.

Indeed, to be effective, strategies for control should target the causes of a problem. The more clearly we can map the causes of organizational misconduct, the better the understandings on which social control can be based. Research and theoretical explanations that isolate one level of analysis for attention automatically and implicitly suggest strategies for control that do not take into account relevant factors at other levels. This is not to say that isolating a particular level of analysis for research is no longer a worthy enterprise: doing so helps us flesh out the nuance of cause. Yet we need to bear in mind both the practical and political implications of our work. When we restrict our analysis to the individual, social psychological, or structural level of explanation, we have isolated one element from many. A partial explanation, no matter how important the finding, leads to a partial, or incomplete, strategy for social control. A rational actor model locates cause at the individual level of analysis, suggesting a strategy that targets responsible individuals: ethics training, punishment, forced resignation, and so forth. Although these are appropriate strategies, they are incomplete because they fail to address other systemic causes located in organizations, industries, professional associations, and networks.

Case studies, analyzed with attention to the social context and possible macro-micro linkages in explaining a particular organizational offense, provide qualitative data about decisionmaking as well as the structures and processes that affect decisions. Case studies can fill gaps in knowledge about how decisions are made in competitive environments. Because of the unusual data about decisionmaking it made available, the 1986 *Challenger* tragedy provided a rare opportunity to examine how macro- and micro-level factors played themselves out in a single incident. This case, although not representative of how decisions are made in all organizations, does not conform to the amoral calculator model. It suggests the need for a social control approach that is broader than a deterrence-centered model of social control. The full impact of the social context on the decision to launch the *Challenger* can only be portrayed by ethnographic-thick description. The summary that follows necessarily abbreviates the complexity of the event and its explanation but nonetheless illustrates a decision model that shows the complex interaction of all levels of analysis in decisionmaking.

The *Challenger* Case: Culture and the Normalization of Deviance at NASA

When organizations produce harmful outcomes that attract public attention, a ritualistic search for the culprit ensues in the aftermath. Usually the (found) culprit is some middle- or lower-level functionary. After NASA's space shuttle *Challenger* disintegrated in a fireball in January 1986, then-President Reagan appointed an investigative commission to determine the cause. Very quickly, the presidential commission learned that the disaster was a failure of the organizational-technical system. The immediate cause was the technical failure of the shuttle's solid rocket boosters, but the technical failure could have been prevented if the NASA organization had not failed first. The commission announced that the failure was a consequence of "flawed decisionmaking." The culprits, in this case, were NASA middle managers who, warned by engineers the night before the launch that the flight was risky in the unprecedented cold temperature that was predicted, overrode the concerned engineers and proceeded with the launch.

In what became the historically accepted explanation of the disaster, the culprits were amorally calculating managers: competitive pressures from the environment, economic strain on the NASA organization, and a tight schedule had NASA managers violating safety rules in order to maintain the launch schedule on which the space agency's resources depended. But research proved the historically accepted explanation wrong. Analyzing NASA decisionmaking on the eve of the launch and in the years preceding it, the presidential commission focused on the obvious signals of danger about the solid rocket boosters—the technical cause of the disaster—that apparently were ignored, dissenting engineering opinions, and engineering memos registering design concerns, all of which seemed damning given the tragic outcome. But hindsight distorted the commission's findings. In retrospect, certain NASA decisions seemed clearly wrong that seemed acceptable to the engineers when they were made. Moreover, the presidential commission misinterpreted key NASA rules and procedures, so that what they defined as actions in violation of NASA safety rules were actually management actions that exactly conformed to rules and procedures. No rules were violated, hence the incident was not an example of organizational misconduct as we are defining it, but this research has relevance for organizational misconduct, nonetheless. The analysis revealed how institutional, organizational, and interactional forces can affect the worldview of individuals in organizations, blinding them to the harm they do. As a consequence, they see benefits, not costs, as the result of their actions.

The *Challenger* disaster was the result not of intentional and calculated deviant actions by amorally calculating managers, but rather of a social context that led managers and engineers alike to normalize technical deviations in formal launch decisions. Decisions that appeared to outsiders as deviant after the disaster were officially acceptable and normal to NASA personnel at the time they were made. Prior to the *Challenger* launch decision, flying with flaws on the solid rocket boosters had become routine. In 1981, on the second mission of the space shuttle program and five years before the debate about the *Challenger* launch, the first in-flight anomaly occurred on the boosters. An anomaly, in NASA language, was an official label for a deviation from the original design predictions for performance. Engineers were required to assess each anomaly, make appropriate changes, then determine if the technical component was, officially, an "acceptable risk."[5] After identifying the cause of the 1981 problem, fixing it, then running tests and doing engineering calculations that convinced them that the risk was acceptable according to engineering standards, they officially recommended launching the next mission. What was important about this event was that the design predicted no anomalies on the boosters; thus none were expected. This first decision established a precedent for accepting technical deviation in the future. Anomalies continued to occur, and even though anomalies became more serious and occurred more frequently, the work group continued to conclude that the design was an acceptable risk and continued to recommend that their superiors "accept risk and fly."

Always their formal decisions to accept risk were grounded in engineering analysis that was then passed up the launch decision chain, presented to their superiors, and defended by the work group. Consequently, the findings of acceptable risk by the work group became a collective definition of the situation throughout the NASA organization. As time passed, flying with booster deviations from design expectations became normal throughout the space agency: a culture developed in which accepting deviation from standards was legitimate. After the *Challenger* disaster, the presidential commission, media representatives, and the general public found NASA decisionmaking incredulous: the repeated pattern of decisions to fly with flaws added to the imagery of amoral calculation because to outsiders it represented willful disregard of safety in order to keep the shuttle flying. But for NASA managers and engineers, the anomalies on the solid rocket boosters and the decisions that were made about them prior to the *Challenger* launch looked reasonable and acceptable as the problems were occurring. Each decision, taken alone, appeared logical and rational, but taken together, they formed a trajectory toward the disaster that was only visible in retrospect.

Ermann and Lundman (1978a) observe that a characteristic of organizational deviance is that norms develop internally that conflict with those of the outside world. What is significant for organizational misconduct from this analysis is that the NASA organization developed a cultural belief system in which the key players in technical decisionmaking about the boosters at all levels of the launch decision chain defined their actions as normative until after the disaster, when they, too, saw clearly their incremental descent into poor judgment. Fascinating were archival documents recording engineering decisions at the time they were made, testimony before the commission, and in-depth personal interviews with key decisionmakers. Consistently, the research demonstrated one fact: as each formal decision of acceptable risk was made in the years before the *Challenger* launch, the work group saw their own behavior as normal engineering.

The Macro-Micro Connection

The normalization of technical deviation in official decisions at NASA is explained by the conjunction of macro- and micro-level factors that affected the worldview of decisionmakers. The case shows how meaning, interpretation, and action at the local level were affected by an enacted work group culture and the culture of production.[6] At the micro level, the evolution of the work group's cultural belief in the risk acceptability originated in everyday interaction about the solid rocket boosters. Two aspects of social context were important. One was uncertainty about the space shuttle technology and the unprecedented character of its design. Because the shuttle was designed to be reusable, and because the engineers doing the hands-on work could not foresee all the forces of the environment to which it would be subject, the vehicle was expected to return from missions having incurred problems. And it did: every mission returned with hundreds of anomalies that needed to be analyzed and corrected before the shuttle could fly again. So when the first deviation from booster design expectations occurred in 1981, the social context was one in which having problems was normal. The discovery of booster damage, although officially treated as a signal of danger, was mitigated in seriousness by the frequency of problems on all technical components on the shuttle. Also, precedent mattered: this first acceptance of technical deviation led to subsequent decisions. As one NASA manager said,

> Once you have accepted an anomaly or something less than perfect, you know, you've given up your virginity. You can't go back. You're at the point that it's very hard to draw the line. You know, next time they say it's the same problem, it's [the booster O-ring] just eroded 5 mils. more. Once you've accepted it, it's very hard to draw the line. [personal interview, June 2, 1992]

The pattern of information about performance after each mission was also important in shaping the official definition of the situation. Whenever an anomaly occurred, the work group responded to it as a signal of danger—an escalated risk. But changes in booster performance occurred gradually, so that the work group incrementally altered the numerical standards that they had initially established, increasing the amount of damage that was acceptable. The incremental character of change in performance contributed to their decisions that it was safe to fly. Had all of the changes occurred at once, the effect would have been a strong signal of danger. But problems occurred incrementally, and although the boosters were experiencing problems, on most flights they were performing exactly as predicted. So the work group sustained their belief in acceptable risk because each signal of danger was followed by successful missions: signals that all was well. Although all anomalies seemed to outsiders after the disaster as strong signals of danger, to insiders as the problems unfolded, the signals were mixed and weak, caused by conditions that were easily reparable. Thus, they officially concluded that flight should continue each time, not that it should be halted.

The work group's ability to see their actions as normal and acceptable was also shaped by macro-level cultural beliefs. Normalizing

the boosters' technical anomalies in official decision was a consequence also of the culture of production: the competitive environment of the space industry, the culture of professional engineering,
and the organizational culture of NASA and of the Marshall Space
Flight Center in Huntsville, Alabama, where the solid rocket booster
project was located. The decisions made in the work group were
shaped by and conformed to institutionalized cultural beliefs that
were shared by engineers and managers alike. Their actions adhered
to these wider belief systems, affirming the correctness of the decisions they were making. They were conforming not only to the decisionmaking precedent they set with the first incident of damage but
also to conventions and understandings that had been instilled in
them both at engineering school and at NASA.

Among the institutionalized cultural beliefs of the culture of production, the following were most prominent in the work group's understanding that flying with flaws was normal and acceptable:

- *Cost, schedule, and safety compromises* Educated and trained to work
  in production systems where products are designed for customers,
  members of the engineering profession routinely "satisfice" where
  design is concerned. The need to be practical and cost-effective and
  to meet schedules results in conventional understandings that the
  best of all designs is not a possibility. Living with compromise is a
  taken-for-granted assumption of engineering. Safety is a priority;
  however, given these other constraints, engineers strive to assure
  that a design or product is not optimally safe but is safe enough.
  Thus, compromises and flying with damage on the boosters were
  consistent with the culture of professional engineering and, within
  that context, were normal and acceptable to the work group at
  NASA.

- *Rule-following* Not only are engineers trained to use engineering
  rules and methods to calculate risk, but they work in bureaucra-
  cies that are production-oriented. As a consequence, rule-following is a taken-for-granted aspect of the daily routine. Because
  NASA is a government bureaucracy that deals with space science
  and risky technology, the normal bureaucratic aspects of routine
  engineering practice are joined by an extraordinary number of
  rules and procedures for coordinating production and assuring
  safety. Within the organization, these rules and procedures affect

worldview: NASA engineers and managers in the work group believed that if they followed all the rules, they would make the vehicle as safe as possible. Thus, their adherence to the rules contributed to their belief that the boosters' anomalies were an acceptable risk.

- *Scientific positivism* Professional engineering is a combination of intuition, hunches, and experiments that ultimately require scientific proof to convince administrators, customers, and regulators. At NASA, quantitative, scientific evidence was highly valued. Moreover, this cultural belief was institutionalized as the required proof of safety in prelaunch decisionmaking. Aerospace engineers at NASA were subject to adversarial challenges by a hierarchical review system prior to each launch that forced them to support their decisions to accept risk with strong, quantitative data assuring the safety of their particular technical components. The insistence on the quantitative was so pervasive and strong within the culture that engineers were chastised if the words "I think" or "I feel" were part of their official presentations. Although intuition and hunch were encouraged at all other times, in launch decisionmaking, scientific positivism reigned. For the solid rocket booster work group, concerns about the increasing anomalies were at the level of intuition: their quantitative data convinced them that the design was an acceptable risk. They had, as they reported afterward, "faith in the tests and the numbers." Thus, scientific positivism also fed into the work group's decisions to accept risk and fly.

The controversial 1986 decision to launch *Challenger* was preceded by years of flying with flaws and accepting risk under conditions that continually pushed the envelope of experience, changing numerical standards to accept more and more extensive damage on the boosters. On the eve of the *Challenger* launch, that pattern was repeated, so that an unprecedented cold temperature was a new signal of danger that was normalized in the official decision that was the outcome of a heated engineering discussion. As before, a small incremental change in risk was deemed an acceptable risk, but this time to devastating effect. The comments of engineers in official testimony, taken after the fact, showed them to have valiantly protested against the launch, finally succumbing to management challenges to the engineering analysis backing their recommendation to delay the launch. Valiantly argue they did, but the outrage they vented to the commission and the press after the disaster is in contrast to their feelings at the end of the discussion, when management reversed the engineers' launch recommendation and decided to proceed with the launch. The engineers were angry that night because they felt they had "lost our autonomy." However, archival documents, testimony, and personal interviews show that on leaving the meeting, they believed that the boosters would experience more damage and that the damage would be beyond what they had noted in previous missions. Many (but not all) were very worried about it. Nonetheless, they did not expect a catastrophe because that night they had *conformed to* the enacted work group culture consisting of their previous decision rules for assessing engineering risk concerning the boosters, the culture of production (the cost, schedule, and safety compromises taken for granted at NASA and in the profession at large), the bureaucratic mandates for launch decisionmaking, and the tenets of scientific positivism.

The launch decision shows the interaction of macro- and micro-level factors, as they intersected to affect local meaning, interpretive work, and action. Individuals were responsible, by virtue of participating in the decision and by virtue of official organizational roles and divisions of labor. But absent was any evidence that would support an explanation of the tragedy consistent with the knowing and calculated risk-taking that are explicit in the amoral calculator model of misconduct. Official sanctions were available and known, therefore calculable, in case of mission failure. All NASA contracts with firms in the aerospace industry state that the contractor is subject to large penalties in the event that their component or personnel are found to be responsible for an accident. Moreover, all participants were aware of additional costs: being personally and publicly responsible for the deaths of the astronauts; losing their jobs; experiencing social condemnation; and incurring costs to both government, contractor, and even the space program. In the *Challenger* launch decision, it would seem that the costs of proceeding when warned against it were so high as not even to require calculation. In fact, they did not expect costs as a result of their decisions because they saw themselves as conforming, not deviant.

Although NASA managers and engineers were normalizing technical deviation in official launch decisions, the case analysis has general implications for the social control of organizations. Sanctions cannot be effective when individual decisionmakers see that their behavior leads to rewards, not costs, or that the costs will be low. The lesson suggested by this case is that the potential deterrent impact of sanctions cannot figure into individual calculations when history and culture congeal so that behavior that is objectively deviant to outsiders is normal and legitimate to many within an organization. When deviance is normalized in organizations, individuals see their actions as conforming, not deviant; they see their actions as accruing benefits, not costs. By definition, the potential deterrent impact of negative sanctions is mitigated.

Organizations, Culture, and Deterrence

The usual disclaimers about the generalizability of a case study must be invoked. The *Challenger* case is unusual for its historic importance. Although its distinctiveness resulted in sensationalistic treatment in the press, its historic significance resulted in official investigations producing sufficient data to support an analysis where macro-micro connections were possible. It is essential to note that the normalization of deviance is *not* a psychological construct; it is an institutional and organizational construct. From this case analysis, it is clear that organizational and institutional contingencies influenced decisions made by all participants. Culture emerged as an important mediator between pressures emanating from the competitive environment and actions taken by employees. Rational choice theory emphasizes the effect of constraints on preferences: decisions will be influenced by opportunity costs forgone as well as legal and normative constraints emanating from social institutions (Cook and Levi 1990; Friedman and Hechter 1988). Rational choice theorists are the first to admit that the power and scope of rational choice theory is limited because insufficient progress has been made toward a theory of preference formation (Friedman and Hechter 1988; Hechter and Kanazawa 1997). Such a theory must rest on an understanding of the definition of the situation the actor holds at the time decisions are made. In this case, culture (and other organizational and institutional factors not brought out in this overview) established preferences that governed choice on the eve of the *Challenger* launch.

If the role of culture in the normalization of deviance at NASA were discovered only in this case, the findings might be explained by the peculiarities of the space agency, its history, and its exotic technical agenda. But a long research tradition suggests that the normalization of deviance is a phenomenon frequently associated with organizational misconduct. The classic research on the topic affirms culture as an appropriate mediating link between environment, organization, and individual choice in instances of organizational misconduct (see Aubert 1952; Bensman and Gerver 1963; Quinney 1963; Geis 1967; Denzin 1977; Ermann and Lundman 1978a; Needleman and Needleman 1979). Although the conceptual language of this research referred to "normative environment," "cultural structure," "normative structure," or "criminogenic environment" rather than "culture," numerous scholars have found support for the existence of organizational cultures in which deviance became normal and acceptable.

Although most of this research does not directly examine decisionmaking, it does establish a strong theoretical basis supporting culture as a mediating link between structure and agency, affecting the cognitive maps of individuals. Geis's (1967) heavy electrical equipment price-fixing case, with much micro-level data on the thought and actions of responsible executives, offers insight into decisionmaking. Geis points out that extraordinary efforts at concealment were a sign of guilty knowledge and intent (read: amoral calculation); nonetheless, the analysis also affirms an industry culture where price fixing was such a taken-for-granted way of life that the conspirators viewed their actions as nondeviant, even while acknowledging their illegality. Nearly three decades later, Baker and Faulkner's (1993) three-case comparison affirms Geis's findings. In contrast with the *Challenger* case, in which deviance was normalized but no rules were violated, for price fixing in the heavy electrical equipment industry deviance was normalized, and illegalities knowingly were committed. Although no rules were violated in the *Challenger* case, the analysis reveals processes of decisionmaking that have significant implications for violative behavior by other organizations.

A social control focus on punishment-oriented strategies intended to deter offenders neglects the social context that leads them to make the choices that they do. Without attention to these other factors, the legal and administrative apparatus—and the public—are wrongly persuaded that once someone is punished or discharged, the problem is solved. Punishment is appropriate; however, as a strategy of social control it does not go far enough. It leaves the more-difficult-to-diagnose goals, policies, cultures, structures, and organizations unchanged, perpetuating the possibility of recurrence. Punishment may be used against both organizations and their employees to accomplish goals other than deterrence: restitution or retribution, for example. But if it is used to accomplish deterrence, then the research affirming the effects of normative environment, cultural structure, and culture raises doubts about its effectiveness, suggesting that the legal and regulatory apparatus might better elevate the importance of other strategies of social control: for example, compliance (the strategy of choice in industries where hazardous materials and risky technologies have the potential for so much harm that punishment after a violation occurs is an undesirable option; Hawkins 1984; Braithwaite 1985), shaming (a strategy designed to both use and alter culture and normative environments; Braithwaite 1989), and alterations of structure, which also affect culture (Stone 1975; Vaughan 1997a, 1997b).

Boundary Work: Elaborating Macro-Micro Connections

In order to develop a base of knowledge about the causes of organizational misconduct that could inform regulatory policymaking, sociolegal scholars need a better understanding of how decisions to violate are made. Previous research on decisionmaking casts doubt on a decontextualized rational choice model of decisionmaking in organizational misconduct (Clinard 1983; Jackall 1988; Grabosky 1989; Braithwaite and Makkai 1991; Paternoster and Simpson 1993, 1996). These are important and useful beginnings, but the links among institutions, organizations, and individual choice are poorly specified (and, in some cases, unspecified). Sociological theory and organization theory emphasize that research designed to target the social context of decisionmaking is the optimal approach. Moreover, both the debate about covert levels of analysis in sociolegal studies and the *Challenger* analysis indicate that examining macro-micro connections is essential to causal understanding. Because causal theory has important implications for social control, a research agenda for the twenty-first century might logically attempt to design research that explores macro-micro links in decisions to violate.

Such a strategy will require sociolegal scholars to engage in boundary work. The concept of boundary work originated with sociologist of science Thomas Gieryn (1983), who investigated how disciplinary boundaries came into being. He found that specialists tried to enhance their distinctiveness and power by marking disciplinary boundaries to clarify how their profession and its interests differed from those of other specializations. These boundaries originated, as Gieryn argues, as strategies of power, competition, and legitimization. An unintended consequence, however, is that, within disciplines, professional training and practice create highly specialized skills, language, and knowledge that bracket intellectual turf and limit the exchange of ideas across disciplinary boundaries. This tendency is exacerbated as professional associations grow large and create intradisciplinary boundaries. Internal subdivisions arise to stimulate communication between those with similar theoretical, methodological, or practical orientations but further segment knowledge. Both intradisciplinary boundaries (within sociolegal studies) and interdisciplinary boundaries (sociology, law, anthropology, cognitive psychology) have resulted in a division of labor that limits understanding about the causes of organizational misconduct. Here are some ways a sociolegal research agenda could span boundaries, facilitating the study of the relationship between environment, organization, and individual choice.

Crossing Intradisciplinary Boundaries

The linchpin of the macro-micro connection is itself a boundary problem: the relationship between structure and agency. Research that seeks to illuminate the connective tissue between structure and agency requires studying cognition: how meanings are constructed and the decisions that result. Case studies and ethnographies are useful because they expose the greatest number of structures and processes, as they intersect in a particular violative act (Ragin 1994). Because both previous research and the *Challenger* analysis show that culture affects how individuals perceive what is rational at a given moment, research that further explores the variable relationships among industry culture, organization culture, professional culture, or work group culture and individual decisions to violate would be worthwhile.

Making advances in this direction requires surmounting some intradisciplinary boundaries. The historic debate about covert levels of analysis in sociolegal studies indicates the existence of conceptual boundaries that restrict research interests to particular levels of analysis. In sociolegal studies as in other disciplines, we are not trained to study all levels of analysis. Choices made in graduate education—university departments, substantive specialties, mentors—create and perpetuate intradisciplinary boundaries by specializing students so they are prepared to study structure or process, but not equally skilled at both. Early professional training tends to be reinforced by department hiring practices and the structure and reward systems of writing and publishing. Consequently, designing and executing studies of decisionmaking that combine levels of analysis are more difficult. One way to bridge this particular boundary is to maintain a sensitivity to the problem and to incorporate as many levels of analysis into a study as the method, data, and substantive problem permit. An exemplar is Simpson (1998), who studied managerial decisionmaking using offense-specific models of corporate crime in a vignette design, varying both organizational characteristics and costs and benefits of violation. Even when designing a project that intentionally limits the research focus to one level of analysis, it is important to incorporate or cite relevant research that pulls in additional levels of analysis to acknowledge the role that these other factors may have played. If the data are primarily micro level, for example, one could draw from literature on structural arrangements implicated in the problem in question (the economy, regulatory structure, industry conditions, cultural understandings about what is culpable). Another solution is to balance personal research preferences about level of analysis with collaborative research by sociolegal scholars who specialize in a different level of analysis.

Another possibility is to look at misconduct in other social settings, crossing another intradisciplinary barrier. Not only do we tend to choose research styles that limit our research to particular levels of analysis, but we also tend to specialize in particular organizational forms: juries, prisons, courts, regulatory agencies, units of government. In the past, research on organizational misconduct concentrated on studies of corporate violations. Admittedly, studying misconduct in corporations whose power protects their boundaries is difficult. Other types of organizations may allow easier access for the kind of ethnographic layered cultural analysis that could be helpful. Historically, sociolegal scholars have examined decisionmaking and cognition in many different socially organized settings. Important insights have come from Sudnow's (1965) study of "normal crimes," Cicourel's (1970) study of juvenile justice, the work of Punch (1985), Van Maanen (1988), and Manning (1977, 1980, 1988) on policing, and that of Ewick and Silbey (1998) on the social construction of legality by citizens. Not only do these studies offer theory and substantive insights that show how social context influences cognition in relation to laws and norms, but they also affirm that deviance and conformity can be successfully studied in organizational forms other than corporations, thus building toward the elaboration of general theory (Vaughan 1992).

Crossing Interdisciplinary Boundaries

Boundary work could include taking advantage of conceptual tools and research from disciplines outside sociolegal studies. Because competition and scarce resources have a known relation to organizational misconduct, economic sociology is a relevant but untapped resource for examining aspects of the environment relevant to organizational offenses. In a conceptualization of the environment useful for exploring macro-micro links, DiMaggio (1994) shows the connection between culture and economy. He emphasizes that culture constitutes economic action, just as it constitutes other logics. Culture constitutes the normative regulation of exchange, the institutional basis of markets, extra- and intraorganizational environments, and the framing and multiple logics of action. Conceptually, DiMaggio's analysis provides a theoretical link between normative and economic environment through institutionalized understandings that are an important aspect of the social context of choice.

At the organizational level of analysis, organization theory is an obvious resource. Although there is consensus among sociolegal scholars that much misconduct takes place in formal organizations, few of the concepts from organization theory and research have been incorporated into the empirical work of sociolegal scholars. Only recently have some of these theoretical tools been brought to bear on research on organizational misconduct (see Baker and Faulkner

1993; Simpson and Koper 1997). Decision theory has a long history in organizational sociology, showing many social contingencies that influence decisions and outcomes. These decision theories provide alternatives to the decontextualized rational actor and amoral calculator assumptions that have dominated discussions of decisionmaking in organizational misconduct. Most well known among these is March and Simon's (1958) model of "satisficing," which identifies limits to rationality in organizational and individual capabilities, muddying considerations of costs and benefits and producing less-than-optimal outcomes (see also Allison and Zelikow 1999; March 1994; Cohen, March, and Olsen 1972; Perrow 1986; Scott 1998). These other decision models could be brought into research designs. In addition, organizational theory has identified many other concepts that influence decisions: information, organizational complexity, interorganizational relations, goal displacement, centralization and decentralization, deadlines, commitment to a line of action, informal organization, and power.

At the micro level, theories from cognitive psychology and social psychology contain still more conceptual tools to use in studies of decisionmaking. These also pose alternatives to a decontextualized amoral calculator model. Most familiar from cognitive psychology are theories of decisionmaking biases and heuristics (Kahneman, Slovic, and Tversky 1982). But sociology has its own battery of theories, beginning with ethnomethodological and social constructionist perspectives. These have, in the past, been central to work in sociolegal studies. Useful in their original form, these perspectives have been elaborated to apply to organizational decisionmaking. For example, Weick (1995) argues that decisions are always selective, an outcome of sensemaking processes that determine which aspects of environment and organization will be taken into account prior to making a choice. Manning (1977, 1992) has focused on organizational communication by studying policing. Building on Weick's sensemaking concept, he has developed a theory of knowing that combines loose coupling, dramaturgy, and semiotics. In Manning's view, communication consists of signs symbolically marking authority, power, and differences. Because another consistent finding in studies of organizational misconduct is the operation of power, Manning's conceptualization may well be an important tool in other socially organized settings where misconduct occurs.

In this essay, I have argued that strategies for the social control of organizations must rest on better understanding of how decisions to violate are made, suggesting a research agenda for sociolegal scholarship that studies the social context of decisionmaking. The unrecognized, covert levels of analysis debate calls attention to the explanatory relevance of all levels of analysis; moreover, it has generated research at all levels that illuminates the importance of each and provides a foundational knowledge on which to build future research. The *Challenger* analysis is an example of how a case study approach can encompass all levels of analysis, showing the mediating role of culture among institutions, organizations, and individual choice. I have also suggested that a research agenda that aims to uncover macro-micro influences on ethnocognition will require boundary work: bridging intra- and interdisciplinary boundaries. Sociolegal scholars are ideally equipped to do this because the sociolegal community is itself interdisciplinary and contains the necessary expertise. In addition, sociolegal scholarship has a long history of studying formal organizations of many kinds. Often, the organization has been the prime unit of analysis (Stone 1975). More frequently, however, the sociolegal issues and theory have dominated, often rendering the organizational setting less visible and unconceptualized. Because the sociolegal community has already accumulated scholarship on formal organizations, studies of decisionmaking in organizational misconduct that strive to incorporate multiple levels of analysis and the connections between them may not only challenge rational actor models and social control strategies but also have theoretical relevance for other sociolegal research interests where decisionmaking is a central concern.

Notes

1. Organizational misconduct is here defined as individuals or groups of individuals who, acting in their organizational roles, violate laws, rules, or administrative regulations in order to achieve the goals of their organization. This definition includes individuals who violate on behalf of their organization *and* for their own benefit but excludes those in organizations who violate laws and rules on their own behalf and in contradiction to organizational goals (embezzlement).

2. For an exemplary discussion of the jurisprudential and philosophical issues that underpin the deterrent approach, see Schlegel (1990).

3. Readers unfamiliar with the historic chronology of these causal explanations and the historic conditions that produced the ideological shifts that produced them (and that they reaffirmed and reproduced) should see Pfohl (1990).

4. In contrast, however, theorists working on general sociological theory *have* articulated the debate and intensely investigated the possibility of synthesis in many books and articles, justifying the term "integrationist" movement as an overt and recognized trend. The references are so numerous that the macro-micro connection legitimately can be said to be institutionalized as a problem (see Ritzer 1990; Alexander et al. 1987).

5. The term "acceptable risk" is an official NASA term.

6. In this discussion, I consider only two of three that were significant in the analysis: the enacted work group culture and the culture of production. Structural secrecy was the third factor and was essential to understanding what happened. In the interest of keeping the overview as simple as possible, this account dwells only on two aspects of the cultural structure. Interested readers may see Vaughan (1990, 225–58; 1996, ch. 8).

References

Abolafia, Mitchel Y. 1997. *Making Markets: Opportunism and Restraint on Wall Street.* Cambridge, Mass.: Harvard University Press.

Agnew, Robert. 1992. "Foundation for a General Strain Theory of Crime and Delinquency." *Criminology* 30(1): 47–87.

Akers, Ronald L. 1985. *Deviance: A Social Learning Approach.* Belmont, Calif.: Wadsworth.

Alexander, Jeffrey C., Bernhard Giesen, Richard Munch, and Neil J. Smelser, eds. 1987. *The Micro-Macro Link.* Berkeley: University of California Press.

Allison, Graham, and Phillip Zelikow. 1999. *Essence of Decision.* Reading, Mass.: Addison-Wesley.

Aubert, Vilhelm. 1952. "White-Collar Crime and Social Structure." *American Journal of Sociology* 58: 263–71.

Ayres, Ian, and John Braithwaite. 1992. *Responsive Regulation: Transcending the Deregulation Debate.* New York: Oxford University Press.

Baker, Wayne E., and Robert R. Faulkner. 1993. "The Social Organization of Conspiracy: Illegal Networks in the Heavy Electrical Equipment Industry." *American Sociological Review* 58: 837–60.

Bardach, Eugene, and Robert A. Kagan. 1982. *Going by the Book.* Philadelphia: Temple University Press.

Bensman, Joseph, and Israel Gerver. 1963. "Crime and Punishment in the Factory: The Function of Deviancy in Maintaining the Social System." *American Sociological Review* 28: 588–98.

Braithwaite, John. 1984. *Corporate Crime in the Pharmaceutical Industry.* London: Routledge and Kegan Paul.

———. 1985. *To Punish or Persuade.* Albany: State University of New York Press.

———. 1989. *Crime, Shame, and Reintegration.* Cambridge, U.K.: Cambridge University Press.

Braithwaite, John, and Toni Makkai. 1991. "Testing an Expected Utility Model of Corporate Deterrence." *Law and Society Review* 25: 7–39.

Calavita, Kitty, Henry N. Pontell, and Robert H. Tillman. 1997. *Big Money Crime: Fraud and Politics in the Savings and Loan Crisis.* Berkeley: University of California Press.

Cicourel, Aaron. 1970. *The Social Organization of Juvenile Justice.* London: Heinemann.

Clinard, Marshall B. 1983. *Corporate Ethics and Crime.* Beverly Hills, Calif.: Sage Publications.

Clinard, Marshall B., and Peter C. Yeager. 1980. *Corporate Crime.* New York: Free Press.

Coffee, John C., Jr. 1977. "Beyond the Shut-Eyed Sentry: Toward a Theoretical View of Corporate Misconduct and Effective Legal Response." *Virginia Law Review* 63: 1099–278.

———. 1981. "No Soul to Damn, No Body to Kick: An Unscandalized Inquiry into the Problem of Corporate Crime Punishment." *Michigan Law Review* 79: 386–459.

Cohen, Michael D., James G. March, and Johan P. Olsen. 1972. "A Garbage Can Model of Organizational Choice." *Administrative Science Quarterly* 17: 1–25.

Coleman, James W. 1987. "Toward an Integrated Theory of White-Collar Crime." *American Sociological Review* 93: 406–39.

Cook, Karen Schweers, and Margaret Levi, eds. 1990. *The Limits of Rationality.* Chicago: University of Chicago Press.

Cullen, Frank T., William J. Maakestad, and Gray Cavender. 1987. *Corporate Crime under Attack: The Ford Pinto Case and Beyond.* Cincinnati: Anderson.

Denzin, Norman. 1977. "Notes on the Criminogenic Hypothesis: A Case Study of the American Liquor Industry." *American Sociological Review* 42: 905–20.

DiMaggio, Paul. 1994. "Culture and Economy." In *The Handbook of Economic Sociology*, edited by Neil J. Smelser and Richard Swedberg. Princeton, N.J.: Princeton University Press; New York: Russell Sage Foundation.

Ermann, M. David, and Richard J. Lundman. 1978a. *Corporate and Governmental Deviance.* New York: Oxford University Press.

———. 1978b. "Deviant Actions by Complex Organizations: Deviance and Social Control at the Organizational Level of Analysis." *Sociological Quarterly* 19: 55–67.

Ewick, Patricia. 1981. "Theories of Organizational Illegality: A Reconceptualization." Yale Working Paper Series 2. Department of Sociology, Yale University, New Haven, Conn.

Ewick, Patricia, and Susan Silbey. 1998. *The Common Place of Law.* Chicago: University of Chicago Press.

Finney, Henry, and H. R. Lesieur. 1982. "A Contingency Theory of Organizational Crime." In *Research in the Sociology of Organizations,* edited by S. B. Bacharach. Greenwich, Conn.: JAI Press.

Fleisher, Arthur A., Brian L. Goff, and Robert D. Tollison. 1992. *The National Collegiate Athletic Association: A Study in Cartel Behavior.* Chicago: University of Chicago Press.

Friedman, Debra, and Michael Hechter. 1988. "The Contribution of Rational Choice Theory to Macrosociological Research." *Sociological Theory* 6: 201–18.

Geis, Gilbert. 1967. "The Heavy Electrical Equipment Antitrust Cases of 1961." In *Criminal Behavior Systems,* edited by Marshall B. Clinard and Richard Quinney. New York: Holt, Rinehart and Winston.

———. 1992. "White-Collar Crime: What Is It?" In *White-Collar Crime Reconsidered,* edited by Kip Schlegel and David Weisburd, pp. 31–53. Boston: Northeastern University Press.

———. 1996. "Definition in White-Collar Crime Scholarship: Sometimes It Can Matter." In *Definitional Dilemma: Can and Should There Be a Universal Definition of White-Collar Crime?* edited by James Helmkamp, Richard Ball, and Kitty Townsend. Proceedings of the Academic Workshop. Morgantown, W.Va.: National White Collar Crime Center Training and Research Institute.

Gieryn, Thomas F. 1983. "Boundary-Work and the Demarcation of Science from Non-Science: Strains and Interests in Professional Ideologies of Scientists." *American Sociological Review* 48: 781–95.

Gottfredson, Michael, and Travis Hirschi. 1990. *A General Theory of Crime.* Stanford: Stanford University Press.

Grabosky, Peter N. 1989. *Wayward Governance.* Woden: Australian Institute of Criminology.

Gross, Edward. 1978. "Organizational Crime: A Theoretical Perspective." In *Studies in Symbolic Interaction,* edited by Norman K. Denzin. Greenwich, Conn.: JAI Press.

Hawkins, Keith O. 1983. "Bargain and Bluff: Compliance Strategy and Deterrence in the Enforcement of Regulation." *Law and Policy* 5: 35–73.

———. 1984. *Environment and Enforcement.* Oxford: Oxford University Press.

Hechter, Michael, and Satoshi Kanazawa. 1997. "Sociological Rational Choice Theory." *Annual Review of Sociology* 23: 191–214.

Helmkamp, James, Richard Ball, and Kitty Townsend, eds. 1996. *Definitional Dilemma: Can and Should There Be a Universal Definition of White-Collar Crime?* Proceedings of the Academic Workshop. Morgantown, W. Va.: National White-Collar Crime Center Training and Research Institute.

Hirschi, Travis. 1989. "Exploring Alternatives to Integrated Theory." In *Theoretical Integration in the Study of Deviance and Crime: Problems and Prospects*, edited by Steven F. Messner, Marvin D. Krohn, and Allen E. Liska. Albany: State University of Albany Press.

Jackall, Robert. 1988. *Moral Mazes: The World of Corporate Managers*. New York: Oxford University Press.

Kagan, Robert A., and John T. Scholz. 1984. "The 'Criminology of the Corporation' and Regulatory Enforcement Strategies." In *Enforcing Regulation*, edited by Keith Hawkins and John M. Thomas. Boston: Kluwer-Nijhoff.

Kahneman, Daniel, Paul Slovic, and Amos Tversky, eds. 1982. *Judgment under Uncertainty: Heuristics and Biases*. Cambridge, U.K.: Cambridge University Press.

Kramer, Ronald C. 1992. "State-Corporate Crime: The Space Shuttle *Challenger* Disaster." In *White-Collar Crime Reconsidered*, edited by Kip Schegel and David Weisburd. Boston: Northeastern University Press.

Leonard, William N., and Marvin Glenn Weber. 1970. "Automakers and Dealers: A Study of Criminogenic Market Forces." *Law and Society Review* 4: 407–24.

Liska, Allen E., Marvin D. Krohn, and Steven F. Messner. 1989. "Strategies and Requisites for Theoretical Integration in the Study of Crime and Deviance." In *Theoretical Integration in the Study of Deviance and Crime: Problems and Prospects*, edited by Steven Messner, Marvin D. Krohn, and Allen E. Liska. Albany: State University of New York Press.

Manning, Peter K. 1977. *Police Work*. Cambridge, Mass.: MIT Press.

———. 1980. *Narc's Game*. Cambridge, Mass.: MIT Press.

———. 1988. *Symbolic Communication: Signifying Calls and the Police Response*. Cambridge, Mass.: MIT Press.

———. 1992. *Organizational Communication*. Hawthorne, N.Y.: Aldine De Gruyter.

March, James G. 1994. *A Primer on Decision-Making*. New York: Free Press.

March, James G., and Herbert A. Simon. 1958. *Organizations*. New York: Wiley.

Needleman, Martin L., and Carolyn Needleman. 1979. "Organizational Crime: Two Models of Criminogenesis." *Sociological Quarterly* 5: 517–28.

Passas, Nikos. 1990. "Anomie and Corporate Deviance." *Contemporary Crises* 14: 157–78.

Paternoster, Ray, and Sally S. Simpson. 1993. "A Rational Choice Theory of Corporate Crime." In *Routine Activity and Rational Choice: Advances in Criminological Theory*, vol. 5, edited by Ronald V. Clarke and Marcus Felson. New Brunswick, N.J.: Transaction Press.

———. 1996. "Testing a Rational Choice Model of Corporate Crime." *Law and Society Review* 30: 549–83.

Perrow, Charles. 1986. *Complex Organizations: A Critical Essay*. 3d ed. Glenview, Ill.: Scott, Foresman.

Pfohl, Stephen J. 1990. *Images of Deviance and Social Control.* New York: McGraw-Hill.

Powell, Walter W., and Paul J. DiMaggio, eds. 1991. *The New Institutionalism in Organizational Analysis.* Chicago: University of Chicago Press.

Punch, Maurice. 1985. *Conduct Unbecoming.* London: Tavistock.

Quinney, Richard. 1963. "Occupational Structure and Criminal Behavior: Prescription Violation by Retail Pharmacists." *Social Problems* 11: 179–85.

Ragin, Charles C. 1994. *Constructing Social Research.* Beverly Hills, Calif.: Pine Forge Press.

Reed, Gary E., and Peter Cleary Yeager. 1996. "Organizational Offending and NeoClassical Criminology: Challenging the Reach of a General Theory of Crime." *Criminology* 34(3): 357–82.

Reichman, Nancy. 1992. "Moving Backstage: Uncovering the Role of Compliance Practices in Shaping Regulatory Policy." In *White-Collar Crime Reconsidered,* edited by Kip Schlegel and David Weisburg. Boston: Northeastern University Press.

———. 1993. "Insider Trading." In *Beyond the Law: Crime in Complex Organizations,* edited by Michael Tonry and Albert J. Reiss, Jr. Chicago: University of Chicago Press.

Reiss, Albert J., Jr. 1966. "The Study of Deviant Behavior: Where the Action Is." *Ohio Valley Sociologist* 32: 60–66.

Ritzer, George, ed. 1990. *The Frontiers of Social Theory.* New York: Columbia University Press.

Schlegel, Kip. 1990. *Just Deserts for Corporate Criminals.* Boston: Northeastern University Press.

Scott, W. Richard. 1998. *Organizations,* vol. 4. Upper Saddle River, N.J.: Prentice Hall.

Shapiro, Susan. 1980. *Thinking about White-Collar Crime: Matters of Conceptualization and Research.* Washington, D.C.: Department of Justice, National Institute of Justice.

———. 1984. *Wayward Capitalists.* New Haven, Conn.: Yale University Press.

———. 1987. "The Social Control of Impersonal Trust." *American Journal of Sociology* 93: 623–58.

Short, James F., Jr. 1989. "Exploring Integration of Theoretical Levels of Explanation: Notes on Gang Delinquency." In *Theoretical Integration in the Study of Deviance and Crime: Problems and Prospects,* edited by Steven M. Messner, Marvin Krohn, and Allen E. Liska. Albany: State University of New York Press.

Simpson, Sally S. 1986. "The Decomposition of Antitrust: Testing a Multilevel Longitudinal Model of Profit Squeeze." *American Sociological Review* 51: 859–75.

———. 1998. *Why Corporations Obey the Law.* New York: Cambridge University Press.

Simpson, Sally S., and Christopher Koper. 1997. "Top Management Characteristics, Organizational Strain, and Antitrust Offending." *Journal of Quantitative Criminology* 13: 373–404.

Staw, Barry M., and Eugene Swajkowski. 1975. "The Scarcity-Munificence Component of Organizational Environments and the Commission of Illegal Acts." *Administrative Science Quarterly* 20: 345–54.

Stone, Christopher D. 1975. *Where the Law Ends.* New York: Harper and Row.

Sudnow, David. 1965. "Normal Crimes." *Social Problems* 12(winter): 255–76.

Sutherland, Edwin H. 1940. "White-Collar Criminality." *American Sociological Review* 5: 1–21.

———. 1949. *White-Collar Crime.* New York: Dryden Press.

Thornberry, Terence. 1989. "Reflections on the Advantages and Disadvantages of Theoretical Integration." In *Theoretical Integration in the Study of Deviance and Crime: Problems and Prospects,* edited by Steven F. Messner, Marvin D. Krohn, and Allen E. Liska. Albany: State University of New York Press.

Van Maanen, John. 1988. *Tales of the Field.* Chicago: University of Chicago Press.

Vaughan, Diane. 1982. "Toward Understanding Unlawful Organizational Behavior." *Michigan Law Review* 80(7): 1377–1402.

———. 1990. "Autonomy, Interdependence, and Social Control: NASA and the Space Shuttle *Challenger*." *Administrative Science Quarterly* 35: 225–58.

———. 1992. "Theory Elaboration: The Heuristics of Case Analysis." In *What Is a Case? Exploring the Foundations of Social Inquiry,* edited by Charles C. Ragin and Howard S. Becker. New York: Cambridge University Press.

———. 1996. *The Challenger Launch Decision: Risky Technology, Culture, and Deviance at NASA.* Chicago: University of Chicago Press.

———. 1997a. "Anomie Theory and Organizations: Culture and the Normalization of Deviance at NASA." In *The Future of Anomie Theory,* edited by Nicos Passas and Robert M. Agnew. Boston: Northeastern University Press.

———. 1997b. "The Trickle-Down Effect: Policy Decisions, Risky Work, and the *Challenger* Tragedy." *California Management Review* 39(2): 80–102.

———. 1998. "Rational Choice, Situated Action, and the Social Control of Organizations." *Law and Society Review* 32(1): 23–61.

———. 1999. "The Dark Side of Organizations: Mistake, Misconduct, and Disaster." *Annual Review of Sociology* 25: 271–305.

Weick, Karl E. 1979. *The Social Psychology of Organizing.* Reading, Mass.: Addison-Wesley.

———. 1995. *Sensemaking in Organizations.* Thousand Oaks, Calif.: Sage Publications.

Wheeler, Stanton, and Mitchell Rothman. 1982. "The Organization as Weapon in White-Collar Crime." *Michigan Law Review* 80(7): 1403–26.

———. 1983. "White-Collar Crime: History of an Idea." In *Corporate and White-Collar Crime: An Anthology,* edited by Leonard Orland. Cincinnati: Anderson Publishing Co.

Yeager, Peter. 1991. *The Limits of Law.* Cambridge, U.K.: Cambridge University Press.

Zucker, Lynn. 1977. "The Role of Institutionalization in Cultural Persistence." *American Sociological Review* 42: 726–43.

Chapter 9

When You Can't Just Say "No": Controlling Lawyers' Conflicts of Interest

Susan P. Shapiro

Conflict of interest in the practice of law is like unprotected sex: you sleep with everyone your lover ever slept with. More precisely, you can be infected by every client you ever had and every client your partners ever had, even partners you do not know and never met, who practice in offices thousands of miles away, and partners of your partners—people who worked at the firm before you arrived and colleagues and clients they worked with in other jobs before they joined the firm. Actually, it is worse than unprotected sex. You can be infected by clients that you or your colleagues merely flirted with, but never slept with, even those who spurned your advances.

How can you possibly stay apprised of the twists and turns of these private and extended social and sexual networks about which most sources of information have reason to dissemble? Yet, in the heat of the moment, you must determine not only whether this new lover and his or her lifelong collection of liaisons pose any risk to you or to any of your colleagues, but whether the dalliance may preclude future relationships with even more desirable lovers, yet unknown, who will reject you or your colleagues when they learn of your sexual history. Quite a daunting analysis even for those more dispassionate and with more time and better data with which to deliberate.

To make matters worse, the counterpart of safe sex is rarely an option in the legal realm. Although condoms (better known in this world as ethical screens or Chinese walls, among other prophylactic measures) are readily available, on only rare occasions do they provide sufficient protection. Without protection, lawyers and their firms can face sometimes dire economic and legal consequences, delivered at the hands of clients, colleagues, adversaries, insurers, disciplinary authorities, and the courts. In light of this treacherous scenario, Nancy Reagan begins to sound eminently sensible. "Just saying no," opting for celibacy, promises the safest course. (Although celibacy, of course, will result in the demise of the human race or, its legal counterpart, dissolution or bankruptcy of the firm.)

Conflict of interest, then, presents a formidable regulatory challenge for lawyers and their firms. Just as varied demographic groups face different risks of contracting the AIDS virus, law firms of different size, age, location, and type and diversification of practice and clientele are unequally vulnerable to conflicts and to the sanctions threatened by those whose interests were abridged, disregarded, or undermined. And, like would-be sexual partners, some firms are more averse to risk, taking more or very different precautions, than others. Because conflicts of interest are ubiquitous in the practice of law and the consequences of indifference are varied, significant, and inescapable, they provide a revealing window into the process of "indigenous" or self-regulation. In this chapter, we peer through that window to observe the varied practices that law firms undertake to identify and respond to conflicts of interest and the sources of variability in and limitations and ironies of such indigenous social control.

The window opens on a random sample of 128 law firms located in the state of Illinois, stratified by firm size and location.[1] In each law firm, I interviewed the person or persons with greatest responsibility for conflict-of-interest issues. In small firms, that was usually the solo practitioner or a name partner. In larger firms, it was usually the managing partner or the chair of the firm's ethics, conflicts, professional responsibility, or new business committee.[2] In 13 percent of the firms, I interviewed more than one individual. Respondents were asked whether, how, and to what extent conflicts of interest arise in their practice and how their firm identifies and resolves potential conflicts when they do.[3] The interviews lasted seventy-five minutes, on average, and most were tape recorded. Of the firms sampled, 92 percent participated in the study.

A Crash Course on Conflict of Interest

Conflicts of interest can arise when the interests of any two clients—past or present—of anyone in a law firm are adverse to each other or to those of any lawyer in the firm.[4] Clients obviously cannot sue each other, even if different lawyers or even different offices of the firm represent them. But adversities of interest can be found even if clients are on the same side: coplaintiffs or codefendants who may experience different amounts of loss, bear different degrees of culpability, or have deeper pockets, better insurance, or different preferences or aversions to risk. Moreover, conflicts of interest are not simply about zero-sum disputes; they arise in so-called win/win situations where two or more clients want to engage in a transaction, do a deal, sell a piece of property, borrow money, acquire a company, and so forth because the terms of agreement are likely to favor one party over the other.

Clients may play no role in a dispute or transaction at all. But conflicts of interest can arise when championing the interests of one client undermines those of another who has no direct standing in the case—what are called "positional" or "issue" conflicts. For example, arguing in a precedent-setting case that client ABC Insurance Company is not responsible for covering Superfund claims filed against its insured, XYZ Chemical Company, may do considerable harm to client TUV Chemical Company, which is having the same insurance coverage dispute with a different nonclient insurance company. Securing a patent for Sony to produce high-definition television may impair client Motorola, which is working on the same process, regardless of whether the firm is advising Motorola on its intellectual property matters at all (it may, for example, be handling a labor matter at Motorola).

Questions about who is *the* client in a complex organization and what to do about the interests of parties with some tie to a client further complicate matters. Lawyers may have fiduciary obligations to a multitude of parties with some direct or indirect relationship to a client, some of whom may be construed as clients by the ethics rules: individuals who are inextricably identified with organizational entities; the partners of a partnership client; family members when the client is a family business; members of a trade association client; major shareholders, boards of directors, or high-level functionaries of a corporate client; parents, subsidiaries, divisions, or branch offices of a large corporation; the spun-off pieces of a divested corporate client; the former as well as the current management of a corporation subject to a hostile takeover; the insurance company that is paying for the defense of an insurance claim against a client. Can lawyers sue or take positions adverse to the interests of these related parties?

Discerning the appropriate obligations toward these attenuated affiliates is difficult enough. Keeping track of constantly shifting webs of affiliations becomes a considerable challenge as marriages and partnerships break apart, alliances develop or disintegrate, and organizations swallow other organizations. Even where the lawyers' relationships and activities have not changed, the web of obligations becomes a kind of moving target because of the shifting networks and boundaries of clients, potential clients, and former clients.

The confusion about who is and who is not a client is further exacerbated by the fact that lawyers' duties to their clients have no "statutes of limitations," no formula whereby responsibilities to protect a client's interests desist. They can continue long after the lawyer/client relationship has ended. As long as lawyers possess relevant confidential information regarding a former client, they are precluded from using it for the benefit of another.[5] So conflicts of interest often outlive lawyer/client relationships.

Although the most thorny conflicts of interest arise from the competing interests of clients, the interests of counselors also collide with those of their clients—over fees, whether and when to settle a case, and over lawyers' personal investments, outside commitments, and loved ones who may be affected by the representation of a client. And firms beget additional conflicts of interest when they merge with or hire laterally from other firms and contaminate the pot with an entirely new collection of past and present clients whose interests may conflict with those served by the hiring firm.

Indeed, the constellation of interests served in a legal practice is continually in flux as disputes and transactions evolve; new evidence is uncovered; new parties join a case, exit, or die; settlements are tendered; verdicts are reached; and organizations and law firms change form, structure, and membership. As cases implicate or touch multitudes of individuals and organizations, repeat-playing clients spread their cases around to different law firms, industry rivals and competitors gravitate to the same specialty firms, firms get larger and swallow up the competition, and country lawyers, enjoying monopolies, are sought out by everyone in town, conflict of interest becomes a ubiquitous feature of the legal landscape and identifying conflicts, a nettlesome problem. To return to the AIDS metaphor, the alternative to "just saying no" is rapidly mapping and analyzing these twisted networks, organizational histories, and individual biographies before the prospective lover loses interest and moves on to another partner.

Because conflicts of interest arise from a multitude of sources, even relatively similar law firms face different risks of encountering particular kinds of conflicts or, indeed, any at all. Moreover, these risks shift over time as firms grow, diversify their practice, attract a different client base, or cope with changes in the economy or market for legal services. So the mapping and deliberative process (indigenous regulation) looks different across firms, reflecting their distinctive setting, structural features, social organization, areas of practice, and clientele.

Incentives

But AIDS is just a metaphor. Given the draconian consequences of contracting AIDS or even HIV, it is understandable why one would carefully scrutinize a potential sexual partner when protection is not available, if not defer gratification altogether. But why do so for a mere violation of ethical rules? Codes of ethics have often been maligned as mere window dressing, at best, or linguistic Trojan horses concealing ulterior motives or hidden agendas, at worst (Abel 1981). In many professions and walks of life there is a long tradition of honoring ethical norms in the breach. What harm is an ethics slap every now and then?

The dilemma might be of mere academic curiosity were it not for the fact that lawyers face substantial economic consequences for taking the wrong course in the face of clashing or potentially clashing interests. Aside from reputational concerns and the risk that conflicts of interest could lead to disciplinary proceedings against law firms as well as individual lawyers (Overton 1990; Schneyer 1991), relatively significant forms of economic self-interest, which cross-cut firms and their individual members, provide incentives for regulating the process by which firms take on new interests (new sexual partners, as it were).

Perhaps the most potent incentive applies in the litigation context, where law firms with demonstrable conflicts of interest can be disqualified from representing their client. In an era of zealous advocacy and hyper-adversarialism, where opponents embrace so-called "scorched earth" or hardball litigation, motions to disqualify law firms tainted by conflicts of interest have become an attractive tactical strategy to increase the cost to one's adversary of contesting a claim (Bateman 1995, 255). The threat of disqualification can impose substantial costs on a law firm and the client it represents. It protracts the litigation and increases its cost, exerts extra pressure on the client to settle the matter rather than having to defend a disqualification motion or find new legal counsel, and, if the lawyers are disqualified, burdens the client to find and prepare a new law firm to represent it in the eleventh hour. In addition to losing face as well as all or part of the fee for the often substantial amount of work already invested in the case, disqualified lawyers also risk a malpractice claim and disciplinary action, as well as permanent loss of the client. It is hard to imagine a monetary fine that could rival the lost investment that a law firm typically makes in a major piece of litigation or in a long-term relationship with a client.[6]

Motions for disqualification are asserted where lawyers fail to recognize or respond to an alleged conflict of interest in a litigation context. In many situations, both in litigation and transactional practice, things do not go that far. Lawyers will discover an unrecognized conflict, an adversary will bring it to their attention, or circumstances will change after the engagement is already under way—giving rise to new conflicts—whereupon the firm may voluntarily withdraw from the matter. The costs to the firm may be substantial here as well. The firm will generally make a financial settlement with the client for the inconvenience and the costs of preparing a new firm to take on the case. Some kinds of fee arrangements that kick in at the conclusion of the representation (such as contingent fees) may be especially punishing to a firm that must step out prematurely. And considerable goodwill and client loyalty are undermined when trusted lawyers suddenly abandon their client midstream, particularly where the conflict easily could have been foreseen. When firms must send away a valued client because of conflicts of interest, they risk losing the client forever to the "replacement firm," which is likely to make moves on their new client and try to forge a long-standing relationship.

Conflicts of interest need not actually materialize to have significant economic consequences. Another financial cost accrues to a firm
that must turn away lucrative new business because of conflicts of
interest created by a petty matter undertaken in the past. By preparing a simple regulatory filing for AT&T, for example, the law firm
cannot later represent MCI in a multimillion dollar dispute with the
telephone giant.[7] Citing a $200,000 piece of litigation that had to be
turned away because it was adverse to the interests of a client in a
$5,000 intellectual property matter (for which the firm still had not
been paid), a lawyer interviewed for this study explained that his
firm decided to overhaul its conflicts system because they were declining too many big cases when the interests of the prospective
clients conflicted with those of current or former clients of the firm.
He unhappily noted that, in his own personal experience, he had to
turn away six or seven of every ten assignments he wanted to take
because of conflicts elsewhere in the firm.

As this respondent's displeasure suggests, the incentive to control
these business conflicts is not merely institutional. Most large law
firms confer financial reward and power on their business-getters or
so-called "rainmakers" and tag partnership and compensation decisions to the lawyer's ability to bring in business to the firm. Few firms
credit attorneys for business they secured but that had to be declined
because it conflicted with interests represented elsewhere in the firm.
As a result, individual lawyers tend to be quite interested in the business contemplated by their colleagues and wary that another's potential bird in the hand will cost them a flock in a nearby bush. These
personal investments in rainmaking, although often a source of tension within the firm, create a proactive vigilance by potentially affected colleagues and another impetus to control firm-wide conflicts
of interest.

The market for professional liability insurance provides an additional economic incentive for self-regulation. In the past two
decades, the cost of malpractice insurance skyrocketed as attorneys
began to break the ban against suing one another.[8] Plaintiff's
lawyers brought large malpractice cases against their brethren. And
government agencies, recognizing the deep pockets of law firms,
coupled with their complicity or at least facilitative role in financial
debacles—especially failures of savings and loan institutions—also
began suing lawyers (Gill 1992). Insurers suggest that conflict-of-

interest charges added to a malpractice claim significantly increase both the size of the claim (generally into the multimillion dollar range) and the likelihood of loss (Attorneys' Liability Assurance Society 1991; Hazard 1990).

This heightened exposure increased not only the cost of liability insurance, but also the difficulty of finding coverage and the incentives to reduce insurance costs by implementing self-regulatory practices.[9] As one respondent in my study explained:

> When malpractice insurance was $1,000 a year, I didn't think about conflicts. [90Ch20–49]

Experience rating plays a role in a firm's ability to obtain insurance coverage and in the premiums assessed. Firms implicated in previous conflicts of interest or with lax self-regulatory procedures can find themselves virtually uninsurable. Many lawyers interviewed in this study explained that they instituted new policies after they had difficulty finding malpractice insurance and noticed that the application forms all seemed to ask the same questions (about policies or procedures that they had not undertaken in the past) or after insurers had excluded coverage for risky practices. Probably more significant, deductibles for malpractice insurance tend to be high, for example, more than $450,000, on average, for members of a large-law-firm mutual professional liability insurance company.[10] The cost of defending a malpractice claim, therefore, is often borne by the law firm rather than its insurer.

I enumerate the incentives for law firms to control conflicts of interest not merely to impugn the assumption that ethics do not matter, but to argue that indigenous regulatory systems respond to a host of normative pressures, inducements, and sanctions. Self-regulation is not merely an instrumental reaction to rules, enforcement practices, the risks of detection, and the certainty and severity of sanctions delivered by organs of the state, which are the central focus of much of the literature on regulatory compliance. Indeed, the state plays little or no role in the social control of conflict of interest in the legal profession. Instead, a diverse collection of private parties—clients, adversaries, competitors, colleagues, malpractice insurers, and (on rare occasions) disciplinary bodies—exert pressures on law firms, each party reacting differently to conflicts of interest, at different stages in the evolution of a conflict, and expressing their displeasure in different ways. Firms that do a lot of litigation, are dependent on very powerful repeat-playing clients, or enjoy geographic or substantive monopoly, for example, face external constraints unlike firms that serve large numbers of one-shotters, have transactional practices, or are interchangeable with the competition. So self-regulatory practices vary across law firms, not only because they face dissimilar numbers and constellations of conflicts, but because they are situated in distinctive normative environments offering a varied mix of incentives and sanctions to which firms respond.

Ideal Types of Social Control

Most of you can probably construct vivid mental images of the metaphor of unprotected sex—imagining yourselves on a desert island without a pharmacy, unexpectedly in the throes of passion with a stranger—undertaking an instant risk assessment; deciding whether interrogating your prospective partner on his or her sexual history may cool the passion or even end the encounter; figuring out which questions would yield meaningful data; trying to fashion the most tactful, expeditious, and nonreactive inquiry; assessing whether your partner is being exhaustive and forthright; conducting another risk assessment; wondering whether, if you "just say no," you will ever have sex again. Maybe you even have the angel and the devil hovering over your shoulders.

The following portraits endeavor to create mental images of the corresponding dilemma faced by different kinds of law firms hoping to avoid a relationship that will entangle them in conflicts of interest. I draw five ideal-type images, perhaps not as dramatic or as evocative as those of the desert island, but that demonstrate the varied ways in which lawyers assess their own risk.

These data-gathering or intelligence systems by which firms identify potential conflicts of interest vary on a number of interrelated dimensions:

- Whether they rely on face-to-face or impersonal means of communication;

- The extent of technological innovation: whether they use paper or electronic records and manual or automated surveillance;

- Whether their analysis is based on human or artificial intelligence;

- Whether they rely on generalized or specialized social control;

- The extent to which the system is "law-like" in a Weberian sense: whether social control is performed by those directly involved or by intelligence staff;

- Whether social control is discretionary or applied universalistically; and

- Whether the resolution is voluntary or imposed.

Law firms fall on a continuum that incorporates these variables. At one end, social control systems have the features listed first or none at all; at the other end, systems implement all of those listed last. We begin with the former.

The Ostrich

In the sexual arena, the ostrich is the sexual outlaw, partners with illusions of immortality who, confident that AIDS cannot happen to them, take no precautions. I encountered few ostriches in the sample, law firms that do nothing, burying their head in the sand, hopeful that conflicts of interest will not arise. It is not that lawyers in these firms make a casual inquiry when the impulse strikes them; they simply do not bother. They learn of conflicts of interest only after they have already developed, usually when a client tells them. These firms, then, do not even fall on the continuum sketched above. The following exchange, prompted by my rather indelicate question directed at the name partner of a downstate firm (specializing in personal injury suits on behalf of plaintiffs and in debt collection), illuminates the ostrich response to conflicts of interest:

> *S:* Would you describe, in the intake of new matters, what process lawyers in the firm go through to evaluate whether there are potential conflicts of interest?
>
> *L: We don't,* all right? The only thing that happens is, first of all, we have a list of doctors, for instance, that we will not sue—not because of any conflict, but because they're our personal doctors or friends or they have some business connection with one or the other of us. But, other than that, *we have no way of finding conflicts.* What happens is that, as far as the injury end of it is concerned, it would be very unusual for

a conflict to occur. As a matter of fact, I don't know how one could occur in the personal injury work, because we don't defend anybody. And, obviously, one plaintiff is not going to be suing another plaintiff. . . . I guess we have had situations where a defendant came in as a plaintiff and was going to sue somebody, and we have discovered that we might represent somebody who's a prospective defendant. And we also got . . . representing somebody that would be suing that and it might be a counter suit. But that's by just happenstance that we would discover that. *There isn't any procedure that we have.* The only other area of conflict—and it's one that does arise from time to time— is we have a Commercial Department in this firm. . . . And they are suing people to collect debts and bills in commercial matters and things of that sort. And, on occasion, there is a client that . . . Let's say I have a railroad client, a guy hurt on the railroad, and he owes a hospital bill or owes a grocer or something. The Commercial Department . . . might have that claim against him. And, when they send the letter or notice to him that they're representing "So-and-So," well, he obviously would know that it's on my letterhead and know that it's my firm, and *he would bring it to my attention.* And we would resolve the matter. We would have to withdraw from one or the other representations. *But we don't have any procedure for discovering that.*

S: So the people in the Commercial Department wouldn't, for example, go through the list of clients or the list of ongoing matters just to make sure that . . .

L: No, they would not. . . . it would be such hard work. They handle, they have a large volume of cases. . . . And they're not big cases at all. They have a very large volume of work. And, if they had to go through our other client lists each time they took a commercial matter, *it would be impossible for them to do.* [65DSM20–49]

This ostrich firm is rather large, by downstate standards, employing between twenty and forty-nine attorneys and located in a medium-size city. I conducted the interview roughly midway through the interviewing process and was, frankly, stunned by a response I had never heard before—even in much smaller and more specialized firms. This firm chose to play Russian roulette. Based on its relatively specialized practice representing one-shotters, the name partner assumed or gambled that there would be few bullets in the gun's chamber and that the cost of extricating discharged bullets would be lower than that of routinely checking that the chambers were empty. I suspect his calculus reflected not only his perception that the gun would rarely be loaded, but also the fact that his revolver tended to discharge less lethal bullets. Representing powerless, unsophisticated clients, often disabled by serious accidents, he probably assumed that they would not recognize a conflict of interest or cause much trouble, if they did. In any event, I met few, if any, other lawyers less risk averse or as certain that implementing a few precautions would be "impossible."

The Elephant

> We have clients who come in from twenty, twenty-five years ago and say, "I'm . . ." and we can say their name. They're amazed that we remember them at all. And I guess that's just part of being an attorney, for one thing. They claim that attorneys remember, or else they wouldn't be attorneys. [127DSS<10]

If the ostrich is a rare endangered species in the law firm world, the elephant is not. I encountered several, especially among small firms. Elephants never forget. They know their clients and assert that they would know immediately if a potential new matter was likely to trigger a conflict of interest. Because these lawyers casually run through a mental checklist before taking on a new case and will consult their records when memory fails, they fall on the continuum—though barely. A solo practitioner and part-time public defender in a downstate community described this sort of intelligence system.

> Given the size of my practice—speaking only of the private practice right now—given the size of my practice, it's not difficult for me to identify a conflict as soon as I hear the name, because I remember, you know, I remember all my clients. Many of these files that I have open stay open, you know, for a year or two. . . . Some years go by when I don't have more than maybe a dozen new files open during the year. . . . And as far as keeping track of those things, I keep track of them in my mind. . . . I mean I just remember what I've done. And, with respect to the public defender, the criminal defense practice, . . . there are few enough criminals in town that they—it's like a revolving door—they keep coming back through the system. And you can remember who you have and who you haven't represented. . . . So you can look through a file as soon as you receive it and see if there's anybody you recognize. And, again, if it's a situation where I've done some work for somebody in the past, defended somebody—that sort of thing—in any significant

fashion, I'll remember the name. . . . I would be surprised if any one of the other [part-time public defenders] do anything differently insofar as identifying conflicts. You know, this town's just small enough and the workload is such that we can remember, you know, you remember people. [91DSL<10]

Most of the elephants explained that, because of the limited size, age, or clientele of their firm, it is easy to keep track of their diverse interests.

There are advantages of a smaller firm, I think, in the conflicts area because, basically, everybody knows everything. And, in larger firms, some people don't even recognize colleagues. [108Ch10–19]

At any given time, I've got 150, 140 files going. And I know every person in every one of my files. You know, you never forget 'em. [86CC<10]

So elephants simply run through a mental checklist before taking on a new case.

I know the names of the people that I have worked with over the past ten years. And a name will either strike a chord of recognition, or it will be a new and different name. So, the first check is just mentally, sort of going through what I have done before, thinking about whether it might be a conflict. [85DSM<10]

Collegial

No matter how unforgetful the elephant, intelligence systems based on memory and personal knowledge begin to break down as firms grow. Even if we are able to keep track of all our dalliances and flirtations and those of our sexual partners, the metaphor of AIDS transmission (as well as the rules of legal ethics) requires that we know all of those of our colleagues and their sexual partners as well. To identify a conflict of interest, we need access not only to all of our own clients and potential clients, their family trees, and assorted interests but also to those of our colleagues. We need to know about the clients they have or have had and, if we want to prevent conflicts that might foreclose future business, we need to know about clients they hope to represent as well. Many firms, therefore, ask that lawyers consult with one another before taking on a new client or matter. In smaller firms, lawyers typically consult face-to-face. In the smallest of firms, colleagues often meet every day to discuss new cases or consult with one another before taking on a new engagement. As the name partner of a Chicago firm described:

> Well, we have [about ten] lawyers. Five associates. With the five associates, maybe there's two or three clients that they've brought in. All the other clients are clients that come in from the partners. And, you know, there's no better microchip than your brain. And, with a firm our size, intuitively I know right away whether we've got a conflict. But we always ask, 'cause we have to ask. . . . And, you know, we talk to each other. And if there are a sufficient number of parties, or principals, or shareholders, or employees, or people, or, you know, related parties that are all people you have to check for a conflict—we'll write a memo. But, for the most part, [we] just walk around and say, "Okay, we got a conflict. Who are we representing here? You know, who owns them? Who do they own?" You know, all the questions you have to ask. . . . It's just not that big. You know, we're not like a, you know, personal injury firm [that] might have 1,000 cases. You know, if [our firm has] 100, that's a lot. [104Ch10–19]

In somewhat larger firms, usually with less than twenty-five attorneys, the partners and associates meet once a week to discuss all new cases and unearth potential conflicts of interest about which colleagues are aware:

> In addition to having a pretty close partnership relationship—I mean, we're all on the same floor and we see each other all the time and we discuss over the cases. In addition to finding it out through direct discussion, the firm also—weekly—goes over new clients with a view toward finding out potential conflicts. We have a weekly meeting. And, at that time, we will describe the new clients that have come in. And, if there is any potential conflict, the attorneys know immediately to speak up and to say that. That way, we include not only the partners who see each other, but also the associates who are at the meeting— they hear it. They know they have the input on it. . . . It's a weekly meeting of all the attorneys. And the very, very first thing that we do—we just completed it this morning—the very first thing that we do in that meeting is to have . . . Our billing clerk reads the names of the files that have been opened this past week. And it's the responsibility of the attorney who opened it to—if there's something new or novel about the case or some help that they want—is to mention the details of the case and the question as to whether or not, in our mind,

there's a conflict. The problem in a firm our size in a community such as [this city] in representing a number of the businesses in the community—in particular, the bank—is whether or not we're ending up suing one of our own clients. And we do run into conflicts of that sort which, for the most part, are minor. We can catch it ahead of time and withdraw. But sometimes, we get very involved—as was the discussion this morning. [54DSL20–49]

In still larger firms, colleagues consult impersonally. Some leave a checklist or clipboard in the reception area of the firm, which lawyers must peruse and sign off on as they come and go:

We have no committee; we have no real centralized management. We really have no system of supervision of conflicts. What we do is we have a form—a new matter conflict-of-interest form. . . . Every time there's a new matter, the lawyer . . . is responsible for filling that out or having his secretary fill it out. And then it sits at the reception desk. And the receptionist polices—only to the extent of being sure everybody initials it. If there is a conflict, if anybody says "yes," it usually gets to me. Just because I'm a senior. But we have no real structure. If everybody says, "no," then it just stays in the file. And we did this primarily . . . Well, I guess the initiative for doing this was not really our own need—as we saw it—but our malpractice carrier insisted on it. It's fine. It's not terribly burdensome. I'm not totally sure that it's sufficient. We're so small that we really—in earlier times—lived off of other people's conflicts. We rarely have a real conflict. [80Ch10–19]

Most other firms adopting an impersonal collegial intelligence model circulate case-specific memoranda or daily or weekly newsletters that list new cases to which their colleagues are expected to respond if they recognize a potential conflict of interest. A member of the executive committee of a fairly large Chicago firm of roughly one hundred lawyers described their system for identifying potential conflicts:

L: We're pretty informal about all this, and maybe we should be more systematic then we are. But what we do is have people circulate a memo to the firm on all new clients, and, more recently, we've been trying to get people to do that as to new matters for existing clients. We do not have a computerized system. We don't try to have names automatically checked against a computerized index. We, of course, have a client and matter index, and I think people, probably fairly routinely, consult that. But I think we depend most on circulating memos.

S: So, say a new client with a new matter approaches a partner in the firm?

L: There will be a conflict memo circulated. And it says, "we've been asked to represent 'So-and-So.' Here are the other people involved. Here's what the matter involves." And then, depending on whether any negative response is heard from anybody in the firm—any reason to raise a flag about it—then the attorney involved will send a memo to me saying, "I propose to undertake this representation and attached is a copy of the engagement letter that we'll have the client sign. Here are the reasons why I believe the client is creditworthy and whatever it is."

S: Do you find that most of the lawyers in the firm are pretty quick about assessing the memos?

L: Oh, I think so. Yes. Yes, yeah, you'll get an answer back pretty quickly, if you circulate it. . . . They're not the only thing that goes around on blue paper, but they're one of the few things that does. . . . I think most people pick up a conflict memo and look at it pretty quickly. It's been my experience that I get comments back pretty quickly on the ones I send around. [21Ch50–99]

Some of the larger firms go even more high tech, with electronic mail messages blaring across lawyers' computer screens or oral messages clogging their voice mailboxes throughout the day as potential new cases arise.[11] Attorneys are expected to check their electronic or telephonic messages, newsletters, or memoranda and sign off on new matters before their colleagues can secure a billing number and begin working on the case.[12]

That communication among colleagues is burdensome is duly noted by many of the respondents. But most find the yield well worth the cost. Indeed, when partners formed the law firm cited in the last example, they intentionally eschewed the other methods of identifying conflicts of interest that they had relied on in the past in favor of circulating intraoffice memoranda.

In a prior firm that a number of us were at—a predecessor firm— . . . people were required, in connection with every new matter, to send in quite a complicated form. If it was a corporate client—listing all the directors and shareholders and I don't know. It was very complicated business. And I think it was probably largely ignored or, at least, certainly not carried out in a methodical way. And I think, to those of us who were exposed to that, that just seemed very complicated, time-consuming for what possible benefit there might be for it. And most conflicts we ever identified came about either because people knew or they looked at the client list, the matter list, or circulated a memo on somebody. And it has always seemed to me that, no matter how elaborate a computer system you have, you can't do away with circulating the memo. Because that's more likely to turn up information about relationships. . . . As I say, I think it's imperative to circulate conflicts memos, whatever sort of system you have. And you're likely to pull whatever knowledge there is out of it. [21Ch50–99]

Colleagues in the majority of firms function collegially, systematically consulting with each other about potential conflicts before taking on a new engagement. But, unlike the elephants, they rely on much more than their memories.

Archival

The problem with elephants or herds of elephants—in the collegial model—is that they sometimes do forget, especially aging or active elephants with a great deal on their mind. Two solo practitioners explained to me why they recently decided to develop a system of records to help identify conflicts of interest, suggesting that memory capacity—at least in a general practice—is rather short-lived:

Well, I've only been in practice now for—in sole practice by myself—for two and a half years. So I am still able to know, when somebody comes in, whether I'm going to have a conflict, because I recognize the parties. But it is getting to the point where I'm forgetting, you know, what I did two years ago. And I may forget names and faces. . . . In fact, this morning I had one—a new client who came in and wanted to have me terminate a partnership agreement. And it so happened that I represented the partner that he wanted to do it in a divorce matter. And, although there is no relationship between the divorce and this business, I referred him to another attorney. Because I recognized the name and knew that that could pose a conflict for me. But that, you know, that's rapidly coming to an end, because I am forgetting what I did in 1991 and '92. And all the names and faces are . . . a little different. [112DSS<10]

I think, informally, I just, I know the names of the people that I have worked with over the past ten years. And a name will either strike a chord of recognition or it will be a new and different name. So the first check is just mentally, sort of, going through what I have done before, thinking about whether it might be a conflict. . . . I was getting to the point that I was not able to remember people from ten years ago. And I was anxious that somebody might slip through my memory. . . . I was looking through some cases, and a person did slip through. . . . And this was almost when I started practice ten years ago. A lady came in and wanted me to get child support set against her husband. And, years later, her husband came in and wanted to modify the support. And, ultimately, he wanted a divorce. He remarried. I did another divorce. And I think it was in the midst of the second divorce that I figured out that "oops!" [laughter] [85DSM<10]

Moreover, however complete and accessible their overflowing memory banks, this firm resource disappears when elephants retire or die or move on to another herd.

We went through a merger in late [recent year]. And two attorneys that practice in [a neighboring city]—and specialize in labor and employment law matters—merged with us. We weren't as systematic or as methodical in going through a conflict check before that merger. Because, quite frankly, at that time, every attorney—darn near; we're still small enough—really had a good handle on who the clients of the firm were. Well, once that merger took place, and we did wind up suing one of their clients. And then we implemented a better system. . . . I don't think we've pulled that brain-dead move in, probably, in a couple of years. [72DSM10–19]

Just because the institutional memory is lost does not mean that the conflicts of interest desist. And keeping track of the herds and ensuring that each member has had an opportunity to comment becomes a laborious process as they multiply. Most firms, therefore, supplement individual and institutional memories and mechanisms for collective feedback and dissemination with some form of archival records. Records represent by far the most common resource on which firms rely for identifying conflicts of interest. Although they are used in the vast majority of law firms, they can look as different as hieroglyphics and complex computer code. The basic distinction is between paper and electronic records and between those created specifically for the social control of conflicts of interest and those developed for another purpose.

The simplest archival system is comprised of a client list that lawyers, secretaries, or receptionists consult to ensure that the adverse party in a prospective matter is not already a client of the firm. Although this practice is most common in small law firms, one of the largest firms in the sample uses essentially the same system:

> In every office we have a list of our clients on microfiche, and it's updated. It's two weeks old. It's never less current than two weeks. And we are automating it. And we think within three or four months, we will be where it's almost same-day. . . . We keep central registration of clients. So I have a new client that comes in to me, knocks on the door, and sits down and talks to me. He says, "[my name], I'd like to bring you something." . . . So the moment the client comes in, we sit down and we begin to talk. And I get a feel for the other parties involved. I'll call my secretary in and give her a note, "Please get the conflict data on . . ." And the client has said, "I'm going to buy a farm from John Jones—farmer living out in DeKalb County." I'll put down "Farmer Jones." "And I've got a loan lined up with the First National Bank of Chicago; I'd like you to help me with them." I write down "First National Bank of Chicago." And while we're talking, I'll tell him, "Well, I'm going . . . to have my secretary check. . . . So my secretary will run out and check. She'll go out. . . . She starts on the microfiche, finds a listing for "J. Jones" and sees that it's registered, say, for [my colleague]—lawyer next door. Well, [colleague]'s out for the moment. So I'll then have her check the fee history upstairs. She puts in a call to our client registration department . . . and then they will have the gap for the last two weeks. . . . I get the information. I see that we have a registration for "J. Jones" and that we have fees. In the current year, we've received a thousand dollars in fees. And I'll be doing the same thing for the First National Bank of Chicago. Okay. And I see we've got some current fees. . . . I can tell the client, "We'll continue on with our discussion. . . . But I'm going to have to check with my partner [names colleague]—as soon as he comes in—to see." [16Ch100+]

Client lists say nothing about the nature of the representation, nor do they disclose the array of parties also implicated in a particular case. It is no wonder that this firm is about to get automated. The notion that its hundreds of lawyers, working in various branch offices, must continually locate one another to gather a few incidental facts—even to rule out nonexistent conflicts of interest—is staggering.

Many firms, typically smaller ones, therefore, develop a second system of paper records to supplement client lists. They create index cards, usually one for each party in a case, that a clerk must check before a new matter can be opened:

> When a new case is brought into the firm, we keep a list of all existing clients of the firm, as well as, we have a five or six part form that we fill out. One of the forms goes in an adverse party docketing system, where we list all parties that have ever been adverse to us in the docketing system. Another part goes into a docketing system of existing clients. So it's relatively easy to know whether there's a conflict on any one of our files. . . . It's not computerized. It's simply kept on what are little index-sized cards like this: Where the yellow copy typically goes to the lawyer handling the matter. And then there's a pink copy that is the adverse party copy. And then I think there's a green copy that is the existing client copy. But it's five or six parts, and we do it that way. It's done manually usually. [121Ch<10]

Most firms retain these index cards forever, long after a case is closed. Some file the cards of opened or closed cases separately; others differentiate between clients and adverse parties. As firms grow and age, the storage and retrieval process can become quite cumbersome. I visited one firm that allocated a special room behind the reception area for what it called the "wheels." The room housed nine massive Rolodex-like devices holding small cards in a rainbow of colors, with each card color-coded by the lawyer working on the case and then alphabetized by the client's name. Information contained on the cards allows the checker to identify the lawyer who worked on the case and the file numbers and the location of the records in which the prior case was stored. The firm's name partner explained that it is used as a backup for what is generally an "elephant" system of conflict identification:

> We've kind of relied on an old system that we've had in identifying our clients as the principal basis on which we check for conflicts—to the extent that we do. Most of the people in the law firm—it's not true any more—for a long time it was true that the people had been around for a long time. And, you know, if you're here on a day-to-day basis, we're small enough so that we kind of knew other people's clients. And you'd go and you see names and whatnot. And if something came in that involved a client that kind of rang a bell, we would begin checking. And we have a thing called the "wheels." . . . And, as we open a file, that label goes on one of the open file wheels in alphabetical order. And that matter will be handled. And as it gets closed, it then goes on

to one of the closed file wheels. So that if somebody needs a file that may have been closed ten years ago, pretty generally, we can find it. We have a numbering system, and we have a storage facility. If I get a matter that involves somebody that—or a client—that I vaguely recognize, I'll go to the wheels and take a look. And then I will check with the attorney that was responsible for that and see whether or not the potential thing—the potential matter—would result in a conflict. . . . I suspect that it is done more in the situation where something jogs a memory. Now, we do have two attorneys who are relatively new— like within the last five, six years—and, if something comes in of substantial nature, they may check to find out whether there is a conflict. And I'd suspect that their first thing would be to send a secretary to the wheels and see whether or not anybody represents somebody on the other side. [74DSL<10]

Larger and more technologically sophisticated firms have abandoned paper trails—at least for contemporary matters—and undertake electronic surveillance. The simplest produce electronic versions of client lists or index cards or use computerized mailing lists or billing records to search for potential conflicts of interest. Although computer browsing through lists or file cards is more efficient than manual retrieval, these records contain very limited information about the nature of the case and the parties involved. More complex surveillance systems rely on specialized conflicts databases that record a storehouse of information about an ongoing case and devise artificial intelligence algorithms to scan the database for indicators of potential trouble. A little more than half of the firms in the sample use conflicts databases. These systems vary tremendously in the amount and richness of information collected and the suppleness and creativity of the artificial intelligence driving the analysis.

At the time of the interview, more than a fifth of the firms were in the process of transition. Some were upgrading their existing conflicts-checking computer software or hardware. Others, like the huge Chicago firm using microfiched records, were negotiating between manual and automated systems—between historical records, stashed in index card files or dusty file rooms, and contemporary records, often stored in different computer files and electronic recordkeeping systems—while

- Waiting to purchase bigger computers with the speed and memory required to initiate multiple, complex searches while simultaneously supporting the firms' billing, word processing, document management, legal research, accounting, networking, and other computer needs;

- Engaging in the tedious multiyear data entry phase of transforming paper records into electronic ones; or

- Trying to cope with an artificial intelligence system that, to their surprise and frustration, is much dumber than its human counterpart.

Indeed, one firm in the sample had just shut down its computerized conflicts-screening system and returned to tried-and-true manual checking:

L2: Right now, the firm's unfortunately at a manual stage. They've been trying to implement a computer stage where they can screen these. But they have individuals that go through thousands and thousands of cards, and they just search manually for the names of all the parties that are listed on the sheet. . . . we've been having some difficulty getting this whole system computerized. I think half the problem is that lawyers' minds think one way and administrative computer people think another, and it's hard to mesh those two mentalities. . . . They just read things a lot different than I do, you know? They're like, "Well, that's in the claimant section of the computer classification." And I'm like, "Who do we represent, you know, who's the party in interest?" And we just were not relating. And I said, "I think our minds just operate differently." So there's kinda been some difficulty getting it computerized.

L1: About six months ago when we first got it computerized . . . Well, what's funny is that they did it without ever talking to the lawyers. So what happened was, all of a sudden, they went computer. And I went ballistic, okay? Because every case in the whole office was kicking out as a conflict, okay? Because they had done so thorough a job that I must have had a hundred a week . . . 150 a week, okay? . . . So then what happened was . . . we were so swamped in information that we had to basically shut the thing down and go back. See, the mechanical system never was broken. It wasn't busted. It was workin' and it always has worked. . . . Well, it took time, you know, time and stuff like that—which is great. That's wonderful. I got no problem with that. But we had never had a conflict problem in identifying the conflicts until we had the computer to help us. [laughter] Then every case

ended up being kicked out for a decision by [L2] or I. And we're looking at these things and none of them are conflicts. But they're saying
they are, so we got to look at 'em. But they weren't. So now we're back
trying to redo the thing, right?

L2: But they're computer people so they want just to have every search
term, you know, that you could possibly think of.

L1: The best example is the plaintiff's lawyer. Here's what they would
do—and it can be a conflict, okay, it can be. . . . For example, let's take
ABC law firm. They're plaintiff's lawyers by and large. They're a very
successful firm, all right? They probably have a hundred or two hundred cases against [our firm], where we're defending somebody, all
right? They were inputting the plaintiff firm and so kicking out every
case in which they were representing a client adverse to a [this firm]
client. But that ain't a conflict. . . . But you know, when you get it on
your desk and somebody's . . . You got to look at it and then you go,
"Well, this isn't a conflict." But it took ten minutes to figure this out, you
know, to go through all this junk that they give you. [6Ch100+]

Cybersurveillance

The most exhaustive surveillance systems incorporate intelligence
features of the elephant, collegial, and archival models, transforming
each to state-of-the-art technology administered by a specialized
staff. The next portrait depicts a soaring high rise overlooking
Chicago's downtown Loop, which houses a large general practice
firm that I will call "Legal Towers," with more than 250 attorneys
working in several offices across the country. The firm has developed
a rather elaborate structure for reviewing prospective cases, which
includes what is generically called a new business committee (comprised of about a dozen attorneys who meet at least weekly), a professional responsibility committee, and a conflicts-analysis staff of
roughly five nonlawyers. The new business committee must approve
all new clients as well as those for which the firm performed no work
in the past year.[13]

Lawyers hoping to bring in new business complete new matter
forms for new clients approved by the new business committee as
well as for prospective cases of ongoing clients that do not require
committee scrutiny. Forms collect information regarding:

- The name and address of the prospective client,
- Type of client (individual, corporation, partnership, fiduciary, association, and so forth),
- Principal business of the client,
- Description of the matter,
- A copy of the litigation complaint,
- Whether the litigation client is a plaintiff, defendant, third-party, or creditor,
- If a former or existing client, the legal services previously performed,
- Prior names used by the prospective client,
- Commonly used abbreviations (for example, AT&T, 3M),
- Parents, subsidiaries, and affiliates of corporate clients,
- Directors, officers, and principal shareholders of corporate clients and of their parents,
- All partners in a partnership,
- All members of an association,
- All beneficiaries of a fiduciary,
- Names of spouses of individual clients,
- Names of any other related parties to which the firm should not be adverse,
- Adverse parties (including corporate affiliates and partners),
- Other parties that might have an interest in the matter (officers, employees, major customers, suppliers, competitors),
- Relationship between the proposed client and any other existing client,
- Potential conflicts of interest of which the lawyer is aware,
- Why the prospective client sought this law firm and who referred it,
- Whether and why the client is switching law firms,
- Other counsel involved in the matter,

- Whether a third party (such as an insurance company) is paying for the representation, and

- Assorted scheduling, staffing, and billing information.

The completed new matter form is sent to the conflicts-analysis staff and a description of the case and the parties involved is published in a weekly report of potential new matters that is circulated to all lawyers in the firm. Colleagues are expected to call immediately if they know of anything that would suggest a problem. The conflicts-analysis staff enter the information disclosed on the form into a conflicts database.

In addition to collecting the information disclosed on new matter forms, the conflicts database includes:

- Information on forms that attorneys are required to complete regarding nonclients and nonmatters (where the firm was consulted about a potential case, but the firm declined the representation or the client chose to go elsewhere),

- Annual reports of officer or director appointments (even for charities or nonprofit organizations) and significant ownership interests of the firm's attorneys and their spouses,

- All subsequent changes or new developments in clients (such as mergers or acquisitions) or matters (additional parties join the litigation) that arise after the case is under way, disclosed in yet another form, and

- Memoranda listing all former clients of lawyers hired laterally from other law firms or government positions.

Firms of this size report anywhere from 5,000 to 20,000 active clients, with as many as a hundred matters open for any given client. And that is just the number of records, not the numbers of data points in each record. Then there are the tens or hundreds of thousands of closed cases collected in the database as well, and one begins to get a sense of the magnitude of the searching process.

When Legal Towers developed this electronic database more than ten years ago, staff recognized that information from closed cases was as essential to conflicts screening as that regarding current matters. But it was difficult to ascertain which cases across the firm's long institutional history were relevant and which were not. So all files going back to the turn of the century were entered into the database. It took five years to convert the records to the new system.[14]

Conflicts analysts next formulate a search procedure, listing the names of clients, related parties, adverse parties, and other entities to be tracked as well as specifying the data sources to be consulted beyond the conflicts database.[15] Initially, the database included generic information on corporate families and relationships—parents, subsidiaries, joint ventures, and the like. But analysts discovered that these relationships changed too frequently, especially in the turbulent 1980s, leading to significant oversights and errors. So all these relational data were methodically stripped from the database. Conflicts analysts now go on-line or check published references in the firm's library—*Moody's, Dun & Bradstreet, Standard & Poor's, Who Owns Whom, the Directory of Corporate Affiliations, Best's Insurance Directory*, and so forth—to find corporate parents, subsidiaries, and other significant relationships.[16] Because the conflicts database is restricted to proper names, it may be necessary to fashion specialized searches on other relevant attributes. For example, particular products produced by competing clients may create conflicts of interest. Say that analysts want to find out whether the firm has ever represented other breweries. They would search standard industry codes collected from census data and obtain a list of every brewery in the country. Then they would run a search of all these names against the conflicts database.

Today law firms can choose among dozens of off-the-rack software packages for conflict-of-interest screening, some of which are linked to billing or docket software. But, when Legal Towers and other large firms went electronic back in the late 1970s and early 1980s, no such software was available. So they hired programmers to develop specialized programs compatible with the firm's caseload and practice, types of records, and artificial intelligence parameters about what abstract evidence indicates a potential conflict of interest. Many large firms have been through several versions of these custom-made programs since then, all of them far more sophisticated than the off-the-rack programs, and most still subject to considerable dissatisfaction by their users.

These software programs work by identifying matches between the specified list of names and all their occurrences in the database—

all possible spellings and misspellings, abbreviations, acronyms, nick-names, and variations. Because false positives (the equivalent of false alarms) are preferable to false negatives (missing true conflicts), pro-grams err in favor of the former. The result, of course, is reams of output involving entities with common or similar names or parts of names ("Smith," "Ford," "Illinois," "& Sons," "University," "General," "Amalgamated," "State," "Lincoln," and so forth) that bear no rela-tionship to the parties touched by a particular matter.[17] And even gen-uine matches do not necessarily bespeak conflicts of interest. The fact that the firm represented John Doe when he bought a house in 1970 probably does not preclude the firm from defending Mary Roe whose automobile struck John's twenty years later. Unfortunately, the artificial intelligence is not up to the task of making that sort of determination. So conflicts analysts generate often weighty stacks of output that reproduce the new matter forms or other records in which so-called "hits" are found and are sent on to be evaluated by human intelligence.

Moreover, because a given matter can involve dozens or hundreds of parties that are repeat players in the legal system—banks, insurance companies, creditors, institutional investors, environmental polluters, and the like—the output and amount of searching time can be sub-stantial. The computer scan of a single piece of complex litigation or a massive bankruptcy may take an analyst a full day, the time it takes to complete about twenty-five simple searches. (Checking an individual with an uncommon name takes five seconds.) The output generated by the firm's biggest search, which took two people three weeks full-time to complete, fills an entire file drawer. On routine cases, turn-around is generally about two to three days. Emergency matters—temporary restraining orders, for example—can be turned around even faster. Analysts receive roughly forty to sixty new matters each week. In addition to these full-blown searches, lawyers may request preliminary searches before they even agree to talk to a prospective client in a prerepresentational meeting, or beauty contest, or before they invest a lot of time undertaking "marketing" activities to attract new clients. It makes no sense to waste time trying to woo the client, only to have to decline the business because of conflicts of interest.

After completing the conflicts search, analysts send an edited ver-sion of the output back to the lawyer responsible for the prospective matter, and he or she must evaluate each hit for its conflict potential.

The output can be massive—especially if the case involves multiple parties, many of whom have a long trail of prior contacts with the firm. The lawyer analyzes the often-inch-thick (or more) stacks of paper, weeding out the false positives and then assessing the remaining hits. Evaluation may require assessing the accounting database and billing records to determine whether the parties are current or former clients, pulling the files of prior cases that are identified as hits to analyze the nature and substance of the former representation, but especially consulting with the attorneys responsible for the cases that gave rise to the potential conflict.

Some prospective matters will self-destruct at this stage. Others may survive only if corrective action is taken (jettisoning tainted pieces of the engagement, securing client consent, erecting ethical screens, and the like). Attorneys responsible for the new matter must sign off on all hits enumerated in the computer output and pass the output and supporting documentation, arguments for why genuine hits are not problematic, and recommendations about how to cure potential conflicts of interest on to the professional responsibility committee, which must approve all new matters. A representative of the committee—or, when the question is controversial, the entire committee—may revisit the issues, review the documentation and case records, undertake legal research, consult with the firm's malpractice insurer or a national ethics expert, weigh the risks and benefits, and debate with colleagues before approving or declining the new matter. It is not unusual for lawyers representing the new and affected clients to disagree about the significance of or the appropriate solution to a potential conflict. Lawyers with ongoing relationships with the affected clients will be reluctant to antagonize them simply to accommodate a colleague, even if the conflict falls short of threatening their ethical obligations. The committee may be called on to mediate these intrafirm disputes and, about ten times a year, especially contentious issues may be referred to the firm's executive committee for resolution.

A matter is not assigned a billing number until after it has received approval from the committee. This serves as a control mechanism. If lawyers begin working on the case before the billing number is assigned, they risk "eating the cost."

The attorney with the greatest hands-on responsibility for conflicts clearance, usually a very senior partner in the firm with the credibility and clout to resolve disputes and enforce committee decisions, will devote a substantial portion of his time to conflicts matters. Although the professional responsibility partner in this firm did not provide an estimate, his counterparts in other firms indicated that they spend often hundreds of hours each year clearing conflicts. Among firms with more than 200 attorneys, respondents, on average, estimated that they devote about 500 hours each year to conflicts clearance (estimates ranged from 75 to 2,000 hours, reflecting to some extent whether they were solely responsible or shared the burden with one or more colleagues).[18]

Taking into account the billable hours of all the attorneys serving on the two committees, the personnel costs of the conflicts analysts, the hours lawyers spend reviewing and clearing the conflicts-screening output generated for new matters they hope to bring into the firm, the outlay on upgrading computer hardware and software, the hourly fees of on-line databases, and the purchase of up-to-date library reference materials, conflicts screening on a single matter can cost thousands of dollars, few of which can ultimately be billed directly to the client. Indeed, on a complex case with many coparties, it may cost more to do a conflicts search than the client will be billed in legal fees. In that instance, prospective clients may be told that it is not to their benefit to be represented by the firm and that perhaps they would like to be referred to a smaller firm.

Legal Towers has developed a form of cybersurveillance that I call "technoblitz": pulling out all the stops technologically, organizationally, and informationally. A "technoblitz" model of organizational intelligence relies on state-of-the-art computer databases and artificial intelligence that screen all prospective new matters; a specialized staff to administer the technical surveillance; a conflicts, new business, professional responsibility, or ethics committee comprised of lawyers to oversee and enforce the self-regulatory process; a party designated to sign off on all new cases; and a mechanism for collegial social control (for circulating all prospective matters to the firm's attorneys and polling their responses). Intelligence systems that use computer databases to screen all new matters for conflicts and have most, but not all, of the other components of the technoblitz model, I call "cyber-surveillance." Most often, the latter do not use specialized staff for computer surveillance—relying instead on file or billing clerks or secretaries—or do not require that someone sign off on new matters, leaving it up to the lawyers to resolve problematic hits unearthed by the computer screening.

This cursory review of the nuts and bolts of "technoblitz" intelligence illustrates how one fairly cautious large law firm responds to the risks of taking on a new engagement. An example offered by a member of the professional responsibility committee of a slightly smaller firm conveys some sense of the often convoluted process of clearing potential conflicts under this intelligence regime:

> I got a call from [a fast food restaurant client], you know, a couple of days ago. And they've got a problem. It wasn't an emergency problem, but they wanted to have an answer . . . They've got a store out in a particular location. They've had some problems with it; there was an injunction entered against them; they were handling it internally . . . The first thing I did was say, "Look, stop. Tell me who is involved." All right? And they gave me a list of people. Now, amongst those people were two property managers, some owners, a pension fund on the East Coast, a mortgage lender—all of which were involved in this property—as well as a large food company that was also in the shopping center and was seeking to restrain the building because of a restrictive covenant—the building of this [fast food restaurant client] there . . . The first thing I did is say, "Look, I don't recognize any of these as being conflicts in our office. But, before you tell me about the situation, let me do a quick check to see if anything . . ." I then filled out this form. I gave the names that he had listed to my secretary. . . . And I asked my secretary, in this case—although normally, I could take more time—to walk it through. So she took it to the various people. They ran it, and they gave a printout immediately, which showed any reference . . . And one of them happened to be [a title company client] and another was [another client]. We had a few matters where we were representing those as well as 150 other matters where there was the word [names a word in the name of the first client—a Chicago street name] in it [laughter] or the word [names a different word in name of first client—a common name for a collectivity] in it, which I had to ferret through. But that gets back to the software problem. Listed along with those names were the attorneys who were in charge of those clients. And I called those attorneys. One happened to be a partner who was out of town. But his secretary got in touch with him, and he called me back and said, "Yes, I represented them several years ago. It hasn't gotten out of our code book yet. But I haven't done anything for two years and certainly nothing in this location, so there couldn't be a conflict." (Thinking that if it's a former client, but it would relate to

that particular piece of property, it could still be a conflict under substantial relationship.) So then I had called another partner who had represented [the second client]. But, again, he said, "No, those aren't current files. We've never done any work for them on this and certainly not a conflict." So, I precleared those conflicts. Then what I did—in order to open up the file, which I did the next day, really—is I ran an official search, you know, sent the file through and did whatever had to be done. And then I put the note in the bulletin, and I put a voice mail in, saying, "If anyone knows any reason . . ." And then I listed all of these various names. And I got a couple of other calls that weren't in the [printout]. [Partner], one of my zoning partners, called up and said, "Gee, we don't represent this company, but I know the principals very well. I think we could get some business from them. How are they involved? And, by the way, they're also the main management agent for [a major discount merchandise company] and all their stores—who we do represent—and we've got a very close working relationship." And then I had to find out specifically, therefore, were they going to be involved? And, as we looked through and sorted through, we realized they had been replaced by [the client with the street name] as the management agent. They weren't even involved any more, and they wouldn't be a party to this at all. But we were being over-cautious, really, in getting all the names. So those are the kinds of things we do . . . Sometimes you walk it through yourself. Sometimes you put the voice mail in yourself. Sometimes the system takes over, and you just fill out these forms; they go through the system; they come back and, two days later, you call the client and say you can handle the matter. [11Ch100+]

The Ecology of Intelligence

One can observe considerable variation across law firms in procedures for ferreting out potential conflicts of interest. Lawyers employing cybersurveillance collect, store, create, retrieve, and cross-check every imaginable sort of electronic datum about new and existing matters, while those in other firms scour client lists and paper records or simply jar their memory banks. Colleagues in some firms communicate personally or electronically daily or, at least, weekly—even while on vacation—to ensure that their firm does not take on a new matter that might trigger a conflict of interest, while lawyers in other firms do not confer at all. Technoblitz firms invest tens or hundreds of thousands of dollars each year in technology, committees, and staff specialists devoted to conflicts of interest, while others leave it up to the discretion of the interested lawyer to seek out and resolve any potential conflicts that might arise. In the former firms, it takes days or weeks to complete a conflicts check and begin work on a case, while in the latter, it often takes seconds. Meanwhile, the ostriches, their heads buried in the sand, are entirely oblivious to the whole scene.

Figure 9.1 depicts the distribution of these intelligence systems through which firms in the sample identify potential conflicts of interest. As noted earlier, one encounters few ostriches or elephants dotting the terrain, and not many more herds of elephants, relying on their collective memories and collegial interactions alone to ferret out conflicts of interest. Together, these methods—or lack thereof— (represented in the three darkest shades) are found in about 15 percent of the firms. Roughly six out of ten firms situate their intelligence process in archival sources (the striped segments on the figure), often supplemented by institutional memories shared among colleagues. These firms are split fairly evenly between those that scan specialized conflicts databases (28 percent) and those that examine paper records, index cards, client lists, or computer records created for other purposes (31 percent). Finally, a little more than a quarter of the firms conduct a form of cybersurveillance (the dots), not quite half of them adopting the more elaborate technoblitz techniques.

Figure 9.1   Intelligence Models

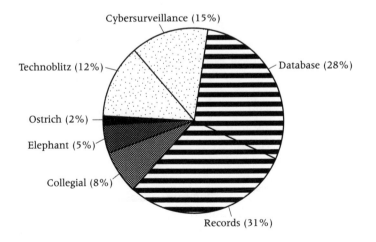

It should come as no surprise that firm size plays a powerful role in accounting for this distribution of intelligence methods. As firms grow, lawyers cannot function as solitary elephants. Partners need a mechanism to learn of the past, present, and future entanglements of their colleagues—whether consulting directly with them or relying on archival records documenting their clients and caseload. Larger firms not only have swollen caseloads; their cases tend to concern more protracted and complex matters involving multiple, often repeat-playing parties—themselves complex organizations continually changing form and structure with mergers, acquisitions, divestitures, and the like, each with different stakes in the transaction or litigation. Under these circumstances, scouring the archives manually to identify all the salient interests becomes increasingly difficult, as does relying on face-to-face communications among colleagues who often work in different sites and time zones. As firms grow, organizational structures develop specialists to undertake the self-regulatory process and adopt forms of cybersurveillance to negotiate through the dense and convoluted paper trail generated by clients, cases, and colleagues.

The profound connection between firm size and intelligence model is portrayed in figure 9.2. From just a passing glance, it is immediately apparent how much the darker bars, representing the largest firms, sink to the bottom of the page where the more comprehensive and more technologically sophisticated intelligence methods are plotted. As one ascends the classification of firm size, the modal intelligence model increases one step: from reliance on records for the smallest of firms (white bars), to databases for medium-size firms (striped bars), to cybersurveillance for large firms (gray bars), to technoblitz techniques for the largest mega-firms (black bars).

Starting at the bottom of figure 9.2, note that 96 percent, all but one of the largest firms employing more than 200 attorneys, adopt a form of cybersurveillance, more than two-thirds of them through all-out technoblitz. Firms with 50 to 199 lawyers comprise most of the rest of the cybersurveillance and technoblitz group and rely as well on the two archival methods. On the other end of the continuum, all the elephants work at the smallest firms; indeed two-thirds of them are solo practitioners. These small firms are also most likely to opt for paper or generalized electronic records to screen for conflicts than for specialized databases. Medium-size firms do the reverse; their archival surveillance methods are more likely to use more sophisti-

Figure 9.2   Intelligence Model and Firm Size

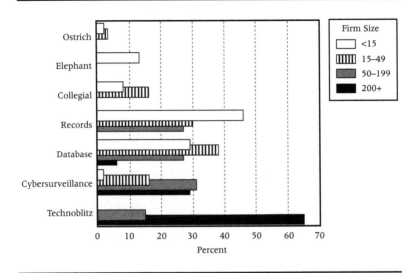

cated databases over paper or general records. Not surprisingly, medium-size firms are also more likely than smaller ones to use collegial methods to supplement their memories in identifying conflicts of interest, since an elephant's ability to know the activities of the rest of the herd is strained as the herd grows. On average, firms that solicit collegial input as a supplement to other intelligence methods (memory, archives, or cybersurveillance) have almost fifty more lawyers than those that do not (the median difference is ten lawyers).

Given the strong correlation between firm size and intelligence method—which would be even higher if the sample was large enough to sort firms into more homogeneous size categories—there is not much variance left to explain. However, one can tease out a few crude variables that account for some of the noise in figure 9.2. The diversity of practice, for example, affects whether medium or large firms develop cybersurveillance methods or rely instead on data archives or collegial interaction to ferret out conflicts of interest. As firms diversify, colleagues may know less about the others' business, because those with disparate expertise interact infrequently, necessitating more comprehensive methods to stay apprised of the interests served by partners in the firm. More significant, diversification spawns ongoing relationships with clients because the firm is now staffed to service more of their legal needs. With individual clients, the diversified firm can represent a family on the purchase of a new home and then handle an auto accident injury, adoption, tax or estate planning, marital dissolution, bankruptcy, and the like. With corporate clients, the diversified firm can make and break contracts, engineer or abort mergers, do securities filings, secure patents and financing, handle sexual harassment claims, defend products liability suits, and so on. With continuing relationships, client interests do not desist as quickly or as predictably, while simultaneously shifting or evolving from matter to matter. As a result, the likelihood that interests of the firm's clients will collide increases considerably. Diversification, then, breeds greater vulnerability to conflicts of interest, on the one hand, and greater difficulty staying apprised of the divergent and shifting interests represented by the firm, on the other. Firms compensate with greater surveillance. Controlling for their size, general practices are more likely to embrace cybersurveillance or technoblitz intelligence schemes than firms offering fewer substantive specialties: Half of the general practice firms employing twenty-five to ninety-nine lawyers adopt these methods, compared with a fifth of more specialized firms; for firms with one hundred or more attorneys, the percentages are 93 versus 66, respectively.

A related feature of the law firm landscape also accounts for differences among large firms: malpractice insurance carriers. Because of their diversified practice—especially specialization in corporate law, securities, and banking, where most malpractice claims occur—deep pockets, and the sheer number and magnitude of cases, large law firms are especially vulnerable to significant malpractice liability.

Up until the late 1970s, most large firms were insured by Lloyd's of London, and a few still are. But, as their premiums continued to rise, largely because of the deteriorating claims experience of large New York City law firms, several firms explored the possibility of creating a mutual insurance company that, through strict selection criteria and loss prevention activities, might keep insurance premiums below those in the for-profit insurance market. The Attorneys' Liability Assurance Society (ALAS) was founded in 1979 by thirty-five large U.S. law firms and headquartered in Chicago.[19]

This mutual insurance company has a vigorous loss prevention program, unparalleled among the for-profit insurers, a significant component of which concerns avoiding conflicts of interest that tend to swell the size of malpractice awards.[20] Given the amount of oversight exerted and self-regulatory guidance offered, ALAS firms look somewhat different from their counterparts that are insured by other malpractice carriers. Indeed, after a few dozen interviews, I could usually guess whether a firm was insured by ALAS by the way my informant described the firm's conflict-of-interest procedures.

Figure 9.3 provides empirical support for my intuitions. The figure differentiates the intelligence models adopted by ALAS and non-ALAS firms, controlling for firm size. Since firms must have at least thirty-five lawyers to join ALAS, the figure includes data only for larger firms. Insurance carrier clearly exerts a significant effect. For all three size categories, 25 percent more of the ALAS firms adopt technoblitz methods (black bars) than their counterparts with different malpractice insurance. And for firms of fewer than 250 lawyers, the combined proportion of high- and low-technology cybersurveillance (black and gray bars) is more than double that of non-ALAS firms.[21] Moreover, the type of insurance carrier accounts for many of the outliers on figure 9.2. Three-fifths of the moderate-size firms pursuing cybersurveillance are ALAS members.

Figure 9.3   Intelligence Model and Insurance

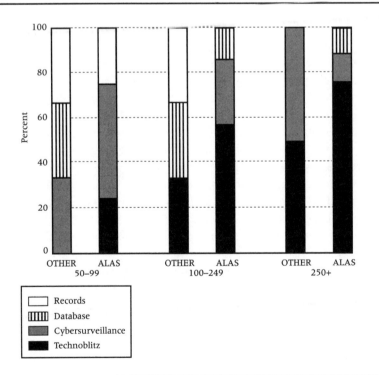

However compelling the empirical and experiential evidence of the impact of insurance carrier on self-regulatory practice, one significant caveat must be addressed, the possibility of a selection effect. Law firms do not select their insurers randomly. Just as health insurers providing the best coverage attract the sickest patients, so too do their malpractice counterparts attract the riskiest firms. The practice profiles of some large firms—especially boutiques that specialize in insurance defense or intellectual property—place them at lower malpractice risk than general practice firms with securities and banking expertise. As a result, the former can usually find much lower premiums in the private insurance market than they would have to pay as a member of ALAS.[22] Similarly, firms that have a less diversified client base or that tend to represent one-shotters may expect fewer conflicts of interest and simultaneously opt for cheaper professional liability insurance *and* invest less in developing an infrastructure to ferret out conflicts. So the relationship between type of insurance and self-regulatory technology may be a spurious one—both artifacts of the firm's practice and client base, on the one hand, and corresponding conflict-of-interest risk, on the other. ALAS membership may serve as a proxy, identifying those firms that face greater risk and invest in both better insurance and a more comprehensive regulatory infrastructure, rather than as the impetus for that infrastructure.

Fortunately for this analysis, there are other reasons for the failure of firms to join ALAS that are unrelated to their vulnerability to liability, in general, or conflicts of interest, in particular.[23] A comparison between these firms, less contaminated by a selection effect, and those affiliated with ALAS would help to disentangle the impact of insurer on self-regulatory practices. Unfortunately, although I oversampled firms with other malpractice carriers, the number of firms that are comparable to ALAS members in size and practice profile is too small to generate stable estimates. Still, the evidence is suggestive. The former are almost 20 percent less likely to adopt technoblitz methods than their counterparts insured by ALAS—a finding (conveniently coinciding with my intuition) that supports both an insurer effect and the likelihood that the effect is slightly exaggerated by a selection effect.

What about the impact of firm location on intelligence method? Stereotypes might lead one to expect that firms in Chicago would be more technologically sophisticated than firms downstate. They would be wrong. Among firms of thirty lawyers or fewer (the range of most downstate firms), exactly the same proportion of Chicago and downstate law firms rely on cybersurveillance or databases, despite the fact that the median Chicago firm in this cluster is slightly larger than its downstate counterpart. Indeed, among firms employing fewer than ten attorneys, the downstate firms are almost twice as likely to employ the highest-technology intelligence method among firms of this size—databases—than those located in Chicago. Of course, a downstate firm of ten attorneys is likely to have a much more diverse practice profile than its counterpart in Chicago. In fact, its profile probably looks more like that of a Chicago firm five to ten times its size. Even the practice of solo practitioners is much less specialized outside of Chicago than in. Once again, then, the risk of encountering conflicts of interest provides a more powerful explanation for intelligence technology than other attributes of the firm.

There are certainly a host of other features of the structure, practice, and clientele of a law firm that one might expect to exert an effect on how it identifies conflicts of interest, for example:

- Caseload and the ratio of cases to lawyers;

- The substantive areas in which it specializes;

- The firm's clients, their characteristics, whether one-shotters or repeat players, and the extent to which they have put all their eggs in this basket or patronize other law firms as well;

- The geographic dispersion of firm offices; and

- The firm's origins—how recently it was founded, whether it spun off from a larger firm, and the like.

Because the sample size is relatively small and the most promising independent variables are so profoundly intercorrelated, it would be futile to continue to explore compelling accounts for how firms construct a social and material technology to identify conflicts of interest. That there are significant patterns of variation is, however, quite clear.

Blind Spots

With the exception of the ostriches, these varied forms of indigenous regulation impose a cost on the structure and internal culture of the

360 Social Science, Social Policy, and the Law

law firm. They expend sometimes substantial resources, affect the allocation of compensation to members of the firm, incite dissension and resentment among colleagues, interfere with rainmaking, protract the process of taking on new engagements, intrude on and strain the relationship between lawyer and client, bridle lawyer autonomy, demand endless paper pushing, and, worst of all, squander valuable time.

So what difference does any of this make? Because it appears that firms construct ever more complex, comprehensive, efficient, specialized, triangulated, and universalistic material and social technology to ferret out potential conflicts of interest as the sheer magnitude of conflicts increases, technoblitz systems have no better track record than herds of elephants—maybe even than ostriches. Suppose Legal Towers can expect that one in three new matters will give rise to a potential conflict of interest (a realistic assumption) and that lawyers in the downstate ostrich firm can expect that a client will bring a conflict to their attention in one case in a thousand. And suppose that Legal Towers's technoblitz technology fails to identify a conflict of interest a mere 0.5 percent of the time (a probably too optimistic false negative rate that I snatched out of thin air). And, of course, ostrich technology fails 100 percent of the time. Then, after a thousand cases—about six months for Legal Towers and who knows how many more for the much smaller downstate ostrich firm—the ostrich will miss a conflict once, and Legal Towers will miss it 1.67 times.

So ostriches do not look so bad after all. Of course, a firm like Legal Towers would be out of business—uninsurable, disqualified from most of its cases, with virtually all of its clients alienated, its profits squandered on massive malpractice awards, its reputation shattered, its partners subject to disciplinary sanctions, if not outright disbarment—if it behaved like an ostrich. And so would many much smaller law firms. It is like the classic example in introductory statistics of the difference between correlation and cause: the fact that there is a strong correlation between the size of a municipal fire department and the number of fires does not mean that fire fighters are out setting fires. Resources are invested where risks are high. The important point, then, is that all these technologies have false negative rates, even if some are far better than others.

> I think the biggest problem that I've found is not the apparent conflict. It's the one that's hard to find. That's the one that really haunts us. No

matter what we do, no matter how much technology we buy, no matter how many people look at sheets, conflicts will occur, and there's not much we can do about it, and it's a terrible problem. [1Ch100+]

All my informants—especially those practicing a kind of cyber-surveillance—acknowledged that their intelligence systems fail and that they do not fail randomly. Their blind spots are systemic. The lesson was made most poignantly in an intellectual property firm. As I waited in the lobby for the interview to begin, the coffee table overflowed with computer and electronics magazines, with pictures of oscilloscopes and meters and resistors and cables and all the paraphernalia I remember from my childhood as the daughter of an electrical engineer.[24] I eagerly awaited learning how lawyers, also trained as scientists and engineers, who secured, defended, and challenged patents for the most complex new technologies would structure their intelligence system. I was stunned to learn that this firm does not use technoblitz methods, not cybersurveillance, not even databases.[25] This firm, whose lawyers are probably more computer savvy than anyone I know, relies on elephants, collegial input, and occasionally records. The firm's name partner explained:

Are you familiar with patent firms? Because there is a huge difference in the kinds of conflicts issues that they face. In a patent firm, you are not interested in the client "name," but in the "product." If you are applying for a patent for a color television, you want to ensure that no one else can produce a color television or get a patent for a color television. You are trying to cover everyone else in the world; they are our enemy. As a result, name searching for conflicts is not very important; rather, product searching is. So, if a new matter comes in regarding a patent for hearing aids, the lawyer will ask whether we have done any other work on hearing aids. [The respondent gets up, goes over to his desk, and comes back with a filled-out new client form. He shows me the sheet.] The sheet comes in to me first. It's likely, though, that the attorney will informally ask other lawyers in the firm about the product—in this case, oil extracting. *We don't do computerized conflicts checking. I am a big believer in computers; don't get me wrong. But you can't check products by computer. You can with names. But names do not help. You can't computerize all the kinds of oil extracting processes. It's just very difficult to computerize.* In addition to my review of all the sheets, copies are circulated to all the lawyers in the firm. It is very rare that something will come up that we didn't know about before. This firm is not that big. I know what's going on. . . . I personally bring in a large percentage of the firm's business, which increases the likelihood that I will know about our clients. . . . If one client wanted to sue another and we didn't already realize it, I would be alarmed. . . . If we had a party like a "Joe Smith," we might check our computer. But, for a major company, we would know if there were any conflicts. [42Ch20–49]

Cybersurveillance is founded on the assumption that interests reside in identities, that names betray conflicts of interest. Often they do. When all the interests can be enumerated and attached to names for a given matter—for example, you have the list of all the coplaintiffs and codefendants in a lawsuit or the name of the buyer, seller, and lender in a real estate transaction—a name search through a database may reliably identify all of the adversities of interest. But there are a number of circumstances where this is not true.

There may be ancillary parties who are not listed or not yet known—witnesses, complicit parties that were not charged, creditors, insurers, partners, major investors or stockholders, competitors, spouses, heirs—but who are likely to be affected by the outcome of the case.

> The database cannot possibly be adequate. We are basically a corporate law firm, serving businesses. One can never know all the parties indirectly involved in a matter when a client comes through the door—even if you ask them. Adverse parties can include boards or trustees whose identities you don't know. Matters of this sort will always have unidentified people. You know they have to be out there, but you don't know who they are. Then there are all sorts of "layered relationships" [corporate families of parents, subsidiaries, and so forth]. [34Ch50–99]

Even where the relevant unit of analysis is a named entity, name searches may have little value. Several family lawyers complained about the difficulty of keeping track of clients who repeatedly remarry and change their surnames. Other names, especially in certain ethnic groups, may be too common to be discriminating.

> Computer databases don't work too well. Seventy percent of Koreans are named Kim, Park, or Lee. So you would need other identifiers. You could use an address, but addresses change a lot—especially when your clientele involves a lot of real estate. [115Ch<10]

Where the matter concerns creating, exploiting, or restricting zero-sum opportunities, the parties affected are potentially infinite and unknowable. What is known is the product or target of opportunity, not those who have an interest in seizing it. In the patent example, the firm cannot possibly know what other corporations are developing the same color television technology or hearing aid or oil extracting process that will be precluded from marketing their intellectual property by the patent secured for the first client. When a client is bidding on a piece of property or trying to acquire a vulnerable company, the lawyers may not know what other clients are seeking the same opportunity. This blind spot is exacerbated as clients spread more and more of their business to disparate law firms. Their varied counselors cannot possibly know about tantalizing opportunities and business prospects that are being developed for their client by competing firms. They cannot protect the interests of a client when they are not privy to all its interests.

Moreover, legal matters do not simply redistribute resources among the parties in contention or lift or levy sanctions. However unintentionally, they sometimes create legal precedent, changing the rules of the game that everyone else must play by. The successful defense of a single client may change the interpretation of a tax rule, raise the standard for deceptive advertising or reasonable care, shorten a statute of limitation, impose new lender liabilities, restrict shareholder's rights, cap damage awards, remove insurance coverage exclusions or exemptions, and the like. Because of the precedential force of case law, if lawyers succeed in altering legal doctrine while advancing the interests of one client, they may hurt other clients whose defense requires a radically different interpretation of the law. But, again, a name search or even a search by industry will not necessarily identify the clients whose interests are likely to diverge from those of the prospective client (assuming, of course, that the case does ultimately change legal precedent).

Because of these limitations of an artificial intelligence that identifies interests with identities and searches on proper names, many law firms triangulate their conflicts surveillance procedures by requiring human intelligence as well.

We don't have a special computerized conflict database. I don't trust them. The available programs have a kind of rigidity in what they are able to search for. And, besides, the database is only as good as what you have input. That's all you are likely to know about. I really believe that human and institutional memory is far better. . . . I like this system [records with collegial input] much better than a computer system. A computer system will give you mechanical reliability, but will the answer be right? Our system will give you the right answer, but the question is how quickly. [43Ch20–49]

Although only a small minority of firms (not even 10 percent) rely exclusively on collegial input to ferret out conflicts of interest, more than half (and more than three-quarters of the firms with more than seventy-five attorneys) employ collegial methods to supplement an archival or cybersurveillance intelligence system. The hope is that lawyers are better able to think in abstract terms, to anticipate the implications of a new legal precedent on a host of unrelated clients, and to know many of the ancillary parties standing on the sidelines that are likely to be indirectly affected by a given matter. At this stage of the computer revolution, human intelligence is still more supple and able to fire across unprogrammed but productive neural pathways, more creative, and more capable of empathy, of anticipating who will be hurt or offended by a given outcome and who will not.

If only humans pay attention. And that's the next problem. Lawyers are busy. They disdain bureaucratic busywork, memos to read, voice mail messages to answer, forms to complete, output to peruse. They have deadlines and trials and motions and depositions and briefs and unhappy clients that command their immediate attention. When their self-interest is threatened by conflicts of interest—they risk losing a lucrative piece of business or antagonizing a valued client because of a new case elsewhere in the firm—their attention may become riveted. But law firm activity is too diverse and fragmented to activate self-interest on every matter. The environmental attorney may compulsively monitor the Superfund or insurance cases, the intellectual property lawyer may monitor the corporate cases, but both may totally ignore the estate planning or divorce cases. Even "conflicts czars" may lapse:

[The database] is a fallback. Because the database—garbage in, garbage out. . . . I mean, I'm as bad as the next one. If I've got a new matter that's coming in—and it's ABC Company versus XYZ—and nine months later there's a new defendant joined in the suit, I'm not going to go back to the file room or the accounting department and tell them "I've got an additional adverse party," so that when we do our next conflict search it comes up. . . . We have a fairly extensive and expensive software system that we bought with an extensive conflict-of-interest database capability. . . . So we have the software capability. It's extremely sophisticated conflict software. But the problem is, I don't think we will get the level of cooperation from the lawyers that we would need to make the software function the way it's supposed to. . . . You have to take reality into account. Lawyers hate all of this. They are offended. You have to come back to the real world. The real world is you've got a busy lawyer sitting, drowning in paper at his desk. He or she is not going to fill out the form I want filled out. He or she—90 percent of the time—will not fill out the conflict clearance form. They're going to say, "Secretary, go fill it out." Garbage in, garbage out. I'm lucky if I get a well thought out conflict clearance form. . . . So I don't think it's realistic to expect—realistically—that people will update conflict information as you go. It would be nice, but I'm no better or worse than anybody else, and I don't. I should, but I don't. [79Ch20–49]

This discussion has focused largely on the danger of false negatives, of missing true conflicts. But false positives are a problem as well. They create inordinate amounts of needless paperwork. They squander attention and goodwill. They burn out lawyers and make them careless and resentful. False positives are even responsible for the social construction of some false negatives when they allow true conflicts of interest to slip through the safety net, drowned out by all the noise that the former produce. Earlier in the chapter, I cited examples of intelligence systems trying to respond to the burden of false positives: of one large law firm that had jettisoned its cybersurveillance system, returning to manual scrutiny of index cards because the sheer number of false positives had inundated the lawyers, and of other firms that circulate only a portion of the new matters for collegial input, concerned that, otherwise, colleagues will not bother to read and respond to the memos at all.

What human intelligence offers in suppleness, abstract synthesis, and imagination, then, it lacks in memory, motivation, reliability, universalism, and speed. For this reason, many firms consider its human input mere icing on the cake, situating its intelligence process in electronic data points unearthed by artificial intelligence. Unfortunately, this reification obscures the fact that the data points are also human constructions. Yet another blind spot, then, concerns the social construction of data or what the last quoted respondent and several others referred to as "garbage in, garbage out."

How does one ensure that all the necessary information is entered into the database and then updated as circumstances change? The best enforcement mechanism available to law firms is to withhold issuance of a billing number—necessary for lawyers to charge their hourly billings, among other less self-interested expenditures like photocopying or telephone charges related to a new matter—until the paperwork is complete. But, although it improves compliance, this strategy produces new biases in the data. First, it gives lawyers an incentive to fill out the forms with minimal or preliminary information rather than waiting until more complete or accurate data become available. It also contributes to the problem, noted above, that ancillary parties, whom lawyers only discover as they become more immersed in the case, often fail to get recorded in the database.

> We've been attempting to find a way to input information that is better than that disclosed on the conflicts sheet. The problem with the sheet is that it includes preliminary information. Once the matter is more well known to the attorney, you tend to get better information. Now, this may take a day or it may take a month. We've been struggling to find a way to capture this information. What we know is that the information in the conflicts sheet that gets input into the database is less comprehensive than what one obtains after reviewing the file at the end of the matter. As a result, we have been reluctant to merely add the sheet to the database. We've been waiting to try to find a way to massage it a bit to be more accurate. But the result is that we have fallen way behind. So we've decided to input the information on the conflicts sheets into the database quickly—just to get caught up—and simply recognize that it is not sufficiently comprehensive. [57Ch20–49]

Second, when new developments arise down the road—a new party joins a lawsuit, one defendant files a counter-claim against another, a client merges with another corporation—there is no bureaucratic occasion or incentive to input amended information into the database, thereby flagging that a conflict of interest is about to develop.

> Last year, we had to . . . turn down a long-standing client of the firm, an ongoing matter, seek replacement of counsel. . . . This was a three-to four-month negotiation process between two long-standing clients of the firm. . . . We've been representing one client in connection with

a contract negotiation . . . which was falling apart. There was a potential for litigation. There was another corporate client on the other side. Wasn't originally on the other side, but acquired the company with which we were dealing. . . . You know, suddenly a conflict arose a year and a half into the engagement. . . . It doesn't come up very frequently, but you'll find these situations where—the instance we had last year where one client buys someone else who's adverse to us, and then you've suddenly got a conflicts issue thrown in our lap. It's hard to figure out how to identify all the conflicts and how to deal with them when they come up, no matter how hard you try. That's the biggest issue for us. [1Ch100+]

Third, it encourages lawyers to do their work off the books, to bypass the docketing process. For example, where they are able to charge their time to an open account—perhaps a related matter for an ongoing client—they can avoid or postpone the paperwork. They're representing ABC Chemical Company on charges of dumping on a site in downstate Illinois, and, when the company is named in another Superfund case in Indiana, the lawyers bill their time under the first case rather than opening a new matter. As a result, the names of the other codefendants on the second site (some of whom may be clients of the firm) never enter the database or get flagged as a potentially significant conflict of interest.

I mean, you discover a lot of things. We discovered that people were using the same matter number for different deals, for instance, that dealt with the same client. But they were reentering . . . they were changing the names of the matters. . . . You know, we had different names for the matter for five different times over ten years. [1Ch100+]

Fourth, conversations in which small bits of confidential information are disclosed—perhaps in a beauty contest or while marketing the firm—that do not result in the opening of a new matter are less likely to find their way into the database.

I got one [malpractice case that I'm defending] going on right now, where a big firm ran a conflicts check and figured out that they did not have a conflict. Then they subpoenaed some documents from one of the witnesses. And in the documents is a letter from another partner in this big law firm. And what he had done is he had given some advice as to the subject matter of this case—real fast—never opened the file. So that's kind of the inadvertent situation. [6Ch100+]

In short, intelligence systems are plagued by systemic blind spots that include bad memory, information overload, inadvertence, disinterest, noncompliance, obfuscation, premature closure on data collection, failure to update, inability to anticipate the social networks implicated in a dispute or transaction, difficulty gathering data on nonmatters (incipient cases that dissolve or go elsewhere, client matters handled in other law firms), and, most important, the fact that the search engine—proper names—is sometimes a poor discriminator and often a bad proxy for interests. Some firms have massaged or tinkered with their technologies to shrink the blind spots or make them less opaque. But false negatives are a fact of life.

Conclusions

So do we sleep with the mysterious stranger? Unfortunately, the risk assessment is not complete. We have now amassed a list of most—but not all—of the dalliances, affairs, intimacies, one-night-stands, flirtations, monogamies, and promiscuities of our prospective partner, our past and present colleagues and their former colleagues, and ourselves. The initial list had lots of problematic characters—fortunately, most of them false positives that we happily discarded. But a few names remain. And there are those nagging false negatives that we have failed to identify. And then there is the matter of our future prospects, those alluring gods and goddesses on the horizon with whom we will find true happiness, but who might reject us—or merely our colleagues—when they learn about this latest tryst. But then we might be able to take some prophylactic measures. Anguishing choices.

In the legal world, analysis does not end with a list of hits or potential hits. Attorneys must decide whether they have uncovered an absolute conflict of interest, one that can be overlooked with the consent of the affected clients, or simply have conjured up a remote possibility that could arise at some point down the road. They might assess the risk that opposing counsel will seek to disqualify the firm for what their adversaries consider a conflict of interest, thereby creating delay and additional cost to their client to defend against even an unsuccessful disqualification motion. They must weigh client relations issues that have nothing to do with ethical rules or their professional responsibilities: whether disclosing an unlikely but conceivable future conflict may drive a prospective client into the arms of another suitor, whether merely asking valued and long-standing clients to waive an insignificant conflict will so anger them that it is better to decline the case than even broach the subject. They might weigh the efficacy of screening tainted lawyers behind so-called Chinese walls to reassure clients of their loyalty and disinterestedness or asking prospective clients for advance waivers, in which they promise to waive unspecified future conflicts of interest as a requirement for taking on their case—two prophylactic measures that have questionable legal standing. Often they must deal with heated intrafirm squabbles as one powerful partner refuses to allow his client to be gored in order to resolve a conflict created by someone else in the firm.

Perhaps most difficult, lawyers often try to read the tea leaves about developments down the road that, were they known at the outset, would lead them to decline the engagement. What is the likelihood that there will be a falling out among parties seeking joint representation that will force the firm to withdraw from the case? What is the risk that new parties with whom the firm has fiduciary obligations will join the lawsuit in the future and thereby conflict out the firm? Is this small pittance of business from this Fortune 500 company likely to snowball into a lucrative relationship, or was it placed strategically to conflict out the firm in an upcoming piece of litigation that the Fortune 500 company plans to bring against a major client of the firm? What is the likelihood that the client who readily agrees to waive the conflict at the outset may be less happy when he or she sees the outcome (fearing that the firm somehow held back—or did not hold back enough—out of loyalty to the other party)? What is the likelihood that taking this matter will preclude the firm from bringing in more lucrative or desirable business in the future by importing a new thicket of interests that must be honored? These are questions for which there is no artificial intelligence.

This research was supported by the American Bar Foundation and National Science Foundation grant SES-9223615. Special thanks to Benjamin Casper for research assistance and to the lawyers who generously shared their time and experience with thoughtful reflection, colorful detail, and unusual candor.

Notes

1. These firms represent a wide swath of practice settings. Many are general practices. But the sample also includes boutiques specializing in litigation, insurance defense, personal injury plaintiffs work, intellectual property, employment litigation, and criminal defense. The firms are distributed as follows:

Number of Firms

Firm size	Chicago	Downstate	Total
1–9	16	19	35
10–19	10	14	24
20–49	16	9	25
50–99	19	0	19
100+	25	0	25
Median	*48*	*10*	*21*
Mean	*139*	*12*	*97*

There are very few large law firms in Illinois outside of Chicago. That is why the downstate sample has so few firms with more than twenty lawyers. In order to get a fuller distribution of types of legal practice that pose unique conflict-of-interest problems, the sample includes extra firms drawn to represent (1) Chicago firms located outside of the so-called "Loop" or downtown area (typically in more ethnic neighborhoods); (2) Chicago branch offices of large out-of-state firms; (3) firms located in the "collar counties" that encircle the Chicago metropolitan area; and (4) small downstate towns that have only a single lawyer or law firm. In order to get some perspective on states other than Illinois, the pilot study included an additional twelve large firms (not reflected in the table) from two other midwestern states.

2. Respondents ranged in age from their late twenties to late seventies, averaging roughly fifty years of age. Ninety-five percent were male. Three-quarters of the female respondents were in firms of one or two attorneys. (This undoubtedly says something significant about the distribution of power by gender in most law firms.)

3. All materials quoted from the interviews are identified in brackets by a unique interview number, assigned consecutively, ranging from 1 to 128, followed by the location of the interview (CH = Chicago, CC = a "collar county" encircling Chicago, DSS = downstate small town, DSM = downstate medium-size city, DSL = downstate large city), and the number of lawyers employed by the firm.

4. For greater detail, see Shapiro (1999).

5. The ethical rules are somewhat more permissive for former than for current clients. The matter that is adverse to the interests of the former client must be *substantially related* to the original representation. In the case of current clients, this substantial relationship test does not apply, and any adversity is forbidden.

6. In a dramatic example reported widely in the press, the Chicago law firm Winston & Strawn was disqualified from representing a corporate client in a dispute over the sale of one of its divisions because a lawyer hired laterally had been counsel to the adversary at his previous firm (Tuite 1993). This lawyer played no role in the litigation at his new firm, which was mostly completed before he joined the firm, but his conflict of interest was imputed to the entire firm. At the time of disqualification, Winston & Strawn had logged more than 10,000 litigation hours and eighty-five days deposing forty-four witnesses, and 70,000 documents had been exchanged in discovery—all or a substantial part of the fee, which it had to absorb. This sort of conflict of interest could have been remedied in Illinois—but in few other states—by erecting a screening device or so-called "Chinese wall" around the lateral hire when he joined the firm. In this particular case, the law firm delayed screening the newly hired lawyer for five weeks—apparently not until its adversary had filed the disqualification motion.

7. Combative parties sometimes use conflicts of interest as a sword, by placing business, holding beauty contests, or sharing confidences with law firms with specialized expertise in order to conflict them out from representing their adversaries in upcoming litigation.

> I think there's a deliberate—and I can't prove this—but I think that there's a deliberate strategy on the part of some in-house corporate departments, you know, to make sure that no law firm in Chicago can sue them, or no big law firm. Many lawyers cite anecdotes or rumors of corporations that intentionally dole out small pieces of business to every major law firm in town to conflict them out of ever taking a case adverse to the corporation. So they give it, you know, a teeny little drop of business to every firm. [36Ch100+]

> Because very easily, in Chicago, you can get a large multinational that can pick off the fifteen largest law firms in Chicago just like [snaps fingers]—give him a little thing here, a little thing there. And the middle-level companies, they can't get a law firm. Or they can pick off every patent law firm in the city of Chicago. Give them this one, give them that one. And you have someone who needs to hire a boutique law firm with specialized knowledge, and all of your good patent law firms are tied up, because this firm has conflicted them out. [16Ch100+]

8. According to one malpractice expert, law students graduating in the 1990s can expect to be sued for malpractice three times during their careers. Another authority, who defends a high proportion of malpractice suits brought against Illinois lawyers, noted that, between 1975 and 1992, there were ten times as many reported malpractice decisions in Illinois as there were in the history of the state before 1975 (Gill 1992). See especially Ramos (1996) who argues that, at $4 billion a year, the cost to insurers of legal malpractice even exceeds that of medical malpractice.

9. Because of the belief that conflicts of interest increase the vulnerability to and magnitude of liability, some insurers encourage or assist their insureds in undertaking self-regulatory measures. Many malpractice insurers offer law firms premium discounts if lawyers attend seminars on loss prevention. Other insurers provide varied loss prevention services to their insureds: on-site seminars and workshops, firm audits, conferences, loss prevention journals, loss prevention personnel to advise attorneys on difficult questions about professional responsibility, and publications, resources, databases, and consulting services to assist firms in developing conflict-of-interest regulatory systems. Some require or strongly "encourage" their insureds to designate loss prevention or risk managers, create special oversight committees, and implement procedures to regulate potential conflicts of interest. The involvement of professional liability insurers in overseeing and micromanaging firms has become so great, that some now refer to them as "regulators" (Davis 1996).

10. Indeed, more than fifty firms affiliated with this mutual insurance company have deductibles that exceed $1 million (Attorneys' Liability Assurance Society 1991, 10). Deductibles are much lower for smaller firms, averaging $5,000 in Illinois, according to one insurance executive (Gill 1992).

11. A few firms, fearing that colleagues will become overloaded with information and disregard the notices altogether, circulate listings only of significant cases. When matters are highly confidential (involving hostile takeovers, for example), the notice may be camouflaged or altered to conceal the purpose of the engagement.

12. The response typically starts out: "How in the hell could we be considering taking on this matter, given . . ." Most firms leave it up to lawyers' discretion to respond, although some require that all partners sign off on a matter before it is opened, even if they are out of the office or away on vacation. Even where voluntary, lawyers have some incentive to review the list. Many jealously track the business generation or "rainmaking" efforts of their colleagues; others want to ensure that the firm does not take a case that might preclude them from bringing in

future business or that might antagonize one of their treasured clients. Because, as noted earlier, lawyers' compensation partially reflects the amount of business they bring into the firm, they are more conscientious in reviewing lists of prospective matters than one might expect from an otherwise dull bureaucratic task.

13. The committee determines whether the matter is philosophically compatible with the practice of the firm, whether there is adequate staffing to undertake the representation, and whether the prospective client is financially able to pay for the necessary legal services.

14. Many other law firms simply retain paper records—usually in card files—on old closed cases. Conflicts checkers then have to peruse manual records as well as the computer database. The process of converting from a manual to an electronic conflict-of-interest system is so complex that the Attorneys' Liability Assurance Society (ALAS), a mutual malpractice insurer comprised of large law firms from across the country, hired a consulting firm in the early 1990s to develop what became a 120-page manual and to offer discounted consulting fees to assist member firms in the transition.

15. Analysts explain that you cannot leave this task to the attorneys, noting that it is amazing what they do not tell you if you do not ask them. They may be working on a contracts matter and will give you the name of only one party. Staffers must often nudge the lawyers to supply complete information and remind them to complete the necessary forms with "have-you-died?" memoranda.

16. The conflicts-analysis staff try to stay abreast of the business news as well, reading the *New York Times, Wall Street Journal,* and various business periodicals on a regular basis, scouring them for news of mergers or other corporate reorganizations involving clients of the firm. Several firms as well as the large-firm mutual malpractice insurer, ALAS, have also developed reliable, affordable, up-to-date databases that can be used for checking these corporate family trees and relationships (Siegel 1994).

17. This problem of false positives and the sensitivity of formulating conflicts software algorithms was what caused the firm cited above to jettison its computerized conflicts-screening system and return to manual checking.

18. As one respondent dramatically observed, these responsibilities consume more and more time:

> When I was first responsible for it, it was no more than, you know, a couple hours a week. I'd get calls once in a while. And sometimes I'd go weeks without getting calls. And now . . . most of my client work I do between 7:00 and 8:30 or 9:00 in the morning and at nights and weekends. And the day is generally devoted to the firm. So, I mean, it's changed dramatically. [pilot02]

19. At the time of this study, 375 law firms and 50,000 lawyers from around the country were covered by this mutual company. A crude comparison of the ALAS membership roster with the *National Law Journal* list of the 250 largest U.S. law firms (the smallest of which employs 130 attorneys) during this period suggests that roughly two-thirds of the firms eligible to join ALAS had done so (Attorneys' Liability Assurance Society 1991; Weisenhaus 1991). The percentage is somewhat higher for Chicago firms (79 percent), probably because ALAS is headquartered here. Because I was concerned about a possible "insurance effect" contaminating my data, I oversampled large firms that had not joined ALAS. As a result, my sample looks more like national insurance trends than those for Chicago. About two-thirds of the sampled firms of more than 130 lawyers were ALAS members, and fewer than half of the firms in the sample eligible to join ALAS had done so.

20. Member firms are required to have one or more loss prevention partners and to send representatives to annual conferences; they are strongly encouraged to form new business committees and adopt other procedures to help screen for conflicts of interest. ALAS publishes and annually updates a weighty loss prevention manual and also circulates to all insured lawyers a loss prevention journal three times a year with reviews of new cases and ethics opinions and other guidance on how to minimize liability risks. As noted earlier, ALAS has hired a consultant to prepare a report for member firms on how to automate manual records used to search for conflicts of interest and has developed a database to help identify corporate families, subsidiaries, and affiliations that are critical for evaluating conflicts of interest. Several ALAS loss prevention counsel visit member firms, conduct loss prevention audits, and provide in-firm seminars as well as day-to-day guidance to lawyers who call with difficult questions concerning professional responsibility.

21. The relationship between ALAS affiliation and high- and low-technology cybersurveillance methods is not merely an artifact of the proclivity of general practice firms to join ALAS. Among the firms of between twenty-five and ninety-nine lawyers, 43 percent of those with a general practice are insured by ALAS, compared with 13 percent of those with a less specialized practice; for firms with at least one hundred attorneys, these figures are 73 and 44 percent, respectively. Still, a strong "ALAS effect" exists even in these less diversified firms. While 40 percent of the ALAS specialty firms of twenty-five to ninety-nine lawyers opt for either type of cybersurveillance, this is true of 14 percent of those with other insurance; the figures for firms of one hundred or more lawyers are 75 and 60 percent, respectively. The ALAS effect is actually slightly higher for the specialized firms than for those with a

general practice. So ALAS affiliation exerts an independent effect on surveillance method.

22. Several respondents told me that, because of their risk profiles, they paid premiums of $2,000 to $3,000 per lawyer lower than those charged by ALAS.

23. For example, some have offices in high-risk jurisdictions in New York City that are excluded from ALAS membership. Others have close ties to insurance company clients and secure their insurance coverage from these clients. Some are fearful about the exposure of some ALAS members over their involvement in failed savings and loans and the possibility of having to bail out the high-risk members of the mutual insurance pool. Others are unwilling or unable to make the substantial capital expenditure initially required to join the mutual company. Some were too small to join ALAS when it was first created and have never bothered to affiliate. For some, the transition from their current insurer to ALAS would create potential exposure for certain acts committed in the past—kind of like changing health insurers when you have a preexisting medical condition—and do not want to have to purchase expensive tail coverage for this exposure. Others are unwilling to abide by the few requirements imposed by ALAS—for example, resigning as officers of client companies.

24. Coffee tables in most other Chicago law firms of this size would include *Fortune, Business Week, Forbes, Time, Newsweek, The Economist, The American Bar Association Journal,* maybe *Sports Illustrated, The New Yorker,* or *The American Lawyer.*

25. Indeed, only one-quarter of the firms in the sample that specialized in intellectual property employed cybersurveillance methods.

References

Abel, Richard L. 1981. "Why Does the ABA Promulgate Ethical Rules?" *Texas Law Review* 59(4): 639–88.

Attorneys' Liability Assurance Society. 1991. *1991 Annual Report.* Hamilton, Bermuda: Attorneys' Liability Assurance Society (Bermuda) Ltd.

Bateman, Randall B. 1995. "Return to the Ethics Rules as a Standard for Attorney Disqualification: Attempting Consistency in Motions for Disqualification by the Use of Chinese Walls." *Duquesne Law Review* 33(2): 249–80.

Davis, Anthony E. 1996. "Professional Liability Insurers as Regulators of Law Practice." *Fordham Law Review* 65(1): 209–32.

Gill, Donna. 1992. "Targeting Lawyers: Legal Mal in the '90s." *Chicago Lawyer* 15(91): 1, 18–21, 63, 82.

Hazard, Geoffrey C., Jr. 1990. "Conflicts Are Often Key in Malpractice." *National Law Journal,* 13(1): 13.

Overton, George W. 1990. "Supervisory Responsibility: A New Ball Game for Law Firms and Lawyers." *Illinois Bar Journal* 78(9): 434–36.

Ramos, Manuel R. 1996. "Legal Malpractice: Reforming Lawyers and Law Professors." *Tulane Law Review* 70(6, Part B): 2583–629.

Schmeyer, Ted. 1991. "Professional Discipline for Law Firms?" *Cornell Law Review* 77(1): 1–46.

Shapiro, Susan P. 1999. *Tangled Loyalties: Conflicts of Interest in the Private Practice of Law.* Unpublished manuscript. American Bar Foundation.

Siegel, Matt. 1994. "The Next Step in Conflicts Checks." *American Lawyer* 16(9): 110–12.

Tuite, Cornelia Honchar. 1993. "Occasionally, Newly Hired Lawyers Can 'Rob' a Firm of Business." *Chicago Daily Law Bulletin*, December 3, 1993, p. 6.

Weisenhaus, Doreen. 1991. "The NLJ 250: Annual Survey of the Nation's Largest Law Firms." *National Law Journal* 14(4): S5–S31.

Index

Numbers in **boldface** refer to figures and tables.

ABC News Special, 147–49, 157
accident victims, as undercompensated, 161–62
"add-on" sanctions, private programs, 54
Administrative Office of the Courts (AOC), 277
administrative process, social science uses, 8
adultery, 71–72, 83–85
affirmative action, 223–24, 227, 230, 232, 245
African Americans, 81, 232, 279–80, 287n11. *See also* racial issues
ALAS (Attorneys' Liability Assurance Society), 356–58, 374–75n21–23
Alcohol, Tobacco and Firearms (ATF) agents, 219
alcohol abuse, 52–54
Alliance to Revitalize California, 150–51
alternative dispute resolution, 186–87, 191–94
AMA (American Medical Association), 175
American Bar Association Code of Professional Responsibility, 27
American Medical Association (AMA), 175
amoral calculator model, 291–92, 293, 299, 313
Andrews, Lori, 188
anecdotes, media reliance on, 146–52
AOC (Administrative Office of the Courts), 277
arbitration, 175, 192, 194, 226

archival method for handling conflicts of interest, 338–44, **353, 355, 357,** 364–65
ATF (Alcohol, Tobacco and Firearms) agents, 219
attorneys. *See* conflicts of interest; lawyers
Attorneys' Liability Assurance Society (ALAS), 356–58, 374–75n21–23
Aubert, Vilhelm, 234
Australia, transportation to, 43
automobile negligence, 178, 180

bad faith cases, 182. *See also* frivolous litigation
Baker, Wayne E., 308
balanced reporting as misleading, 157–59
Baldus, David, 22–23, 262–73, 276, 281
barbaric punishments, 75
bar disciplinary procedures, 155–56
Beattie, John, 49, 63n4
Beccaria, Cesare, 295, 298
Becker, Gary, 237
behavior: of juries, 178–83; law's impact on, 11–12; regulation of deviant, 25–28, 198–99, 201. *See also* organizational systems, misconduct of
behaviorism, 4, 31n5
beliefs, and identifying prejudice, 223
Bennett, W. Lance, 141, 151–52
Best v. Taylor Machine, 202
Bey, State of New Jersey v., 277, 278

bias in sociolegal relations: criminal justice system, 232–35, 238–45, 275–78; jury attitudes, 179–82; legal reporting, 18–19; moral issues, 22, 246–50; organizational outcomes, 226–37; personal prejudice, 213–25; pressures on decisionmakers, 237–46, 251–52*n*13; research issues, 21–24, 210–13, 216–18, 237–38

Bienen, Leigh, 261, 268

Blumberg, Abraham, 6–7

Blumstein, James, 180

Bobbitt, Lorena, 90

Born, Patricia, 196–97

boundary work for organizational conduct, 310–12. *See also* organizational systems, misconduct

Bovbjerg, Randall, 180, 195–96

breach of contract cases, 182

Brookings Institution, 154

Burstin, Helen, 189

Bush, George, 146

businesses, societal biases concerning, 179, 181–82, 212, 230

Butz, Earl, 216

California, 58, 150–51, 240

cameras at executions, 76

Coase, Mirium, 117–18

capital punishment. *See* death penalty

causation issues: amoral calculator model for, 291–92, 293, 299, 313; individual crime and deviance, 294–96; organizational misconduct, 298–99, 307–9, 313; shift away from, 10–11

celebrity and trials, 89–90

Challenger space shuttle disaster, 299–307

Chance, 276

character witnesses, Coase case, 122–24

Chicago Evening American, 76

Chief Executive, 153

Cicourel, Aaron, 312

circumstantial evidence, Coase case, 119–27

Civil Justice Reform Act of 1995, 202

civil law, social science uses, 8. *See also* litigation, civil

civil rights, 245–47

class, social, and biases in legal system, 189, 232–35, 238–45, 248

clients, legal, complexities of identification, 324–25

Coase, Avi, 116–17

Coase, Daniel, 101–33

Coase, Sarah, 118–19

Coase case: circumstantial evidence, 119–27; defense, 102–8, 114–19, 129–31; expert testimony, 119–22, 126–27; indictment, 113–14, 133*n*3; judges, 127–32, 133*n*1; prosecution, 103, 108–13

code language for discrimination, 215

Cohen, Felix, 30*n*3

Cohen, Richard S., 280, 281, 282–83

collegial method of handling conflicts of interest, 334–38, **353,** 354, **355,** 364

colonial period: entrepreneurs, 43, 50; execution vs. transportation, 14–15, 41–42, 45–50, 61; justice as public, 71–73, 74

Colonists in Bondage (Smith), 43–44

common crime vs. white-collar crime, 238–45, 252*n*14, 297–98. *See also* criminal justice system

communication, and handling of conflicts of interest, 334–38

community corrections, 54–56, 57

comparable worth issue, 229

compensation in civil cases, 20, 161–62, 182, 187–90

competitive pressure, and organizational misconduct, 292–93

compromises, and organizational misconduct, 304

computerized methods of tracking conflicts of interest, 344–52

conceptualism vs. realism, 2

confidence intervals, 272–73, 277

conflicts of interest: as combative legal tool, 371*n*7; and ecology of intelligence, 352–59; incentives for controlling, 326–30; introduction, 322–23; and limits of risk assessment effectiveness, 368–69; methods of identifying, 326–52; and organizational blind spots, 359–68; origins of, 324–26; variation in regulation of, 27–29

constructivist approach, 31*n*5

Consumer Attorneys of California, 150, 151

context: and bias problems, 216–18, 238–40; and cognitive appreciation of norms, 312; image and fact-finding, 106, 113–14, 128–29; and perceptions of barbaric punishment, 75; and unequal pressures on decisionmakers, 245–46

contingency fees, 185

control, social. *See* social control

convergence of logistic regression models, 278–79

convicts, colonial trade in, 14–15, 41–42, 46–50, 61

corporations, societal biases concerning, 179, 181–82, 212, 230

correctional facilities, 50–54, 56–60, 74–75

Corrections Corporation of America, 51, 55

costs: criminal trials, 130–31; of harassment, 143; liability insurance, 154, 172–73; tort system, 153–54, 195; transportation of convicts, 43, 49–50

counter-intuitive factual complexity, 105

court decisions, validity and viability of, 7. *See also* U.S. Supreme Court

Crime and the Police in England: 1700–1900 (Tobias), 46

criminal justice system: codification of, 69–70; common vs. white-collar crime, 238–45, 252*n*14, 297–98; as entertainment, 70–73; entrepreneurial opportunities in sentencing area, 41–42; extra-legal causes of legal inequality, 16–17; formal vs. informal, 92–93; individual crime and deviance, 294–96; juvenile, 56–60, 215, 241–42; measurement of discrimination in, 212–13, 226–29, 230, 232–37; media relation to, 68–69, 76–78; privatization, 51–54, 56–60, 74–75; social science uses, 8; structural inequalities in, 6; trial dramas, 89–92. *See also* Coase case; death penalty

culpability estimates, 277, 278–79

cultural beliefs, organizational, and control of deviant behavior, 27, 304–5, 310–11

custody and technology, 52, 56

cybersurveillance method of handling conflicts of interest, 344–52, 354, **355**, 357, 362–64

Daniels, Stephen, 172, 182, 202

Danzon, Patricia A., 184, 192

death penalty: likeliness of seeking, 22; measurement of discrimination in, 230–31; opposition to, 48; social science role in, 23, 259; transportation as alternative to, 46–50; U. S. Supreme Court views on, 235, 261, 275–78. *See also* executions; New Jersey

decisionmaking: inequalities in pressure on decisionmakers, 237–50, 251–52*n*13; in organizational misconduct, 308, 309–14. *See also* policy making

deconstructive approach, 30*n*3–4

defendants, 17, 185, 215

defense, criminal, 91, 102–8, 114–19, 129–31, 131–32

defensive medical practice, 160–61, 173, 195, 199

"deliberate detachment" posture, 31*n*7

Denny, Reginald, 236

desegregation, 223

deterrence of negligent behavior: individual conduct, 25–28, 198–99, 201; organizational conduct, 292, 293, 295, 296, 298

deviant behavior, regulation of, 25–28, 198–99, 201. *See also* criminal justice system; organizational systems, misconduct of

Dewey, J., 3

Diamond, Shari, 259

DiFrisco, State of New Jersey v., 277, 278

DiMaggio, Paul, 312

Dimsdale, Thomas, 86–87

direct action, 85–89

discriminant-based method for death penalty testing. *See* special master to U.S. Supreme Court

discrimination. *See* bias in sociolegal relations

disqualification, legal, and conflicts of interest, 327

doctors, 179, 200. *See also* malpractice, medical

drug testing, 53

due process rights vs. social organizations, 6

East Texans Against Lawsuit Abuse, 150
economic issues: and discrimination, 237; transportation vs. execution, 14–15, 41–42, 43, 50, 61; and white-collar crime, 240
Edelman, Murray, 141
education issues, 7, 226, 259
Eisenberg, Theodore, 182
electric chair, 74, 94n6
elephant method of handling conflicts of interest, 333–34, **353,** 354, **355**
empirical research. *See* research, socio-legal
employment: measurement of discrimination in, 227–28, 229–30, 231–32, 245; personal prejudice in, 211–12, 214–15, 220–21
empowerment of jury, 15–16, 79, 93
England, transportation from, 41–46
entertainment as function of criminal justice system, 70–73
entrepreneurs: early American, 43, 50–51; as innovative and responsive, 61–62; juvenile institutions, 56–60; opportunities in criminal sentences, 41–42; prisons, 51–52; treatment programs, 52–54
environmental groups, biased media coverage of, 212, 230
equality vs. legality, 245–46
equal time, journalistic, 156–57
equitable compensation. *See* compensation in civil cases
Ericson, Richard, 53
Ermann, M. David, 302
ethics, codes of, and conflicts of interest, 326–30. *See also* moral issues
ethnicity vs. class in discrimination determination, 248. *See also* racial issues
ethnomethodological perspective, 237–38, 313
Evans, Donald, 53
evidence, circumstantial, Coase case, 119–27
Ewick, Patricia, 312
executions: electric chair, 74; hanging, 72–73, 74, 75, 76; lynching, 87–88, 97n26; media presence, 76; vs. transportation, 14–15, 41–42, 46–50, 61
expedition of litigation, and voluntary arbitration, 194

expert testimony, Coase case, 119–22, 126–27

fact control, 105–8
fact-finding, and lawyers, 16–17
factories, prison, 51
factual ambiguity and inequality, 131–32
fairness, journalistic, 156–57
Fairness and Accuracy in Reporting, 164
Falkner, Robert R., 308
Fallmer, Clara, 84
Fallows, James, 152
Farber, Henry, 184
fault principle in tort law, 174, 175–76, 195, 200–201
federal law enforcement, complexities of language in, 238–39
fee-shifting initiatives, 162, 163
Feldberg, Michael, 86
Fisher, Amy, 90
Florida, fee-shifting policy, 163
FMC, 153
frame of interaction, and judgment of bias, 216–17
frequency of claims in civil cases, 195
frivolous litigation, 142–45, 161, 184–86, 201
Fuhrman, Mark, 219
functionalism, 4, 31n5
Furman, Rosemary, 158
Furman v. Georgia, 235

Galanter, Marc, 8, 202
Gannon, Thomas, 197–98
"gap" between law's intent and practice, 19–20, 171–76
Geis, Gilbert, 297, 308
gender differences, temporary insanity, 84–85
Georgia, Furman v., 235
Georgia, Gregg v., 261
Gieryn, Thomas, 310
Goerdt, John, 180, 182
Goetz, Bernhard, 88
Goffman, Erving, 216
Gotti, John, 90
government issues: and appearance of fairness, 243; crime and economics, 14; in federal law enforcement, 238–39; and juvenile corrections, 60;

and legal realism, 2, 4; private sector treatment program, 52–56; social change and law, 5 (*See also* policy-making; U.S. Supreme Court)
Gray, Hannah, 71
Great Society, 5
greed, of lawyers, 148–49
Gregg v. Georgia, 261
Gronfein, William, 197–98
Gross, Felicia, 183

hanging, 72–73, 74, 75, 76
harassment, cost of, 143
Harris, State of New Jersey v., 278, 280
Harvard School of Public Health, 187, 188–89
Hauptmann, Bruno, 90
Health, Education and Welfare, Department of, 187
health care issues, insurance, 192, 195–99. *See also* malpractice, medical
health maintenance organizations, 192
higher education, and complexities of representative mix, 249
Hirschi, Travis, 294
Holmes, O. W., 2
Holt, Sam, 87
Howard, John, 48
Hsieh, Chee Rhuey, 184, 186
Huber, Peter, 153, 154

ICJ (Institute for Civil Justice), 177
Illinois, 174, 323
image-making in Coase case, 105–8, 113–14, 127–32
indentured servitude, 42–44
index-of-outcomes test, 264, 268–76, 277–82
Indiana, tort reform in, 197, 200–201
indictment, Coase case, 113–14, 133n3
individual vs. organizational causation, 291, 294–96
industry, societal biases concerning, 179, 181–82, 212, 230
inequalities in sociolegal system: and criminal defense, 131–32; documentation problems with, 21–22; extra-legal causes of, 16–17; prejudice and handling of racial, 222–23; and pressures on decisionmakers, 237–50, 251–52n13; structural, 6

injury, liability issues, 160, 184, 187
insanity defense, 91
Institute for Civil Justice (ICJ), 177
institutionalist approach, 31n5
institutions, sociolegal, 6, 14–15, 226–37. *See also* organizational systems, misconduct of; organizations; prison system
instrumentalism, 18
insurance: loss ratio for companies, 196; medical, 192, 195–99. *See also* liability
integrationist movement in crime causation, 295
intelligence methods for handling conflicts of interest: archival, 338–44, **353, 355, 357,** 364–65; collegial, 334–38, **353,** 354, **355,** 364; cybersurveillance, 344–52, 354, **355,** 357, 362–64; ecology of, 352–59; elephant, 333–34, **353,** 354, **355;** ostrich, 331–33, 353, **355,** 360
interdisciplinary boundaries to organizational misconduct, 312–14
intradisciplinary boundaries to organizational misconduct, 310–12
Israeli trial example, 16–17, 101–33

Jacob, Herb, 8
Jamail, Joe, 148, 157
Japan, number of lawyers in, 145
job training programs, prison, 52–54
journalism. *See* media
Joyce, Craig, 190
judges: Coase criminal trial, 127–32, 133n1; and juries, 82; and juvenile justice, 58–59; pretrial judicial fact assessment, 103, 104; reliance on social science research, 258–59; and sociology's role, 7
juries: as empowered vs. public, 15–16, 79, 93; performance and behavior of, 178–83; size of in relation to social science research, 259; and tort system, 20, 159–60, 172–73; and unwritten laws, 82–85
jury-determined settlement, 192–93
Justice without Trial (Skolnick), 6
juvenile justice system, 56–60, 215, 241–42

Kagan, Robert A., 291–92, 293
Kahl, Lester, 76

Keating, Charles, 151
Kemp, McClesky v., 23, 33*n*12, 267
Kessler, Daniel, 198, 199–200
Key, Philip Barton, 83
Kimmel, John, 83–84
Kinney, Eleanor, 197–98, 201
KKK (Ku Klux Klan), 88
knowing, theory of, 313
Koenig, Thomas, 182
Kritzer, Herbert, 185
Ku Klux Klan (KKK), 88

La Due, Charlie, 84
laissez-faire politics, collapse of, 2
Langbein, John, 157
language, and discovery of prejudice, 215–16
Lapham, Lewis, 164
law and order dilemma, 6
law and society: action vs. words, 2–3; historical analysis, 13–16; revision of existing paradigms, 9–13; tort law changes, 194–201
Law and Society Association, 4–5, 8
law enforcement. *See* criminal justice system
Law Enforcement Assistance Administration (LEAA), 52
lawsuits. *See* litigation, civil
lawyers: bar disciplinary procedures, 155–56; difficulties in fact-finding for, 16–17; greed of, 148–49; litigation amongst, 328–29; media coverage of regulation, 162–63; number of, 145; for plaintiff and liability insurance, 173. *See also* conflicts of interest
LEAA (Law Enforcement Assistance Administration), 52
learning theory, 296
legal community, failure to use social science research, 259–60
legality vs. equality, 245–46
legislation, social science uses, 8. *See also* government issues
Leo, John, 143, 154
liability: costs of, 154, 172–73; and increase in civil court cases, 178–83; inflated risk perception, 160; and legal conflicts of interest, 328–29, 355–58, 372*n*8–10; and payments for injury, 184; product, 159–64, 173, 180, 182;

provider, 199; and tort reform movement, 172–75
Lindbergh kidnapping, 90
Litan, Robert, 154
litigation, civil: as epidemic, 144–46; and frequency of claims, 195; frivolous lawsuits, 142–45, 161, 184–86, 201; and jury behavior, 20, 178, 181–82; lawyer-to-lawyer, 328–29; and liability issue, 178–83; mediation process, 193; and policy issues, 161–64; and social class, 189; voluntary arbitration, 192, 194. *See also* malpractice, medical
Llewellyn, Karl, 30*n*3
Lloyds of London, 356
Loeb-Leopold case, 79
Loftin, State of New Jersey v., 280
logistic regression approach in proportionality test, 271–72, 278
"loser-pay" systems, 162
loss ratio for insurance companies, 196
lower classes and legal system, 189, 241–42
"lowest common denominator information," 141
low-security custodial programs, 54–56
Lundman, Richard J., 302
lynching, 87–88, 97*n*26

MacNeil, Robert, 147
macro- vs. micro-levels of analysis, in organizational misconduct, 294–99, 302–7, 309–14
Majors, Lloyd, 73
Mallott, Robert, 153
malpractice, legal, 328–29, 356–58, 372*n*8–10
malpractice, medical: actual incidence of, 188–89; arbitration vs. tort action, 175; and defensive medical practice, 160–61, 173, 195–99; difficulties in expediting cases, 194; jury behavior in, 178, 180–81, 182; lack of claims, 161–62; and liability insurance, 154, 173; "map" of legal terrain, 20; as over-reported, 159; reforms in, 190–201; settlement vs. trial in, 183; and tort law changes, 194–201; tort system map, 177, 178
mandatory sentencing, 243

Manning, Peter K., 312, 313
"manufactured defense," Coase case, 105
March, James G., 313
Marshall, Robert, 262, 269
Marshall, State of New Jersey v., 262–68
Marshall Space Flight Center, 304
Martin, Joanne, 172, 182, 202
Martini, State of New Jersey v., 277, 278
Marxist theory, 296, 298
Massachusetts, juveniles in custody, 58
mass toxic torts, 178
May, Marlynn, 189–90
McCarthy, John P., 282
McClellan, Mark, 198, 199–200
McClesky, Warren, 33*n*12
McClesky v. Kemp, 23, 33*n*12, 267
McConnell, Mitch, 142
McDonald, Douglas, 59
McDonald's Corp., 143–44, 160
McFarland, Daniel, 83
McLaughlin, John, 143
McMahon, Maeve, 53
media: balanced reporting as mislead-
    ing, 157–59; biases of, 212, 226, 230,
    232; formal vs. informal criminal jus-
    tice system, 92–93; newsworthiness of
    issues, 152–59; pressure for fairness
    from, 243; public's relation to law,
    18–19, 68–69, 139, 141–52, 159–64;
    and sociolegal research use, 140–41;
    trial coverage, 76–78
medical negligence. *See* malpractice,
    medical
memory, institutional, and handling of
    conflicts of interest, 333–34
Menéndez brothers, 90
Mertonian theory, 296
Meschievitz, Catherine, 193
Michigan, litigation process, 193, 196,
    197–98
middle class, treatment in juvenile jus-
    tice system, 241–42
Miller, Jerome, 57
minimum- and medium-security
    prisons, 51
misconduct. *See* deviant behavior;
    negligence
mitigating factors in death penalty
    assessment, 275
moral issues: amoral calculator model,
    291–92, 293, 299, 313; cognitive ap-

preciation of norms, 312; outrage at
    racism, 219; and search for prejudice,
    22, 218–25, 246–50. *See also* conflicts
    of interest
Morgan, James, 72
multivariate models, 269, 282

NAACP (National Association for the
    Advancement of Colored People), 87
Nader, Ralph, 150, 151
NASA (National Aeronautics and Space
    Administration), 26–27, 299–307
National Association for the
    Advancement of Colored People
    (NAACP), 87
National Police Gazette, 76
National Race Survey, 220
negligence: automobile, 178, 180; indi-
    vidual conduct, 25–28, 198–99, 201;
    organizational conduct, 292, 293,
    295, 296, 298; and rates of injury,
    187. *See also* malpractice, medical
New Jersey: index-of-outcomes ap-
    proach, 268–76; integration of social
    science and law in, 283–84; problems
    in meeting proportionality, 276–83;
    race and proportionality of death
    penalty in, 261–68; as research target,
    260–61
New Republic, 79
news media. *See* media
New York Daily News, 76
nigger, ironic uses of, 221
non-profit corporations, jury sympathy
    for, 179
normalization of deviance in organiza-
    tions, 300–309

Oakland Tribune, 76
objectivity and legal realism, 3–4
odds ratio method for death penalty
    proportionality, 280, 283
operationalism, 31*n*5
Orange County, California, bankruptcy
    of, 240
organizational systems, misconduct of:
    causes and control, 298–99, 307–9,
    313; definition, 314*n*1; macro- vs.
    micro-levels of analysis, 294–98,
    302–7, 309–14; NASA and *Challenger*
    case, 300–302; social control mecha-
    nisms, 291–94

organizations: and conflicts of interest, 333–34, 359–68; and discrimination outcomes, 226–37; theory of, 312–13
Osborne, John E., 89
ostrich method of handling conflicts of interest, 331–33, 353, **355,** 360
Ostrom, Brian, 180, 182
oversight agencies, role in determining bias, 242

Parrott, Big Nose George, 89
pejorative terms, 215–16, 221
Peller, Gary, 30*n*3–4
penal code, and function of criminal justice system, 69–70, 93
penalty trial cases. *See* death penalty
penitentiaries, 50–54, 56–60, 74–75
perception, changed by lawyers, 16–17
personal involvement, and judgment of bias, 217
personal knowledge, and handling of conflicts of interest, 333–34
Peterson, Mark A., 182
Phoenix New Times, 155
physical findings from police investigation, Coase case, 111–13
Physician Payment Review Commission, 179
physicians, 179, 200. *See also* malpractice, medical
Piazza, Thomas, 220
plaintiffs: Coase case, 103, 108–13; and frivolous lawsuits, 185; jury attitudes toward civil, 181–82; recovery rates for, 198
plea bargaining, 102–3, 243
police, organizing of, 75
policymaking: colonial transportation, 14–15; discrimination pressure on, 237–50, 251–52*n*13; ineffectiveness of sociolegal research on, 170–71; and law as object of direct social action, 11; and legal realism, 2, 4; litigation reform and inadequate information, 161–64; media reporting vs. scholarly journals, 140–41; for prisons, 50–51; social science's role, 5–9, 17–18, 24, 202
political issues: and appearance of fairness for government, 243; crime and criminal justice, 68

popular culture, social research's effects, 248
Portland Press Herald, 155
positivist science and law's rationality, 3
poverty and treatment in legal system, 189, 241–42
power operations in organizations and misconduct, 313
prejudice, personal, 213–25. *See also* bias in sociolegal relations
premises liability, 180
President's Council of Economic Advisors, 146
press. *See* media
pretrial screening panels, 191–92
prison system, 50–54, 56–60, 74–75
private investigators, Coase case, 122
privatization: low-security custodial programs, 54–56; of prison system, 51–54, 56–60, 74–76
probation, 52–56
product liability, 159–64, 173, 178, 180, 182
professional training, and boundaries to organizational misconduct, 311
proportionality of death penalty. *See* New Jersey
prosecution, Coase case, 103, 108–13. *See also* plaintiffs
provider liability, effects of reductions in, 199
public opinion and the law, 18–19, 68–69, 139, 141–52, 159–64
Punch, Maurice, 312
punishment. *See* executions; prison system; transportation
punitive damages, trends in, 159–60, 182–83

Quayle, Dan, 142, 145, 146

racial issues: and attribution of prejudice within groups, 220, 222–25; criminal justice system bias, 226; and death penalty in South, 22; and juvenile justice, 59; moral outrage at racism, 219; and pay scales for black vs. white women, 232; race riots of 1992, 251*n*10–11; and subtlety of bias in legal cases, 237. *See also* New Jersey
Radzinowicz, Leon, 46

"rainmakers," 328
Ramseur, State of New Jersey v., 261–62
Rand Corporation's Institute for Civil Justice (ICJ), 177
Rand researchers, 153, 161
rational choice theory, 294, 295, 296, 298, 307–8, 309
realism, legal, 1–9, 10, 11, 30*n*3
Reasoner, Harry, 154
reform, legal: and information deficits, 161–64; and realism, 2; reduction in public aspects of criminal justice, 72; and social science uses, 8–9; tort system, 172–76, 184–86, 190–201
regulation, and deviant behavior, 25–28, 198–99, 201
regulatory agencies, inequality of social justice pressures on, 242
representative social composition, difficulties in obtaining, 249
research, sociolegal: bias discovery in sociolegal relations, 21–24, 210–13, 216–19, 237–38; dissemination into legal arena, 19, 20–21; ethnomethodological perspective, 237–38, 313; fields of study, 25; limitations of, 170–71, 201–2; and media, 140–41; and popular culture, 248; proper presentation, 164; regulation effectiveness, 27, 28; revision of focus, 10; role of, 7–9, 12, 13, 23, 170, 258–61, 266; tort system, 171–76; value for policymaking, 5, 6
return-to-custody facilities, 54–56
review procedures, and discovery of prejudice, 219
Rice, Jeffrey, 192
righteousness, and discrimination, 246–50. *See also* moral issues
riots and mobs as direct action, 86
risk assessment, 26–27, 160, 301, 368–69. *See also* conflicts of interest
Rodgers, Esther, 72
Rolph, John, 283
Roosevelt, Theodore, 2
Rose, Mary, 183
Rosenblum, Victor, 8
Rothman, David, 50, 61
Rottman, David, 180
rule-following, and deviance in organizational behavior, 304–5

Russell Sage Fellows, 170
Rustad, Michael, 182

Saks, Michael, 189
sample size, and proportionality test, 270, 275
Sanders, Joseph, 190
San Francisco Examiner, 156
San Jose Mercury News, 152
Sarat, Austin, 170–71
Sarma, Syam, 182
satisficing model, 313
savings and loan scandal, 240
scholars, sociolegal: outreach to press, 163–64; pressure to shift from gaps to normal patterns, 171. *See also* research, sociolegal
Schugart, Alan, 151
Schwartz, Gary, 199
scientific positivism, 305
screening panels, pretrial, 191–92
Seattle Times, 156
selection effect in conflict of interest management, 358
selective reporting, 159
sensationalism, in legal reporting, 18–19
sensemaking concept, 313
sentencing. *See* death penalty
settlements, 183–84, 186–87, 192–93
sexism, 220–21, 226
shame as punishment, 74–75
Shanley, Michael, 182
Shapiro, Susan P., 248
Shau, Eli, 111
Sheppard, Sam, 95*n*11
Sherwin, Richard K., 107
shippers, colonial transportation, 45
Sholz, John T., 291–92, 293
Shua, Jonathan, 101–33, 110–11
Shua, Paul, 108–9
Shua, Ronda, 109–10
Shuck, Peter, 163
Sickles, Dan and Teresa, 82–83
Silbey, Susan, 312
Simmons, Walter, 193–94, 198
Simon, Herbert A., 313
Simpson, O. J., 70, 89, 163, 219, 236
Simpson, Sally S., 311
60 Minutes, 154, 158
size of legal firm, and intelligence method for handling conflicts of interest, 354–60

skewed coverage, media, 142
Skolnick, Jerome, 6
slavery, 42–44
Sloan, Frank, 180, 181, 184, 185, 186, 195–96
Smith, Abbot Emerson, 44
Sniderman, Paul M., 220
Snyder, Ruth, 76
social class, and biases in legal system, 189, 232–35, 238–45, 248
social constructionist perspective, 313
social control: and blind spots for firms in conflict of interest, 359–68; and causation of crime, 298–99; colonial transportation as, 14–15; ecology of intelligence for conflicts of interest, 352–59; methods for handling conflicts of interest, 330–52; in organizational systems, 291–94; problems of tracking conflicts of interest, 368–69. *See also* organizational systems, misconduct of
social justice, inequalities in, 242–43
social organizations vs. due process rights, 6
social psychological theories, 295
social relations, reordering of, 24–29
social science, role of, 7–9, 12, 13, 23, 170, 259–61, 266
sociolegal research. *See* research, sociolegal
special master to Supreme Court, 262–73, 281
Spurr, Stephen, 198
state government. *See* government issues
State of New Jersey v. Bey, 277, 278
State of New Jersey v. DiFrisco, 277
State of New Jersey v. Harris, 278, 280
State of New Jersey v. Loftin, 280
State of New Jersey v. Marshall, 262–68
State of New Jersey v. Martini, 277
State of New Jersey v. Ramseur, 261–62
Stengel, David, 189–90
Stossel, John, 147–49, 157
structural analysis of law, 13, 16–17, 295
Sudnow, David, 312
suffering, jury perceptions of, 181–82
summary jury trial vs. jury-determined settlement, 192–93

supervised treatment programs, 52–56
Supreme Court, U.S., 5, 235, 261, 262–73, 275–78, 281
surveillance and technology, 52, 56
Sutherland, Edwin H., 235, 296, 297–98

Taragin, Mark, 180, 183, 186–87
Taylor Machine, Best v., 202
"technoblitz" intelligence for handling conflicts of interest, 350–53, 354, **355, 357**
technology, modern penal management, 52, 56
television. *See* media
temporary insanity, 82–85
Texaco Corporation, 219
Texas Trial Lawyers, 150
Thaw, Evelyn Nisbet, 84
Thaw, Harry, 84
theater: direct action as, 86, 88; trial as, 15–16, 70–71
"The Practice of Law as a Confidence Game" (Blumberg), 6–7
The Thin Blue Line, 107
Tort Policy Working Group, 176–77
tort system: awards, 20, 159–60; claims epidemic, 144–46; costs of, 153–54, 195; debate on behavior of, 176–86; equitable compensation in, 187–90; historical analysis, 171–76; introduction to debate, 170–71; and punitive damages, 182; reforms assessment, 190–201; settlement outside tort system, 186–87; trends in, 201–3. *See also* malpractice, medical
Towery, Jim, 149
toxic substance cases, 178, 180, 182
Transportation Act of 1718 (English), 49
transportation vs. execution, colonial, 14–15, 41–42, 46–50, 61
treatment programs, private, 52–56
trials as theater, 15–16, 70–71. *See also* criminal justice system; litigation, civil
The Trouble with Lawyers (ABC News), 147–49
Tukey, John, 280, 281, 282, 286n284

unwritten laws, 82–89, 93
urbanization, and privatization of punishment, 75–76
U.S. Department of Justice, 176

U.S. Dept. of Health, Education and Welfare, 187
U.S. News and World Report, 154
U.S. Office of Technology Assessment, 161
U.S. Supreme Court, 5, 235, 261, 262–73, 275–78, 281

validity, of court decisions, 7
value-neutral inquiry and legal realism, 3–4
Van Maanen, John, 312
variable uses in proportionality test, 270
Vauden, Nicolas, 72
Vaughan, Diane, 291–315
verdicts, misleading reporting of, 159
viability, of court decisions, 7
victim undercompensation, lack of media attention to, 161–62
Vidmar, Neil, 183, 192
vigilante movements as direct action, 86, 87, 88
Viscusi, W. Kip, 196–97
voluntary arbitration, 192, 194

Wackenhut Corporation, 51, 55
Wallace, Mike, 158
Wall Street Journal, 147–49, 161

Watergate scandal, 239
Weber, Max, 86
Weick, Karl E., 313
Weisberg, Herbert, 275–76
Wheeler, Stanton: and bar discipline, 157–58; historical patterns, 42, 61; importance of social science in law, 1, 12, 170; and tort reform, 201
whipping, 75
White, Michelle, 184
White, Stanford, 84
"white caps," 89
white-collar crimes, 232–35, 238–45, 252n14, 297–98
whites, historical transformation of racial attitudes, 223–25
white supremacy and lynching, 87
Wilson, Pete, 142
Wilson, Woodrow, 2
Wisconsin, 193, 196
work camps, 54–56
Wright, Paul and Evelyn, 83–84

"yellow press," 76
Yntema, Hessel E., 3

Zuckerman, Stephen, 195–96